48889
W13N

Productivity and Wages in Indian Industries

Productivity and Wages in Indian Industries

By

Dr. Laxmi Narayan

Reader

Department of Economics

DDU Gorakhpur University

Gorakhpur–273 009

(India)

DISCOVERY PUBLISHING HOUSE

NEW DELHI-110002

First Published-2003

ISBN 81-7141-703-5

© Author

Published by

DISCOVERY PUBLISHING HOUSE
4831/24, Ansari Road, Prahlad Street,
Darya Ganj, New Delhi-110002 (India)
Phone: 23279245 • Fax: 91-11-23253475
E-mail:dphtemp@indiatimes.com

Printed at :
ARORA OFFSET PRESS
Laxmi Nagar, Delhi-92.

Preface

This book is an outcome of my Ph.D. Thesis titled "Trends in Labour Productivity and Wages in Indian Manufacturing Industries". I express my deep gratitude to Dr. P.C. Shukla, Reader Department of Economics, D.D.U. Gorakhpur University, Gorakhpur, who was my supervisor for doctoral research, for his invaluable guidance, profound knowledge of the subject and continued interest in this research work. I shall ever remain grateful to him for his deep sense of personal attachment and ever increasing encouragement. I express my deep gratitude to Prof. Ashok Srivastava, Head Dept. of Economics, for his ever encouraging attitude. The stimulus provided by teachers Sri J.P. Shukla, Sri J.N. Yadav, Dr. Y.K. Singh and Dr. Sandeep Kumar and special mention. I express my sincere thanks to Dr. N.K. Mishra, Lecturer, DAV College, Gorakhpur for his invaluable advice. The library facilities provided by various institutes especially Ratan Tata Library, Delhi School of Economics, Institute of Economic Growth, Delhi and A.N. Sinha Institutes of Social Sciences, Patna need special acknowledgment. I am also thankful to my colleagues Dr. Surender Singh, Rajesh Chaurasia and Satish Kumar Dubey for their help in work. I express my thanks to my parents, wife and sons for their encouragement and help in various ways. Lastly, I express my sincere thanks to Discovery Publishing House for bringing out the publication of book in through professional manner.

The productivity studies have attached the attain of many because it indicates the efficiency in resource utilization in an economy which ultimately determines the amount of surplus generation. The productivity and wages plays an important role in the process of economic development. Given the pivotal role of human resources in productivity growth. It is imperative to have a thorough understanding of the productivity and the reward to the human resources. The focus of the present book is on examining this relationship between wages and productivity.

The wage-productivity relationship assumes greater importance in a developing country like India where wage and income policy is facing a real conflict between demand of the workers for higher wages and need of the economy for higher rate of capital formation, only a sustained rise in the level of productivity can provide the resources for development and expansion of the economy/industry consistent with the legitimate aspiration of workers for rising their level of living. In the present phase of post-liberalization reforms, marked by jobless growth in India and widespread recessionary trends in global economy, this work assumes greater importance and relevancy. In theory, the relationship between wages and productivity seem plausible and convincing. The marginal productivity theory and efficiency wage hypothesis shows the linkage of one with other. In practice, productivity plays a limited role in wage determination. This has resulted in an anti-work culture in the country.

The main problem in linking wages with labour productivity is the identification of the contribution of labour in increased productivity. This has been pointed out by various wage boards, wage committees etc. It may be realised that an income policy can not be divorced from Workers expectation. However, an indiscriminate upward movement of wages, or payment of monetary wage-supplements, may be reflected in the cost of production and consequently in the price of the products. The inflationary pressure following such an increase would largely neutralize the gain in wages. So, the workers instead of worrying over wages, should strive to secure significant gains in productivity so as to ensure price stability which is conductive to a continual rise in real wages. Rise in wages without an increase in productivity would merely result in pushing up prices and costs.

The role of human factor, in economic development and productivity growth is widely accepted. Some people mention capital and technology as important factors but human resources are most important. The capital can be misused by human misappropriation and the high technological standard can never be maintained without matching human resources development and constant upgrading of human efforts. The labour is a distinct factor of production as it is both the creator and end user of wealth. The price of labour is a unique parameter that is highly complex to determine and depend upon many factors. The present work attempts to understand the relation between wages and some of these important factors.

This book will be very helpful for the students of Industrial and Labour economics, the planners, the businessman, the researcher in field of productivity and wages, and for all those who wants to save the country from being a high cost economy.

Dr. Laxmi Narayan

Acknowledgement

By the grace and blessings of Almighty, it is my pleasant duty to express my gratitude to those who have helped me at various stages of this research work.

During the process of research, the influence of my Supervisor, Dr. Prakash Chander Shukla, has been a guiding light. I have been greatly benefited by his guidance, profound knowledge of the subject and his continued interest in my work. I shall ever remain grateful and indebted to him, for his deep sense of personal attachment and the ever-increasing encouragement that he has given to me.

I express my deep gratitude to Dr. Ashok Kumar Srivastava, Head, Department of Economics for granting me permission to undertake this research work and for his ever encouraging attitude. There is a special pleasure in acknowledging the stimulus provided by Sri J.P. Shukla, Sri S.N. Yadav, Dr. Y.K. Singh and Dr. Sandeep Kumar of the department of economics. They were always eager to help me whenever I have approached them.

I would also like to acknowledge my indebtedness to Sri N.K. Mishra, Lecturer, D.A.V. College, Gorakhpur for his scholarly advice and valuable suggestions, especially in data processing. I also acknowledge my thanks to Sri Nihal Ashraf, Library Assistant at A. N. Sinha Institute of Social Sciences, Patna for helping me in collection of relevant literature.

With a sense of appreciation, I feel myself highly indebted to the staff of the libraries of Rattan Tata Library, Delhi School of Economics; Institute of Economic Growth, Delhi; Indian Council of Social Science Research, Delhi; V.V. Giri National Labour Institute,

Noida; Giri Institute of Development Studies, Lucknow; D.D.U. Gorakhpur University, Gorakhpur; M.D. University, Rohtak and Punjab University, Chandigarh for allowing me to use the library facilities at their institutions.

Although, it is hard to list the name of all my colleagues who helped me in different ways at various stages of my study. I express my special thanks to Mr. Kailash Shukla, Mr. Surender Singh Yadav, Sri Rajesh Chaurasia, Miss Vandana Tripathi and Mr. Satish Kumar for their constructive suggestions and valuable advice. I am thankful to Ex. Office Assistant Mr. Shiromani Tiwari and present office staff of Department of Economics, D.D.U. Gorakhpur University, for their constant support in more than one way throughout the work.

Last, but not the least, above all, I express my sincere gratitude to my parents for their blessings which nourished me to see this moment. The constant encouragement provide by my father needs special acknowledgement. During the research work, I could not give enough attention to my brothers Subhash Chand and Balwan Singh. They have provided me moral support and continuous encouragement. I also feel indebted to them. I am also thankful to my wife Munish Yadav who has provided me with congenial atmosphere for study and looking after household chores. I also feel indebted to my sons Sanjay and Kuldeep who continuously felt my indifference towards them.

Laxmi Narayan

Contents

1

Introduction and Problem Setting

1.1 Introduction

One among several positive fallouts of the Indian economic reforms of the 1990s is the rediscovery of the idea of productivity. Although the concept was known in the 1950s and the National Productivity Council was set up, it was almost forgotten due to the licence-permit raj[1] and highly conflict-prone industrial relations. Increasing productivity has emerged as a new national priority, where the efforts of all converge to accelerate the process of economic growth and raise the standard of living.[2]

Indeed productivity enters, in one way or other, virtually in every broad economic problem; it affects costs, prices, profits, output, employment and investment and thus, occupies a crucial role in economic development. Its measurement, therefore, has come to be accepted as a rational basis for development planning as well as motivating productive efficiency. The use of productivity indices in the analysis of factors that promote productivity and in the analysis of dynamic economic relationship, as a background for prediction and policy decisions, is well recognised now and being increasingly used at the firm, industry and economic level.[3] We learn from productivity statistics about such significant variables as, the nature and magnitude of employment, production, earnings of labour force and per worker productivity. A government in possession of such information can be wisely guided by the available information for making sounder economic decisions. It is well-known fact that productivity data play an increasing role in the collective bargaining between labour and management.[4]

It is now widely recognised that in order to monitor the progress of a sector, industry or organisation, it is essential to make scientific appraisal of trends in productivity, the efficiency with which resources are converted into goods and services. For the total economy to be highly productive, the route is to raise the productivity of each major resource as capital, material, human and leadership.

The role of human factor in economic development has been widely accepted. It is rightly pointed out that "in productivity efforts, the most important is the Human factor, some people mention 'Capital' as the most important for industrial development and others quote Technology as the driving force for productivity improvement. Yes, they are important, but capital could be misused by human misappropriation, and the high technological standard can never be maintained without matching human resource development and constant upgrading by human efforts."[5] So, the exponents of the theory of 'productivity of labour' regard it as one of the basic indicators of economic development, as the major determinant of the national income and as an important tool for the analysis of economic and social problems. Historically also, the greatest interest has always centred around the relationship between production and labour, the universal source, and, the term productivity is frequently used without qualification to refer to this ratio.[6]

At present, the concept of labour productivity is widely accepted and is recognised as an indispensable factor for rapid economic development. In the history of economic thought, discussion on labour and its role in economic development is quite old. Adam Smith, Ricardo and Karl Marx established a fundamental relationship between labour theory of value, production, distribution, accumulation and economic development. Thus, economic development is viewed as an aspect of man's struggle against nature. The change in mode of production has shifted the attention from exchange to production and gave an impetus to the idea that labour was the source or cause of wealth or value. It is the search for the role of labour in economic development that led the classicists to build up the edifice of political economy on the foundations of the labour theory of value. This approach led to the discovery of labour both as a creator and measure of wealth, a market, a pressure group and subject of social protection, created new institutions and also contributed for rapid economic development in a capitalist economy. This makes it more than a factor of production because the quantity and quality of labour is a cause and consequence of economic development.[7]

Productivity analysis has proved to be very useful at the various level of economic organisation and productivity measurement is an important tool of economic and social analysis. It is the best way for studying the rate of growth of an economy and for judging the stage of economic development attained by a nation. Through inter-regional and international comparisons of productivity, efforts have been made to locate the factors responsible for rapid growth and competitive strength.

There are numerous obvious reasons for giving so much importance to labour productivity. Labour is the most important and universal factor in the production process, and labour time possesses an apparent universality regardless of production unit, industry or nation. It is a relatively simple concept, since by relating the output to the labour input along, reduces the difficulties of adding together unlike things. It is emphasised that "The labour productivity index is compsite. In the final analysis it reflects the realisation of many other economic objectives (reduction in the cost of production, advantageous location of the industry, degree of specialisation, effectiveness of capital equipment and so on)."[8] It is the measure of industrial efficiency in general, reckoned in terms of one specific factor. It is rightly remarked, "behind labour productivity lies all the dynamic forces of economic life: technical progress, accumulation, enterprises, and the institutional pattern of society."[9]

In the post-liberalisation phase marked by virtually jobless growth in India and recessionary trends in the global economy, the studies pertaining to employment, wages and productivity in a labour abundant country has assumed increasing importance and relevance. A thorough probe into the changes in productivity appears to be imperative, for it indicates the efficiency with which resources are converted into commodities and services that men want. Higher productivity is the means of achieving better level of economic well-being and national strength. Given the pivotal role of human resources in economic development, a thorough understanding of the relationship of its productivity improvement and the reward it obtains from its contribution to output is exceedingly important.

Labour as distinct factor of production, as it is defined in the textbooks of economics, did not exists prior to the advent of industrialisation. Since, there was absence of labour market, therefore, the reward of work and supply of work-effort was based on customary principles and on non-economic considerations. The industrial revolution gave rise to labour market replacing subsistence economies and creating an 'economic man'; who primarily gets his stimulus through market-led rationality. Therefore, workers as well as employers started responding to market forces in making their decisions regarding supply of work-effort and demand for work. The breakdown of the system of reward of workers based on the customary principles necessitated the evolving of new principles on which the reward of work will be based. Since then, several attempts have been made to identify the criteria that can be used for rewarding workers. One can say, for the sake of brevity, that the entire science of economics is a grand attempt to evolve a suitable criterion for rewarding labour.[10]

This endeavour for evolving suitable criteria for reward of work led to continuous, still unresolved debate. Various wage theories emerged to explain the basis of labour reward. With few exceptions, as for Marxian wage concept, a large body of them since the thirteenth century have advocated without much reluctance a low wage. The wage system, in modern sense, did not take shape till the industrial revolution in Europe.

The earliest explanation of wages, by mercantilist and physiocrats, was their idea of subsistence wages. In 1776, Adam Smith expounded the idea of 'labour theory of value'. He recognised that there was a level below which wage level could not go. Wages of labour, however, will vary depending on skill and nature of job. He believed that reward to a person is determined by his contribution to the creation of wealth. Smith while not advocating a low wage *per se* advocated the idea of *laissez-faire* which strengthened the forces of cut-throat competition. Other concepts of wages that came from the classical school of thought included "Subsistence Theory of Wages" (Iron Law of Wages) and "Wage-Fund Theory", which served as bulwarks against workers' demands for higher wages and improved living conditions. It was at this stage that a good part of the ethical and moral arguments give way to economic explanations such as capital formation and rate of growth of profits.

For Marx, the main economic problem was to explain the distribution of the relative shares of the total output between capital and labour. Unlike Ricardo and his predecessors, who tried to explain the distribution purely as a result of economic forces, Marx was among the first writers in political economy to draw attention to the historical and social elements that played a significant part in the evolution of two classes, the capitalists and the workers. He argued that in the process of production, whereas other factors transform themselves, it is the labour alone which transforms itself more than what it receives. The capital, thus, was nothing but the dead labour. The excessive use of capital would cause a falling rate of profit; because of over production, which would ultimately lead to the breakdown of capitalism.

According to marginal productivity theory, the rate of increases in real wages and the rate of increase in real productivity should be similar or the same in long run. Hicks and Marshall had advanced the 'law of marginal product' that affirmed that the wages of labour tends to be equal to his net product. This is regarded, even today, by most modern economist as the most fundamental principle of the theory of wages. This implies that any increase in real wages can takes place only through improvements in productivity.

The efficiency wage hypothesis also established the link between wages and productivity in reverse direction. Wage rate, as per this theory, acts as a motivating factor for the improvement of the workers' productivity. The rise in productivity acts as a deciding factor for the adoption of improved technology as a result of which the workers' skill improves leading to improvement of wage rate.

The empirical evidence and historical experience, however, have shown that the entire galaxy of wage theories has been unable to capture and represent the dynamism of wage determination in progress. In theory, the relationship between wages and productivity seems plausible and convincing and as such, the role of productivity in wage determination cannot be undermined. In fact, the wage determination must be linked with productivity simply because the workers must get his share out of the increased productivity. In practice, however, productivity plays a limited role in wage determination.

Notwithstanding the practical difficulties, the wage-productivity relationship assumes greater importance in a developing country like India where wage policy is faced with a real conflict between the needs of the workers for larger consumption and the demand of the economy for a higher rate of capital formation. In changing system of consumption, production and distribution; productivity is, by and large, to be considered guiding factor in determining wages. Thus, productivity analysis occupies a central place in the study of wage policies and problems. A rise in wages (beyond certain limits) without a corresponding rise in productivity would either lead to the stagnation in the economy (by reducing the rate of returns on capital) or force a rise in prices which would ultimately keep the real income of workers and there standard of living at the same level. On the other hand, rise in wages backed by a corresponding rise in productivity would contribute to overall gains not only for the economy but for the workers also. Only a sustained rise in the level of productivity can provide resources for development and expansion of the economy/industry consistent with the legitimate aspirations of workers for raising their level of wages.

In principle, there is a complete agreement that rising productivity is a valid justification for higher wages. However, the increase in the wages cannot be linked to the increase in the labour productivity in a mechanical way. Labour productivity alone provides little guidance for practical/operational purposes unless specific assumptions are made about the productivity of other factors. It may be noted that if capital productivity declines, proportional increase in wages cannot be allowed without depressing the rate of return on capital and if it (capital productivity) is rising even more than proportional increase in wages can be granted consistent with a stable or even rising rate of return. Therefore, the analysis of capital productivity is as significant as labour productivity in the analysis of wage-productivity relationships.[11] Thus, wages and earnings can not be linked to labour productivity alone without reference to capital productivity or total factor productivity, specially in Indian industries where there have been massive increase in capital stock in relation to labour. Therefore, capital productivity and total factor productivity are as significant as labour productivity in the study of wage-productivity relationship. The increase in wages without reference to productivity of other factors may leads to a fall in the rate of return on capital that may slacken the investment (because rate of profit would fall). The employers in India, in this regard put more emphasis on linking wages to productivity with the aim of reducing the labour cost as also to raise profitability at a higher level. But, the employees argue in favour of labour productivity from the point of view of existing low wages. To this, they have strongly asserted that productivity of labour in India has constantly increased, but the gains of which were not shared by the workers.[12]

In the absence of any principle governing the distribution of productivity gains among labour, capital and consumer, it is important to examine, at least the existing position of the share of the labour in the overall trend of productivity gains in different industries in India. There are many studies at the level of aggregate of manufacturing and at the dis-aggregation up to two-digit level but there are few studies regarding individual industry at three-digit level, particularly in recent past. A study of the individual industries at three-digit level is necessary to have a better understanding of the relationship between wages and labour productivity to delineate the area for remedial action.

The crux of wage-productivity relationship revolves around the positive effects of the changes in wage rate on the behaviour of the rate of productivity. Another view is that the rise in the rate of productivity leads in the long run to the rise in the rate of wages. Despite the considerable controversy to which the marginal productivity theory has been subjected, most economists are more or less in agreement with the idea that wages and productivity should be positively related. But whether productivity determines the wages or the wages determine the productivity is a question of endless debate. The present study is a humble effort which aim at addressing the above mentioned issues.

1.2 Scope of the Study

The study is an attempt to analyse the trends in wages and productivity in five selected three-digit industries from organised manufacturing sector and organised manufacturing sector as a whole. It is a time series study based on the secondary data from Annual Survey of Industries (ASI). The study covers the period from 1973-74 to 1995-96. The period has been consciously chosen for the reasons that National Industrial Classification (NIC), 1970, to classify industries, is being followed from 1973-74 and the latest data available at the time of study being of 1995-96. The scope of the study is restricted to the data on wage-cost-productivity nexus in selected industries. The industries selected for the study are sugar industry (206), paper and paperboard industry (280), fertilisers and pesticides industry (311), motor vehicles industry (374) and watches and clocks industry (382).[13]

1.3 Selection of the Industries

The selection of the industries for the study is guided by number of factors. The selected industries represent the varied aspects of Indian manufacturing industries. Sugar and paper & paperboard industries are consumer non-durable industries while watch industry is a consumer durable goods industry. Fertiliser industry is a basic goods industry whereas motor vehicle industry is a capital goods industry. Sugar industry is an important agro-based industry from food products group depending on agriculture (from supply side) whereas fertiliser industry is from chemical and chemical products group, predominantly depending on agriculture (from demand side). The paper and paperboard industry is one of the oldest industries in India. It covers one of the most important segments of India's industrial economy and is treated as basic sector. It is also one of the items covered by Essential Commodities Act. Most of the units of paper & paperboard industry are in private sector. Motor vehicle industry is from transport equipment group and most of its units are having foreign collaboration (financial or technical). Watch industry is from the category of other industrial group and this industry has developed during the plan periods only. Sugar industry is one in which from 1960-85, the increase in value added has been less than the increase in capital and labour inputs, and it is the only industry (among the industries covered by Ahluwalia (1992) where growth in labour input has been more than the growth in capital input. Fertiliser industry is one of the few industries with remarkably high growth in capital input. Watçhes and clocks industry is selected for its highest increase in value added and total factor productivity. Fertiliser and sugar industries are under the strict government regulation and price administration. With the exceptions of watches and clocks, these industries are subject to considerable administrative and policy interventions of government including in the matter of pricing, distribution and wage bargaining.

1.4 Objectives of the Study

The main objective of the present study is to explore the relationship between wages and productivity in selected three-digit industries. It has been argued that wages of the organised sector workers are shooting through roof. The workers in organised sector are a privileged lot enjoying an array of protective labour legislation, and they (organised labour) get away with a disproportionately large share of the national produce by way of wage increases and added perquisites. The argument runs further to say that organised labour cling on to their protected jobs through union militancy and aggressive collecting bargaining. Thus, major blame is put on labour arguing that their high wages does not have any relationship with their contribution to output, i.e., productivity. It is in this context that this study is undertaken to find the link between wages and productivity in the selected industries in Indian manufacturing sector. In this endeavour, our objectives in the present study can be classified as follows:

* To analyse the trends in value added, fixed capital employment and share of labour in value added in the proposed industries.
* To examine the trends in productivity (labour, capital and total factor), impact of technological change on labour productivity and elasticity of substitution in the proposed industries.
* To analysis the trends in money and real wage rate on one hand and rate of returns on capital on other hand.
* To measure the gains in productivity and examine the relative share of labour and capital in productivity gains.
* To examine the relationship between wages and productivity and to analyse the individual and combined impact of various variables on wages.

1.5 Hypothesis

The present study is guided by testing of the following hypothesis.

* The wage increase in industries does not have any relationship with the increase in productivity.
* There is no casual relationship between wage rate and labour

productivity and vice-versa in the proposed industries.

* There is a negative association between labour productivity and unit labour cost.
* The increase in wage cost to the industries does not have any effect on the level of employment in the industries.
* The capital deepening will lead to an increase in the labour productivity.

1.6 Methodology

The gross value added will be used as the measure of output for present study. The total number of persons employed will be used as the measure of labour input and gross fixed capital will be taken as the measure of capital input. The capital input has been measured using perpetual inventory accumulation method. The study during the discussion of methodology will highlight the issues relating to (a) measurement of output, i.e., why gross value added is used (b) measurement of inputs, i.e., why total number of persons employed and gross fixed capital are preferred.

Partial factor productivities of labour and capital will be obtained by dividing the index of output by the index of input. Increase in labour productivity is decomposed in two parts using Solow method, i.e., the increase in labour productivity due to capital intensity and residual attributed to the technical change. Capital intensity is measured as the ratio of gross fixed capital to labour input.

Since, these partial factor productivities suffer from inter-factor substitutability; a measure of overall efficiency, total factor productivity will be measured using Kendrick, Solow and Translog methods. Total factor productivity is defined as the ratio of output to weighted inputs. There are two approaches to total factor productivity measurement. A non-parametric index number approach and a parametric production function approach. The index number approach, generally, does not proceed by specifying an explicit production (or a dual cost) function; rather its strategy is to compute separate input and output indexes from observed prices and quantity data and use them for measurement of total factor productivity. As a result of this, TFP measurement by this approach is free from all the biases of explicit functional form.

However, index number approach shares most of the limitation of specific functional forms and their maintained hypothesis underlying specific index number formulae. Therefore, the alternative approach to productivity measurement, i.e., parametric production function approach will also be used, where various forms of production functions mainly, Cobb-Douglas, CES and VES are fitted and estimates of productivities will be obtained.

The use of gross value added by single deflation i.e., the deflation of total output and total input by same price index, may not represent true productive efficiency of industry. The change in relative prices of output and input may give biased result by this method, so the productivity trends using gross value added by double deflation method will also be calculated. The input price index for this purpose will be derived using weighted combination of various components of inputs for the industry concerned.

The productivity gains between two periods will be measured as the difference between change in actual output and change in potential output at the base year efficiency. The gain accruing to factors are measured as the difference between change in factor compensation at constant product prices and the compensation that would have been, if compensated at the base year rate. Factors share in output will be obtained by multiplying the relative share of each factor in total factor input by the respective index of relative factor price.

Once the productivity trends and productivity gains are analysed, the study will try to analyse the trends in factor compensation. Money wages/earnings have been deflated by consumer price index for industrial workers (CPIIW) to get real wages to study the welfare aspect of workers. The money wages/earnings are deflated by product price index (termed as product wages/earnings) to analyse the real wage cost burden to industry. To examine reinvestment potentiality of industry through plough back of internal resources/funds, rate of returns on capital are deflated by machinery price index. The trends in labour compensation are compared with the trends in labour productivity to test the hypothesis that factor reward depends on their productivity.

Annual trend rate have been computed using semi-logarithmic function of the form $Y = ab^t$. The inter-temporal comparisons of trend rates are done by fitting separate functions for sub-periods. To clearly delineate the trends, graphical representation of data is done using various forms of graphs.

The Granger test of causal relationship will be used to test the causal relationship between wages and productivity. The arbitration in lag selection will be removed using Akaike final prediction error method. The wage function and employment function for selected industries are also estimated for understanding the inter-relationship between wages, labour productivity and employment.

The multiple regression analysis using log-linear form has been used to examine the statistical relationship between wages and productivity and other variables. Since, it is a time series study, presence of auto/serial correlation in the residuals may affect the validity of the estimates. So Durban-Watson (DW)/Durban-H (DH) statistics for each regression has been calculated to examine the presence of auto/serial correlation. Whenever, this test indicates the presence of auto/serial correlation, the equations are re-estimated using 'Prais-Winsten' and 'Cochrane-Orcutt' methods. However, the results of the regression giving higher adjusted R^2 among both are only reported.

1.7 Data

The basic data source for the study is the Annual Survey of Industries (ASI), Central Statistical Organisation, Government of India. The data for price index are taken from Office of Economic Adviser, Ministry of Industry, Udhyog Bhawan, New Delhi and from *CIER's Industrial Databook.* The data for consumer price index are taken from *Indian Labour Journal.* The data related to union activities and industrial disputes are collected from Indian Labour Statistics, Labour Beuro, Ministry of Labour, Shimla. The data for the calculation of weights for computation of the input price index are taken from the *'Input-Output Transactions Table (1989-90)'* from Central Statistical Organisation.

1.8 Limitation of the Study

The main limitation of the study is that we could not adjust labour input for quality differences (i.e., difference in skill, efficiency, age etc.). Another limitation of study is the aggregation bias inherent in our data source. Only the aggregated data at industry level were available and firm level data are not available. Moreover, the reporting factories may not be giving accurate figures or they may be following divergent accounting practices. Other limitation of the study relates to our measure of capital input. Due to the non-availability of the data on age composition of assets, we have adjusted capital stock series by using gross-net ratio, which may not represent real capital stock. Moreover, the capital series could not be corrected for discarding of assets due to non-availability of data. Another possible limitation of the study is that productivity effects could not be separated from scale effects. Presence of large-scale economies may overstate the productivity measurements.

1.9 Organisation of the Study

The entire study has been divided into eight chapters. The first chapter is introductory in nature. It explains the need of the study on wage-productivity relationship and prepares the building block of the study. Chapter-2 of the study is related to the methodology for measurement of productivity. Different methods of estimating productivity, using both index number approach and production function approach have been discussed at length. The measurement of output, input and other variables used in study have also been presented in this chapter. Chapter-3 discusses about wage-productivity relationship at length. Besides theoretical and empirical evidence, this chapter also discusses the views of various authorities on the relationship. The productivity trends obtained by various methods are discussed in Chapter-4. The experiences of earlier studies on productivity are also presented in this chapter. Productivity gains and their distribution among labour and capital are presented in Chapter-5. This chapter also studies the relative factor price movement. Chapter-6 investigates the trends in factor compensation (wages and rate of return) in selected industries. This chapter also covers the comparison of wages and labour productivity. The wage functions and employment functions are also presented in this chapter. Chapter-7 deals with the exploration of relationship between wages and other variables besides productivity. The test of causal relationship between labour productivity and wage rate is also presented in this chapter. Summary of findings and concluding remarks are presented in Chapter-8.

References

1. Ahluwalia concluded that the industrial policy framework was main reasons for the productivity slowdown in the mid sixties. For details, see Ahluwalia (1985), pp. 147-165.
2. S.A. Khader (2000) *"Strategic Perspective for Building Productivity Culture."* Yojna, Vol. 44, No. 5, p. 13.
3. M.K. Singh (1989) *Labour Productivity in Indian Industry.* New Delhi: National Publications, p. 1.
4. Kehar Sanga (1964) *Productivity and Economic Growth.* Bombay: Asia Publishing House, p. 36.
5. J. Miyai quoted in Khader (200), op. cit., p. 11.
6. International Labour Organisation (1951). *Methods of Labour Productivity Statistics*. Geneva, p. 12.
7. G. Saibaba and L.K. Mohan Rao (1992) *"Labour Productivity and Trade Unions in India."* The Indian Journal of Labour Economics. Vol. 35, No. 4, p. 407.
8. G. Prudensiky (1964) *"Labour Productivity: Concept, Factors and Growth Reserves"*, in Diatchenkp and J.T. Dunlop (Eds.) Labour Productivity. New York: McGraw Hill Publication, p. 4.
9. W.E.G. Salter (1969) *Productivity and Technical Change.* Cambridge: Cambridge University Press, p. 1.
10. S.C. Aggarwal, (1998[a]) *Human Resources in Public Enterprises: A Wage-Productivity Approach.* New Delhi: Anmol Publishing Pvt. Ltd., p. 4.
11. J.N. Sinha, and P.K. Sawhney, (1970) *Wages and Productivity in Selected Indian Industries.* New Delhi: Vikas Publishing House, p. 5.
12. K. Mohanty, (1993) *Wages and Productivity in a Developing Economy.* New Delhi: Discovery Publishing House. p. 8.
13. Figures in bracket refer to the corresponding NIC three-digit classification numbers.

2

Data and Methodology

2.1 Introduction

Productivity growth is very important for the progress of a nation because it denotes the stage of the development of the country and future-standing of a nation. Productivity studies at the national level enables us to enquire into the trends and prospects of rise in the standard of living, growth of different sectors as well as employment pattern and possibilities. The analysis of productivity at the industry or plant level forms the basis for determining its competitive position. It is also helpful in locating low productivity factors and in deciding upon the idea of standard technique and organisation. Productivity data may be useful in devising a correct policy of distribution. The factual data on the growth of productivity is expected to minimise controversies in the sphere of collective bargaining and thus help in resolving wage disputes (MK Singh, 1989, p. 1). The economic literature is full of the issues relating to the theory and measurement of productivity. Solow (1957), Fabricant (1959), Kendrick (1961), Nadiri (1972) and Jorgenson and Gliriches (1972) among others had tried to explain the growth of output productivity growth.

Studies on productivity acquire a great significance in the context of the growth of developing economies. These economies are characterised by an acute shortage of resources *(particularly capital)* and must use the available resources as best as they can. Also generation of surplus, which plays an important role in their growth, depends crucially on the efficiency with which resources are used.

Measures of productivity, in so far as they reflect advances in knowledge, brings out how effective total production and organisation of production has been in circumventing the problem of resources scarcity and in achieving efficient use of resources. The estimates are affected, to a great extent, by the measurement of variables involved in the productivity analysis mainly, output and inputs. This chapter will discuss at length about the measurement of these variables for present study and the methodology for the productivity estimates.

This chapter is divided into seven sections. Section 2.2 gives the details of data source. The next section 2.3 relates to the methodology for measurement of output. Whereas section 2.4 deals with the measurement of inputs. Section 2.5 describes the methodology for measurement of productivity and is divided in sub-sections relating to the measurement of partial productivity ratios and total factor productivity. Section 2.6 gives an account of the measurement of other variables used in the study.

2.2 Sources of Data

The main data source for this study is the Annual Survey of Industries (ASI). The definitions of terms expressed are same as used by ASI. It is pertinent to know the coverage and scope of ASI. The survey is conducted annually under the statutory provisions of the Collection of Statistics Act, 1953 and the rules framed thereunder in 1959, except in state of Jammu and Kashmir where it is conducted under the State Collection of Statistics Act, 1961 and the rules framed thereunder in 1964. The field-work of the survey is carried out by the Field Operations Division (FOD) of the National Sample Survey Organisation (NSSO) through its network of zonal, regional and sub-regional offices located in different parts of the country. But the responsibility of framing the instructions, processing of data and publications of reports thereon are the responsibilities of the Central Statistical Organisation (CSO).

The ASI extends to the entire country except the State of Arunachal Pradesh, Mizoram and Sikkim, and Union Territory of Lakshdweep. It covers all factories registered under section 2m(i) and 2m(ii) of the Factories Act, 1948, employing 10 or more workers using power and those employing 20 or more workers but not using power on any day of the preceding 12 months. The reference period for the ASI for the years covered in the study is the accounting year of the factory. The primary unit of enumeration in the survey is individual factory. The ASI frame is based on the lists of registered factories/units maintained by Chief Inspector of Factories in each state. For the purpose of ASI, the factories in the frame are classified into two sectors, viz., the census and the sample sectors. While the factories employing 100 or more workers constitute the census sector, the remaining factories constitute the sample sector (it was 50 or more workers with the aid of power up to 1986-87). Once a factory is classified into census/sample sector, its status is not altered for a period of three years, i.e., till the frame is revised, though change in employment might warrant it. While all the industries in census sector are enumerated every year, the factories under sample sector are enumerated as per sampling design.

There are the problems of comparability of ASI data over time. The National Industries Classification (NIC)-1970 was used to classify the industries up to ASI 1988-89 but NIC-1987 is being followed from ASI 1989-90. While this change in classification does not affect the comparability of industries, but the motor vehicle industry (No. 374 in NIC-1970) is splitted in two parts (i.e., No. 373 for manufacture of heavy motor vehicles and coach works and No. 374 for manufacture of other four wheelers) in NIC-1987 and fertilisers and pesticides industry classification No. 311 in NIC-1970 is changed to 301 in NIC-1987. All the factories in the ASI are classified according to the values of the principle products manufactured by them but in subsequent surveys there may be shift to industries from one industrial class to other.

The data for the various price indices has been taken from monthly bulletin of *Index Numbers of Wholesale Prices in India* from the Office of the Economic Advisor, Ministry of Industry, Government of India, Udyog Bhawan, New Delhi and from *CIER's Industrial Databook* by making suitable and necessary adjustments. The data pertaining to consumer price index are obtained from various issues of *Indian Labour Statistics* and necessary adjustments have been made for the purpose of study. The weights for calculation of input prices are taken from *Input-Output Transactions Table (1989-90)* from CSO. The data on number of mandays lost and number of workers involved are taken from the various issues of *Indian Labour Statistics*.

2.3 Measurement of Output

The measurement of productivity is affected by the definition and quantification of output. Like all economic aggregates, measurement of output also raises certain conceptual problems namely, the problems of aggregation, adjustment for quality change, evaluation of output produced at different point of time, heterogeneity of products, technological change, change in product mix and change in the price of products an by-products. Various choices arise while measuring output among the different measures of output, viz physical product, gross output, value added and gross value added. We will limit our discussion on the various choices and reasons for selecting the particular measure for the study. This section is further sub-divided into two sections. Section 2.3.1 deals with the issues involved in the measurement of the output and section 2.3.2 deals with the measurement of output for the present study.

2.3.1 Issues Involved in the Measurement of Output

Physical output would give a better measure of productivity, since in this case, one is not confronted with the problem of making adjustment for change in money value in measuring productivity over a period of time. But an industry produces a diverse set of goods, each of which is expressed in different units, thereby making this measure impractical. Hence, aggregation of output can only be visualised in terms of value only. The important choice arise between value added and gross output. If the later is chosen then it becomes necessary to measure production function in terms of labour, capital and materials. Majority of the studies have chosen 'value added' as a measure of output, advancing following arguments in its favour.[1] (1) It facilitates comparison of results for different industries with different material intensity. (2) It facilitates aggregation of output across industries. (3) Inclusion of materials as an argument in production function leads to the problem of dominant variable, in such formulation almost all the variation in output tends to get explained by materials, thereby obscuring the relation of greater importance (i.e., of physical and human capital utilisation).

A view on the role of materials is implicit in the choice between gross production and value added as the measure of output. Within the framework of production functions, the value added procedure is consistent with two polar assumptions about the role of the materials: (1) The elasticity of substitution between materials and value added in $Y = G\{F(K, L), M\} = G\{V, M\}$ is infinite, allowing one to rewrite it as $Y = F(K, L) + M$ or $V = Y - M = F(K, L)$; and, (2) The elasticity of substitution between materials and output is zero, materials, being used in fixed proportion to output, such that $M = aY$. This model can be written as $Y = [F(K, L), M = aY]$ which implies that $Y - M = V = Y(1 - a) = (1 - a) F(K, L)$ and that value added procedure is again appropriate so long as 'a' is either a constant or is uncorrelated with the value of a capital and labour. The last requirement is the essence of separability whereby the marginal product of materials must be independent of the marginal product of the other two inputs (i.e., labour and capital inputs).[2]

Thus, it can be seen that the use of value-added function is premised on the existence of value-added function, which in turn requires the separability between materials and value added. Pradhan and Barik (1998) have tested the existence of value-added function for the aggregate manufacturing sector and reject its existence.

The total gross output includes all goods and services produced without deduction for intermediate products consumed in the process or for capital consumption. But real product estimates is preferred to total gross output because the real product estimates in relation to real factors costs alone indicates change in efficiency with which basic factor resident in the industry are used to add value to intermediate products.

A further choice arises between net value added and gross value added. The former is net of capital consumption. From the standpoint of economic welfare, the production of capital goods required to offset capital consumption is not required for its own sake, but is necessary to maintain capital stock intact. Denison (1969, p. 2) regards both gross and net measures as legitimate for productivity analysis. He, however, preferred net measure arguing: "In so far as a large output is a proper goal of the society and objective of policy, it is the net product that measures the degree of success in achieving this goal. Gross product is larger by the value of capital consumption. There is no more reason to wish to maximize capital consumption—the quantity of capital used up in production—than there is to maximize the quantity of any other intermediate product...."[3]

Kendrick (1973, p. 18) shows that trends are not affected significantly by use of gross value added in lieu of theoretically preferable net value added. Griliches and Jorgenson attempt to rationalize use of gross value added as preferable to net measure. They argued, "Exclusion of depreciation of capital introduces an entirely arbitrary distinction between labour and capital input, since the corresponding exclusion of the stock of labour service is not carried out."[4] The present study will use gross value added as the measure of output. The use of gross value added, as a measure of output, is justified on the grounds that from the data available, it is very difficult to make a proper estimate of capital consumption. The figure on 'depreciation' that are given in our data source (ASI) are at the rate allowed by the income tax authorities for assessing taxable income and are seldom a representative of true capital consumption or decline in the capital stock as the real capital consumption is quite different from the book value of depreciation. Secondly, by taking gross value added we are measuring both factor returns net of depreciation, thereby avoiding the bias in weighting system.

The next important choice arises in the deflation procedures adopted to make correction for price changes to arrive at the real value added. Many Indian studies recognised the need for double deflation but did not go about it due to scarcity of data.[5] Bruno (1978, 1984) and Rao (1996) points out that the use of single deflated value added, leads to biased estimates. The single deflation method is valide only if price of materials relative to the price of output, are more or less constant. When the price is changing, Bruno (1978, 1984) and Rao (1996[a]) have noted that estimated productivity will vary inversely. Bruno (1984) and Rao (1996[a]) have given a formal expression of the relationship between changes in the relative prices of the materials and value added by single deflation. It clearly shows that the problem is serious only if the relative prices of materials fluctuate. Bal Krishnan and Pushpangadan (1998, p. 2243) argue that recent development in productivity measurement demands for double deflation, and they even questioned what was till then the accepted wisdom concerning productivity growth using single deflation.

Gross value added (our measure of output denoted by GVA) is arrived at by adding the value of depreciation in net value added, i.e., deducting total input from total output. Now to arrive at the value of real value added if we deflate the value of GVA by WPI of the concerned industry product, the method is what is known as single deflation. Symbolically, GVA is given by :

$$GVA = P_{t.} Q_t - P_{mt.} M_{t.} \quad ...(2.1)$$

Where P_t is the price of output Q_t and P_{mt} is the price of material input M_t. Now if we deflate the GVA by the WPI of concerned product (P_t/P_o), then we will have real GVA given by:

$$RGVA_{SD} = (P_{t\cdot} Q_t - P_{m.t.} M_t)/(P_t/P_o). \quad ...(2.2)$$

Here, when we deflate GVA by output prices, we are ignoring the effect of material price and thereby implicitly assuming that the movement of price indices of GVA and material prices are similar. The problem arises due to the fact that the movement of these prices is hardly similar and change in the relative price will affect the RGVA. If the prices of material increase over time relative to product prices, it would reduce the RGVA. Thus, best method should be to deflate gross output-by-output prices and material inputs by input prices, their difference would give us RGVA. Symbolically:

$$RGVA_{DD} = P_{t.}Q_t/(P_t/P_o) - P_{m.t.}M_t)/(P_{mt}/P_{mo}).$$
$$= P_oQ_t - P_{mo.}M_{t.} \quad ...(2.3)$$

Thus, in double deflation the materials are weighted by base year material prices and gross output by base year output prices and their difference would give RGVA by double deflation.

Now again as discussed earlier, and recent advance in productivity theory suggests that use of single deflation would not give correct estimate of RGVA. The most of earlier studies have though recognised the desirability of using double deflation for arriving at real value added figure but avoided using it in the absence of suitable material or input deflator.[6] But, Balkrishnan and Pushpangadan (1998) emphasised that, though the data requirements are substantial but by no means insurmountable. His material price index is for aggregate manufacturing and does not serve our purpose for individual industries.[7] Pradhan and Barik (1998) derived material price index of the individual industries by using structural coefficient of industries from 'Input-Output Transactions Table'.

But, this measure (double deflation) also does not give an error free measure; Rao (1996[a]) has shown that there are biases in the measurement because the weights are fixed. Besides this, the problem of aggregation is inherent in data Source (ASI). He remarked :

"A measure of aggregation bias is ineviatable...even disaggregation up to plant level can not be of any help because many firms/enterprises produce a mixed products rather than a single homogenous product. Besides there may be problem of non-standardization of goods, quality changes, introduction of new product in the output and obsolescence of existing product over time all leadings to some sort of bias in output."[8]

2.3.2 Measurement of Output for Present Study

In the present study, we will use gross value added measure instead of gross output because our main interest is the study of factor's efficiency and the pattern of remuneration to different factors. In this context, Sinha and Sawhney have also emphasized that "Since the ultimate objective of our study is to provide a basis for factor incomes, the value added measure is more meaningful since it yield a magnitude which is distributable among factors operating within the industry while the value of raw material accrues to the person outside the industry concerned."[9]

The ASI gives data on gross value of output, gross value of input and depreciation. Deduction of total input and depreciation from total output derives the value of net value added. Theoretically, net value added is the contribution of labour and capital in the production process. The depreciation is added back to get the gross value added. This study will prepare two indices of gross value added based on single deflation and double deflation. This can be justified because to cater for the difference in relative price movement, gross value added by double deflation is best measure but, the gross output arrived at by the use of double deflation is not, what is available for distribution between labour and capital, and hence estimates by single deflation is required to get the real output distributable among labour and capital. The *material price index* is the weighted average of the WPI of concerned inputs and the weights for inputs are derived from the *Input-Output Transactions Table 1987-88*. But, for the organised manufacturing sector we have used the material price index as given by Balkrishnan and Pushpangadan (1994, p. 2029). The series, beyond 1988-89, has been extended by using the weights given by them (p. 2032). And for single deflation and deflation of output we have used WPI of concerned industry.

2.4 Measurement of Inputs

The measurement of inputs is equally important in the productivity analysis because productivity estimates are very sensitive to the measurement of inputs. A discussion on the various problems in measurement of inputs and selecting the best alternative is very important. This section is further sub-divided into three sub-sections. Section 2.4.1 discusses at length about the measurement of labour input and measurement used for the present study. Whereas section 2.4.2 discusses the issues involved in the measurement of the capital input and section 2.4.3 deals with methodology used for the present study.

2.4.1 Measurement of Labour Input

Apart from aggregation problem, labour measurement has less difficulty than the measurement of capital. Physical measure of labour input exit in the form of employment or man-hours and therefore, the problem of converting value to constant prices does not arise. The treatment of depreciation does not arise, as the labour efficiency is not considered to deteriorate with age. Moreover, changes in the utilisation of labour are better recorded than the capital.

Sometimes, a methodological problem regarding the unit of measurement is raised. Three alternative measure of labour input are available; 'man-hours' or 'man-days' worked, 'workers' and 'employees'. The most important choice arises between man-hours and number of persons engaged (workers or employees). Denison (1961) noted that the man-hours are better measure than employment to represent changes in disutility or cost of labour. However, he claimed that employment is a better measure of effective labour input than man-hours to represent the contribution of labour to output. He remarked that the employment is a labour input, that is crudely adjusted for one form of quality change—the quality of one hour's work that is due to the shortening of working hours. The effect of a shorter work hour on hourly production is to work through several channels—reduction of work fatigue and more importantly stimulation of management efficiency and substitution of capital for labour. Again for long-term comparisons, the choice favours employment because the progressive reduction in man-hours per week leads to an increase in labour intensity, which in turn increases output per man-hour.

The present study will use the number of persons (workers or employees) as input measure. Besides the theoretical consideration, our choice is guided by the availability of data. The ASI gives data on number of persons employed and mandays worked. Mandays represent the total number of days worked and not the number of days paid for, during the year. It is obtained by summing the number of persons of specified category attending in each shift over all the shifts worked, on all days. The man-hours data are usually calculated by multiplying the mandays worked by a constant of eight hours (which may not be the actual duration of the shift). The series thus obtained may not represent the man-hours actually worked. Moreover, man-hours series covers only workers and leaves out 'persons other than the workers'.

The next important choices arises between the workers and employees. The ASI gives data on workers, persons other than workers and total number of persons employed during a year. For labour input either the number of worker or total number of persons employed can be taken. However, the measure of labour input in terms of total number of persons employed implicitly involves the unrealistic assumption of prefect substitutability between the workers and persons other than the workers. But if we take number of workers as a measure of labour input, the share of capital income is likely to be overstated. Gangopadhyay and Wadhwa (1998, p. L47) pointed that since the share of capital income is defined residually, using wages to compute the share of labour income would imply that benefits which are a part of emoluments and therefore accrue to labour, would actually counted as capital income.

The 'Labour Bureau' does not favours the inclusion of the persons other than workers in the measure of labour input on the grounds that they form very small portion of total employees in the factory and the number of such persons is fairly stable to the number of workers. The persons other than workers include supervisor, technician, managers, clerks and other similar types of employees. On the other hand, Sinha and Sawhney (1971) noted that their services are as important for the execution of work in the factory as the operators who are directly engaged in the various stages of production process.

Based on the above discussion the present study will use the total number persons engaged as the measure of labour input. It may be pointed out that there are various limitations of our measure of labour input. Labour differs in quality due to age, sex, skills, job experience, education and occupational composition of labour force. The assessment of quantitative importance of each factor in the technological progress is almost impossible. Griliches (1967) assumed that efficiency differences in different class of labourer are reflected in their rate of remuneration and suggested for making adjustment. Goldar (1986, p. 49) argued that considering the imperfection of labour market it may be possible that differences in remuneration need not be representative of efficiency differences for Indian manufacturing and accordingly, it is hard to see why a weighted index of labour using remuneration of different classes as weights be a better measure of labour input than the number of person employed. It has been argued that two most important factors improving the quality of labour are learning process and education but it is very difficult to incorporate them in a production function.

Based on above discussion and scarcity of data, no attempts have been made to adjust labour input for quality differences, that is a limitation of our measure of labour input. However, it may be noted that very few attempts have been made to adjust labour input for quality change at this level of aggregation. Gupta (1987) have used the concept of workers equivalent to adjust for some sort of quality difference between 'workers' and 'persons other than workers'. His measure of employment in workers equivalent is given by:

$$E = L_w + (W_{nw}/W).Lnw. \qquad ...(2.4)$$

Here W_{nw} / W is the ratio of wage rate of non-worker to that of workers. L_w and L_{nw} is the number of workers and persons other than workers. This explicitly assumes that rate of remuneration reflects the quality difference of persons which may not be a good assumption in Indian context.

2.4.2 Measurement of Capital Input

The calculation of capital input is the most difficult part of the work in the scheme of productivity analysis. The measurement of capital throws various problems of definition and measurement besides usual problem of aggregation and heterogeneity associated with it. It should be stressed at the outset that there is no entirely satisfactory or universally accepted way of measuring capital input. Not only there are serious theoretical problems related to the very idea of measuring capital but also even actual practices show a wide divergence. Thus the estimation of capital input is a controversial issue both in theory and practice.

The present study does not go in details about the definition and theoretical aspect. Asit Banerjee (1975, pp. 4-6) provides a detailed description of theoretical problem, the place of capital in production process and the historical perspective of theory of capital.[10] Goldar (1985) provides a very useful review of both the theoretical problems and shortcoming of existing estimates of capital stocks for manufacturing sector.[11] We limit our discussion on the empirical issues involved in the measurement of capital. We shall discuss the certain critical issues in selecting suitable estimate for present study among the various concepts of capital measurement.

Physical measurement of capital is not possible for the reasons that there are numerous kinds of capital expressed in different physical units of different quality. The only feasible way of measuring capital is indirect. Then the question arises, should the capital be valued in terms of its costs or in terms of its contribution to production. Denison (1957) strongly favours the first method for the productivity analysis. If the capital is measured in terms of its costs then the increase in the quality of capital will be reflected in the technical progress term rather than the measure of capital input. The major measurement problem arises because capital is not of the same vintage. If the capital is measured in terms of its contribution to the production then the increase in the efficiency of capital as a result of technical advance will be incorporated in the measurement of capital itself. This will make capital productivity constant, which is of no use.

The next important choice is whether to include working capital or exclude it from capital input. In productivity measurement the fixed capital is usually taken into account in calculating capital inputs. In this context, Sinha and Sawhney remarked:

> "While the importance of working capital to industrial productivity cannot be denied, the inventory and cash holdings are more often determined by supply and market expectations than technological pipeline requirements and have, therefore, far less bearing on productivity than fixed

investment. Also the available data on inventories and cash are as on the last day of the year and not the average holding of working capital through the year which alone may be appropriately related to the annual flow of output."[12]

Thus, it is extremely difficult to have a precise measure of working capital as applicable for whole year and its exclusion is justified on these grounds. But the exclusion of working capital from the capital input is criticised on the following grounds:

"The exclusion of the later (working capital) is defensible only if its ratio to fixed capital remains unchanged over time which demonstrably not the case: not only is this ratio is non-negligibly large but varies significantly over the period... The aggregation of working capital and fixed capital may be defended on the grounds that even if they enter in the production function as separate arguments, optimisation would render their marginal products equal."[13]

The next important question is whether capital stock should be inclusive of capital depreciation or not. The researchers are not unanimous on this question. The economic rational desires to have an estimate of net capital stock if a fairly suitable measure of economic depreciation can be estimated. The Labour Bureau uses capital net of depreciation on the grounds that there is a quantitative deterioration of old machine which lost their productive capacity with time and requires greater expenditure for repair and maintenance (Subramanium, 1977, p. 352).

Beri (1961) noted that in case of old plants and equipment, repair and maintenance charges mount up, so their contribution to net output falls and he suggests that the real value of capital stock, net of accumulated depreciation allowances is to be regarded as a more suitable measure of capital input than the gross value of the capital. Sinha and Sawhney (1970, p. 20) emphasized that the net capital measure will be meaningful only if the rate of depreciation allowed, corresponds to the decline in the real product yielding capacity of various items in the stock, this is far from the truth; in fact, the available estimates of depreciation are either tax-based accounting concepts or based on certain rule of thumb. Therefore, they do not reflect the decline in the capacity of real stock to product. Kennedy and Thirlwal in their survey article have justified the use of gross capital stock on the grounds that the flow of capital services does not decline with age at the rate frequently suggested by the allowance for depreciation. They remarked[14] "*Net* measure of capital tends to assume that the services derived from capital deteriorate with age much more than they actually do. Ideally one would like to have a net measure of capital which makes the allowances for depreciation but not obsolescence, but lack of evidence renders this scarcely practicable." Consequently, gross rather than net capital stock, will be more closely related to the capital services consumed by the industry.

The use of gross capital stock assumes to have the same efficiency from the time of purchase until they are fully written off, when their usefulness is assumed to be zero. This is also not a realistic assumption. However, it is the fact that a large amount of expenditure is incurred by the business firms on repair and maintenance, where main objective is to keep assets in more or less similar productive capacity. Hasim and Dadi (1973, p. 10) noted that a large part of such maintenance cost is treated as current cost and is deducted from gross value of output to obtain gross value added. Accordingly they argued that, since the main objective of such expenditure is to keep the productive capacity of capital assets more or less intact, such expenditure should be treated as re-investment. If so, then the so-called 'gross value added' is in fact net value added, and under such a situation there is no need to subtract depreciation from gross capital stock so as to correct for capital consumption. The use of gross fixed capital is especially applicable in the case of Indian manufacturing industries where the figures on depreciation does not represent the actual capital consumption. Moreover, as George Rosen (1959) puts it "in fact, in underdeveloped countries a machine is probably more often used at approximately constant levels of output for a period far beyond the accounting life of the machine, measured by the normal depreciation, until it is eventually discarded or sold for scrap.[15]

There are two steps in calculation of capital input, namely (1) estimation of the value of fixed assets, and (2) estimation of flow of services from these assets. Obviously it is not the stock of capital but the services of capital, which is to be treated as a factor of production. But the measurement of real services of capital is even more difficult than the measurement of capital stock. The estimation of flow of services is based on the assumption that there is a constant relation between the stock of fixed capital and flow of its services. If the stock data have to represent correctly the flow of capital services, it is required that the ratio of capital services to capital stock be same for all types of assets, and also the assets prices (used as a weights for measuring stocks) be proportional to services prices. Goldar (1986, p. 54) argues that to the extent this does not hold in reality leads to the errors in the measurement of capital input. The estimation of gross fixed capital series is usually done by the use of Perpetual Inventory Accumulation Method (PIAM). The estimate requires the estimation of gross fixed capital for the benchmark year and the estimation of investment for subsequent years. The first part of this process is controversial whereas second part is comparatively easy, once gross fixed capital for benchmark year is calculated. The empirical estimates for benchmark year gross fixed capital stock differs. Asit Banerji (1975) estimated the gross fixed capital stock for benchmark year (1946) by multiplying the book value of 1946 by a constant of two. To obtain gross fixed capital (GFC) for subsequent year he adds deflated gross yearly investments (at 1946 prices) to the benchmark year cumulatively. Goldar (1986) questions this method on the grounds that multiplying by two is arbitrary and asks, why this multiplication is only for the year 1946 and not for the subsequent years. Moreover, he argued that Banerji assumes zero rate of discarding implying that all machines working in 1946, however old they might have been, continued to serve up to 1964.

The majority of the Indian studies[16] have used the gross-net ratio, obtained by Hasim and Dadi, for estimation of gross fixed capital for benchmark year. To explicitly account for the cumulative depreciation, Hasim and Dadi have gone into the detail using a sample of 1000 balance-sheets of firms and obtaining the ratio of purchase value to book value of fixed capital stocks (known as gross-net ratios) for 41 three digit ASI industries, separately for three categories of assets (1) building and construction, (2) plant and machinery and (3) other assets. These ratios are used to derive gross fixed assets at purchase prices for the year 1960. Goldar (1986) questions this method and argues that Hasim and Dadi have seriously overestimated the value of fixed capital stock especially for the earlier part of the series. He also questions the use of price index of manufacturing articles and noted that a price index based on machinery and construction prices would obviously be much more appropriate. Goldar (1985) claimed his superiority over the earlier estimates on three grounds (a) greater attention to the valuation of base year capital, (b) more appropriate capital goods price deflator and (c) correction of capital series for discarding of assets. He estimated the capital stock in year t (denoted by K_t) as:

$$K_t = K_Q + \sum_{t=1}^{T} (I_t - DS_t). \qquad ...(2.5)$$

Where K_o is the gross capital stock for benchmark year, I_t is the gross investment (at the base year prices), DS_t is the amount of fixed assets discarded during year 't'. The procedure of estimating I_t series is the same as done by Banerji. But for the calculation of K_o and DS_t, Goldar does not follow a consistent procedure. At one place (Ch. IV) he uses the gross-net ratio calculated from the report of taxation enquiry commission and at one place (Ch. V) he had used the double of book value at base year and again he had used the gross-net ratio of Hasim and Dadi for arriving at the estimates for industries and industrial groups. Similarly he had taken rate of discarding as $DS_t = 0$; and $DS_t = K_{t-1}$. The measurement of assets discarded, as well as average life of capital is again arbitrary here.[17]

The next important question is the construction of correct price index for capital goods and it is here we are faced with some of the difficult problems. Asit Banerji (1975, p. 5) argued that the main problem is to separate the influences that increase the productivity of capital goods from one that increases the productivity in the production of capital goods. Technological progress makes the problem of deflation more difficult by giving rise to the insoluble index number problem. Ruggles and Ruggles (1961) noted, the idea that real capital can be measured by what it would cost in the base year to produce the given year stock, is not meaningful, as the comparison becomes impossible because of technical change. It may be noted that for preparing price index of capital some specified items of capital of specific quality are chosen and market prices indices of these items are worked out. An average index of individual machinery price indices based on appropriate weights, gives the average price index of machinery. The use of later implies that the prices of items not included in the specific selected items, have also moved parallel to those of the specified items. Subramanium (1970, p. 353) argues that a price index worked out in the above manner suffers from severe limitations. First, machine of the same description produced at different points of time may be different in specifications and quality. The increase in the price index of the same type of machine may partly be due to improvement in the quality, increasing the quantity of capital embodied in that price. The use of its price index as deflator will give a lower estimate of the real value of capital. Secondly, when a new efficient (perhaps automatic) machine is developed, the old type of machine is no longer in demand (a typical case of obsolesce) and its price will go down in the market. At the same time the real inputs required for production of old type would not have declined correspondingly. Thus, the use of price index based on the prices of specified items of machines available in the base year as deflator both for old type and new type machine will give inaccurate estimates of real capital employed. Thirdly, the use of base year weighting may prove be defective. The cost of production of newly introduced capital goods may have fallen very fast. The price index based on an early year would, therefore, be relatively too high and the resulting quantity of capital too low.

Next in the measurement problem is the choice between corrections of capital for under-utilization of capital. Kendrick (1973) and Denison (1974) have strongly argued against the correction for the capacity utilization in productivity studies. Kendrick remarked:

> "In contrast to the human population, the entire living population of capital goods (those that have not been discarded, including items in the active 'standby' status) is available for productive use at all times, and involves a per annum cost, regardless of degree of use. The purpose of capital assets is for use in production of current output and income. The degree of capital utilization reflects the degree efficiency of enterprises and the social economy generally. Hence, in converting capital stocks into inputs, we do not adjust capital for changes in the rates of capital utilization, and thus these are reflected in changes in the productivity ratios."[18]

Denison (1974 has also argued against correcting the capital series by capacity utilization in the productivity studies on the grounds that that capacity utilization fluctuates with the variations in the pressure of demand.

2.4.3 Measurement of Capital Input for the Present Study

In present study value of gross fixed stock at constant price has been taken as the measure of capital input. The ASI gives data on working capital, fixed capital, invested capital and productive capital. Fixed capital represents the depreciated value of fixed assets owned by the factory on the closing day of the accounting year. Fixed assets are those, which have a normal productivity life of more than one year. Fixed capital includes land including leasehold land, buildings, plant and machinery, furniture and fixtures, transport equipments, water system and other fixed assets such as hospitals, school etc. used for the benefits of the factory workers. Working capital is the sum total of physical working capital and cash deposit in hand and banks, and the net balance receivable over amount payable at the end of accounting year. It excludes unused overdraft facilities, fixed deposits irrespective of duration, advances for acquisition of fixed assets, loans and advances by proprietors and partners irrespective of their purpose and duration, long-term loans including interest thereon and investments. Physical working capital is the total inventory comprising of raw materials and components, fuel and lubricants, spare stores and others, semi-finished goods and finished goods as on the closing day of the accounting year. However, it does not include the stock of materials, fuels, stores etc. supplied by others to the factory for processing and finished goods processed by factory from the raw materials supplied by others. Productive capital is the total of fixed capital and working capital as defined above while invested capital is the total of fixed capital and physical working capital as defined above.

Our measure of capital stock excludes the working capital in conformity of the discussion in last section. Again we use gross stock rather than net stock for the reasons discussed in last section. We have not corrected our series of capital stock for under-utilisation of capital. It may be noted that majority of Indian studies have not corrected their capital stock for capacity utilisation.[19] Besides theoretical consideration discussed above, the non-availability of reliable estimates for the manufacturing sector weighted our choice. It is assumed that the flow of capital services is proportional to the capital stock. The perpetual inventory accumulation method (PIAM) is used for the generation of capital stock series. This method requires the estimation of fixed capital for the benchmark year (K_o) and the gross investment series deflated by a suitable price deflator (I_o).

The estimation of capital stock for benchmark year is a difficult and controversial issue. The ASI data on fixed capital relating to a particular year is the depreciated value of capital stock accumulated over the years. This value of capital has been acquired over different point of time and is the summation of historical cost of the component of the capital goods valued at historical prices. To get the estimates of gross fixed capital for the benchmark year at the constant prices, we require the age structure and price indices for different years. For present study to solve this problem, we have made use of gross-net ratio given by Hasim and Dadi for the various three-digit industries. We first obtain the value of (i) Land (ii) Building and Construction (iii) Plant and Machinery (iv) other Assets from ASI 1960.[20] Hasim and Dadi provide estimates of gross-net ratio for last three categories of assets. Now taking the ratio of land equal to unity and multiplying the value of these assets by their corresponding gross-net ratio and then adding up together we get the gross fixed assets, at purchase prices, for particular industry. For industry No. 399 (watches and clocks) we have taken the corresponding ratio of miscellaneous industries. Having estimated gross fixed capital at purchase price for different industries, we multiplied these figures by ratio of current to purchase price for the year 1960. We have got the ratio of current to purchase price of fixed capital for different two-digit industries by dividing the figure of gross fixed capital at current prices for the year 1960 by the gross fixed capital at purchase price for same year as given in Dadi.[21] The ratio for the industries at three-digit industries is assumed to be same as for two-digit industries. This way we get the gross fixed capital at 1960 price. Now to convert these figures for the price of 1973-74 we have multiplied these figures by the price index of 1973-74 with base 1960 = 100. In this way we got the gross fixed capital in 1960 at the 1973-74 prices (K_o), we could get a time series of gross fixed capital at constant prices if we have a series of gross investment of capital stock for different years. The series of gross investment (I_t) by following formula :

$$I_t = (B_t - B_{t-1} + D_t)/P_t. \qquad ...(2.6)$$

Here I is the gross investment, B is the book value of fixed capital, D is the book value of deprecation, P is the price deflator (wholesale price index for machinery and machinery goods) and t is the time subscript. Having estimated gross investment (I_t) the time series of gross fixed capital can be had by cumulatively adding the gross investment. Symbolically:

$$K_t = K_0 + \sum_{t=1}^{T} I_t. \qquad ...(2.7)$$

In this way we can develop the series of gross fixed capital for present study. For year 1972-73 we have taken average of 1971-72 and 1973-74. However it may be noted that this capital stock is not corrected for the assets discarding, in the absence of good studies on the mortality rate and time pattern of fixed assets. This is the reason that most of the Indian studies have ignored the problem of assets discarding.[22]

2.5 Measurement of Productivity

Productivity can be defined as the efficiency with which inputs are transformed into useful output within the production process. Productivity can be measured by either comparing the output with the services of a single factor (Partial Productivity Ratio) or by comparing all the inputs combined to some standard form to the output (Total Factor or Multifactor Productivity). These ratios are generally compared with the corresponding ratios of different times or places. The productivity ratios are generally normalised to some base year, resulting in a productivity indices over time. The partial productivity ratios are simply the average product of labour or capital. Total factor productivity is more comprehensive approach and has been extensively used. Section 2.5 is further sub-divided into three sub-sections. Section 2.5.1 deals with the partial productivity ratios which is further sub-divided into labour productivity ratio (2.5.1a) and capital productivity ratio (section 2.5.1b). Section 2.5.2 deals with the total factor productivity measure by non-parametric methods (section 2.5.2a), using Kendrick, Solow and Translog methods and section 2.5.2b deals with the production function estimates using C-D, CES, VES and Transcendental Logarithmic production function respectively.

2.5.1 Partial Productivity Ratios

The partial productivity ratios are the simplest measure of productivity and are derived by dividing the output by relevant factor input. Naturally, there can be as many partial productivity ratios as there are inputs. The most commonly used and widely reported partial productivity ratios are labour productivity ratio and capital productivity ratio. The partial productivity ratio relates output to the input of a single factor and it does not tell us anything about the other factors. The increase in partial productivity ratio means that over a period of time more output is possible with decreasing amounts of inputs or with same inputs or same output with lesser inputs. The inverse of these partial productivity ratios implies unit requirement of factor concerned for per unit of output. The study of a partial productivity ratio is very helpful in measuring the saving in use of that particular factor over a period of time. These ratios indicate the average productivity of that particular factor. As long as, all partial productivity ratios move in the same direction, a general idea can be had about the direction of overall productive efficiency but when different ratio moves in the opposite directions, no definite idea can be made about the overall productive efficiency, and they can be misleading. Moreover, it is the marginal productivity and not the average productivity *(represented by partial productivity ratios)* which is important in determining the factor remuneration, factor's share etc. Unfortunately, unlike average ratios, marginal ratios cannot be estimated directly in pure statistical sense. In practice we cannot make other thing constant or change them equi-proportionally. This is not to suggest that they are not useful at all, but just to point out that care and caution must be taken while interpreting and using them for decision-making. However, Rosen (1958, p. 18) has suggested that if data do not permit an estimation of marginal ratio, average ratio may be used as a very rough estimate for the approximation of marginal ratio. But caution must be taken while using them.

2.5.1a. Labour Productivity

Labour productivity may be defined as the ratio of output to the ratio labour input, while there is no ambiguity regarding the definition of labour productivity but its measurement differs due to various definition and quantification of numerator and denominator of the ratio, i.e., output and input. The definition and measurement issues are discussed in the section 2.3 and 2.4. Symbolically, labour productivity in any year may be defined as :

$$AP_{Lt} = V_t / L_t. \qquad ...(2.8)$$

and a change in labour productivity between two periods can be measured by the ratio of productivity in two periods, symbolically:

$$R_L = V_t/L_t \div V_O/L_O \qquad ...(2.9)$$

Where AP_{Lt} is the labour productivity in year t; V_t is the value of output; L_t is the value of labour input, R_L is the index of labour productivity; t and o refers to the time subscript in standard index number terminology.

Labour productivity should be interpreted with utmost caution, as labour is only, one of the factors of production. Changes in labour productivity should not be interpreted as the changes due to labour alone. Labour productivity carries with it a strong connotation of workers efficiency in popular thinking which may be quite misleading.[23] A sharp distinction may however be drawn between labour efficiency and labour productivity in respect of their qualitative and quantitative difference. In fact, the concept of output per person is representative of the efficiency of enterprises in the utilisation of labour force, rather than the efficiency of labour in the unit of time which is related to its abilities and will to work. Beri (1968, p. 97) has remarked that labour productivity measure of efficiency is quite misleading, especially in the underdeveloped countries, where labour is cheaper and abundantly available and there has been greater amount of capital increase. Fabricant (1970) argued that a rise or fall in efficiency may result from host of factors and this change in efficiency in the use of resources can not be determined by comparing changes in output with change in labour alone. They pointed out the inadequacy of labour productivity as a measure of overall efficiency. The critics object that it *(labour productivity measured by V/L)* does not measure anything peculiar to labour and that increased capital or materials may raise labour productivity while labour itself remain passive (Salter, 1969, p. 2). The labour productivity is not necessarily, is the measure of labour efficiency, it may be boosted by the injection of modern technology, and that it cannot, *ipso facto,* made the justification of equivalent wage increases. Subramanium argued that when an appreciable increase in labour productivity is noticed, our first line of enquiry should be directed towards ascertaining the cause of it—towards verifying whether a large, perhaps uneconomic, increase in capital is at the bottom of it (1977, p. 341).

The improvement in labour productivity index may result due to various factors such as capital intensity of technology, better capacity utilisation, economies of scale, use of better technology, size of market, employment of better trained manpower, changes in raw material and many other factors. Thus, there may be a case where labour productivity has increased even when there is no improvement in quantity and quality of labour input. Sinha and Sawhney (1970, p. 14) argued that an increase in labour productivity, measures the saving in the cost of labour used in producing a given output but whether it amounts to reduction in real cost of production, depends upon the direction of changes in the cost of other factors of production. Thus, labour productivity so obtained should not be purely relied in linking wages with the productivity (directly or proportionally).

It has been argued that once the concept of labour productivity suffers from substantial limitation, then why there is a continued interest in labour productivity. The main reasons for this is that the labour input is easier to compute and is more reliable. Labour is the only active factor which is directly productive. Other factor inputs such as production means are passive by nature, they improve the productivity of labour, in the course of production. Ultimately it is the human factor, which governs and organise all other factors.

2.5.1b. Capital Productivity

The capital productivity index has obvious significance for the productivity analysis as it reflects the efficiency in the utilisation of capital. Capital productivity may be defined as the ratio of total output to the total input. Symbolically:

$$AP_{Kt} = V_t/K_t. \quad ...(2.10)$$

and a change in capital productivity between two periods can be measured by the ratio of capital productivity in two periods, symbolically:

$$R_K = V_t/K_t \div V_o/K_o. \quad ...(2.11)$$

Where R_K is the index of capital productivity. This measure also has all the limitations of labour productivity ratio and partial productivity ratios discussed in preceding paragraphs.

2.5.2 Total Factor Productivity

Productivity is a measure of how well labour, capital and other inputs are utilised to produce output. Total Factor Productivity may be viewed as the relationship between real product and real tangible factor cost. It identifies the contribution to an increase in output made by the factors, other than increase in total inputs. The meaning of productivity measures depends on the definitions accorded to the output and inputs, the methodology by which the concepts are statistically implemented including the weighting pattern used to combine unlike units of outputs and inputs, and the manner in which inputs are related to output. In the empirical analysis the phrases *Technological Progress* and *Total Factor Productivity* are often used interchangeably, though a useful distinction can be made between them.[24] Technological progress may be defined as the advance in the knowledge relating to the art of production. It may take the form of new goods, new processes or newer mode of organisation. Total Factor Productivity (hereafter referred as TFP) may be defined as the ratio of output to a weighted combination of inputs. Thus, changes in TFP may take place for a number of reasons other than the advance in knowledge. It contains the effect of technical progress and of better utilisation of capacities, learning by doing, improved skill of labour, better maintenance procedures, better organizational skills, better labour management relations, etc. and is, hence, a better measure of technological change and the change in efficiency with which technology is applied to the production. The methodology for measurement of total factor productivity may be classified into two broad categories viz (i) A non-parametric index number approach and (ii) a parametric production function approach. The study will analyse productivity in the selected industries using both these approaches.

2.5.2a. Index Number Approach

The index number approach, generally, does not proceed by specifying an explicit production (or a dual cost) function; rather its strategy is to compute separate input and output indexes from observed prices and quantity data and use them for measurement of TFP. As a result of this, TFP measurement by this approach is free from all the biases of explicit functional form. Total factor productivity growth may be denied as the difference between the growth in output and the growth in aggregate inputs. The residual measure can be obtained only if the weights for aggregation are known. A unique set of weight has been derived analytically by Solow (1957). He demonstrated that residual growth would become a measure of technical progress, provided the share of value of inputs in total revenue may be used as the weights for the aggregation. Under the conditions of competitive equilibrium and disembodied technical progress, this residual would measure the outward shift in the production function over time. The Kendrick measure of TFP growth is the application of this specific functional form of production. With the application of duality theory, TFP growth measures the difference between the changes in the input price by way of Translog index. The different indices would differ due to weighting pattern used and different assumption about the elasticity of substitution implicit in the underlying production function. The present study will prepare the following indices of TFP (i) Kendrick index, (ii) Solow index, and (iii) Translog index.

(I) KENDRICK INDEX

Kendrick measure of TFP is an arithmetic measure because here tangible factor input is an arithmetic average of labour and capital input. As Kendrick puts it "the fact that our total factor input index is the weighted arithmetic mean of labour and capital input indices (rather than geometrical mean) implies a logarithmic linear relationship within successive sub periods."[25] This measure of TFP is based on the linear production function of the form:

$$V = aL + bK. \qquad ...(2.12)$$

Where V is output, L and K are labour and capital respectively, and a and b are coefficients of labour and capital. A weighted input index is prepared by combining labour and capital inputs using appropriate weights. The weights may either be the prices of labour and capital or the percentage share of labour and capital in the total value added. The weighted inputs of labour and capital in each year are added to get total input index. Then, an index of output as also of total input is prepared. The ratio of output to total input index will yield the arithmetic TFP index. Symbolically, it may be expressed as:

$$TFPK_t = V_t/(a_o L_t + b_o K_t). \qquad ...(2.13)$$

Where V_t is an index of output, L_t and K_t are indices of capital and labour in year t and $TFPK_t$ is the Kendrick index for time t. However as Mehta (1980) points out that this function poses some uncomfortable theoretical problems. By re-arranging terms, equation (2.13) can be written as:

$$V_t = TFPK_t\,(a_o L_t + b_o K_t). \qquad ...(2.14)$$

From this it can be seen that regardless of how fast capital is growing in relation to the labour this ratio remains same. Thus, marginal rate of substitution is assumed to remain constant regardless of the changes in factor proportions. The assumption of linear production function, prefect competition, prefect substitutability between labour and capital are implied. The weights here are not derived from a statistical function but are the estimated factor's share in income. The value of $TFPK_t$ in the base year would be equal to one by definition.

(II) SOLOW INDEX

Solow's geometric index of TFP is given by the parameter A (t) in the multiplicative production function of the form:

$$V = A\,(t)\,L^{\alpha}K^{\beta}. \qquad ...(2.15)$$

Taking logarithmic and differentiating w.r.t. time we have:

$$V'/V = A'/A + \alpha\,L'/L + \beta K'/K. \qquad ...(2.16)$$

Where dot (') represents derivations with respect to time. For discrete changes the above equation may be written as:

$$\Delta A/A = \Delta V/V - [\alpha\,(\Delta\,L/L) + \beta\,(\Delta\,K/K)]. \qquad ...(2.17)$$

Where $\Delta A/A$ is the rate of change of TFP; $\Delta V/V$ is the rate of change of output; $\Delta L/L$ and $\Delta K/K$ is the rate of change of labour and capital; α and β are the share of labour and capital in total income. Thus, rate of change of TFP is the difference between the rate of change of output and the weighted sum of the rate of change of inputs. Under the assumption of constant return to scale we have $\alpha + \beta = 1$ and the equation can be written as:

$$V/L = A(t).(K/L)^{\beta}. \quad ...(2.18)$$

and the TFP is given by:

$$\Delta A/A = (\Delta V/L)/(V/L) - \beta(\Delta K/L)/(K/L) \quad ...(2.19)$$

Thus, under the assumption of constant return to scale the rate of TFP is the difference between rate of change of output per unit of labour and rate of change of capital per unit of labour multiplied by capital share in output. Thus, Solow's geometric index assumes a more general neo-classical production function where the elasticity of substitution need not to be constant, but technical change is of Hicks-neutral type under the assumption that factor are paid according to their marginal products. Once computation of $\Delta A/A$ is done for different year with the help of the equation (2.19), an index of TFP {A (t)} for each year can be derived from the identity:

$$A(t+1) = A(t)(1 + \Delta A/A), \quad ...(2.20)$$

measuring cumulative effect of shift over time. A (0) is one by assumption representing base year technology.

Solow's model can also be used to separate the effect of technical progress and capital accumulation in TFPG. The basic procedure is to estimate the contribution made to growth in output by increase in inputs of labour and capital by multiplying the observed increase in factor price, and deducting the result from the overall growth in output. To decompose labour productivity change due to technological progress and due to capital intensity. We uses the equation:

$$(\Delta V/L)/V/L = \Delta A/A + \beta(\Delta K/L)/(K/L). \quad ...(2.21)$$

which shows that labour productivity is compounded of two elements (i) changes in capital intensity and (ii) changes in technical progress. To find out how much of change in labour productivity is due to technical progress we proceed as follows

(i) Total rise in labour productivity is calculated by:

$$\Delta V/L = (V/L)_t - (V/L)_o. \quad ...(2.22)$$

(ii) The labour productivity in year t is deflated by A (t) of the same year. This is net of technical change and attributable to capital intensity. Symbolically:

$$\Delta V/L_{K/L} = [(V/L)_t/A\ (t)] - (V/L)_o. \quad ...(2.23)$$

(iii) Here, $V/L_{K/L}$ is the increase in labour productivity solely due to capital intensity (K/L ratio).

(iv) The remainder of the change in labour productivity and changes due to capital intensity give the rise in labour productivity due to technical progress. Symbolically:

$$(\Delta V/L)_{tp} = \Delta\ V/L - \Delta\ V/L_{K/L}. \quad ....(2.24)$$

Thus, Solow index can be used to decompose the effect of increased per capita capital and the technical progress on labour productivity.

Ahluwalia (1991, p. 63) noted that Solow's concept of TFP growth is unambiguous for infinitesimally small shift in technology in continuous time. Empirical estimates, however, are based on a discrete set of price and quantity data. In order to solve this problem a 'flexible' functional form of production function is required. One such functional form is Transcendental Logarithmic (Translog) production function for which Tornquist discrete approximation is exact.

(III) TRANSLOG INDEX

The Translog index of total factor productivity is derived from Translog production function under the assumption of constant return to scale and competitive equilibrium. It also assumes that factor price are paid according to their marginal productivity. This index is the discrete version of continuous divisia index. Divisia index satisfy both factor reversal and time reversal test for the index number. Its functional form is derived as follows.

Considering an aggregate production function with two factors of production which is homogeneous of degree one, we have:

$$Y = F\ (K, L, T). \quad ...(2.25)$$

Denoting factor prices by P, marginal shares of factor input can be defined as:

$$S_K = (P_K.K)/(P_Q.Y). \quad ...(2.26)$$

and

$$S_L = (P_L.L)/(P_Q.Y). \quad ...(2.27)$$

Under constant returns to scale:

$$S_K + S_L = 1. \quad ...(2.28)$$

The rate of technical change may be defined as the rate of growth of output w.r.t. time holding inputs constant. Symbolically:

$$S_T = \delta LnY/\delta t. \quad ...(2.29)$$

Under constant returns to scale, the rate of technical change can be expressed as the rate of growth of output less a weighted average of rate of growth of inputs (capital and labour) and weights being their respective shares. Symbolically:

$$S_T = (\delta LnY/\delta t) - [(S_K LnK/\delta t) + (S_L LnL/\delta t)] \quad ...(2.30)$$

Where S_T is the divisia index of the rate of technical progress and the figures in bracket [ ] in above equation, may be written as $\delta LnI/\delta t$, is the divisia index of input. Thus, TFP is measured here as the difference between the rate of growth of value added and rate of growth of inputs (total factor input). The above equation is for the continuous time framework and to apply it for real world, a discrete time approximation is needed. The Translog index is a discrete version of continuous divisia index. In this average rate of technical change is defined as follows:

$$\Delta S_T = \Delta LnY - (\hat{S}_L \Delta LnK + \hat{S}_L \Delta LnL). \quad ...(2.31)$$

Here

$$\hat{S}_K = \tfrac{1}{2}[S_K(t) + S_K(t-1)]. \quad ...(2.32)$$

$$\hat{S}_1 = \tfrac{1}{2}[S_L(t) + S_L(t-1)]. \quad ...(2.33)$$

$$\Delta\, LnY = LnY(t) - LnY(t-1). \quad ...(2.34)$$

$$\Delta\, LnK = LnK(t) - LnK(t-1). \quad ...(2.35)$$

$$\Delta\, LnL = LnL(t) - LnL(t-1). \quad ...(2.36)$$

And ΔS_T is called the Translog index of the rate of technological change.

However there are certain biases, which affects the accuracy of the productivity measurement in non-parametric approach. It fails to distinguish scale effects from the effects of neutral technical progress. If economies of scale prevail, TFP overestimates effects of neutral technical progress and underestimates the effects in the presence of diseconomies. Another issue that is overlooked is that all technical change is disembodied and thus, ignores the effects of dynamic interactions between technical change and capital accumulation.[26] In view of shortcomings of these TFP measures by use of non-parametric approach, we have restored to an alternate measure using production function approach (parametric method).

2.5.2b. Production Function Approach

Production function approach to productivity measurement is more advantageous because it can handle the problems arising due to non-separability of inputs and output, non-neutral technical change, non-constant returns to scale and non-proportionality of input prices of their respective marginal productivity in a explicit manner. A production function shows the technological relationship between the maximum output obtainable from a given set of inputs and the relationship between the inputs themselves in the existing state of technological change. In this approach to productivity measurement the various components of productivity can be estimated directly by econometric estimation. The production function can be used to measure the efficiency of production technology, returns to scale, the degree of economies to scale, the degree of capital intensity of technology and the degree of substitution between factors of production. The direct estimation of production function has an advantage as it is not necessary to assume competitive equilibrium in order to derive estimates of productivity growth. The parameters of a specified function can be estimated through regression analysis.

(I) COBB-DOUGLAS PRODUCTION FUNCTION

One of the most commonly estimated functional forms in the Cobb-Douglas production (C-D) function written as:

$$V = A(t)K^{\alpha}L^{\beta}e^{u}. \qquad ...(2.37)$$

Where α and β are coefficient of labour and capital, A (t) is the efficiency parameter and u_i is the stochastic disturbance term following usual properties. Before the production function can be estimated some functional form has to be given to the term A(t). The most commonly used in practice has been $A(t) = Ae^{\lambda t}$ where λ is the measure of technical change in output per period [λ measures the proportionate change in output per period when input level are held constant]. It is very important here to point out the limitations of this representation of technical change. It assumes neutral technical progress and that the technical progress is exogenous and disembodied (this neglects the usefulness of investment for technical progress).

This function is linear in the logarithmic of the inputs, output and time. Thus, we have:

$$Ln^{27}V = a + \alpha LnL + \beta LnK + \lambda t + \mu_i. \quad ...(2.38)$$

The estimation of this equation yields values of α, β and λ. λ provides estimates of TFPG and is the rate of exponential technological change. Sum of the partial elasticities ($\alpha + \beta$) indicates the extent of economies or diseconomies to scale. The returns to scale are constant, increasing or decreasing if the value of $\alpha + \beta$ is equal to unity, more than unity or less than unity respectively.

Marginal product of labour (MP_L) and capital (MP_K) can be obtained by differentiating the equation (2.37) with respect to labour and capital. We obtain:

$$MP_L = \delta V/\delta L = \alpha V/L. \quad ...(2.39)$$

$$MP_K = \delta V/\delta K = \beta V/K. \quad ....(2.40)$$

Since profit maximization entails that marginal productivity of labour is equal to the real wage rate and marginal product of capital is the price per unit of capital, it would imply that:

$$MP_L = w/p = \alpha V/L. \quad ...(2.41)$$

Or share of labour in total output:

$$\alpha = (w/p). (L/V). \quad ...(2.42)$$

Similarly

$$MP_L = r/p = \beta V/K. \quad ...(2.43)$$

And share of capital in total output

$$\beta = (r/p). (K/V). \quad ...(2.44)$$

Equation (2.42) and (2.44) shows that in this production function factors shares are constant. From equation (2.41) and (2.43) we can obtain the capital-labour ratio, and capital-output ratio.

$$K/L = (\beta/\alpha).(w/r) \quad \text{and} \quad K/V = \beta p/r. \quad ...(2.45)$$

Thus, it shows that the ratio of capital of labour depends on the ratio of the factor prices and not their absolute levels. Similarly the capital-output ratio depends only on the ratio of the price of output to the price of capital.

We have used the ratio form of C-D function. Under the assumption of constant returns to scale this equation is derived from equation (2.37):

$$Ln(V/L) = a + \beta \, Ln(K/L) + \lambda \, t + \mu_i. \quad ...(2.46)$$

When the assumption of constant returns to scale is relaxed we have:

$$Ln(V/L) = a + \beta \, Ln(K/L) + (\alpha + \beta - 1) \, LnL + \lambda \, t + \mu_i \quad ....(2.47)$$

Here zero, positive or negative coefficient of LnL denotes that the returns to scale are constant, increasing or decreasing.

(II) CONSTANT ELASTICITY OF SUBSTITUTION (CES) PRODUCTION FUNCTION

The C-D function assumes elasticity of substitution as unity, which is a particularly restrictive property because this means that capital can always be substituted for labour (or labour for capital). This may not be the case, the data may have very low or very high elasticity and it will not be appropriate to fit C-D function. Beside this, one of the purpose of productivity study is to examine the extent to which factor substitution is possible. The CES production function, which allows for non-unitary elasticity of substitution, may be written as:

$$V = A_0 e^{\lambda t} \, [\delta L^{-\rho} + (1 - \delta) \, K^{-\rho}]^{-v/\rho} \, .e^{u.} \quad ... (2.48)$$

Where λ is efficiency parameter, δ is the distribution or labour intensity parameter, v is the scale parameter, ρ is related to elasticity of substitution given by $\sigma = 1/(1 + \rho)$; where σ is constant by assumption and its value lies between the rage of 0 and ∞. Also ν, γ, ρ, δ are non-negative constants and δ must not exceed unity, i.e., $0 < \delta > 1$. CES production function reduces to C-D form when σ approaches unity (ρ approaches zero) and to Leontief-type production function when σ approaches zero (ρ approaches infinity). The technical progress in this function is also Hicks-neutral and disembodied.

There is no direct method by which a simple logarithmic transformation gives a log linear form (which would give a direct estimable exact representation as in the case of C-D function), most investigators have approached its estimation via marginal productivity conditions. The marginal productivity theory gives an adequate explanation of wage determination. It is well-known that the price of labour under the conditions of profit maximization is equal to its marginal product. The labour force would be increased up to a point at which the reward paid to the marginal unit of labour (marginal wage) would be equal to the contribution made by the unit (marginal productivity of labour). Hence $MP_L = W/L = w$; under the assumption of constant returns to scale ($\nu = 1$), we have:

$$dV/dL = [(1-\delta)/A^{-\rho}].\ [(V/L)^{1+\rho}]. \qquad ...(2.49)$$

From the above equation we get :

$$V/L = aw^{\sigma}. \qquad ...(2.50)$$

Where $a = A^{-\rho}/1 - \delta$; $\sigma = 1/(1 + \rho)$.

Taking logarithmic and introducing time trend, we get:

$$Ln(V/L) = a_0 + \sigma\ Ln\ w + \lambda\ (1 - \sigma)\ t + u \qquad ....(2.51)$$

If the assumptions of constant returns to scale are relaxed, we derive the following relationship:

$$Ln(V/L) = a_0 + a_1 Lnw + a_2\ LnL + a_3\ t + u. \qquad ..(2.52)$$

Where

$$a_1 = \nu/(\nu + \rho);\ a_2 = \rho(\nu - 1)/(\nu + \rho);\ a_3 = \lambda\rho/(\nu + \rho).$$

From this relationship, we can get the value of parameters (λ, σ, ν) as:

$$\lambda = a_3/(1 - a_1);\ \sigma = a_1/(1 + a_2);\ \nu = [a_2/(1 - a_1)] + 1.$$

A more direct approach may be considered by taking a Taylor series expansion about $\rho = 0$ as shown by Kmenta (1967) and following linear approximation may be obtained:

$$LnV = LnY + \nu\delta LnK + \nu\ (1 - \delta)LnL - \nu\ \rho\ \delta\ (1 - \delta)$$

$$[Ln\ K\text{-}Ln.L]^2. \qquad ...(2.53)$$

(iii) Variable Elasticity of Substitution (VES) Production Function

The CES production function assumes that the elasticity of substitution is a constant throughout and that the existence of relationship between value added per labour and wage rate is independent of capital stock. This may not be a case, when capital-labour ratio varies due to changes in the factor price ratio, it is possible that the elasticity of substitution varies with capital-labour ratio. Kazi (1974, p. 235) has shown that ACMS production function overestimates the elasticity parameter and underestimates the efficiency parameter. He argued that estimates of 'elasticity of substitution' from the CES production relationship gives the *gross elasticity*, that is, it also includes part of variation due to K/L in the average product.

The VES production function explicitly permits the capital-labour ratio to be an explanatory variable of productivity. The estimation form of VES production can be written as:

$$Ln(V/L) = b + b_2 \, Lnw + b_3 \ln (K/L.+ lt + \mu \quad ...(2.54)$$

Where elasticity of substitution is given by $b_2/(1 - b_3/S_K)$ and S_K is the share of capital in gross value added. The associated production function may be written as:

$$V/L = A \, [\delta K^{-\rho} + (1-\delta)\eta (K/L)^{-b_3/1+\rho} . L^{\rho}]^{-1/\rho} \quad ...(2.55)$$

(iv) Transcendental Logarithmic Production Function

A more general specification production function is the Translog production function developed by Christensen, Jorgenson and Lau (1973). It is a flexible functional form imposing, relatively few *a priori* restrictions on the underlying technology. The elasticity of inputs is allowed to vary with the level of inputs. The function is written as:

$$LnV = \alpha_0 + \alpha_L LnL + \alpha_K LnK + \alpha_t t + \tfrac{1}{2}\beta_{LL}(LnL)^2 + \tfrac{1}{2}\beta_{KK} LnK)^2 + \beta_{LK}(LnL)(LnK) + \beta_{Lt}(LnL).t + \beta_{Kt}(Lnk).t + \tfrac{1}{2}\beta_{tt}t^2. \quad ...(2.56)$$

Where α and β are the parameters of the production function.

Here, the first four terms are of the C-D production function and last three terms relates to the assumptions about technological progress and nature of bias in technical progress. The other quadratic and interaction terms provide information on the curvature of production function. The elasticity of value added w.r.t. labour and capital are given by:

$$\delta LnV / \delta LnL = \alpha_L + \beta_{LL} LnL + \beta_{Lk} LnK + \beta_{Lt} t. \quad ...(2.57)$$

$$\delta LnV / \delta LnK = \alpha_K + \beta_{LK} LnL + \beta_{Kk} LnK + \beta_{Kt} t. \quad ...(2.58)$$

These equations show that the elasticities of value added w.r.t. labour and capital are not constant but depends upon the input levels (Log L and Log K) and time (t). Under competitive equilibrium, the marginal productivity condition requires that elasticity of value added with respect to each input is equal to the respective factor share in value added. Thus, in this production function, elasticity of substitution is a function of input level and is not constant, as factor shares changes with input level.

The rate of technical progress or TFPG in the Translog production function is given by:

$$\delta \text{LogV} / \delta t = \alpha_t + \beta_{Lt} \text{LogL} + \beta_{Kt} \text{LogK} + \beta_{tt} t. \qquad ..(2.59)$$

Where α_t is autonomous TFPG, β_{Lt} and β_{Kt} defines the bias in the TFPG. If both β_{Lt} and β_{Lt} are zero, then the technical progress is of Hicks-neutral type. If β_{Lt} is positive then the share of labour increases with time and there is a labour using bias and if β_{Kt} is positive than the share of capital increases with time and technical progress is having a capital using bias. This function is not estimated for present study, as number of observations are less and the estimates may not give consistent results.

2.6 Measurement of other Variables

In this section, we will discuss the measurement of other variables used in productivity analysis in subsequent chapters. Various variables involved are unit wage cost, capital intensity and trade union activities.

2.6.1 Unit Labour Cost

The real problem is not the impact of rising labour cost on total costs. Rather, it is the change in unit labour cost which is significant. Unit labour cost represents the cost of production of unit output paid to labour input by employer. This can be obtained by dividing total emoluments by total output. Alternatively, it can also be obtained by dividing wage bill by gross value added. We will use the second measure of unit labour cost for study because it is expected that both the measures will show almost same trend, and this measure will help us in comparing increase in labour cost in relationship to gains in labour productivity.

2.6.2 Capital Intensity

Capital intensity of an industry refers to the technology used in the industry. Capital intensity of industry is generally measured by ratio of capital to labour input. It can also be measured as a ratio of capital to output. For present study we will measure capital intensity, in an industry, by dividing the value of gross fixed capital by the number of employees, i.e., our measure of labour input. Symbolically:

$$\text{Capital Intensity } (k_t) = K_t/L_t. \qquad ...(2.60)$$

Where k stands for measure of capital intensity.

K stands for measure of gross fixed capital.

L stands for number of persons employed.

Better technology results in higher productivity enabling greater output with given capital and other resources, or the constant output with a smaller use of resources. In this connection, the uses of capital-intensive and labour-intensive techniques of production are important. These techniques are directly or indirectly related to capital-output ratio (K/V) and labour-output ratio (L/V). Capital-output ratios have been used in various growth models. Here capital to GVA ratio has been referred as capital-output ratio or capital coefficient which relates only a single factor to the product. Such capital-output ratio (K/V) may easily be related to capital-labour ratio (K/L) or capital intensity. Here:

$$K/V = K/L \div V/L. \qquad ...(2.61)$$

If by increasing the value of K/L, the productivity of labour is increased more than proportionately, the value of capital output ratio is decreased *(or capital productivity increased).*

2.6.3 Rate of Factor Compensation

Earnings per employee and rate of returns to capital have been used as the rate of factor compensation for labour and capital. Earnings per employee which has been used frequently as wages and wage rate in the study is obtained by dividing the total emoluments (wages + salaries + fringe benefits) by the number of total employees. The various measure of labour compensation namely (i) money wages per worker, (ii) money earnings per employee, (iii) real consumption wages per worker, (iv) real consumption earnings per employee, (v) real product wages per worker and (vi) real product earnings per employee will be discussed in Chapter-6.

The rate of return on capital is measured by dividing the value of difference between gross value added and total labour compensation by gross fixed capital. Symbolically:

$$r_t = (V_t - W_t)/K_t. \quad ...(2.62)$$

Where Vt = Gross Value Added (GVA) at current prices.

Wt = total wage bill.

K_t = capital inputs, i.e., gross fixed capital at constant prices.

It has to be noted here that entire non-wage income does not accrue to capital alone. It includes other items such as depreciation on capital, rate of interest, taxes etc. However, they constitute only a small part of income accruing to capital. Therefore, ratio $(V_t - W_t)/K_t$ can be taken as the broad measure of rate of return on capital. The various measure of rate of return on capital namely (i) rate of return at current prices, (ii) rate of return at constant product prices and (iii) rate of return at constant machinery prices are discussed in Chapter-6.

The methodology for measurement and distribution of productivity gains is explained in Chapter-5. The wage function and employment function and the comparison of wages and labour productivity trends, by devising the wage-productivity index and by using ratio of growth rates of wages and labour productivity, are explained in Chapter-6. The methodology for causality test and the test of wage-productivity relationship is explained in Chapter-7.

References

1. Griliches and Ringstad (1971) have advanced these arguments and invariably quoted by many studies including Goldar (1985), Ahluwalia (1991), Ramjas (1992) and Aggarwal (1998).
2. P. Balakrishnan, and K. Pushpangadan (1998), 'What Do We Know about Productivity Growth in Indian Industries?' *Economic and Political Weekly*, August 15-22, p. 2242.
3. Denison, E.F. (1972), 'Some Major Issues in Productivity Analysis.' *Survey of Current Business*, Vol. 49(5), May, p. 2.
4. Z. Griliches, and D.W. Jorgenson (1967), 'The Explanation of Productivity Change: Capital Input.' *Review of Economic Studies*, Vol. 34, July, p. 256.
5. Ahluwalia (1991), Goldar (1985), Ramjas (1992), Aggarwal (1998) have used gross value added by single deflation.
6. It is evident that the single deflation by Goldar (1985) who uses WPI for deflation procedure purpose captures the movements of relative price changes in the value added. He uses WPI of aggregate manufacturing for deflation purpose, whereas Ahluwalia (1991) uses the WPI of concerned industry, but does not go for double deflation.
7. The input compositions are different for different industries.
8. J.M. Rao (1996[b]). 'Indices of Industrial Productivity Growth: Dis-Aggregation

and Interpretation.' *Economic and Political Weekly*, December 7, p. 3177.

9. J.N. Sinha and P.K. Sawhney (1970). *Wages and Productivity in Selected Indian Industries*. New Delhi: Vikas Publishing House, p. 16.
10. A. Banerji (1975). *Capital Intensity and Productivity in Indian Industry*. New Delhi: Macmillan Co. of India Ltd., pp. 4-6.
11. B.N. Goldar (1986). *Productivity Growth in Indian Industry*. New Delhi: Allied Publishers Pvt. Ltd., pp. 50-61.
12. Sinha and Sawhney (1970), op. cit., p. 19.
13. J.M. Rao (1996[a]). 'Manufacturing Productivity Growth: Method and Measurement.' *Economic and Political Weekly*, November 2, p. 2934.
14. Kennedy and Thirlwal (1972). 'Survey in Applied Economics: Technical Progress.' *Economic Journal*, Vol. 82, part-1, p. 30.
15. George Rosen (1959). *Industrial Change in India*. Bombay: Asian Publishing House, p. 42.
16. These ratios are used by Ahluwalia (1985, 1991), Kadak (1986), Balkrishnan and Pushpangadan (1994, 1998), Dholakia & Dholakia (1995) and Gangopadhyay & Wadhwa (1998) among others. Ahluwalia (1985, p. 187) remarked "though there are problems of inadequate coverage with the Dadi and Hasim study, theirs were the best estimates available...."
17. He had criticised Asit Banerjee on the grounds that use of multiplication by two is arbitrary.
18. Kendrick (1973), op. cit., p. 26.
19. Bharmanand (1982), Goldar (1985), Ahluwalia (1985, 1991), Balkrishnan & Pushpangadan (1994, 1998), Rao (1996[a]) among others have not corrected their capital series for capacity utilisation.
20. Year 1960 is chosen solely due to availability of gross-net ratio by Hasim and Dadi for the year (1960).
21. M.M. Dadi (1971). *Income Share of Factory Labour in India*. Ph.D thesis submitted to the M.S. University of Baroda, pp. 98-99.
22. Only Hasim & Dadi (1973) and Goldar (1985) have recognized this problem. Recently NPC research division (1997) has also used the rate of discarding while calculating capital series.
23. It is labour productivity purely in statistical sense, any factor affecting output and labour input may have an influence on labour productivity.
24. Goldar (1986), op, cit., p. 2.
25. Kendrick (1973), op. cit., p. 15.
26. Ganti Subrahmanyam (1984). 'Some Conceptual Issues in Productivity Measurement.' *Prajnan*, Vol. 13, No. 2, p. 182.
27. 'Ln' in this equation and elsewhere denotes natural logarithmic with base 'e'.

3

Productivity and Wages: Theoretical and Empirical Evidence

3.1 Introduction

Productivity plays a very important role in the process of economic development and ultimately determines the standard of living of the people in the country. The changes in wage rates and profits due to changes in productivity governs the growth of productivity itself and the economy of a nation. While on one hand an increase in productivity facilitates an increase in the wage rate, an increase in wage rate leads to an increase in productivity (Patel and Gandhi, 1998, p. 917). The wage-productivity relationship can assume the form of a circular self-generating mechanism where increase in productivity leads to increase in wages and an increase in wages motivates the worker to further increase productivity.

The linking of wages to productivity is very often questioned. The answer appears to be obvious that if labour productivity could be identified then wages should not be allowed to lag behind it. Wages are the major source of income to the worker. Today, the worker, especially in organised manufacturing sector, is not satisfied with the wages he receives. He expects to be protected against the galloping inflation. He wants to improve his standard of living by sharing in the gains of economic progress in the country. He is politically awakened and is ready to protect to secure his rights. In this endeavour, he as strong political allies. An income policy cannot be divorced from his expectation or from the economic situation. However, an indiscriminate upward movement of wages, or payment of monetary wage-supplements, may be reflected in the cost of production and consequently in the price of the product. Such gains may not be of any avail to the workers since inflationary pressures following such an increase would largely neutralise the increase in money wages and adversely affect the volume of employment. An increase in real wages can take place only through improvements in productivity and the linking of wages to such gains in productivity (Suri, 1976, p. 68). It is in this context that the changes in money and real wages and their relationships with unit costs and productivity need to be examined.

In this chapter the relationship between wages and productivity in theory and practice will be discussed. The experience of some earlier empirical studies will also be discussed. The chapter is divided into four sections. Section 3.2 deals with the theoretical aspect of the wage-productivity relationships whereas, section 3.3 deals with the views of various authorities on wage-productivity relationship. Section 3.4 deals with the earlier studies on wage-productivity relationship in Indian industries. Section 3.5 deals with the role of wages in industrial disputes.

3.2 Wage-Productivity Relationship: Theoretical Perspective

Economic theory of underdevelopment is not quite explicit on the role of wages in the process of industrialization. Wages constitute a source of mass consumption and those who believes that capital formation requires a reduction in consumption argue that wages must be either stable or even decline to achieve a higher rate of growth of per capita income (Palekar, 1974, p. 2). The wages in economic analysis is the price paid for labour as a factor of production. The labour is a distinct factor of production as it is both the creator and end user of wealth. The price of labour is a unique parameter that is highly complex to determine and depends upon many factors.

Mercantilists wanted hard work and efficiency from labourers but advocated only subsistence wages, just sufficient for his living. According to the subsistence theory of wages, the subsistence level determines wage rate and that in long run wage rate will remain equal to the subsistence level. This theory does not accept the importance of productivity. Physiocrates considered that the level of wages is the function of labour supply and the size of wage fund available.

They do not give any importance to the industry and considered that agriculture is only capable to producing surplus.[1] According to Adam Smith, in a primitive society, wages are determined by the productivity of labour. In the beginning of the nineteenth century, a new wage theory, *the wage fund theory* emerged (popularised by Adam Smith, JS Mill, Ricardo and other classical writers) supplementing the subsistence theory rather than replacing it. According to this theory, wages depends on two things; (1) The wage fund or circulating capital set aside for the purchase of labour and (2) the number of labourers seeking employment. Wages therefore, cannot rise unless either the wage fund increases or the number of workers is reduced. But since, the theory takes the wage fund as fixed, wages could rise only by the reduction in the number of workers, which is against the interest of working class. This theory also neglects the possibility of flow of extra remuneration from greater productivity. The most forceful refutation of the wage fund theory came from Walker who argued vigorously that wages were paid out of the product of labour and not from previously accumulated capital. *The residual claimant theory* advanced by Walker and explained by Jevons held that wages are residue left over after the other factors of production are paid. Though not explicitly, stated, this theory accepts the possibility of increase in wages through increase in productivity of labour. German philosopher Karl Marx contributed the *theory of surplus value* in his celebrated book 'Capital'. For Marx, the main economic problem was to explain the distribution of the relative shares of the total output between capital and labour. His unique idea was his conception of the relation of wages to the value of product that labour produced. Building on the thesis 'labour creates all value', Marx maintained that the total value produced by labour (use value) was greater than what is received by him in wage payments (exchange value). This excess, called *surplus value,* is retained by capitalist or employer. Marx believed that this system breaks down as it works upon itself to squeeze out its own source of energy (by excessive use of capital, profits would be squeezed). This will be replaced by the classless society, where means of production would be collectively owned and used with no exploitation of labour. In such a society, the rule of distribution would be *from each according to his ability, to each according to his needs.*

It is the *marginal productivity theory,* which establishes direct link between productivity and wages. According to this theory, price of labour (wages) is determined by its marginal utility to employers. Thus, the wages paid are equal to the productivity of labour force. Neo-classical writers and marginal economists in explaining the wage determination and wage differential for various grade of labour used this theory. Taussig gives the modified version of this theory. According to him, the wage is equal to the marginal productivity of labour minus the amount of discount of the advances made to the workers. These theories acknowledged the direct link between wages and labour productivity. The wage rate is determined by the interaction of supply and demand in the labour market under the assumption of perfect competition in labour and commodity market, free mobility and rational behaviour. Hicks (1964) points out towards certain peculiar quality of labour. He emphasised that "the only wage at which equilibrium in labour market is possible is a wage which equals the value of marginal product of labourers."[2] In same vein, Marshall pointed out that "the wages of labour tends to equal 'the net product' of man's labour...the value of produce that he takes part in producing after deducting all the other expenses of producing it."[3] According to this theory, wage differences would reflect the productivity difference of different class of labour. Generally there has been wide acceptance of the marginal productivity theory's emphasis upon capital formation as the basic source of long-term advances in real wages. There is much less acceptance of the theory as a short-term explanation in the wage determination. In the long run, capital-labour ratio determines the average level of wages. Labour productivity, according to this view, depends on the tool labour has. The tools are provided by the capital investment. If the capital investment of workers is larger, productivity and wages will be higher.

If we take the wages as a price of labour, then as per demand-supply criterion (advanced for wage determination), the wage rate should be able to clear the labour market (i.e., to provide full employment). The neo-classical theory fails to explain the coexistence of the high wages and unemployment. The *efficiency wage hypothesis* explains the involuntary unemployment. According to this hypothesis, labour productivity depends upon the real wage paid to them. If wage cuts harm productivity, then cutting wages may end up raising labour cost (because labour productivity will eventually fall). This theory establishes the link between labour productivity and wages in reverse direction. Here the cause is wages and effect is productivity against the marginal productivity theory where cause is productivity and effect is wages. Akerlof and Yellen (1986) provided four different macroeconomic approaches that justify relationship between wages and productivity.[4]

There are basically two routes through which the relationship between productivity and wage rate (from improved wages to improved productivity) may arise.[5] First, there is the case where a wage increase raises the efficiency of workers, and second, there is a case where a wage increase improves the efficiency of management. The first to these mechanisms is generally referred to as the *economy of high wages* and second is termed as the *shock theory.* According to the economy of high wages argument, improved wages lead to higher level of marginal productivity at given level of employment through improvements in workers nutrition and health. This effect has frequently been found to be of importance in the context of less developed countries. The basic argument lying behind the slack hypothesis is that the productivity of management is shocked into improving as the wage rate payable to the workforce increase. Underlying this hypothesis is the assumption that the employer firm is operating with a degree of slake or inefficiency, which has the potential to be reduced when the organisation becomes threatened in some way. Whether wages and labour productivity are linked via either economy of high wages or shock effects, the analysis suggests that labour's marginal physical product schedule shifts upwards as the wage rate is increased.

3.3 Wage-Productivity Relationship: Views of Wag Fixing Authorities

The great financial depression of 1930s led Keynes to denounce the doctrine of *laissez-faire* and advocate the increasing importance of the state intervention. It became, in fact, increasingly evident that if the mass of the people were to rise above the level of mere wage slaves, they would have to be protected against the evils of free and unrestricted competition, by greater measure of interference and regulation of industry on the part of society. The earliest measures of wage regulation were aimed mainly at removing very low and oppressive wages.

Once introduced, state intervention continued. Sooner or later, it became a special feature of wage determination in many countries of the world, at least for certain categories of workers and under special circumstances. The political and economic developments of the present century till 80s had, all the more, necessitated the assumption of wider state activities in this direction. In particular, the gradual change in the state functions, wider applications of democratic ideals and principles, establishment of socialist states, increase in the size of permanent class of wage-earners, increase in the number of industrial strife to the determinant of the interests of the community to large and occasional disruptions in the harmonious functioning of the economic system, have led the state to adopt more positive measures in order to regulate wage rates.[6]

Keeping in view the changing social philosophy concerning economic justice and fair play, the state intervened in the realm of wages with a view to protect workers in low wages industries. Occasionally, the purpose behind state intervention has been the maintenance of industrial peace in the sphere of wages—the main bone of contention between employers and workers. Sometimes, especially during periods of economic depressions, state regulation of wages has been designed to speed up the pace of economic recovery. Similarly, preventing an inflammatory spiral and maintaining economic stability during war times has been another objective of regulation of wages by the state. The most comprehensive object of state regulation of wages, which has found expression in large number of countries, even in the capitalist societies, not to speak of the socialist ones, has been the pursuit of a national income distribution policy and fitting the wage-structure *therein* and using the wage policy as an instrument of planned economic development.[7] One of the objectives that an income policy seeks to achieve is to introduce more stability into wages and salaries, so that income trends more clearly aligned to the productivity trends. Hence, wages and labour productivity are always expected to be positively correlated and higher the labour productivity, the higher will be the wages in an industry and vice-versa.

In the determination of wages in Indian industries, the productivity-wage relationship has been one of the most vexed and indecisive problems. It has been theoretically agreed by parties that wages should move so as to bear a positive relationship with productivity. The Royal Commission on Labour, the Fair Wages

Committee, the Committee on Sharing the Gains of productivity, the Study Group on Productivity and Incentives, and the Five-Year Plans have, therefore emphasised the significance of the factor in the domain of wages.[8] The workers, employers and economists too regarded 'productivity' as one of the criteria in wage determination. But when the question of the practical application of this principle comes before wage fixing authorities, the whole issue boils down to the state of indifference in view of the conflicting argument put forward by the employers and employees. While the importance of productivity-wage relationship cannot be denied, we don't find any accepted approach to wage-productivity relationship in India (for that matter anywhere except annual improvement factor at some places). The wage fixing authorities don't appear to have given importance to productivity. Productivity is referred as one of the factors determining actual wages.

The central wage boards considered the productivity factor, that is, whether wages should be linked to performance. For example, Sugar Wage Board observed: "In a progressive economy, wage should ever be the function of productivity. In the major organised industries, gradually the stage is being reached when further wage increases can come only out of increased productivity. It is imperative that the worker realises that no real wage increase can flow out of the government decree. Higher productivity alone can bring down the cost of production, afford higher wages and arrest inflationary trends" (*Sugar Wage Board,* para 193). The Wage Boards,[9] however, observed that term 'productivity of the industry' is a complex issue as productivity is the end product of a combination of factors and it is not an easy task to distinguish the contributing factors and still more difficult to distinguish the degree of importance of these factors *(Sugar Wage Board,* para 183, *Cement Wage Board,* para 5.14). In the view of the complex nature of productivity, the wage boards, while admitting that there was an overall increase in the productivity, found it very difficult to apportion the increase in productivity between the various factors of production including labour *(Sugar Wage Board,* para 183; *Cotton Textile Wage Board,* para 36 & 88; *Jute Wage Board,* para 7.46; *Iron and Steel Wage Board,* para 5.8-5.10). In this context, the Boards endeavoured to elucidate the complex nature of productivity by citing an example, as in the case of labour productivity, apart from preparedness of the workers to work, the productivity of labour depends upon a number of factors such as degree of rationalisation, the extent of modernisation, the quality of raw materials used, the working conditions, the availability of necessary finance, managerial skill and organisation as well as industrial policy of government (*Sugar Wage Board,* para 183; *Cotton Textile Wage Board,* para 36; *Cement Wage Board,* para 5.14, *Iron and Steel Wage Board,* para 5.11).

The adjudication authorities have also, by and large, disregarded the productivity factor in their rewards relating to wages.[10] The reason assigned for their indifference to this factor related to the difficulties of the measurement of productivity of labour and fixation of production standards. But this overall disregard of productivity in wage determination is bound to prove detrimental to industrial progress and economic stability and disadvantageous to employers as well as employees in long run.

The planning commission seems to recognise this fact. It points out that, ''Rate of progress has to be determined not only by the need of workers but by the country resouces...on the side of labour their should be a keen realisation of the fact that, in an underdeveloped economy, it can not build for itself and for community a better life except on the foundation of a higher level of productivity to which it itself has to make substantial contribution."[11] Again it is emphasised in Third Plan that, "Neither the exercise of their organized strength in industrial conflict nor laws and the intervention of the state can help the workers much in realizing their aspiration. Their gain can arise only out of strength and dynamism of the economies, the only enduring basis for which is the rising level of productivity."[12] The Eighth Plan also echoed the same sentiments when it pointed out that, "Improvement in the productivity of workforce also assumes greater significance in our economy where low productivity and low incomes of a large mass of employed constitute a much higher dimension than employment."[13] The plan also recognise the mismatch between wages and productivity, it points out that, " The level of changes in wages and salaries often have no relationship with productivity and wages, thus, do not function as instruments that induce efficiency."[14] The plans also recognise the need of wage incentives to increase productivity and efficiency. The Seventh Plan observed, "An appropriate environment has to be created so as to encourage and promote greater efficiency, higher productivity and faster industrial growth through a well coordinated system of incentives...."[15]

There is a strong case for wage-productivity linkage. Though it has been recognised that the relationship between wages and productivity is not direct, rising productivity is likely to have a favourable effect on the wage level at least for two reasons. First, an increase in productivity may create additional demand for labour if that results in corresponding increase in average productivity (of course the demand curve for product should be sufficiently elastic). Second, rise in productivity will increase generally the profitability of industry and therefore its capacity to pay. The profits in an industry determine the grant of wage increase and the rate of return. The profits in turn may itself be determined by the price of product and positive productivity gains. The profits cannot be sustained over a long time by relative increase in product prices. Normally, it is the productivity improvement that becomes the main source of rise in real earnings in the industry and is amenable to influence to some extent. A wage system linked to productivity is one of the few ways open to industry to stimulate greater efficiency and enhance employers earning without adverse effects, like stagnation and inflation.[16] There is no shortcut method for economic development and higher real wages for workers except increased productivity. The National Commission on Labour observed, "Any sustained improvement in wages cannot be brought without increasing productivity. The real wages of any group of workers cannot be unrelated to their productivity unless inroads into the share of other groups are made. The urgency of improving productivity level to sustain increases in real wages cannot be overemphasised."[17] In spite of the difficulties in measuring labour productivity, the NCL declared that wage change beyond certain level must reflect productivity changes.

It is also important to remember that wages should not go up to the extent of compelling employer to replace labour by capital since, unemployment is the worst problem facing the country today. Fair wages committee observed: "Objective is not to merely determine wages which should be fair in abstract, but to see that employment at the existing level not only maintained but if possible increased."[18] A system based on productivity-wage relation help in achieving this goal and enable the industry to work with efficiency. It is desirable to establish some positive relationship between productivity and wages in the interest of both employers and employees. Payment of wages without reference to productivity may undermine the long-term interests of workers because an industry cannot hope to expand unless it earns a reasonable rate of profit. The employers are generally reluctant to revise wages upward in the absence of rise in the productivity. They maintained that an upward revision of wages, unrelated to productivity, would affect adversely both the present and future level of production and employment. In the absence of proper procedure to link wages to productivity, in long run, an irrational wage structure may evolve. Such a structure is likely to bring about instabilities in the price level and the level of employment and production. Both employers and trade unions, therefore, should accept productivity-wage linkage as a healthy norm. Beyond the minimum wage level the wages are to be adjusted with productivity in order to meet the development needs and ensure stability in the economy.

Fair wages committee unanimously recommended that fair wages should on no account be less than the minimum wages. Wages, in its view, must not merely provide for the bare subsistence of life but for preservation of efficiency of the worker, which is the lower limit of the fair wage, the upper limit is equally set by what may broadly be called the capacity to pay and in between this upper and lower limit the following factor would be taken into consideration namely (i) the productivity of labour, (ii) the prevailing rates of wages in same or similar occupation in neighbouring localities, (iii) level of national income and its pattern of distribution and (iv) the place of the industry in the national economy.[19] It has been argued that productivity does not play a deciding or dominant role in wage fixation and its main utility as a criterion lies not so much in deciding upon a particular level of wages as appropriate for future, as in checking up whether wages fixed on the basis of other criterion are fair, in a broad sense, having regard to contribution and claims of labour and capital from time to time. It is aptly remarked in this context: "The wage level has to be fixed so as to ensure a basic minimum, irrespective to any other considerations. A linkage between wages and productivity could possibly be considered only while deciding higher wages, for higher achievement and productivity."[20] Though, rising productivity is the foundation of a rising level of real earnings in the long run, there is no automatic or generally observed relationship between the two during short periods. The employers can pay wages in money terms only, the real context of which is at the mercy of general price level. The general price level depends on many factors related to the process of economic development and is largely outside the control of individual industries. In an economy already subjected to inflationary pressure, larger money wages may, in most cases, merely raise the price level without raising real wages.

The above discussion shows that wages should be linked to productivity in some way. But, various arguments have been put forward suggesting the futility of such an exercise. It is accepted that the differential rate of productivity growth are largely due to technological and economic factors, and therefore, they do not on the whole reflects differences in the contribution of employees to production. The wage-productivity linkage is said to create a chaotic wage structure. The level of productivity may be higher in some industries, and very low in some others depending on technological progress. If wages were strictly iinked to productivity, the wage rates would be disproportionately high in some industries and low in others requiring the same skill and responsibility. It has been correctly observed that an increase in productivity does not automatically leads to rise in wages. The connection between wage and productivity is not so close and direct as it appears and what is the most that can be said is that increased productivity increases the possibility of higher wages or it permits an increase in the wage rate without increasing labour costs per unit. The degree to which increases in productivity leads to increases in wages is determined by factors like relative bargaining power of the parties and the extent of public control. Here, it is not the matter of automatic and objective connection, but of deliberate 'gearing' of wage movements with the productivity movements. Thus, the relationship between productivity and wages may better be seen as an aspect of perspective policy formulations and deliberate use of productivity criterion in regulating wages, rather as a theoretical analysis of a hypothetical situation (MK Singh, 1989, p. 202).

3.4 Wage-Productivity Relationship: Empirical Evidences

Several studies have been conducted to empirically test the relationship between wages and productivity. The number of these studies is so large that it is very difficult to list them all. In this section, an attempt has been made to briefly describe a few significant studies conducted in India on the link between wages and productivity. Most of the studies confirm the existence of close relationship between the two.

In highlighting productivity, wages, labour cost and share of labour, and value added by manufacturing, the National Commission on Labour remarked that, "Increases in money wages to industrial workers since independence have neither been associated with a rise in real wages, nor have real wages increases been commensurate with improvement in productivity. Simultaneously, wage costs as a proportion to total costs to manufacturing have registered a decline and the same is true about workers share in value added by manufacturing."[21]

Fonesca (1964) analysed determination of money wages using data for the period 1953-63. In his regression analysis money wages paid to workers was taken as dependent variable (X_1) while independent variables were degree of unionisation (X_2), cost of living index (X_3) and productivity (X_4). His result shows that money wages are largely influenced by productivity followed by cost of living index. He observed that a rise in labour productivity still fails to raise industrial wages. The share of labour in value added by manufacturing in the industrial sector also appears to show a stagnating or falling trend. In other words, gains from increase in productivity have been unequally divided.

Johri and Aggarwal (1966) in a study on inter-industry wage structure in 29 industries for the period 1950-61 found that the correlation had a positive association between wages and productivity although the strength of association was decreasing over time. They conclude that the evidence strongly suggests that higher the labour productivity, higher would be wages and vice-versa. In a similar study by Sawhney (1969) covering 29 industries for the period 1953-63 also supports the findings of Johri and Aggarwal. In the explanation of inter-industry wage differential his study arrived at the conclusion that wage rate in different industries are significantly influenced by the corresponding level of labour productivity and his finding was supported by the correlation coefficient (both partial and simple) and regression analysis.

Sivamaggi (1968) has examined wages, labour productivity (value added divide by man-hours) and cost of production for the period 1951-61 based on CMI and ASI data for seven major industries (including paper & paperboard and sugar). The result shows that labour productivity has increased due to an increase in capital intensity and improvements in management techniques. Rise in real wages overall and industrywise, lagged behind the improvements in productivity. The wage components of total industry cost was small and wage cost ratio declined during the period.

Papola (1970) tested the hypothesis that labour productivity is a factor affecting money wages. In his regression analysis for cotton textile industries, he has taken wage rate as dependent variable and demand for labour (X_2), production of cloth (X_3), productivity (X_4), capacity to pay (X_5) and cost of living (X_6) as independent variables. His study concludes that cost of living seems to have the highest degree of influence on wage rate followed by capacity to pay. Productivity seems to be only a marginally significant variable for determination of wages and other criteria do not exert any significant influence. In another study Papola (1972) tried to explain inter-state differences in money wages by taking money wages as dependent variable and productivity (X_1), rate of return (X_2), capital intensity (X_3) and average size of units (X_4) as independent variables. His result shows that productivity and rate of return are found to contribute significantly to wage variation only in few states and the significance of capacity is also generally low. Capital intensity only emerged as a significant factor explaining differences among wages.

Vermas study (1971) on analysis of factors contributing to wage differences between manufacturing industries also supports the finding of earlier studies. His cross-section analysis of 209 industries for year 1964 (from ASI 1964) included five explanatory variables including labour productivity measured by value added per worker. The result of regression analysis shows that the wage differed among industries, primarily due to the fact that in some industries the level of productivity was higher than other industries.

Another study for aggregate manufacturing sector is by Suri (1976) for the period 1959-69. His dependent variable was money wages paid to workers and independent variables were cost of living index (CPI), productivity index (value added by manufacturing per man-hour worked at current prices), employment index, capital-output ratio (at current prices) and the index of degree of unionisation. His index of money wages excludes fringe benefits. His result of correlation analysis shows that except the degree of unionisation, all other variables are having a positive and statistically significant correlation with money wages. The result of regression analysis suggests that changes in money wages are largely explained in terms of changes in the cost of living index and productivity index. The productivity index has higher explaining power than cost of living index.

Madan (1977) shows that, for the period 1951-70, in general, the earnings of workers are observed to have been sticky and slow to respond to productivity movement in the downward direction, they seem to have responded, however, to the upward trend in productivity over time. He concluded: "An improvement in the real earnings of labour is, nevertheless, seems to have occurred at greater rate during period of rapid increase in productivity than during the periods of slow productivity growth."[22] The study goes on to observe that if significant improvement in real earnings of workers is to be achieved, the industry should have an adequate rate of increase in productivity. Increase in productivity is, thus, a *sine qua non* for the rise in worker's earnings, as it should be for an improvement in other factor's rewars, including returns on capital.

The study conducted by Promod Verma (1979) further concluded that the productivity (value added per worker) has increased at a faster rate than wages during 1961-75. The comparative movements in wages, productivity and price indicate that workers consistently received declining share in the output of industry. The study also points out that the gap between productivity and wages was widened during 1964-66 and again accelerated from 1969 onwards. He also concluded that productivity is a significant variable in the operation of wage system. Oomen and Evenson's study (1979) of agro-based industries in India shows a positive association between capital intensity and labour productivity, and increase in marginal productivity of labour above wage rate. This shows that wages are lagging behind the increase in productivity in these industries.

Verma and Subbayamma's study (1985) shows a wide inter-industry wage differential and dominate influence of labour productivity in explaining wage differential and in determination of wage rate. On the other hand, Veena Bhatnagar's study on engineering industries in India revealed that wage rate does not directly affect labour productivity and vice-versa. The study also points out the rigidities in downward movement of wages and remarked that increase in labour productivity does not seem to be a result of a rise in wages to any significant extent.

Tulpule and Dutta's study (1988) analysed the trends of real wages in manufacturing in India for the period 1960-83. The study found a high correlation (+ 0.81) between real wages per workers and labour productivity. They refuted the claim that workers are appropriating a disproportionately large share of wealth, arguing that real wages rose only marginally faster than the national per capita real income and beside that the labour productivity increased faster than real wages.

Verma's study (1992) using multiple regression analysis having wages as dependent variable and labour productivity, consumer price index and capital intensity as independent variables shows that capital intensity has both positive and statistically significant influence on wages. While productivity and CPI shows a positive impact, their magnitude is low. When real variables (labour productivity and capital intensity) are taken into account the result shows that real productivity still exercise some influence on real wages although this has admittedly become weak. His result shows that productivity is still the most crucial factor explaining wage variations across the states and industries besides increasing influence of capital intensity in explaining wage variations. The study concluded: "Wage behaviour in the industry is influenced by such factors as productivity, capital intensity and inflation. Over the years, the importance of these factors has been varying. During the 50s and 60s, consumer prices played a very important role in determining wages. At the same time, productivity also had an impact on wages. Prices and productivity continued to have a sway over wages until late 70s. In more recent years, capital intensity has also emerged as a factor explaining wage movement."[23]

Jose's study (1994) of 19 two-digit manufacturing industries, employing about 7.6 million workers in the factory sector, for the period 1970-71 to 1987-88 based on ASI data indicated that the 1970's was a period of relative stagnation or even declines in the productivity levels among a number of industries whereas during 1980s there came about sharp acceleration in productivity rates, which was quite conspicuous among high wage industries. On the earning front, the study brought out that any rise in real earnings was quite moderate ranging between 2% to 3% per annum and by and large, restricted to high wage industries. The study concludes: "By and large, the 1970s was a period of relative stagnancy in real earnings among most industries. In several cases any perceptible rise in real earnings came about only from early 1980s onwards while in some high wage industries the rise started as early as the mid-1970s."[24] The study also observed that it was productivity change that made it possible to bring any improvement in real earnings of employees and noted a high degree of association between the index number of real earnings and productivity in most industries.

Kannan (1994) shows that in factory sector as a whole growth of product wage has been more than compensated by the growth of labour productivity. This augur well for capital accumulation and future growth. At the level of disaggregation at two-digit level also, out of 18 industry groups covered, the growth of labour productivity has been more than the growth of product wage in 15 (except cotton, jute and paper). The study shows that growth in consumption wage is uniformly lower than the growth in product wage. This indicates that the relative prices of wage goods (mainly foods) are higher than the goods produced by workers in the industry. This points out to a more basic constraint in industrialisation, i.e., the ability to increase the real consumption of workers along with the increase in productivity. This points out that wages as a cost element is increasing faster than as representing income to workers.

Bhattacharya and Mitra (1994) have estimated wage function for public and private manufacturing for the period 1970-71 to 1990-91. The regression analysis shows that labour do not get full compensation for increase in labour productivity and prices in private manufacturing, whereas, in public enterprises wage rate is fully adjusted to prices and only partial adjusted to labour productivity. Aggarwal (1998) also, while examining the wage-productivity nexus in selected public sector enterprises in India, concluded that the real wage increase has been generally slower than the increase in their labour productivity. The rise in real wage rates in many cases has been even slower than the increase in national per capita income.

Gangopadhyay and Wadhwa (1998) in a recent paper has shown that rate of growth of wage earnings has been falling along with employment, reflected in the falling share of wages in net value added between two sub-periods 1973-83 and 1984-93. The capital deepening has been accompanied by gains in labour productivity and gains in productivity have been associated with falling unit labour cost. They pointed out that their measure of labour productivity (output per worker) could increase in three different ways. One, labour can become more skilled over time, embodying greater amount of human capital. Two, new capacities may come up with better technologies that increases the quantity of output from the same amount of inputs, including labour. Third, new techniques that substitute capital for labour can also increase output per worker. While the first two are usually good for labour, the third may increase unemployment. The authors remarked that it is likely that all three happen simultaneously (that makes separating individual effect difficult) while we can easily identify whether capital per worker is going up or not, separating output effect of new technology and better human capital cannot be simply done. For testing the hypothesis of adoption of capital-intensive techniques, they argued that if increase in labour productivity is associated with a falling share in wages. Then reason may be that, with industrial growth, to protect themselves from the burden of fixed labour cost during down swings, industries may go in for more capital-intensive technologies substituting capital for labour. This is because, the incremental capital-output ratio will be going up, and correspondingly there will be an increase in the ratio of output to labour. We will thus, have a situation of increased labour productivity being associated with falling share of wages. Similarly a fall in labour productivity will be associated with a rising share of wages in value added because with a fall in output, given the technologically irreversibility, the share of wages in net value added goes up and profit, the other part of net value added, will be squeezed.

3.5 Wages and Industrial Relations

Verma (1992) pointed out that during the period 1939-60 the industrial conflicts were influenced by wages and consumer price index and for the period 1961-78 the conflicts were influenced by wages, inter-union rivalry and political events in the country. Wages and wage related issues have been major source of industrial disputes in Indian industries. The data presented in Table 3.1 reveals that on an average 28.1 per cent of total industrial disputes are caused due to wages and 7.9 per cent due to bonus related issues. Though the percentage share of wages and bonus as causes of industrial disputes has decreased from average of 30.0 per cent and 8.9 per cent in first half to 26.1 per cent and 6.9 per cent in second half of the period. This does not, in any way, indicate the harmonious relation between employers and employees. The indiscipline as a cause of disputes has increased significantly from 9.8 per cent to 16.0 per cent during the period.

Table 3.1: Percentage Distribution of Industrial Disputes by Causes

Year	Wages & Allowance	Bonus	Personal & Retrenchment	Indiscipline	Leave & Others
1973-74	34.1	10.3	24.3	5.7	25.6
1974-75	36.1	6.2	26.5	6.2	25.0
1975-76	32.0	7.9	29.9	8.9	21.3
1976-77	23.4	13.8	29.9	9.9	23.0
1977-78	31.2	15.2	23.0	8.8	21.8
1978-79	28.7	9.9	24.2	10.7	26.5
1979-80	31.9	8.8	21.7	9.1	28.5
1980-81	28.4	7.3	24.4	8.9	31.0
1981-82	29.7	8.4	22.4	9.9	29.6
1982-83	30.0	5.8	21.6	11.8	30.8
1983-84	27.7	6.0	21.4	13.3	31.6
1984-85	26.6	7.7	18.8	13.4	33.5
1985-86	21.8	7.0	22.4	15.6	33.2
1986-87	24.3	9.2	22.0	14.3	30.2
1987-88	27.6	7.7	17.1	14.0	33.6
1988-89	27.8	6.9	17.0	15.8	32.5
1989-90	24.6	6.3	19.7	15.9	33.5
1990-91	24.9	4.1	16.4	16.1	38.5
1991-92	24.5	3.9	17.4	18.1	36.1
1992-93	23.0	8.0	17.5	21.2	30.3
1993-94	26.8	7.0	20.3	18.7	27.2
1994-95	30.0	7.8	16.4	15.4	30.4
1995-96	30.9	7.6	19.7	14.0	27.8
Average					
1973-95	28.1	7.9	21.5	12.9	29.6
1973-84	30.0	8.9	24.0	9.7	27.4
1985-95	26.1	6.9	18.7	16.0	32.2

Source : Indian Labour Statistics (various issues)

Table 3.2 : Loss of Production, Wages and Mandays in Industrial Disputes

Year	No. of. Disputes	Mon-days Lost (in Million.)	Wage Loss (in Rs. Crore)	Production Loss (in Rs. Crore)	Wage Loss Per Man-day	Production Loss Per Man-day
1973-74	3370	20,626	31.91	153.86	15.47	74.60
1974-75	2938	40,262	31.64	209.63	7.86	52.07
1975-76	1943	21,901	33.81	177.6	15.44	81.09
1976-77	1459	12,746	12.33	92.31	9.67	72.42
1977-78	3117	25,320	21.81	284.48	8.61	112.35
1978-79	3187	28,340	24.89	285.32	8.78	100.68
1979-80	3048	43,854	46.14	443.02	10.52	101.02
1980-81	2856	21,925	27.56	297.14	12.57	135.53
1981-82	2589	36,584	46.83	628.76	12.80	171.87
1982-83	2483	74,615	33.24	357.42	4.45	47.90
1983-84	2488	46,858	50.05	430.07	10.68	91.78
1984-85	2094	56,025	67.2	528.05	11.99	94.25
1985-86	1755	29,239	36.42	374.5	12.46	128.08
1986-87	1892	32,748	45.31	823.59	13.84	251.49
1987-88	1799	35,358	53.88	639.69	15.24	180.92
1988-89	1745	33,947	61.95	694.23	18.25	204.50
1989-90	1786	32,663	49.97	495.31	15.30	151.64
1990-91	1825	24,086	33.39	348.35	13.86	144.63
1991-92	1810	26,428	39.36	579.87	14.89	219.42
1992-93	1714	31,259	35.3	533.41	11.29	170.64
1993-94	1393	20,301	37.68	660.66	18.56	325.43
1994-95	1201	20,983	29.22	481.99	13.93	229.70
1995-96	1066	16,290	54.31	454.59	33.34	279.06
Average						
1973-95	2155	31,842	39.31	433.65	13.47	148.74
1973-84	2631	35,755	35.62	323.97	10.74	94.63
1985-95	1673	29,944	45.33	551.19	16.08	198.31

Source: *Indian Labour Statistics (various issues)*
Note: *Column 6 = Column 4/Col. 3.*
Column 7 = Column 5/Col. 3.

There is considerable loss of mandays and production due to these industrial disputes (strikes and lockouts).[25] Chaudhuri and Bhattacherjee (1994) have studied the feedback effects between strikes and nominal wages in Indian industries during period 1960-86. Their results indicated that wages were significantly affected by strike activities, strikes were not affected by wages during the period. Table 3.2 reveals that for the period the average yearly loss of mandays have been Rs. 3,18,420 lakh in 2,155 disputes resulting in the average loss of Rs. 433.65 crore of production and Rs. 39.31 crore of wages (per mandays loss of wages and production has been Rs. 13.47 and Rs. 148.74). Although the number of disputes was decreasing over the period along with the decrease in mandays loss but there has been a considerable loss of production and wages due to strikes and lockouts throughout the period.

References

1. They argued that man cannot create anything. They completely ignored the productivity of capital.
2. J. R. Hicks (1964) *The Theory of Wages*. London: Macmillan and Company Limited, p. 8.
3. Marshall, p. 58 (first edition) c.f. Hicks (1964).
4. These approaches provides the benefits of higher wages by (1) reduced shirking of work employers due to a higher cost of job loss (2) lower turnover (3) improvement in the average quality of job applicants, and (4) improved moral. For more details about these approaches see Akerlof and Yellen (1986), pp. 1-12.
5. S.C. Aggarwal (1998[a]) *Human Resources in Public Enterprises: A Wage-Productivity Approach*. New Delhi: Anmol Publishing Pvt. Ltd, pp.17-18.
6. Ibid., p. 19.
7. Ibid., p. 20.
8. *Report of the Committee on Fair Wages*, para 15; *Report of the National Commission on Labour*, para 15.10, p. 222; *Report of the Committee on Sharing Gains of Productivity*, March, 1967, pp. 8-9; *Report of the Study Group on Productivity and Incentives*, pp. 79-81.
9. See for details P. Chakraborty (1966) *Indian Central Wage Boards Analysis*. Calcutta: Gupta and Company Pvt. Ltd.
10. See Labour Bureau (1983) *Supplement of Industrial Awards in India.*
11. *First Five Year Plan* (1951-56), Government of India, p. 571.
12. *Third Five Year Plan* (1961-66), Government of India, p. 261.
13. *Eighth Five Year Plan* (1992-97), Government of India, p. 116.
14. Ibid., p. 21.
15. *Seventh Five Year Plan* (1985-90), Government of India, p. 23.
16. The increase in wages have an inflationary element in it (cost inflation), the wages can rise without corresponding rise in prices if productivity increases at the rate faster than the price. Thus, linking of wages to productivity can help in curbing wage pull inflation in the economy. For more discussion on wage pull inflation see Misra (1981) p. 262; also see Orliker (1988) for relationship between productivity and inflation.

17. Government of India (1969) Report of the National Commission on Labour. Ministry of Labour, *Employment and Rehabilitation*, p. 15.
18. Government of India (1949) *Report of the Committee on Fair Wages*. Ministry of Labour, p. 13.
19. Ibid., p. 15.
20. K.V. Iyer (1981) cf. S.I. Sundaram (1987) *National Wage Policy*. Delhi: B.R. Publishing Corporation, p. 31.
21. *National Commission on Labour Report* (1967), op. cit., p. 225.
22. B.K. Madan (1977) *The Real Wages of Industrial Labour in India.* New Delhi: Management Development Institute, p. 51.
23. P. Verma, (1992) *Trends and Structure of Wages in Indian Industries. Productivity*, Vol. 33, No. 2, p. 275.
24. Jose, A.V. (1992) Earnings, Employment and Productivity Trends in the organised Industries in India, *The Indian Journal of Labour Economics*, Vol. 35, No. 3, p. 213.
25. It may be noted that usually the mandays lost are calculated taking into strikes and lockouts. No publicity is given to the loss of production due to go slow, this means that the figures give an underestimation of actual figure.

4

Productivity Trends in Selected Industries

4.1 Introduction

In this chapter an attempt has been made to measure and analyse the partial as well as total factor productivity in selected industries. Two sets of productivity indexes, one based on real value added arrived by single deflation and other based on real value added by double deflation[1], will be analysed. This is required because it is increasingly realised that the productive efficiency of the industry can only be measured by correcting the real value added for the differential price movements of materials and products, also the measurement biases[2] are less in this method. The real value added arrived at by single deflation does not consider the movement of input (materials) price and assumes that movement of input price is similar to output price. This is not a plausible assumption, the double deflation method that takes into accounts this difference in price movements, thus, is a better method for productivity analysis. But the real value added, thus arrived, is not what is really available for distribution among labour and capital and the productivity gains, measured by this method, will not exhaust among labour and capital. This necessitated the measurement of productivity indexes based on the real value added measured by single deflation.

The scheme of the chapter is as follows. The chapter is divided in five sections. Section 4.2 deals with the brief review of some earlier studies relating to the Indian manufacturing industries. The detailed discussion about the estimates of productivities using both, parametric and non-parametric, methods is presented in section 4.3. The results of partial productivity ratio of labour productivity and capital productivity along with the total factor productivity indexes using Kendrick (TFPK), Solow (TFPS) and Translog (TFPT) methods are presented in this section. The estimates of C-D, CES and VES production functions are also presented in this section. Section 4.4 deals with the inter-industry differences in productivity growth in selected industries. Section 4.5 provides the conclusions drawn from the discussion in previous sections.

4.2 Earlier Studies on Productivity in Indian Industries

This section gives a brief review of some earlier studies on the productivity for the Indian manufacturing sector, and for the industries selected for the study. The review will deal with both parametric and non-parametric studies. Earlier studies on productivity in Indian industries can be broadly classified in two broad categories. The first category concerns partial and total factor productivity and the second category deals with production functions. Section 4.2.1 deals with the partial productivity and total factor productivity studies based on non-parametric methods whereas section 4.2.2 deals with the productivity studies using parametric methods (production functions).

4.2.1 Partial and Total Factor Productivity Studies

Goldar[3] provides a comprehensive review of productivity studies in Indian manufacturing sector for period covering fifties and mid-sixties We will not cover these studies here. However, it may be noted that barring the study of Hasim and Dadi (1973) all other studies show a rising trend in labour productivity, falling trend in capital productivity and decline in overall efficiency (total factor productivity). These studies attributed the growth of labour productivity to the capital deepening (increased capital-labour ratio) as shown by Singh (1966) for period 1951-63, Shivamaggi, Rajgopalan and Venkatachalam (1968) for period 1951-61, Rajkrishna and Mehta (1968) for period 1946-66 and Banerji (1975). Hasim and Dadi's study for period 1946-61 shows rising trends in labour productivity and capital productivity accompanied by rising trends in capital intensity and total factor productivity contrary to other studies. The study also points out the constancy of capital-output ratio and presence of technological change in Indian manufacturing industries. Their results differ from earlier studies, mainly due to a more accurate measure of capital stock from book value of CMI/ASI.

Brahamanand (1982) has measured partial and total factor

productivity for all the sectors of the economy. His estimates pertaining to registered manufacturing sector shows an increase in capital intensity, rising trends in labour productivity and declining trends in capital productivity. It shows that TFP has increased during 1950-51 to 1970-71 but thereafter has been declining. The TFP growth rate for whole period was a negative 0.2 per cent. Goldar (1986) showed rising trends in labour productivity and capital intensity, and falling trends in capital productivity. His estimates of TFP growth of the large scale manufacturing for period 1959-79 are 1.3 per cent for Translog and Solow index and 1.1 per cent for Kendrick index. Kadak (1986) also supports the findings of Goldar where the increasing trends in labour productivity (at the rate 5.17 per cent) and capital intensity (at the rate of 14.07 per cent) are associated with decreasing trends in capital productivity (at the rate of negative 8.38 per cent). His estimates of TFP shows declining trends, for both Kendrick and Solow indexes.

Ahluwalia (1985) shows that labour productivity has increased at the rate of 2.5 per cent. Except food products, beverages and petroleum products all other groups (two-digit industries) have shown rising trends. Her decomposition of labour productivity shows that majority of the increase in labour productivity was due to increased capital intensity (3.1 per cent). The TFP growth during period was negative 0.6 per cent for Solow and –0.4 per cent for Translog index.

The studies covered above are related to the period preceding to the period of our study. For the studies corresponding to the period of present study, Ahluwalia's study (1991) stands out as a pioneering and comprehensive study. The dominant feature that emerges from the analysis of long run trends in partial factor productivities in the manufacturing sector is that of a sharp increase in capital intensity (K/L ratio), at the rate 4.9 per cent accompanied by falling capital productivity (rising capital-output ratio), at the rate of negative 2.5 per cent and moderately rising labour productivity at the rate of 2.2 per cent per annum. She observed a decline in TFP growth at the rate of 0.3 per cent for the period 1965-66 to 1979-80 although according to her, there has been turn around in TFP growth since 1980 with TFP increasing at the rate of 3.4 per cent per annum in the first half of eighties. During this period, there have been change in partial productivities where increased labour productivity and capital intensity was associated with a rising or stable capital productivity (not the declining capital productivity, as observed earlier).

After this study of Ahluwalia most of the studies focused on testing the turn around hypothesis as put forth by her. But based on NAS data another study by Goldar (1995) showed that the TFP growth for organised manufacturing sector was 1.55 per cent per annum for the period 1970-71 to 1980-81, which rose at the rate of 3.85 per cent during 1980-81 to 1985-86 and further to 5.05 per cent per annum during 1985-86 to 1990-91. An increase in the productivity growth during the 80s, according to Goldar, was mainly due to an increased inflow of advanced technology and import of capital goods. But Balakrishnan and Pushpangadan (1994) demonstrated that such a turn around in productivity growth in confirmed only when the estimates are derived by using the real value added series based on single deflation and no such turn around is found when double deflation procedure is used for measuring the real value added. Rao (1996[a]) noted that when double deflation was used, TFP increased at the rate of 4.6 per cent for the period 1973-74 to 1980-81 and –0.2 per cent for the period 1981-82 to 1992-93, the overall growth rate being 2.2 per cent for the whole period (1973-74 to 1992-93). But, when TFP was estimated by single deflation the result showed that the TFP declined at the rate of 0.2 per cent for the period 1973-74 to 1980-81 and increased at the rate of 2.1 per cent for the later period with overall growth rate of 1.3 per cent. This clearly supports the findings of Balakrishnan and Pushpangadan and suggests the importance of double deflation in productivity measurement.[4] Gangopadhyay and Wadhwa's study (1998) using Translog index shows that TFP increased at the rate of 3.61 per cent for the periods 1974-93. For the periods 1974-80, 1981-86 and 1986-90, TFP increased at the rate of 1.17 per cent, 5.44 per cent and 5.01 per cent respectively. For the sub-period, corresponding to liberalisation period in India 1991-93, the growth in TFP was at the rate of 3.88 per cent. In a recent paper, Mitra (1999) shows that TFP growth for the period 1966-67 to 1992-93 has been either sluggish (if positive) or negative across a large number of industries and states.

There have been a number of productivity studies at the level of specific industries. As our main interest lies in productivity trends of the selected industries, we will confine ourselves to the results pertaining to the industries covered in the present study, mainly to know the productivity trends prior to the period under study. Sugar and paper &

paperboard industries were among the industries studied by Sinha and Shawney (1970) for the period 1950-63. The results related to sugar industry shows that labour productivity based on gross output increased at the rate of 4.7 per cent and based on net distributable output (our measure of GVA_{SD}) increased at the rate of 3.9 per cent whereas, corresponding trend rate of capital productivity was 1.2 per cent and 0.4 per cent respectively. The TFP growth for the industry was only 0.5 per cent based on gross output and 0.4 per cent based on net distributable output (NDO). Whereas, in paper and paperboard industry TFP increased at the rate of 0.9 per cent (0.7 per cent based on gross output), labour productivity at the rate of 2.1 per cent (3.9 per cent based on gross output) and capital productivity at the rate of 0.03 per cent (1.6 per cent based on gross output). These two industries are also included in the study of Asit Banerji (1975). Results pertaining to sugar industry show that capital deepening contributed significantly towards increasing labour productivity, as obvious from high rate of growth of K/L ratio (5.0 per cent) and a fairly close rate of growth of labour productivity (3.9 per cent). The Solow index of TFP shows an insignificant trend rate of 0.1 per cent per annum and capital productivity shows a declining trend at the rate of –1.1 per cent. Paper & paperboard industry also shows similar trends where rapid increase in capital-labour ratio (10.4 per cent) was accompanied by significantly rising trends in labour productivity (6.0 per cent) and declining trends in capital productivity (4.4 per cent). TFP (Solow index) also shows a declining but statistically insignificant trend rate of 0.3 per cent per annum.

Ahluwalia (1991) shows that in sugar, khandsari & gur labour input (6.5 per cent) increased faster than the capital input (6.3 per cent) with a modest increase in value added (4.0 per cent). The performance of the industry has been unsatisfactory with a decline in labour productivity (–2.3 per cent), capital productivity (–2.1 per cent) and TFP (–2.3 per cent) along with a decline in capital intensity. Fertilizers industry was the one, where rapid growth of factor inputs (14.4 per cent and 6.4 per cent for capital and labour respectively) was associated with the rapid growth of value added (13.0 per cent). In this industry, TFP growth was at the rate of 1.3 per cent and labour productivity increased at the rate of 6.3 per cent per annum. The industry experienced capital deepening as shown by 7.5 per cent growth in capital-labour ratio and growth rate of capital productivity being negative, 1.0 per cent per annum. Watches and clocks was one of those industries which experienced rapid growth in TFP. This industry shows highest increase in value added (18.9 per cent) associated with highest increase in capital input (17.2 per cent), and labour input increased at the trend rate of 11.0 per cent. The increase in labour productivity (7.1 per cent) in this industry is associated with a positive trend in capital productivity (1.5 per cent) and TFP (3.8 per cent). The capital-labour ratio in the industry increased at the trend rate of 5.5 per cent per annum. In paper & newsprint industry labour productivity and increase (1.5 per cent) was associated with declining capital productivity (2.0 per cent) and TFPG (–0.7 per cent), indicating most of the rise in labour productivity is due to capital deepening (K/L ratio increased at the trend rate of 3.7 per cent). The value added, labour input and capital input in the industry increased at the rate of 5.9 per cent, 4.4 per cent and 8.9 per cent respectively. In heavy vehicles & motorcar industry increase in value added (7.3 per cent) is associated with increase in labour productivity (1.3 per cent) and capital intensity (K/L ratio at the rate of 3.7 per cent and capital input at the rate of 9.9 per cent). The capital productivity (–2.4 per cent) and TFPG (0.9 per cent) shows a declining trend during the period.

4.2.2 Production Function Studies

A comprehensive survey of production function estimates for Indian manufacturing industries may be found in Somayajulu and George (1983) and Goldar (1986). Somayajulu and George surveys the production function studies, classifying them according to returns to scale (increasing, decreasing or constant), elasticity of substitution, partial and total factor productivity. Their reviews are detailed and exhaustive. We confine our analysis to comparing the estimates of functions with some more recent estimates. However, it may be pointed out that the most of the estimates are based on Cobb-Douglas specification, which assumes constant elasticity of substitution between labour and capital and Hicks-neutrality of technical change. Banerji (1975) has made systematic attempt to test the assumptions underlying the C-D specification and found empirical support for these assumptions. Goldar estimates of C-D production function for 1951-65 shows constant return to scale and statistically insignificant capital coefficient. He attributed this partially to multicollinearity and partially to errors in measurements of capital. Elimination of trend component by including a separate time trend might have led to an underestimation of capital coefficient and an overestimation of coefficient of time.[5] His result for CMAS function does not give any consistent result for elasticity of substitution due to presence of multicollinearity. Rajlaxmi (1985) has estimated VES production function for Rajasthan and India and found that VES is the correct form of production function for estimating elasticity of substitution. Her result shows that elasticity of substitution has been declining over time.

The most exhaustive study of production function for the Indian industries has been done by Ahluwalia (1991). Her estimation of C-D production function (ratio form) for manufacturing industries consistently indicate constant return to scale and TFP growth not significantly different from zero for the period up to 1982-83. There is an evidence of distinct upward shift in the TFP growth after 1982-83. The coefficient of capital is in the range of 0.35 to 0.43 and is statistically significant. This suggests that labour's share is in the range of 0.57 to 0.65. The assumption of unitary elasticity of substitution underlying C-D production function is not rejected when it is estimated using CES production function. The result of panel data for 64 industry groups with Translog specification, rejected the hypothesis of Hicks-neutrality of technical progress and found labour using bias in the technical progress. Her explanation of turn around in TFP may be summed up: "As the rising fiscal deficit in the eighties created resurgent demand conditions, the reorientation of the policy framework and the toning up of infrastructure enables a supply response to the rising demands through productivity improvements. The agriculture sector also played a supportive role in the process."[6] In a recent paper Gangopadhyay and Wadhwa (1998) estimated production function for aggregate manufacturing using panel data by pooling cross-section and time series data for 18 two-digit industries for the period 1973-74 to 1992-93. The estimates of TFP growth, estimated at the means of variables, shows a trend rate of –0.20 per cent (compounded annually). Their results also show a labour saving ($B_{LT} < 0$) and capital-using ($B_{KT} > 0$) bias in technological progress. The results also indicate that technical change is not Hicks-neutral but capital augmenting. This contradicts the result of Ahluwalia who finds a labour using and capital saving bias in technical progress. They explained this to the changing behaviour of Indian industry since 1985. The hypothesis of production function being of C-D variety and that of constant returns to scale are also rejected. They have searched for structural break, up to year 1992, but did not find any support for the hypothesis of structural break after year 1982-83 as advanced by Ahluwalia.

4.3 Productivity Trends in Selected Industries

In this section, we will analyse the productivity trends and productivity estimates by estimating single factor productivities of labour and capital and total factor productivity for the selected industries and for organised manufacturing sector as a whole. The productivity estimates will be obtained by using real value added (our estimate of output) arrived at by applying both single deflation and double deflation methods. Section 4.3.1 deals with the productivity estimates in the organised manufacturing sector as a whole. Sections 4.3.2 to section 4.3.6 deal with the productivity estimates in the selected industries. The *Cochrane-Orcutt* and *Prais-Winsten* methods have been used to eliminate autocorrelation, from the estimates using parametric approach, whenever *Durban-Watson statistics* test rejects the hypothesis of zero autocorrelation. Only re-estimated results of best estimates (high R^2) between *Cochran-Orcutt* and *Prais-Winsten* methods are reported. The *F* values for 'OLS' and *Rho* values for *Cochran-Orcutt* or *Prais-Winsten iterative* estimates are reported. We have divided the period in two parts—1973-74 to 1984-85 and 1985-86 to 1995-96—for the analysis of results in non-parametric approach[7] and for inter-temporal comparison.

4.3.1 Organised Manufacturing Sector

The gross value added by single deflation in organised manufacturing sector increased at the rate[8] of 8.36 per cent. Labour input in the industry has increased at the trend rate of 1.95 per cent whereas capital input in the industry has increased at trend rate of 6.98 per cent. The average share of worker in total employment has been around 78 per cent and their share is declining over time, from 80.1 per cent in 1973-74 to 74.6 per cent in 1995-96. This indicates that employment of 'persons other than workers' is increasing at higher rate than 'workers'. The results of productivity estimates are analysed below.

4.3.1a. Estimates of Factor Productivities

The detailed time trends of partial factor productivities and total factor productivities using single deflation and double deflation are presented in Tables 4.1 and 4.2. Column-2 of Table 4.1 shows that index of labour productivity has fluctuated up to 1980-81 (102.97) but thereafter it has continuously increased except a minor dip in 1991-92 and was at 298.6 in 1995-96 with trend rate of 5.21 per cent. The index of capital productivity has shown fluctuations throughout the period and capital productivity has remain almost stagnate during the period. The index has increased at insignificant trend rate of 0.26 per cent. Productivity seems to have picked up in second half, where labour productivity and capital productivity index has increased at much higher rate (6.57 per cent and 1.14 per cent respectively) than in first half (3.12 per cent and 0.42 per cent respectively). The total factor productivity has increased significantly in the period as all three indexes of TFP have increased at significant growth rates of 1.99 per cent, 2.21 per cent and 2.16 per cent for the indexes of TFPK, TFPS and TFPT respectively, and as expected, the increase has been more noticeable in the second half. Capital-labour ratio in organised manufacturing sector has increased from 0.6123 in base year to 1.5837 in 1995-96 showing an increase of more than two and half time (Column-2 Table 4.5). The index of capital intensity (capital-labour ratio) has steadily increased to 258.6 in 1995-96, at the exponential trend rate of 4.94 per cent and the increase has been more in the second half (5.38 per cent) of the period than in the first half (2.69 per cent). Chart 4.1 shows that graphs of labour productivity and capital productivity have moved in harmony. Thus, the increase in labour productivity seems to have been made possible due to 'more machine per worker effect'. *It is important to note that in a situation where capital-labour ratio is increasing overtime, the analysis of partial productivity changes would overstate the increase in labour productivity and understate the increase in capital productivity.* To separate the effect of increase in labour productivity due to '*more machine to work with effect*' from the '*pure increase in labour productivity effect*' we have decomposed the increase in labour productivity using Solow method. Column-2 of Table 4.6 shows that value of labour productivity has increased from Rs. 0.09282 lakh in 1973-74 to Rs. 0.27714 lakh in 1995-96 showing a net gain of Rs. 0.18432 lakh. The decomposition shows (Table 4.27) that 37.3 per cent of the change in labour productivity has been due to increased capital intensity and technical progress accounted for the 62.7 per cent of increase in the labour productivity. The contribution of capital intensity in increased labour productivity has been more for period from 1973-84 than the contribution for the period of 1985-95.

Table 4.1 : Estimates of Indexes of Factor Productivity (Single De-flation) and Capital Intensity: Organised Manufacturing Sector

Year	Indexes of Partial Factor Productivity		Indexes of Total Factor Productivity			Capital Intensity
	Labour	Capital	Kendrick	Solow	Translog	K/L
1	2	3	4	5	6	7
1973-74	100.00	100.00	100.00	100.00	100.00	100.00
1974-75	101.72	101.35	101.52	101.53	101.52	100.37
1975-76	112.28	90.84	99.64	98.93	99.32	123.60
1976-77	108.11	105.82	106.87	105.54	106.86	102.17
1977-78	110.42	107.09	108.61	107.25	108.59	103.11
1978-79	127.29	117.55	121.87	120.67	121.76	108.28
1979-80	113.76	104.24	108.44	107.29	108.32	109.13
1980-81	102.97	91.81	96.65	95.42	96.55	112.15
1981-82	117.66	99.27	107.01	106.00	106.86	118.52
1982-83	129.46	105.62	115.45	114.47	115.28	122.58
1983-84	149.48	110.83	125.88	125.52	125.76	134.88
1984-85	147.00	102.25	119.00	118.40	119.12	143.77
1985-86	160.03	100.61	121.47	121.79	122.27	159.07
1986-87	167.48	99.18	122.24	122.96	123.49	168.86
1987-88	170.37	98.14	122.08	123.04	123.58	173.60
1988-89	191.07	102.70	130.65	132.76	132.88	186.04
1989-90	205.02	106.94	137.32	139.92	139.88	191.72
1990-91	223.11	106.29	140.26	143.69	143.44	209.90
1991-92	214.21	96.56	129.44	132.52	132.67	221.85
1992-93	235.41	102.58	138.80	142.51	142.47	229.50
1993-94	267.42	108.37	149.50	154.57	153.78	246.76
1994-95	281.10	108.59	151.63	156.97	156.13	258.86
1995-96	298.57	115.54	161.16	166.83	165.94	258.64
Annual Trend Rates (% Per Annum)						
1973-95	5.21	0.26+	1.99	2.21	2.16	4.94
	(18.74)	(1.326)	(11.189)	(11.725)	(11.804)	(19.03)
1973-84	3.12	0.42+	1.56*	1.53*	1.56*	2.69
	(4.50)	(.679)	(2.730)	(2.633)	(2.724)	(4.291)
1985-95	6.57	1.14	2.71	3.07	2.96	5.38
	(19.182)	(2.981)	(7.678)	(8.475)	(8.488)	(27.92)

Source: Data computed from appendix tables A-1, A-7, A-13 & A-19 as per methodology explained in Chapter-2.

Notes:
1. The growth rates are calculated by fitting exponential function of the form $Y = ab^t$.
2. Figure in brackets are t-values of estimates and are significant at 1 per cent level of significance unless otherwise specified.
3. *Significant at 5 per cent level; + Insignificant.

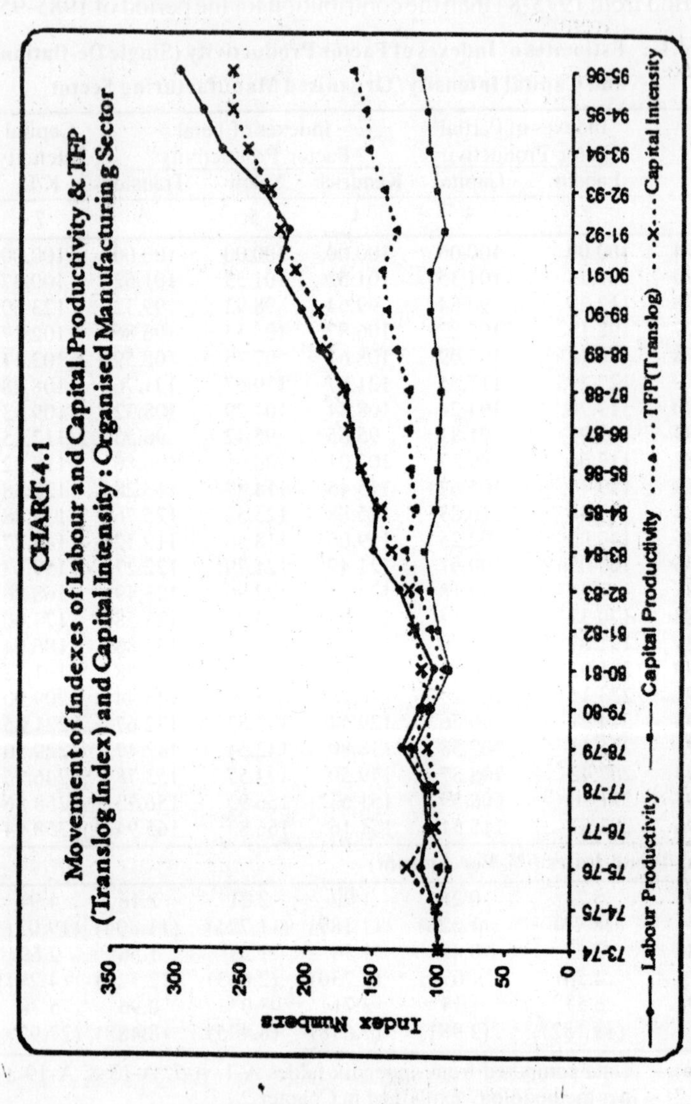

Sources: Plotted from the data in Table 4.1.

CHART-4.2

Comparision of Indexes of Labour Productivity by Single Deflation and Double Deflation: Organised Manufacturing Sector

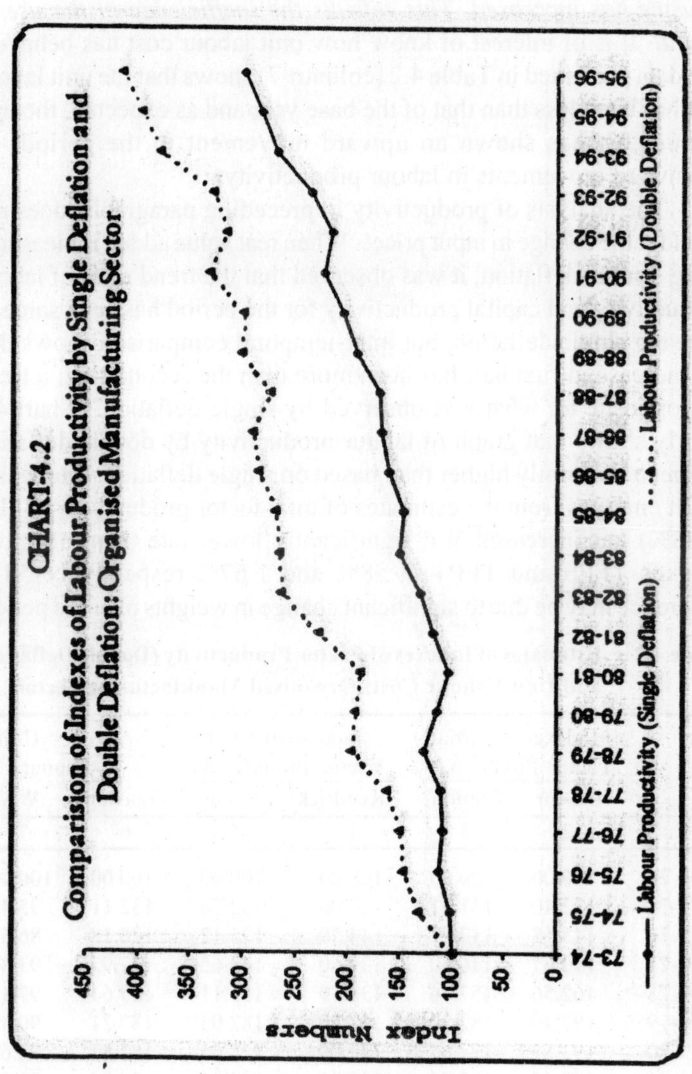

Sources: Plotted from the data in Table 4.1 and Table 4.2.

The insignificant increase in capital productivity along with increasing capital intensity reveals that capital-output ratio in the industry has increased. This reflects the inefficiency in the use of capital. It is of interest of know how unit labour cost has behaved. The data presented in Table 4.2 (column-7) shows that the unit labour cost has been less than that of the base year and as expected, the unit labour cost has shown an upward movement in the periods of downward movements in labour productivity.

The analysis of productivity in preceding paragraphs does not consider the change in input prices. When real value added is measured using double deflation, it was observed that the trend rates of labour productivity and capital productivity for the period has been same as by using single deflation, but inter-temporal comparison shows that the increase in first half has been more than the second half, a trend just opposite to, what was observed by single deflation.[9] Chart 4.2 clearly shows that graph of labour productivity by double deflation has been uniformly higher than based on single deflation. Interesting result emerges from the estimates of total factor productivity; TFPK (0.33%) has increased at a significantly lower rate than other two indexes TFPS and TFPT (1.58% and 1.67% respectively). The difference may be due to significant change in weights over the period.

Table 4.2 : Estimates of Indexes of Factor Productivity (Double Deflation) and Unit Labour Cost: Organised Manufacturing Sector

Year	Indexes of Partial Factor Productivity		Indexes of Total Factor Productivity			Unit Labour Cost
	Labour	Capital	Kendrick	Solow	Translog	W/V
1	2	3	4	5	6	7
1973-74	100.00	100.00	100.00	100.00	100.00	100.00
1974-75	132.40	131.91	127.06	132.20	132.11	95.42
1975-76	145.57	117.77	144.79	125.12	126.18	86.55
1976-77	149.67	146.50	129.50	143.65	147.92	93.84
1977-78	162.56	157.66	131.19	155.11	159.64	97.15
1978-79	197.40	182.30	151.75	182.95	187.21	90.49
1979-80	193.89	177.67	140.09	178.65	182.83	92.61
1980-81	187.34	167.04	130.31	168.91	173.05	95.20
1981-82	228.35	192.67	153.11	198.62	202.10	87.63
1982-83	264.29	215.61	167.98	224.49	227.75	90.90
1983-84	265.87	197.12	163.00	207.94	212.50	84.74

conti.

1	2	3	4	5	6	7
1984-85	269.98	187.79	159.38	200.48	205.43	94.14
1985-86	284.99	179.16	166.00	195.34	200.62	86.59
1986-87	290.12	171.81	163.26	189.54	195.05	88.06
1987-88	274.04	157.86	144.59	174.96	180.42	88.02
1988-89	302.58	162.64	153.24	183.82	189.08	81.43
1989-90	300.78	156.89	142.01	178.46	183.71	76.50
1990-91	332.48	158.40	146.93	184.42	189.43	72.28
1991-92	316.55	142.68	133.81	167.44	172.72	68.52
1992-93	329.26	143.47	127.88	169.63	174.98	68.71
1993-94	379.45	153.77	139.69	185.62	190.41	59.03
1994-95	397.16	153.43	135.13	186.94	191.77	60.09
1995-96	415.82	160.77	127.79	195.85	200.91	59.83
Annual Trend Rate (% Per Annum)						
1973-95	5.51	0.55+	0.33+	1.58	1.67	–2.11
	(15.72)	(1.032)	(.882)	(3.299)	(3.418)	(8.521)
1973-84	8.71	5.86	3.25	6.37	6.54	–0.62+
	(12.59)	(6.274)	(4.281)	(7.736)	(7.729)	(1.611)
1985-95	4.03	–1.28*	–2.33	–0.08+	–0.11+	–4.47
	(7.84)	(2.648)	(5.515)	(.115)	(.209)	(12.11)

Source : Data computed from appendix tables A-1, A-7, A-13 & A-19 as per methodology explained in Chapter-2.

Notes : 1. The growth rates are calculated by fitting exponential function of the form $Y = ab^t$.

2. Figure in brackets are t-values of estimates and are significant at 1 % level of significance unless otherwise specified.
3. *Significant at 5 % level; + Insignificant.

4.3.1b. Production Function Estimates

The estimates of production functions for the organised manufacturing sector are summarised in Table 4.3. The estimates by OLS method showed a high degree of autocorrelation. Therefore, *Cocharen-Orcutt* and *Prais-Winsten* iterative procedures (as available in SPSS PC+) are applied to get rid of autocorrelation whenever the hypothesis of no positive autocorrelation was rejected by *D-W statistic*. However, the results from both method do not differ significantly and the results of the method having higher explaining power are reported. The result shows that coefficient of capital (LnK/) is significant in all the equations indicating that labour productivity is significantly related to capital intensity. The coefficient of labour (LnL) is significantly different from zero indicating that the hypothesis of constant return to scale are rejected and that organised manufacturing sector has experienced increasing returns to scale. The insignificant coefficient of trend variable indicates the absence of neutral technical progress. The estimates of CES production function show that coefficients of labour (LnL) and wage rate (Lnw) are significantly different from zero but the coefficient of wage rate (Lnw) is not significantly different from

Table 4.3 : Production Function Estimates: Organised Manufacturing Sector

Dependent Variable-Ln V/L
Number of observation-23

Functional Forms	Constant	Coefficient of Ln K/L	LnW	LnL	Time	Adj. R^2	D-W Statistics	F/Rho
1	2	3	4	5	6	7	8	9
Estimates Without Trend Variable								
CD-I	−2.281	1.037	-	-	-	.9529	1.716	.2182+
	(4.060)	(21.132)						(.998)
CD-II	6.348	0.928	-	.3358*	-	.9552	1.704	.3015+
	(−3.476)	(14.36)		(2.501)				(1.378)
CES-I	−2.814*	-	1.439	-	-	.7728	2.043	.6919
	(1.869)		(8.248)					(4.286)
CES-II	−2.102	-	1.464	−0.058	-	.7322	2.009	.6992
	(.6823)		(6.608)	(4.064)				(4.261)
VES	−3.771	0.632	.711	-	-	.9325	2.089	.5708
	(4.706)	(5.808)	(4.220)	-	- -		-	(3.030)
Estimates With Trend Variable								
CD-I	1.416+	0.696	-	-	.0178*	.9485	1.647	.3087+
	(0.691)	(3.694)			(1.873)			(1.415)
CD-II	26.98*	1.715	-	1.109+	−.0527*	.9659	1.807	.2236+
	(2.312)	(3.914)		(.6823)	(1.801)			(0.973)
CES-I	3.145*	-	.706	-	.0304	.8667	2.164	.6492
	(1.748)		(2.919)		(3.761)			(3.726)
CES-II	9.924	-	.738	.452*	.0396	.8709	2.076	.7137
	(3.0176)		(3.479)	(2.516)	(4.818)			(4.323)
VES	−2.407+	.553	.649	-	.0061+	.9287	2.066	.5756
	(1.011)	(3.261)	(3.254)		(0.613)			(3.086)

unity. It, therefore, implies that there is evidence of increasing returns to scale and elasticity of substitution is close to unity, i.e., the assumption of unitary elasticity of substitution implicit in CD function is not rejected. The technical progress calculated from

CES function is 15.5 per cent, it is an overestimation and does not supports the finding of CD function. The results of VES production function show that both capital intensity and wage rate are significantly related to labour productivity and the partial elasticity of wage rate is more than capital intensity. Technical progress as computed from VES production function is 1.36 per cent, which is close to the estimates by index number approach. It may be concluded that organised manufacturing sector is characterised by increasing returns to scale and the elasticity of substitution is not more than unity resulting in the inability of the industry to absorb unemployment.

Table 4.4 : Estimates of Function Explaining Sources of Productivity Change: Organised Manufacturing Sector

Explanatory Variable	Constant	Coefficient of Ln V	Ln w	Ln K/L	Time	Adj R^2	D-W Statistic	F/Rho
Ln V/L	−4.429	.674	.209	.797	−.0410	.9982	1.848	3250.3
	(8.160)	(16.172)	(4.103)	(19.238)	(11.357)			(4,18)
Ln V/K	3.942	.737	−.400	.130+	.0334	.9964	1.881	1321.0
	(3.917)	(7.356)	(3.272)	(1.309)	(3.851)			(4,18)
TFPK	−1.502*	.581	.284	.102*	−.0343	.9851	1.928	356.55
	(2.261)	(11.391)	(4.564)	(2.012)	(7.754)			(4,18)
TFPS	−2.533	.619	.273	.188	.0385	.9890	2.010	486.96
	(4.031)	(12.834)	(4.639)	(3.911)	(9.226)			(4,18)
TFPT	−2.024	.601	.273	.149	−.0360	.9881	1.868	456.35
	(3.201)	(12.389)	(4.610)	(3.087)	(8.294)			(4,18)

Source: Estimated using data in table 4.1, 6.1 and appendix. Table A-7.

Notes : 1. The figure in parenthesis refers to the corresponding t-values.

2. All t-values are significant at 1% level of significance unless otherwise specified.

3. *Significant at 5% level; + Insignificant.

4.3.1c. Sources of Productivity Change

The results presented in Table 4.4 shows that labour productivity is significantly related to value added. Thus, we find the support for Vedroon Law. Value added, wage rate and capital intensity are closely related to labour productivity and to all the measures of TFP. The increase in value added may increase productivity over the period because of (a) technical progress and (b) economies of scale (both internal and external). The positive association of labour productivity with wage rate indicates that higher wages results in higher productivity (supporting efficiency wage hypothesis). The positive and significant association between labour productivity and capital intensity may be due to 'more machine to work with effect'. The coefficient of time is negative in all equations. This implies that labour management relation and other institutional factors have adversely affected productivity in the organised manufacturing sector.

Table 4.5: Capital Intensity (Capital-Labour Ratio) in Different Industries

Year	Manufacturing Sector	Sugar	Paper & Paperboard	Fertiliser & Pesticide	Motor Vehicles	Watches & Clocks
1	2	3	4	5	6	7
1973-74	0.61234	0.56646	0.79515	2.34202	0.51204	0.28350
1974-75	0.61459	0.31610	0.83811	2.45797	0.53304	0.24953
1975-76	0.75686	0.28052	0.87051	2.66937	0.55844	0.31644
1976-77	0.62561	0.24252	0.90371	2.85172	0.57830	0.31510
1977-78	0.63137	0.26908	0.83830	3.17936	0.58948	0.30787
1978-79	0.66305	0.34041	0.90308	3.27744	0.59320	0.29666
1979-80	0.66822	0.32358	0.87041	3.03630	0.55997	0.29724
1980-81	0.68676	0.25347	0.95695	3.24223	0.58310	0.39190
1981-82	0.72573	0.28037	0.98747	3.83642	0.60546	0.43262
1982-83	0.75061	0.36965	0.99739	3.72547	0.62217	0.40642
1983-84	0.82591	0.59726	1.19713	3.72390	0.71538	0.43646
1984-85	0.88033	0.71905	1.39707	4.35978	0.76444	0.57305
1985-86	0.97403	0.79790	1.37604	4.10641	0.82937	0.58928
1986-87	1.03399	0.83958	1.52722	5.08327	0.87863	0.61417
1987-88	1.06302	0.80284	1.53252	4.86410	0.96256	0.69001
1988-89	1.13920	0.81135	1.86469	4.85905	0.97225	0.75502
1989-90	1.17395	0.88360	1.78487	4.97893	1.05178	0.78061
1990-91	1.28532	0.92890	1.85932	5.59612	1.09426	0.99050
1991-92	1.35848	0.94982	1.91171	6.44028	1.18354	0.92375
1992-93	1.40529	1.00711	1.94706	6.02643	1.25360	0.99883
1993-94	1.51103	1.15558	2.10245	6.51738	1.38488	1.16354
1994-95	1.58508	1.27158	2.73599	6.84452	1.34683	1.20912
1995-96	1.58376	1.22703	2.35410	6.93049	1.47476	1.06457

conti.

1	2	3	4	5	6	7
Annual Trend Rates (% Per Annum)						
1973-95	4.94	7.82	5.74	5.05	5.19	7.82
	(19.03)	(8.534)	(19.76)	(29.97)	(20.87)	(22.86)
1973-84	2.69	3.84[+]	3.98	5.15	2.82	6.06
	(4.29)	(1.271)	(5.518)	(11.09)	(5.884)	(6.254)
1985-95	5.38	5.04	5.72	5.01	5.90	7.51
	(27.79)	(8.888)	(7.834)	(5.01)	(24.91)	(9.718)

Source : Data computed from appendix Table A-1 to A-6 and A-13 to A-18 as per methodology explained in Chapter-2.

Notes : 1. The growth rates are calculated by fitting exponential function of the form $Y = ab^t$.

2. Figure in brackets are t-values of estimates and are significant at 1% level of significance unless otherwise specified.

3. + Insignificant.

Table 4.6 : Labour Productivity (Real GVA_{SD} - Labour Ratio) in Different Industries

(Value in Rs '00000)

Year	Manufacturing Sector	Sugar	Paper & Paperboard	Fertiliser & Pesticide	Motor Vehicles	Watches & Clocks
1	2	3	4	5	6	7
1973-74	0.09282	0.08804	0.13678	0.25364	0.13865	0.09737
1974-75	0.09442	0.04638	0.17697	0.21964	0.13560	0.11286
1975-76	0.10422	0.05025	0.15691	0.19084	0.13122	0.14739
1976-77	0.10035	0.04431	0.13717	0.23597	0.16177	0.16466
1977-78	0.10249	0.04842	0.13064	0.26024	0.16304	0.14609
1978-79	0.11815	0.07130	0.13361	0.34532	0.16508	0.15286
1979-80	0.10559	0.05571	0.12378	0.29456	0.12771	0.14693
1980-81	0.09558	0.02908	0.11839	0.24547	0.12932	0.18959
1981-82	0.10921	0.04932	0.11780	0.32836	0.15810	0.19444
1982-83	0.12017	0.10554	0.07559	0.40566	0.21225	0.28044
1983-84	0.13875	0.18195	0.10123	0.39461	0.18655	0.21826
1984-85	0.13644	0.17344	0.13904	0.58533	0.19215	0.25863
1985-86	0.14854	0.16950	0.12015	0.46540	0.18753	0.27673
1986-87	0.15545	0.18861	0.15475	0.48418	0.20782	0.28437
1987-88	0.15814	0.18993	0.13985	0.52206	0.19542	0.29225
1988-89	0.17735	0.26703	0.17620	0.61405	0.20940	0.29859
1989-90	0.19030	0.26847	0.23019	0.66124	0.23098	0.34482
1990-91	0.20709	0.20818	0.24913	0.81814	0.25550	0.34358
1991-92	0.19883	0.21800	0.21135	0.87219	0.24554	0.47862
1992-93	0.21851	0.23158	0.17979	0.83579	0.23901	0.29889
1993-94	0.24822	0.31339	0.18672	0.78443	0.27066	0.36408
1994-95	0.26092	0.41892	0.24812	0.94540	0.31199	0.39966
1995-96	0.27714	0.31334	0.29471	1.20396	0.47187	0.40776

1	2	3	4	5	6	7
Annual Trend Rate (% Per Annum)						
1973-95	5.21	10.88	2.96	7.99	4.28	6.32
	(18.85)	(8.613)	(3.576)	(17.67)	(9.221)	(13.83)
1973-84	3.12	8.64*	–3.80*	7.64	3.11*	8.28*
	(4.537)	(1.974)	(2.703)	(4.979)	(2.720)	(7.355)
1985-95	6.57	6.84	6.76	9.06	7.10	3.97
	(19.19)	(4.112)	(3.980)	(9.865)	(5.406)	(3.226)

Source : Data computed from appendix Table A-1 to A-12 as per methodology explained in Chapter-2.

Notes : 1. The growth rates are calculated by fitting exponential function of the form $Y = ab^t$.

2. Figure in brackets are t-values of estimates and are significant at 1% level of significance unless otherwise specified.

3. *Significant at 5% level.

4.3.2 Sugar Industry

The gross value added by single deflation in sugar industry has increased at the rate of 9.69 per cent. Labour input in the industry has declined at trend rate of 1.07 per cent whereas capital input in the industry has increased at trend rate of 6.66 per cent. The average share of workers in total employment has been 68.4 per cent. The frequency distribution of the industries by the year of initial production presented in Appendix Table A-30 shows that before 1900 there were only two industries. The decade of 1930s saw that more than 73 industries started their production. Since then the number of factories in the industry continued to increase and in the decades of seventies, 97 and in eighties, 75 factories started their production. The productivity estimates for the industry are analysed below.

4.3.2a. Estimates of Factor Productivities

The detailed time trend estimates of partial productivities and total factor productivity based on single deflation along with capital intensity are presented in Table 4.7 and are depicted in Chart 4.3. Column-2 of the Table 4.7 shows that labour productivity index has been less than the base year up to 1981-82 and thereafter the index of labour productivity has shown an increasing trend, and it was 475.82 in 1994-95. The average annual trend rate of labour productivity is 10.88 per cent for entire period. The average annual trend rate in first half (8.64 per cent) has been more than the second half (6.84 per cent).[10] In value terms, labour productivity has increased from Rs. 0.08804 lakhs in base year to Rs. 0.31314 lakhs in 1995-96. It was the lowest at

Rs. 0.02908 lakh in 1980-81 and the highest in 1994-95 at Rs. 0.41892 lakh (Column-3, Table 4.6). Column-3 of the Table 4.7 shows that the index of capital productivity has shown an increasing trend but the increase has not been uniform. The index fluctuated throughout the period but it was more than that of the base year throughout except for the year 1974-75 and 1980-81. The capital productivity has also increased at the trend rate of 2.83 per cent and the increase in capital productivity was more in the first half than in the second half. Estimates of Kendrick, Solow and Translog indexes of total factor productivity have shown similar trends. The annual trend rates for these indexes turn out to be 6.61 per cent, 7.38 per cent and 6.10 per cent respectively. Estimates for sub-period reveals marked inter-temporal differences in trend rates. Average annual trend rates of indexes for period 1973-84, at the rate of 6.78 per cent, 8.52 per cent and 5.97 per cent, has been markedly higher than the average annual trend rates for the period 1985-95, at the trend rate of 3.45 per cent, 4.02 per cent and 3.79 per cent respectively for TFPK, TFPS and TFPT. Chart 4.3 shows that all the indexes of productivity has shown similar up and down movements. The capital intensity in the industry has increased from 0.56646 in base year to 1.22703 in 1995-96 at average annual trend rate of 7.82 per cent; the increase has been 3.84 per cent for the period 1973-84 and 5.04 per cent for the period 1985-95. Column-7 of Table 4.7 shows that index of capital intensity has been less than 100 up to 1982-83. The index has fluctuated up to 1980-81 and thereafter it has shown increasing trend except some fluctuation in between and was 216.62 in 1995-96. The significant rise in capital intensity may overstate the increase in labour productivity and it seems that part of increase in labour productivity has been due to increased capital intensity. To know the contribution of capital intensity in increased labour productivity, we have decomposed the increase in labour productivity using Solow method. Data presented in Table 4.7 shows that 76.6 per cent of the increase in labour productivity has been contributed by increased capital-labour ratio and technical progress accounted for remaining 23.4 per cent only. The decomposition during sub-periods shows that during 1973-84 technical regress has pulled back the increase in labour productivity, made possible by capital intensity (121.6 per cent). But in later half technical progress has contributed 65.5 per cent of the increase in labour productivity. It is interesting to know about what happen to unit labour cost of production. *Here, it would be worthwhile to point out that rise in labour productivity is no guarantee in decline in unit labour cost (W/V), which is obtained by dividing the wage bill (total emoluments) by gross value added (both at same price). Simultaneous rise in labour productivity and unit labour cost is possible if wage rate increases at a faster rate than labour productivity.* Behaviour of unit labour cost presented in column-7 of Table 4.8 shows that index of unit labour cost has been fluctuating for the period and it has been more than that of the base year up to year 1980-81, for year 1984-85 and then from 1990-91 to 1992-93. The annual trend rate of unit labour cost had been -1.68 per cent and the decline has been more in the second half than in the first half. The comparison of these trend rates shows that relatively more increase in productivity indexes in the first half has not resulted in corresponding decline in unit labour cost as compared to the second half where with small growth rate in productivity indexes could result in more decline in unit labour cost. *This shows that rising labour productivity is no guarantee to the reduction in unit labour cost.*

Table 4.7 : Estimates of Indexes of Factor Productivity (Single Deflation) and Capital Intensity : Sugar Industry

Year	Indexes of Partial Factor Productivity		Indexes of Total Factor Productivity			Capital Industry
	Labour	Capital	Kendrick	Solow	Translog	K/L
1	2	3	4	5	6	7
1973-74	100.00	100.00	100.00	100.00	100.00	100.00
1974-75	52.68	94.40	68.42	75.69	71.03	55.80
1975-76	57.08	115.26	77.43	86.30	81.46	49.52
1976-77	50.32	117.54	71.66	81.34	76.98	42.81
1977-78	55.00	115.78	75.68	84.41	80.01	47.50
1978-79	80.98	134.76	102.22	113.92	105.81	60.09
1979-80	63.28	110.77	81.46	91.55	84.55	57.12
1980-81	33.03	73.82	46.37	56.39	48.88	44.75
1981-82	56.02	113.18	76.00	93.22	78.99	49.50
1982-83	119.87	183.70	146.35	183.04	144.51	65.26
1983-84	206.66	196.00	200.97	250.19	188.52	105.44
1984-85	196.99	155.19	172.76	208.80	162.85	126.94
1985-86	192.52	136.67	158.75	193.08	150.76	140.86
1986-87	214.23	144.54	171.24	209.19	162.97	148.22
1987-88	215.73	152.21	177.22	215.94	168.26	141.73

conti.

1	2	3	4	5	6	7
1988-89	303.29	211.75	247.57	302.36	235.08	143.23
1989-90	304.93	195.48	236.11	286.35	223.71	155.99
1990-91	236.45	144.19	177.37	212.75	168.72	163.98
1991-92	247.61	147.67	183.09	220.50	174.81	167.68
1992-93	263.03	147.95	187.21	227.91	180.47	177.79
1993-94	355.95	174.49	230.92	291.63	225.46	204.00
1994-95	475.82	211.96	288.71	370.42	281.92	224.48
1995-96	355.89	164.30	221.45	286.57	215.92	216.62
Annual Trend Rate (% Per Annum)						
1973-95	10.88	2.83	6.61	7.38	6.10	7.82
	(8.613)	(4.474)	(7.155)	(8.098)	(7.217)	(8.635)
1973-84	8.64*	4.62*	6.78*	8.52*	5.97*	3.84+
	(1.974)	(2.312)	(2.126)	(2.752)	(2.054)	(1.272)
1985-95	6.84	1.71+	3.45*	4.02*	3.79*	5.04
	(4.112)	(1.119)	(2.243)	(2.476)	(2.451)	(8.857)

Source : Data computed from appendix Table A-2, A-8, A-14 & A-20 as per methodology explained in Chapter-2.

Notes:
1. The growth rates are calculated by fitting exponential function of the form $Y = ab^t$.
2. Figure in brackets are t-values of estimates and are significant at 1% level of significance unless otherwise specified.
3. * Significant at 5% level; + Insignificant.

The analysis so far has ignored the price of material input for the industry. The price of main input, sugarcane, in the industry has increased at a rate much higher than the price of sugar. This is reflected in the productivity movement as presented in Table 4.8. Column-2 of the Table 4.8 shows a trend rate of 13.42 %. The results indicate that indexes based on single deflation depressed the real productivity advance. The differentiated price movement is more visible in later half of the period. Chart 4.4 also shows that in the later half of the period the gap between both lines have widened. The capital productivity index based on double deflation has increased at trend rate of 5.19 % and index moved slowly in the later half of the period. The difference in price movement is also reflected in the measure of TFP as indicated by the movement of TFPK, TFPS and TFPT indexes of total factor productivity.

CHART-4.3

Movement of Indexes of Labour and Capital Productivity & TFP (Translog Index) and Capital Intensity : Sugar Industry

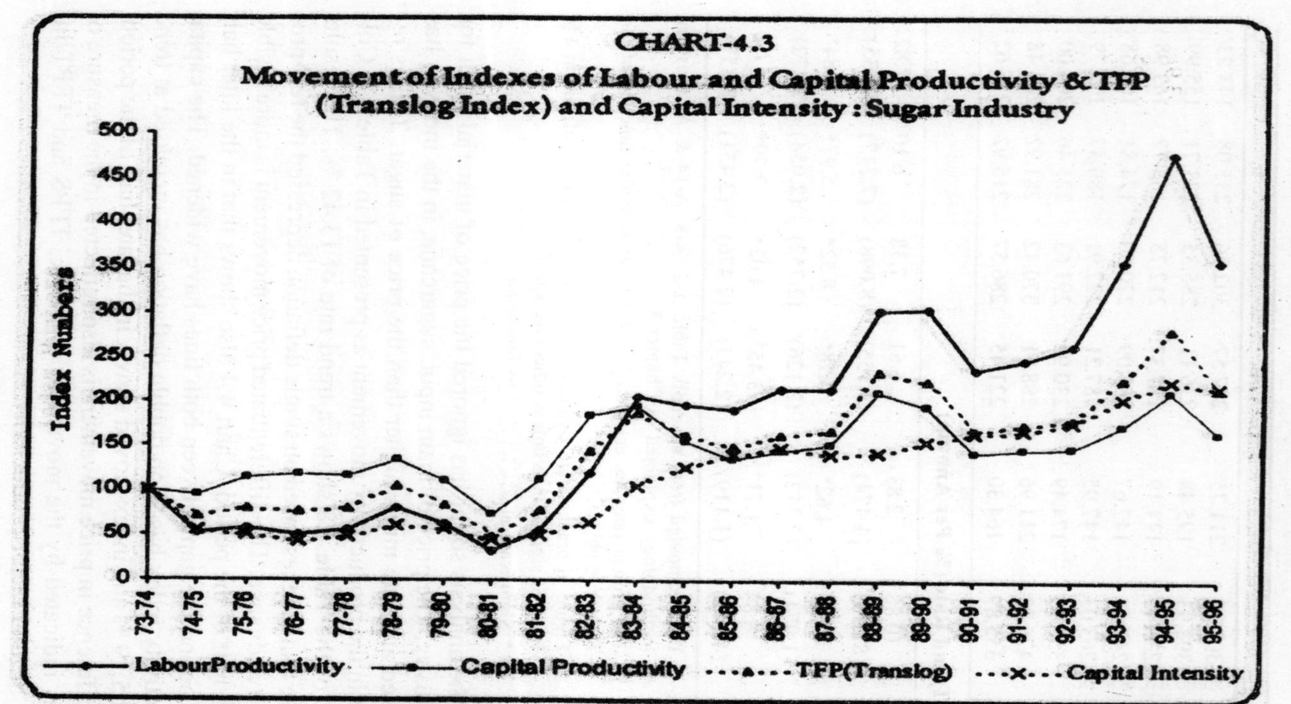

Sources: Plotted from the data in Table 4.7.

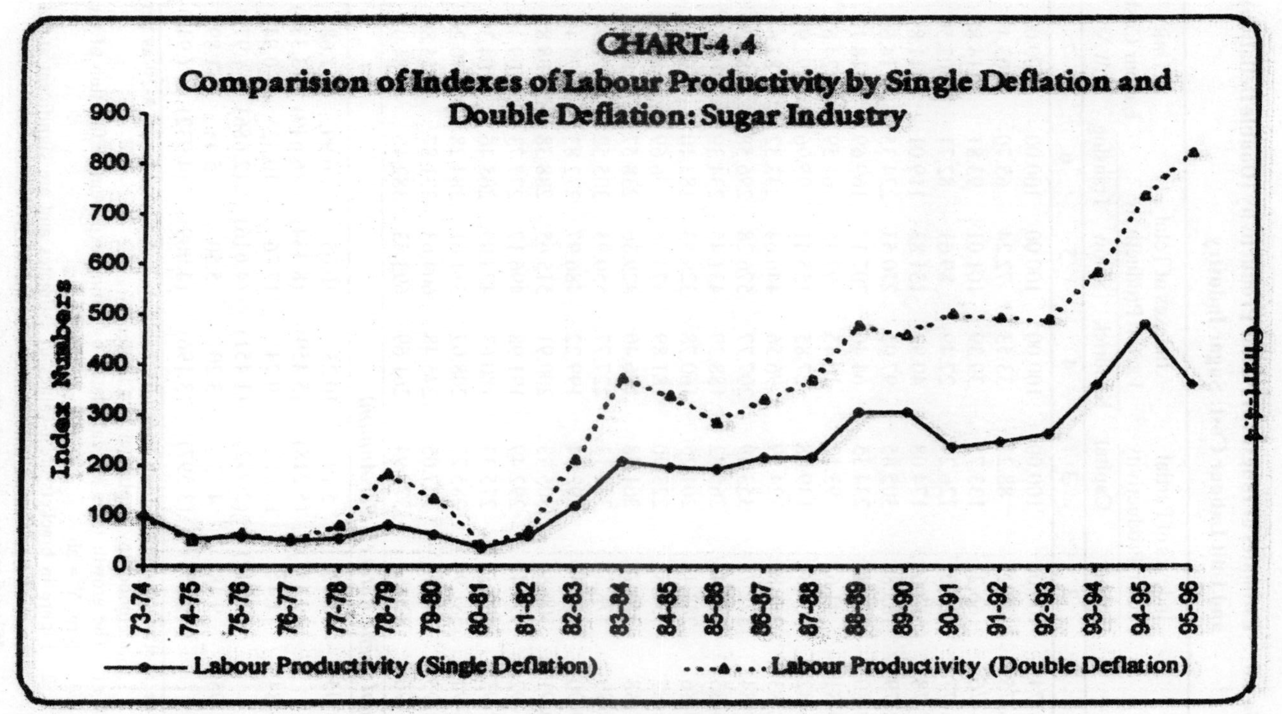

CHART-4.4
Comparision of Indexes of Labour Productivity by Single Deflation and Double Deflation: Sugar Industry

Sources: *Plotted from the data in Table 4.7 and Table 4.8.*

Table 4.8 : Estimates of Indexes of Factor Productivity (Double Deflation) and Unit Labour Cost: Sugar Industry

Year	Indexes of Partial Factor Productivity		Indexes of Total Factor Productivity			Unit Labour Cost
	Labour	Capital	Kendrick	Solow	Translog	W/V
1	2	3	4	5	6	7
1973-74	100.00	100.00	100.00	100.00	100.00	100.00
1974-75	49.22	88.21	33.53	72.24	65.70	103.49
1975-76	66.23	133.75	39.39	101.01	93.81	114.88
1976-77	54.05	126.24	27.49	89.61	82.71	103.50
1977-78	82.69	174.08	40.92	131.83	119.01	111.89
1978-79	183.80	305.85	97.05	270.53	224.35	114.69
1979-80	133.87	234.35	64.46	207.17	169.69	118.12
1980-81	41.67	93.12	16.45	97.36	61.59	124.61
1981-82	68.84	139.08	27.85	155.41	95.96	92.97
1982-83	211.82	324.59	96.56	446.64	243.32	87.64
1983-84	372.71	353.49	207.77	576.28	296.58	87.20
1984-85	337.43	265.82	188.39	431.45	234.39	108.59
1985-86	283.47	201.25	160.78	329.53	183.10	91.53
1986-87	331.85	223.90	181.89	373.68	206.69	88.15
1987-88	370.74	261.58	186.40	429.36	238.57	96.26
1988-89	478.58	334.13	227.77	550.93	305.52	71.94
1989-90	456.32	292.54	199.22	486.97	272.83	76.49
1990-91	500.86	305.43	200.91	515.65	288.38	108.85
1991-92	490.45	292.49	191.98	496.17	277.73	109.36
1992-93	489.33	275.33	180.63	473.05	265.46	104.39
1993-94	581.96	285.27	208.07	511.61	284.28	70.26
1994-95	734.15	327.05	245.48	604.63	331.87	55.80
1995-96	820.84	378.94	261.69	693.53	382.16	84.03
Annual Trend Rates (% Per Annum)						
1973-95	13.42	5.19	10.23	10.05	6.99	–1.68
	(9.437)	(5.218)	(5.459)	(8.334)	(6.649)	(3.336)
1973-84	14.44*	10.21*	9.74⁺	17.76	10.32*	–0.94⁺
	(2.712)	(2.992)	(1.451)	(4.616)	(2.686)	(.972)
1985-95	9.48	4.23	3.20	5.50	5.45	–1.89⁺
	(9.556)	(3.597)	(3.196)	(4.909)	(4.932)	(.948)

Source : Data computed from appendix Table A-2, A-8, A-14 and A-20 as per methodology explained in Chapter-2.

Notes : 1. The growth rates are calculated by fitting exponential function of the form $Y = ab^t$.

2. Figure in brackets are t-values of estimates and are significant at 1% level of significance unless otherwise specified.

3. *Significant at 5% level; ⁺Insignificant.

4.3.2b. Estimates of Production Function

Estimates of productivity presented in last section were based on the assumption of competitive equilibrium and the presence of constant returns to scale. Production function estimates presented in this section would provide a check on these assumptions besides giving TFP estimates. Production function estimates presented in Table 4.9 shows that the coefficient of LnK/L is significant and more than unity in restricted CD-I function, in both equations (with time trend and without time trend). When the assumptions of constant return to scale are relaxed in CD-II, the coefficient of LnL is insignificant in both equations with or without trend variables), thereby indicating presence of constant returns to scale. The rate of TFP given by CD functions turn out to be 1.44 per cent, which is less than the estimates by non-

Table 4.9: Production Function Estimates: Sugar Industry

Dependent Variable—Ln V/L *Number of observation-23*

Functional Forms	Constant	Coefficient of Ln K/L	Ln w	Ln L	Time	Adj. R^2	D-W Statistics	F/Rho
Estimates Without Trend Variable								
CD-I	-1.138	1.325	-	-	-	.9039	1.513	.3327**
	(2.596)	(14.123)						(1.578)
CD-II	-2.402^{+}	1.393	-	.174^{+}	-	.8873	1.523	.3355**
	(1.439)	(10.536)		(.764)				(1.552)
CES-I	-.631*	-	1.139	-	-	.9260	1.724	.2778^{+}
	(1.860)		(16.647)					(1.294)
CES-II	-.467^{+}	-	1.132	-.024^{+}	-	92.16	1.720'	.2815^{+}
	(.366)		(12.89)	(.132)				(1.279)
VES	-.964	.587*	.656	-	-	.9387	1.634	.2576**
	(2.732)	(2.116)	(2.762)				(1.162)	
Estimates With Trend Variable								
CD-I	-.726^{+}	1.194	-	-	01.137^{+}	.8906	1.497	.3271^{+}
	(1.076)	(6.793)			(.913)			(1.509)
CD-II	3.804^{+}	.940^{+}		-.625^{+}	0.144^{+}	.8977	1.541	.2888^{+}
	(.255)	(.552)		(.390)	(.126)			(1.280)
CES-I	-.049^{+}	-	.962	-	.0227	.9328	1.660	.2507^{+}
	(.096)		(6.969)		(1.482)			(1.135)
CES-II	3.423**	-	.696	-.442*	.0384*	.9609	1.525	183.70
	(1.675)		(3.335)	(1.848)	(2.319)			(3.19)
VES	-.657**	.418**	.729	-	0.0088*	.9607	1.513	179.21
	(1.427)	(1.698)	(3.533)		(.709)			(3.19)

parametric methods. Assumption of constant return to scale is also not rejected by the estimates of CES production function, as coefficient of LnL is insignificant. The coefficient of Lnw is significant in all forms of CES function and is close to unity indicating the presence of unitary elasticity of substitution. The elasticity of labour productivity with respect to wage rate is positive and statistically significant indicating that increase in wage rate has affected labour productivity positively. Computed value of technical progress is 59.7 per cent in CES-1 which is clearly an overestimation but the estimates of CES-II gives TFP as 12.63 per cent which is close to the estimate in last section. The estimates of VES production function also shows that the coefficient of Lnw is significant but the coefficient of LnK/L is significant at 10 per cent only. Computed value of TFPG of 1.15 per cent is close to the value given by CD function but smaller than the estimates of CES.

Table 4.10 : Estimates of Function Explaining Sources of Productivity Change : Sugar Industry

Explanatory Variables	Constant	Coefficient of LnV	Ln w	LnK/L	Time	Adj. R^2	D-W Statistics	F/Rho Value
LnV/L	−4.504	1.004	−.005+	.994	−.0647	.9952	1.615	.7789
	(26.353)	(29.82)	(.119)	(19.459)	(15.456)			(5.121)
LnV/K	.101+	1.004	−.005+	−.006+	−.0647	.9855	1.615	.779
	(.598)	(29.822)	(.119)	(.117)	(17.496)			(5.122)
TFPK	−2.368	1.001	0.54+	.477	−.0706	.9884	1.657	.8229
	(11.632)	(25.534)	(1.131)	(7.881)	(15.452)			(5.972)
TFPS	−2.079	1.041	−.002+	.426	−.058	.9786	1.556	.8546
	(7.546)	(20.02)	(.027)	(5.247)	(9.127)			(6.788)
TFPT	−2.076	.999	.015+	..452	.0689	.9916	1.734	.6528
	(11.844)	(27.604)	(.345)	(8.652)	(19.164)			(3.553)

Source: Estimated using data in Tables 4.6, 6.3 and appendix Table A-8.
Notes: 1. The figure in parenthesis refers to the corresponding t-values.
2. All t-values are significant at 1% level of significance unless otherwise specified.
3. * Significant at 5% level; ** Significant at 10% level; + Insignificant.

The estimates of production function in last section indicate that labour productivity is more responsive to wage rate as compared to capital-labour ratio. It seems to support *efficiency wage hypothesis.*

4.3.2c. Sources of Productivity Change

The results of functions explaining sources of productivity change presented in Table 4.10 indicate that not only labour productivity and total factor productivity but also the capital productivity is positively related to value added. Thus, we found the support for the Vedroon law. The coefficient of Lnw is negative and insignificant and coefficient of LnK/L is significant except in the function explaining capital productivity. The time variable is negative and significant indicating the deterioration in institutional factor in productivity advance. It seems that value added in these functions has captured the effect of wages on productivity, therefore the negative wage rate coefficient is obtained. The models have high degree of autocorrelation as explained by significantly high value of '*rho*'.

4.3.3 Paper and Paperboard Industry

The gross value added by single deflation in paper and paper- board industry has increased at the rate of 5.23 per cent. The capital input in the industry has increased at much faster trend rate of 8.08 per cent than the labour input at trend rate of 2.21 per cent. The average share of workers in total employment has been 68.4 per cent. The numbers of factories in this industry, which started production before 1950, was only 14 but number of the factories has rapidly risen after independence, particularly after seventies. In the decade of eighties 515 new factories started their production (Appendix Table A-30). The productivity estimates for the industry are analysed below.

4.3.3a. Estimates of Factor Productivities

The data on partial and total factor productivity in paper & paperboard industry are presented in Tables 4.11 and 4.12. Column-2 of Table 4.11 shows that labour productivity measured as real gross value added by single deflation increased by 117 per cent at the average annual trend rate of 2.96 per cent. The index does not show any consistent trend, years of rising productivity are followed by the years of decreasing productivity and it has remained less than the base year from 1977-78 to 1983-84 and in year 1985-86. In value terms labour productivity has increased by 115 per cent from Rs. 0.13678 lakh in 1973-74 to Rs. 0.29471 lakh in 1995-96 showing a net gain of Rs. 0.15793 lakh for the period (column 4 of Table 4.6). The index of capital productivity has shown the declining trends at the rate of 2.64 per cent and the index has fluctuated throughout the period. The total factor productivity has also shown the declining trends, as all the three measures of TFP, Kendrick, Solow and Translog has shown declining trends at the rate of 1.61 per cent, 0.15 per cent and 0.48 per cent respectively (shown in columns 4, 5 and 6 of Table 4.11). Inter-temporal comparison shows marked differences in the productivity movement in the industry for period 1973-84 and 1985-95. Labour productivity declined at the trend rate of 3.80 per cent and capital productivity declined at the trend rate of 7.49 per cent for the period 1973-84. Total factor productivity for the period also declined at trend rate of 6.18 per cent, 5.98 per cent and 6.00 per cent for TFPK, TFPS and TFPT indexes respectively. Whereas in period 1985-95 labour productivity has increased at average annual trend rate of 6.76 per cent and capital productivity at the trend rate of 0.98 per cent. Total factor productivity has also shown increasing trend at the rate of 0.99 per cent, 2.94 per cent and 2.89 per cent respectively. Capital intensity in the industry has increased from 0.7952 in 1973-74 to 2.3541 in 1995-96 (column-4 of Table 4.5). Capital intensity has shown continuously rising trends with minor fluctuation and index has increased at trend rate of 5.74 per cent. Increase in second half (5.72 per cent) is significantly higher than in first half (3.98 per cent). The graph of capital intensity in Chart 4.5 lies above the graph of labour productivity. This shows the presence of excess capital in the industry. Decomposition of labour productivity shows that most of the increase experienced in labour productivity is the result of increased capital intensity. Solow decomposition shows that 77.5 per cent of the increase in labour productivity is due to increased capital intensity and technical progress accounts for only 22.5 per cent of the increase in labour productivity. But, during the period 1973-84, technical regress has pushed down the increase in labour productivity. In period 1985-95, the increase in capital intensity accounted for 28.4 per cent of the increase in labour productivity and technical progress accounted for 71.6 per cent. Here, it is worthwhile to see that what happen to labour cost of unit production. Column-7 of Table 4.12 shows a downward trend for entire period. The trend rate of downward movement being 1.03 per cent, but there are ups and downs in between and the index has been above base year from 1977-78 to 1983-84 and in the year 1985-86 and 1987-88. The index has shown an increasing trend for the first half at trend rate of 3.47 per cent and it had declined during the later half at annual trend rate of 4.21 per cent. It is striking to note that except period 1983-84 to 1985-86 the ups and downs in unit labour cost are inversely related to total factor productivity, i.e., to say that most of the times unit labour cost tendsto rise as TFP shows declining tendency and vice-versa. This seems to indicate the wage rigidity and sticky behaviour of wages. Comparison of trend rates of unit labour cost and labour productivity shows that increase in labour productivity has reduced the unit labour cost & vice versa.

Table 4.11 : Estimates of Indexes of Factor Productivity (Single Deflation) and Capital Intensity: Paper & Paperboard Industry

Year	Indexes of Partial Factor Productivity		Indexes of Total Factor Productivity			Unit Labour Cost
	Labour	Capital	Kendrick	Solow	Translog	K/L
1	2	3	4	5	6	7
1973-74	100.00	100.00	100.00	100.00	100.00	100.00
1974-75	129.39	122.76	124.30	125.93	124.71	105.40
1975-76	114.72	104.79	107.47	107.96	107.54	109.48
1976-77	100.28	88.24	91.99	91.45	91.62	113.65
1977-78	95.51	90.59	92.35	91.47	91.60	105.43
1978-79	97.69	86.01	90.16	89.09	89.44	113.57
1979-80	90.50	82.67	85.40	84.52	84.78	109.47
1980-81	86.55	71.92	76.83	75.55	76.42	120.35
1981-82	86.12	69.35	74.99	73.67	74.58	124.19
1982-83	55.26	44.06	49.61	46.82	47.60	125.43
1983-84	74.01	49.16	57.77	58.50	58.17	150.55
1984-85	101.65	57.86	67.48	74.92	72.68	175.70
1985-86	87.85	50.76	61.71	65.50	63.41	173.06
1986-87	113.14	58.91	70.54	80.19	76.57	192.07
1987-88	102.25	53.05	66.31	72.29	69.05	192.73
1988-89	128.83	54.93	67.63	81.92	76.91	234.51
1989-90	168.30	74.98	88.28	109.38	103.60	224.47
1990-91	182.14	77.89	91.28	115.05	108.80	233.83
1991-92	154.53	64.27	77.31	95.20	90.45	240.42
1992-93	131.45	53.68	65.97	79.73	75.97	244.87
1993-94	136.51	51.63	64.49	78.44	74.87	264.41
1994-95	181.40	52.72	65.26	88.18	82.65	344.09
1995-96	215.47	72.78	85.97	113.71	109.86	296.06
Annual Trend Rates (% Per Annum)						
1973-95	2.96	–2.64	–1.61	–0.15+	–0.48+	5.74
	(3.576)	(3.949)	(2.701)	(.209)	(.679)	(3.157)
1973-84	–3.80*	–7.49	–6.18	–5.98	–6.00	3.98
	(2.703)	(6.802)	(5.931)	(4.475)	(5.039)	(3.98)
1985-95	6.76	0.98+	0.99+	2.94**	2.89**	5.72
	(3.980)	(.613)	(.714)	(1.786)	(1.773)	(7.833)

Source : Data computed from appendix Tables A-3, A-9, A-15 and A-21 as per methodology explained in Chapter-2.

Notes: 1. The growth rates are calculated by fitting exponential function of the form $Y = ab^t$.

2. Figure in brackets are t-values of estimates and are significant at 1% level of significance unless otherwise specified.

3. * Significant at 5% level; ** Significant at 10% level; + Insignificant.

CHART-4.5

Movement of Indexes of Labour and Capital Productivity & TFP (Translog Index) and Capital Intensity : Paper and Paperboard Industry

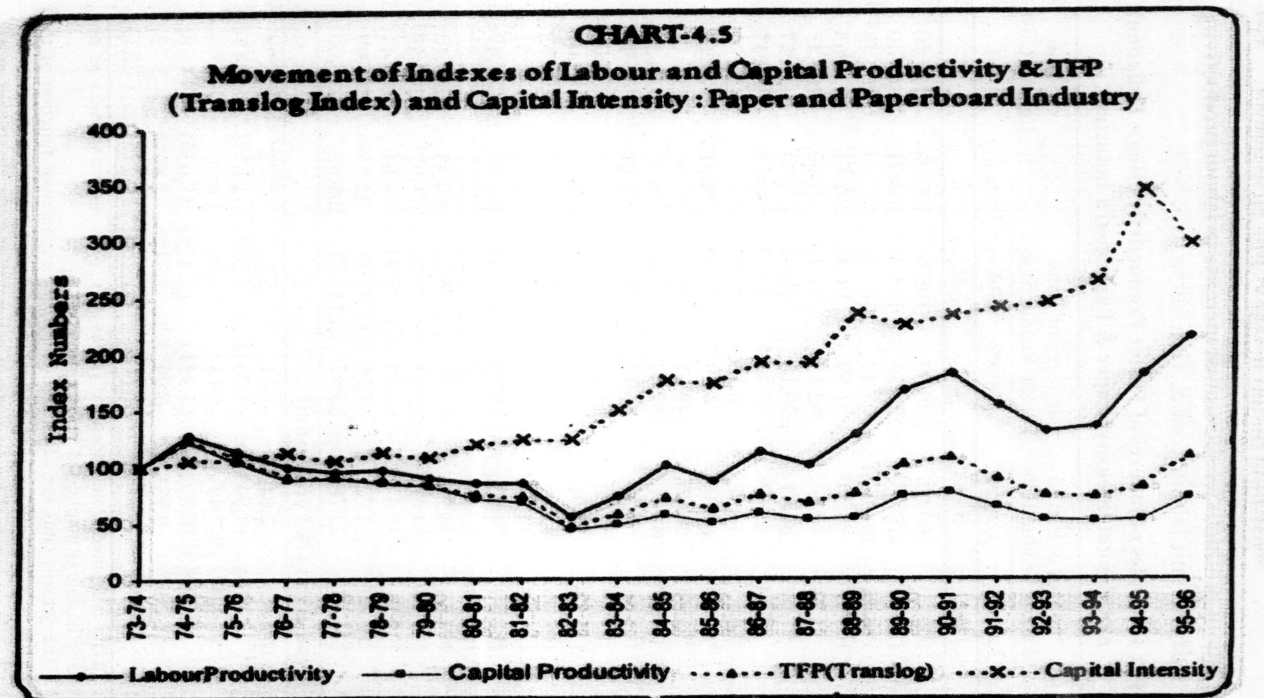

Sources: Plotted from the data in Table 4.11.

CHART-4.6

Comparision of Indexes of Labour Productivity by Single Deflation and Double Deflation: Paper and Paperboard Industry

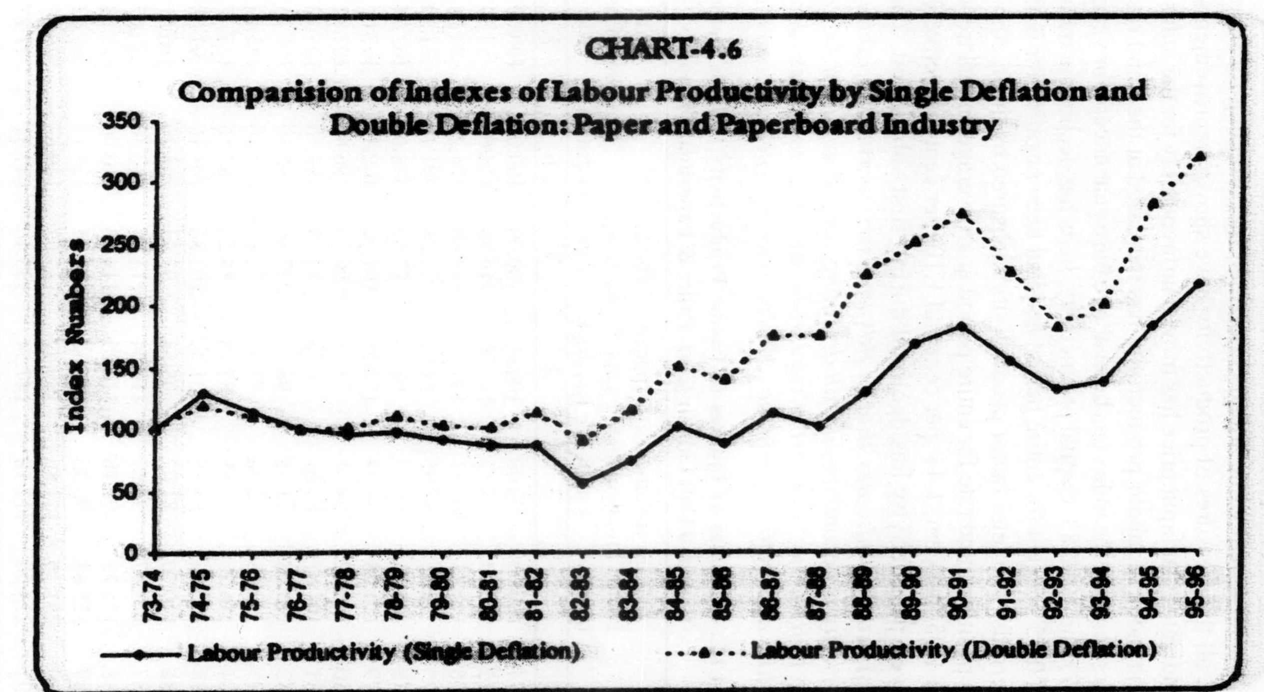

Sources: Plotted from the data in Table 4.11 and Table 4.12.

When the real value added is obtained by correcting for input prices, all the measures of productivity have shown improvements. This indicates that input price has moved unfavourably for the industry. The index of labour productivity has increased at the trend rate 5.37 per cent and the index has been above base year except for years 1976-77 and 1982-83. Capital productivity, here, has declined at trend rate of 0.35 per cent for entire period and had been negative for both sub-periods. The total factor productivity measured by this method shows positive trend rate for entire period at an average annual trend rate of 1.05 per cent, 1.44 per cent and 1.10 per cent respectively, however, productivity has declined during first sub-period. *The analysis so far indicates that in this industry increasing labour productivity is accompanied with declining capital and total factor productivity along with rising capital-labour, this indicates ideal capacities and inefficiency in the use of resources, especially capital.*

Table 4.12 : Estimates of Indexes of Factor Productivity (Double Deflation) and Unit Labour Cost: Paper & Paperboard Industry

Year	Indexes of Partial Factor Productivity		Indexes of Total Factor Productivity			Unit Labour Cost
	Labour	Capital	Kendrick	Solow	Translog	W/V
1	2	3	4	5	6	7
1973-74	100.00	100.00	100.00	100.00	100.00	100.00
1974-75	120.32	114.15	116.30	116.86	116.03	67.39
1975-76	111.13	101.51	104.77	104.60	104.28	80.28
1976-77	99.96	87.95	91.92	91.28	91.43	94.39
1977-78	102.03	96.77	98.60	97.52	98.05	102.74
1978-79	111.58	98.24	102.65	101.72	102.10	107.00
1979-80	103.02	94.11	97.13	96.36	96.62	102.92
1980-81	101.82	84.61	90.08	88.78	89.56	105.12
1981-82	113.98	91.78	98.70	97.46	98.10	107.45
1982-83	90.66	72.28	77.96	76.83	77.50	153.59
1983-84	116.20	77.18	87.78	88.26	87.56	123.47
1984-85	150.66	85.75	101.47	103.86	101.16	92.08
1985-86	140.30	81.07	95.58	97.93	95.29	116.91
1986-87	175.87	91.57	110.64	114.84	110.38	95.67
1987-88	175.73	91.18	110.25	114.43	110.00	115.58
1988-89	225.83	96.30	121.32	128.25	121.17	91.02
1989-90	251.10	111.86	139.72	147.07	139.62	75.57
1990-91	274.00	117.18	147.54	155.46	147.31	71.27

conti.

1991-92	226.34	94.14	119.17	124.79	118.96	80.29
1992-93	182.43	74.50	94.63	98.73	94.51	87.55
1993-94	201.15	76.08	97.98	102.77	98.17	89.20
1994-95	282.57	82.12	110.24	120.13	111.57	75.35
1995-96	320.93	108.40	142.28	150.30	143.68	64.41
Annual Trend Rates (% Per Annum)						
1973-95	5.37	–0.35^{+}	1.05*	1.44	1.10*	–1.03**
	(5.370)	(.819)	(2.310)	(2.964)	(2.392)	(1.631)
1973-84	1.17	–2.70	–1.53*	–1.48*	–1.55*	3.47*
	(1.0940)	(4.026)	(2.093)	(1.877)	(2.105)	(2.403)
1985-95	5.52	–0.19^{+}	0.88^{+}	1.20^{+}	1.00^{+}	–4.21
	(3.090)	(.125)	(.599)	(.743)	(.636)	(3.467)

Source : *Data computed from Appendix Tables A-3, A-9, A-15 and A-21 as per methodology explained in Chapter-2.*

Notes: *1. The growth rates are calculated by fitting exponential function of the form $Y = ab^t$.*

2. Figure in brackets are t-values of estimates and are significant at 1% level of significance unless otherwise specified.

*3. * Significant at 5% level; ** Significant at 10% level; $^{+}$ Insignificant.*

4.3.3b. Estimates of Production Function

Production function estimates, presented in Table 4.13, shows the presence of decreasing returns to scale in the industry as the coefficient of LnL is negative and significant in all the equations of CD function. Coefficient of K/L is positive and significant in the industry except in CD-II, with time trend. The coefficient of Lnw is significant in all estimates of CES function but it is significant at 10 per cent level VES production function without trend variable. The estimates of trend variable do not give any satisfactory results. The trend coefficient is insignificant in all equations. CD-II function gives the value of trend variable -3.37 per cent and the computed value of Hicks-neutral technical progress from CES-II function is 1.09 per cent whereas, VES production function gives the value of technical progress 6.55 per cent. The elasticity of labour productivity w.r.t. wage rate is positive and statistically significant. The elasticity of substitution in the industry has been more than unity and is significant. This indicates that capital in industry can be substituted with ease and there are scopes of employment generation in the industry.

Table 4.13: Production Function Estimates: Paper and Paperboard Industry

Dependent Variable-Ln V/L
Number of observation-23

Functional Forms	Constant	Coefficient of LnK/L	Lnw	LnL	Time	Adj. R^2	D-W Statistics	F/Rho
Estimates Without Trend Variable								
CD-I	0.324	.856	-	-	-	.2803	1.502	.6933
	(0.229)	(3.190)						(4.376)
CD-II	.485	.944	-	−.996*	-	.4953	1.577	.3896*
	(3.066)	(4.759)		(2.333)				(1.844)
CES-I	3.266*	-	1.715	-	-	.5515	1.885	.3213**
	(2.198)		(5.390)					(1.517)
CES-II	−2.407*	-	2.088	−.524	-	.7482	1.813	33.79
	(2.051)		(7.900)	(2.827)				(2.20)
VES	-1.856^{+}	$.287^{+}$	1.101^{+}	-	-	.4132	1.822	.5102
	(.939)	(1.136)	(1.859)					(2.856)
Estimates With Trend Variable								
CD-I	.638	1.125	-	-	−.0298	.3100	1.541	.595
	(.301)	(2.381)			(1.066)			(3.227)
CD-II	9.208	.549		−1.549	−.0337	.5191	1.619	.3089
	(1.488)	(.820)		(1.906)	(.655)			(1.378)
CES-I	−5.909	-	2.319	-	−.0145	.7173	1.697	.28.84
	(3.052)		(5.318)		(1.477)			(2,20)
CES-II	3.834	-	1.402	−1.209	.0292	.7753	1.748	23.63
	(.750)		(2.315)	(2.306)	(1.253)			(3,19)
VES	−7.733	.889	1.841	-	0.551	.7524	1.668	23.29
	(3.803)	(1.970)	(3.880)		(2.441)			(3,19)

4.3.3c. Sources of Productivity Change

Functions explaining sources of productivity change as presented in Table 4.14 indicate that productivity is positively and significantly related to value added and wage rate. Coefficient of LnK/L is insignificant in functions explaining TFP but is positively and significantly related to labour productivity and negatively and significantly related to capital productivity. This indicates that capital intensity has though increased labour productivity but has negatively affected capital productivity. The negative coefficient of time variable indicates decline in institutional factors in productivity advances.

4.3.4 Fertilizers and Pesticides Industry

The gross value added by single deflation in the industry has increased at the rate of 10.96 per cent. Labour input in the industry has increased at trend rate of 2.75 per cent whereas, the capital input in the industry has increased at trend rate of 7.94 per cent. The average share of workers in total employment has been 64.5 per cent. The productivity estimates for the industry are analysed below.

Table 4.14 : Estimates of Function Explaining Sources of Productivity Change: Paper and Paperboard Industry

Explanatory Variable	Constant	LnV	Lnw	Ln/KL	Time	Adj. R^2	D-W Statistics	F/Rho Value
Ln V/L	-4.585	.980	.505	.527	-.0599	.9804	1.716	267.9
	(7.408)	(14.664)	(3.093)	(4.021)	(9.270)			(4,18)
Ln V/K	.198+	.980	.505	-.473	-.0599	.9732	1.716	199.3
	(.032)	(14.664)	(3.093)	(3.602)	(9.270)			(4,18)
TFPK	-.229+	.818	.487	-.234**	-.0547	.9428	1.658	91.47
	(.325)	(10.718)	(2.613)	(1.566)	(8.635)			(4,18)
TFPS	-2.584	.946	.560	-.0739+	-.0645	.9419	1.514	87.92
	(3.399)	(11.523)	(2.795)	(.459)	(8.132)			(4,18)
TFPT	-1.815	.961	.513	-.0627+	-.0689	.9516	1.714	106.99
	(2.684)	(13.140)	(2.871)	(.436)	(19.164)			(4,18)

Source: Estimated using data in Table 4.11, and 6.5 and appendix Table A-9.

Notes: 1. The figure in parenthesis refers to the corresponding t-values.

2. All t-values are significant at 1% level of significance unless otherwise specified.

3. * Significant at 5% level; ** Significant at 10% level; + Insignificant.

4.3.4a. Estimates of Factor Productivity

The estimates of trends in productivity based on single deflation and double deflation along with trends in capital intensity and unit labour cost are presented in Tables 4.15 and 4.16. Estimates of labour productivity show that labour productivity in industry has increased from Rs. 0.2536 lakh in base year to Rs. 1.2039 lakh in 1995-96 (column-5 of Table 4.6). Index of labour productivity presented in column-2 of Table 4.15 shows a significant rising trend. The index has registered an increase of around 375 per cent at average annual trend rate of 7.99 per cent. Index has not shown any consistent trend during the period and it been less than 100 for period 1974-76 and for year 1980-81. Inter-temporal comparison shows that labour productivity increased at faster rate in later half (9.06 per cent) as compared to first half (7.64 per cent). The index of labour productivity with double deflation has moved at a markedly high annual trend rate of 11.68 per cent registering in increase of around 691 per cent. This reflects that the price of input to the industry has moved faster than the price of output thereby affecting performance of industry. Chart 4.8 shows that graph of labour productivity by double deflation has shown sharp divergence in period 1986-87 to 1990-91. Index of labour productivity with double deflation in 1973-84 has increased at a phenomenal trend rate of 20.12 per cent and for 1985-95 it has increased at trend rate of 4.78 per cent only. This shows that during the first half the price of input has increased at a much higher rate than the output price and during the second half price of input moved slower than output price. This again points out the importance of double deflation in productivity measurement. Index of capital productivity also does not show consistent trend and the index has been less than base year up to 1983-84, except 1982-83, and in years 1986-87 and 1987-88. Capital productivity in the industry has increased at trend rate of 2.80 per cent for entire period and 2.37 per cent and 3.87 per cent for sub-periods. The total factor productivity based on single deflation has shown a significantly rising trend and all three indexes of TFP, namely Kendrick, Solow and Translog have increased at annual trend rate of 3.32 per cent, 4.15 per cent and 4.02 per cent respectively. The indexes of total factor productivity have moved faster in later half than in the first half. Total factor productivity based on double deflation has increased at annual trend rate of 6.91 per cent, 7.03 per cent and 6.57 per cent respectively for TFPK, TFPS and TFPT. *It is interesting to note that the total factor productivity has remained stagnate in later half.*

Table 4.15: Estimates of Indexes of Factor Productivity (Single Deflation) and Capital Intensity: Fertilisers and Pesticides Industry

Year	Indexes of Partial Factor Productivity		Indexes of Total Factor Productivity			Capital Intensity
	Labour	Capital	Kendrick	Solow	Translog	K/L
1	2	3	4	5	6	7
1973-74	100.00	100.00	100.00	100.00	100.00	100.00
1974-75	86.59	82.51	83.42	83.08	83.56	104.95
1975-76	75.24	66.01	68.42	66.70	68.30	113.98

conti.

1976-77	93.03	76.41	80.15	79.23	80.49	121.76
1977-78	102.60	75.58	81.36	80.65	81.96	135.75
1978-79	136.14	97.29	104.43	105.20	106.32	139.94
1979-80	116.13	89.58	95.60	95.63	95.99	129.64
1980-81	96.78	69.91	75.59	74.99	76.26	138.44
1981-82	129.46	79.03	86.20	90.29	89.80	163.81
1982-83	159.93	100.54	107.52	113.60	113.60	159.07
1983-84	155.58	97.85	106.54	110.54	110.54	159.00
1984-85	230.77	123.97	135.35	149.25	144.55	186.15
1985-86	183.49	104.65	116.36	125.76	120.52	175.34
1986-87	190.89	87.95	102.44	107.93	106.80	217.05
1987-88	205.82	99.10	114.19	119.80	118.98	207.69
1988-89	242.09	116.69	131.99	141.01	140.05	207.47
1989-90	260.70	122.63	140.77	149.15	148.02	212.59
1990-91	322.56	134.99	156.67	170.55	167.59	238.94
1991-92	343.87	125.05	143.11	162.21	160.08	274.99
1992-93	329.52	128.06	143.23	163.80	161.92	257.32
1993-94	309.27	111.14	124.87	142.70	142.44	278.28
1994-95	372.73	127.54	142.89	166.05	164.81	292.25
1995-96	474.67	160.41	176.91	209.72	207.67	295.92

Annual Trend Rate (% Per Annum)

1973-95	7.99	2.80	3.32	4.15	4.02	2.05
	(16.68)	(6.303)	(7.901)	(9.075)	(9.202)	(29.30)
1973-84	7.64	2.37**	3.11*	3.94*	3.69*	5.15
	(4.979)	(1.652)	(2.270)	(2.591)	(2.573)	(11.089)
1985-95	9.06	3.87	3.58	4.83	5.00	5.01
	(9.685)	(3.665)	(3.448)	(4.617)	(5.01)	(8.787)

Source : Data computed from Appendix Table A-4, A-10, A-16 and A-22 as per methodology explained in Chapter-2.

Notes:
1. The growth rates are calculated by fitting exponential function of the form $Y = ab^t$.
2. Figure in brackets are t-values of estimates and are significant at 1% level of significance unless otherwise specified.
3. * Significant at 5% level; ** Significant at 10% level; + Insignificant.

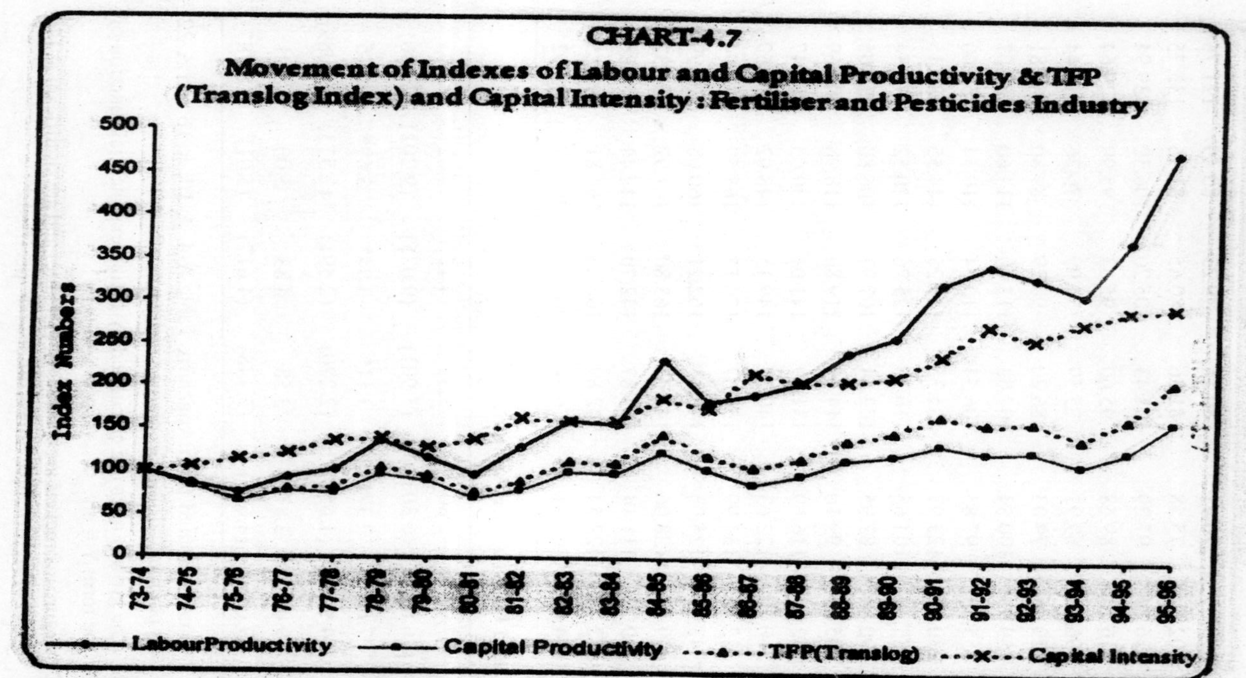

Sources: Plotted from the data in Table 4.15.

CHART-4.8

Comparision of Indexes of Labour Productivity by Single Deflation and Double Deflation: Fertiliser and Pesticides Industry

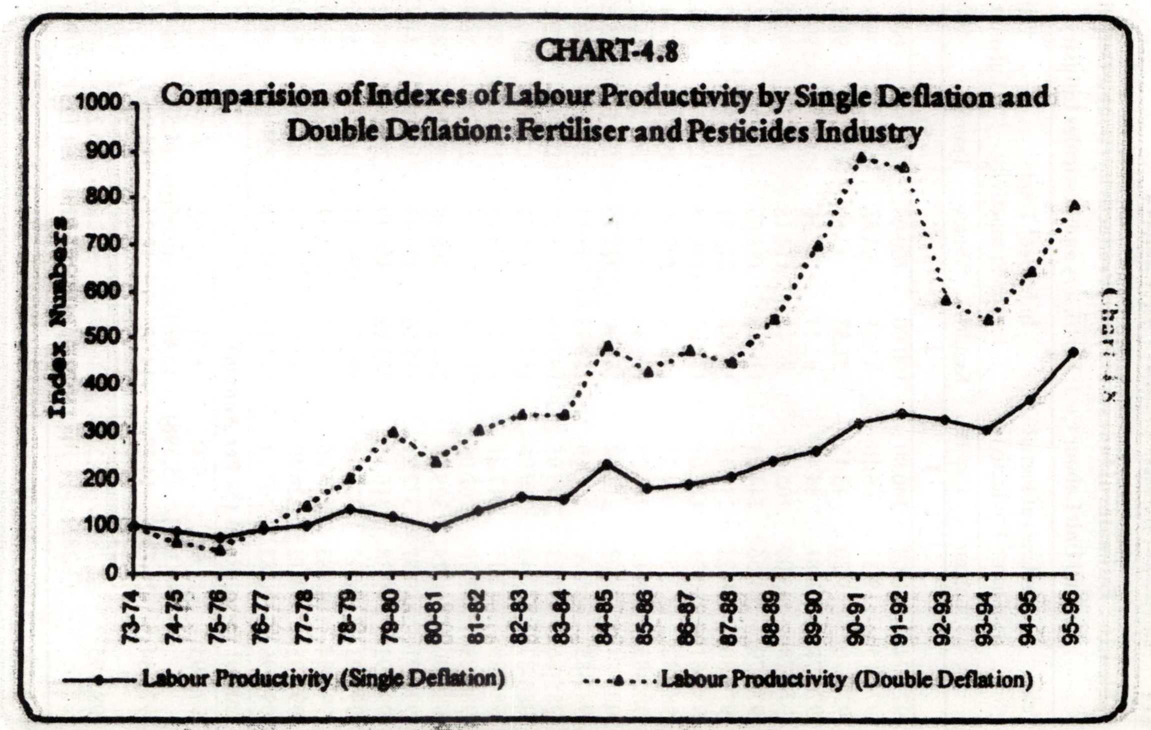

Sources: Plotted from the data in Table 4.15 and Table 4.16.

Table 4.16 : Estimates of Indexes of Factor Productivity (Double Deflation) and Unit Labour Cost: Fertilisers and Pesticides Industry

Year	Indexes of Partial Factor Productivity		Indexes of Total Factor Productivity			Unit Labour Cost
	Labour	Capital	Kendrick	Solow	Translog	W/V
1	2	3	4	5	6	7
1973-74	100.00	100.00	100.00	100.00	100.00	100.00
1974-75	69.37	66.10	47.21	65.86	47.22	79.81
1975-76	49.20	43.17	31.53	42.69	31.78	98.55
1976-77	102.81	84.44	62.74	87.56	63.56	90.01
1977-78	143.08	105.40	80.40	114.18	81.22	92.76
1978-79	201.56	144.03	110.65	158.00	111.59	82.40
1979-80	298.72	230.42	173.88	243.91	176.70	94.79
1980-81	236.75	171.01	131.05	178.54	132.08	93.13
1981-82	302.57	184.71	146.74	199.08	145.11	73.47
1982-83	336.11	211.29	166.86	226.38	165.57	60.12
1983-84	338.08	212.62	167.90	227.79	166.60	75.62
1984-85	486.96	261.59	212.93	293.15	208.02	62.50
1985-86	431.23	245.95	197.99	275.17	194.49	80.57
1986-87	477.42	219.96	183.77	245.71	177.78	90.20
1987-88	452.15	217.71	180.59	242.18	175.11	87.64
1988-89	543.70	262.06	217.34	291.44	210.76	76.99
1989-90	700.24	329.39	274.27	368.88	265.52	83.71
1990-91	889.37	372.21	315.56	426.93	303.16	81.84
1991-92	869.38	316.15	273.28	358.49	260.50	68.21
1992-93	584.97	227.34	194.77	262.44	186.22	59.59
1993-94	542.83	195.06	168.87	224.24	161.02	59.05
1994-95	644.12	220.40	191.98	255.93	182.79	56.16
1995-96	790.82	267.24	233.14	311.31	221.88	48.47
Annual Trend Rates (% Per Annum)						
1973-95	11.68	6.31	6.91	7.03	6.57	–2.11
	(10.133)	(5.598)	(5.884)	(6.056)	(5.583)	(4.632)
1973-84	20.12	14.23	14.03	15.24	13.81	–3.43
	(7.341)	(5.195)	(4.338)	(5.367)	(5.367)	(4.270)
1985-95	4.78*	–0.21⁺	0.52⁺	0.28⁺	0.23⁺	–5.60
	(2.282)	(.103)	(.254)	(.139)	(.113)	(6.709)

Source: Data computed from Appendix Tables A-4, A-10, A-16 and A-22 as per methodology explained in Chapter-2.

Notes: 1. The growth rates are calculated by fitting exponential function of the form $Y = ab^t$.

2. Figure in brackets are t-values of estimates and are significant at 1% level of significance unless otherwise specified.

3. ⁺ Insignificant.

It is worthwhile to analyse the trend in capital intensity, in the industry, as it has shown high capital-labour ratio in beginning. The graph of capital intensity (Chart 4.7) has been above the graph of labour productivity up to 1983-84. This indicates the underutilisation of capital. Capital-labour ratio has increased from 2.3420 in base year to 6.9305 in 1995-96 (column-5 to table 4.5). Index of capital intensity has increased by around 193 per cent at annual trend rate of 5.05 per cent. Index has shown consistently rising trend with minor exceptions. Decomposition of labour productivity, as given in Table 4.26, shows most of the increase in labour productivity is due to increase in technical progress (66.3 per cent) and capital productivity accounts for 33.7 per cent of the increase in labour productivity. During first sub-period capital intensity accounted for 41.8 per cent of the increase and during later half capital intensity accounted for 34.7 per cent . It is of interest to see if rising labour productivity has resulted in the reduction of unit labour cost. Trends in unit labour cost presented in Column-7 of Table 4.16 shows declining trends at trend rate of 2.11 per cent and the rate of decline is more in 1985-95 (–5.60 per cent) than in 1973-84 (–3.43 per cent). The comparison of ups and downs of unit labour cost and total factor productivity indicates that both of them seem to have moved inversely, except in the years 1974-75, 1977-78, 1980-81, 1986-87, 1991-92 and 1993-94. This indicates that productivity in these years has moved slower than wages.

4.3.4b. Estimates of Production Function

The estimates of production function presented in Table 4.17 show that coefficients of LnK/L are significant in functions without trend variable. Introduction of trend variable reduced the numeric value and statistical significance of estimates[11] even turning coefficient of LnK/L negative in CD-11.[12] Estimated value of TFPG is 4.67 per cent and 13.11 per cent respectively for CD-I and CD-II. Estimates of CES production function shows that coefficient of wage rate is significantly different from zero. Its numeric value is more than unity for estimates without time trend but not significantly different from zero and less than one for estimates with trend variable. Thus, the hypothesis of unit elasticity of substitution is not rejected. Estimates of VES production function also show significant coefficient of wage rate. Thus, we find support for hypothesis that wage rate in industry has positively affected productivity. Values computed from estimates gives TFPG as 9.55 per cent, 11.07 per cent and 5.26 per cent respectively by CES-I, CES-II and VES production functions that are correct only in terms of direction.

Table 4.17 : Production Function Estimates: Fertilisers & Pesticides Industry

Dependent Variable-Ln V/L
Number of observation-23

Functional Forms	Constant	Coefficient of Ln K/L	Ln w	Ln L	Time	Adj. R^2	D-W Statistics	F/Rho
Estimates Without Trend Variable								
CD-I	−3.278	1.631	-	-	-	.9146	1.495	$.1643^{+}$
	(5.795)	(15.065)						(.745)
CD-II	−4.174	1.490	-	.324**	-	.9103	1.442	$.1964^{+}$
	(4.343)	(8.912)		(1.533)				(.873)
CES-I	$.735^{+}$	-	1.205	-	-	.7784	1.698	.4663*
	(1.098)		(8.904)					(2.357)
CES-II	−2.146*	-	1.084	.400**	.8326	1.835	.3409	.3409**
	(1.949)		(6.919)	(1.381)				(1.580)
VES	−2.706	1.066	.437*	-	-	.9263	1.598	$.1856^{+}$
	(4.601)	(4.321)	(2.235)					(.823)
Estimates With Trend Variable								
CD-I	$.922^{+}$	.712*	-	-	.0467**	.9243	1.5107	$.1664^{+}$
	(.401)	(1.424)			(1.878)	.9440		(.7353)
CD-II	11.325*	$-.565^{+}$		−.953*	.1311		1.577	123.9
	(2.370)	(.812)		(2.206)	(3.029)	.9521		(3,19)
CES-I	2.280	-	.466	-	.0510	-	1.626	218.37
	(3.393)		(2.961)		(5.357)	.9347		(3,19)
CES-II	4.961	-	.343*	.466**	.0727	-	1.681	.1762*
	(2.655)		(1.776)	(1.451)	(4.471)			(.759)
VES	$.965^{+}$	.296†	.456	-	.0370**	.9501	1.531	141.05
	(.421)	(.601)	(2.832)	-	(1.464)	-	-	(3,19)

c. Sources of Productivity Change

Estimates of functions explaining sources of productivity change show that all the measures of productivity are significantly affected by value added. Capital intensity is significant in explaining only changes in labour productivity and has not affected other measures of productivity. Time variable is negative and significant in explaining changes in all the measures of productivity. Coefficient of wage rate is insignificant other than in functions explaining TFPS and TFPT.

Table 4.18 : Estimates of Function Explaining Sources of Productivity Change: Fertilisers and Pesticides Industry

Explanatory Variable	Constant	LnV	Lnw	Ln/KL	Time	Adj. R^2	D-W Statistics	F/Rho Value
Ln V/L	–5.322	.961	.0015+	1.162	–.0762	.9752	1.646	.486
	(5.501)	(9.533)	(.014)	(6.143)	(5.199)			(2.294)
Ln V/K	–.716+	.961	.162+	.0015+	–.0762	.9205	1.646	.486+
	(.826)	(9.533)	(.857)	(.0142)	(5.199)			(2.295)
TFPK	.821+	.859	.1836+	.1212+	.0699	.9317	1.868	.462*
	(.865)	(8.753)	(.990)	(1.234)	(4.891)			(2.148)
TFPS	–2.018*	.997	.397*	.0155+	–.0795	.9338	1.666	.5013*
	(1.939)	(9.147)	(1.952)	(.140)	(5.027)			(2.389)
TFPT	–1.753*	.954	.382*	.0099+	–.0757	.9430	1.674	.4697
	(1.810)	(9.503)	(2.056)	(.098)	(5.181)			(2.914)

Source : *Estimated using data in Table 4.15 and 6.7 and appendix Table A-10.*

Notes: 1. *The figure in parenthesis refers to the corresponding t-values.*
2. *All t-values are significant at 1% level of significance unless otherwise specified.*
3. ** Significant at 5% level; ** Significant at 10% level; + Insignificant.*

4.3.5 Motor Vehicles Industry

The gross value added by single deflation in the industry has increased at the rate of 6.98 per cent. Labour input in the industry has increased at trend rate of 2.59 per cent whereas capital input in the industry has increased at trend rate of 7.92 per cent. The average share of workers in total employment has been 70.9 per cent. The number of factories in motor vehicles industry has phenomenally increased after the decade of 1960s, as shown by Appendix Table A-30. The productivity estimates for the industry are analysed below.

4.3.5a Estimates of Factor Productivity

Estimates of factor productivities with single deflation along with capital intensity are presented in Table 4.19. Column-2 of the table shows that index of labour productivity has fluctuated during the period. The index has been less than base year up to 1975-76 and for years 1979-80 and 1980-81. The average annual trend rate of labour productivity has been 4.28 per cent, which is significant at 1 per cent level of significance. The index of capital productivity as presented in Column-3 of Table 4.19 shows that the index has been less than base

Table 4.19 : Estimates of Indexes of Factor Productivity (Single Deflation) and Capital Intensity: Motor Vehicles Industry

Year	Indexes of Partial Factor Productivity		Indexes of Total Factor Productivity			Capital Intensity
	Labour	Capital	Kendrick	Solow	Translog	K/L
1	2	3	4	5	6	7
1973-74	100.00	100.00	100.00	100.00	100.00	100.00
1974-75	97.80	93.95	95.75	95.71	95.80	104.10
1975-76	94.64	86.78	90.33	90.24	94.43	109.06
1976-77	116.67	103.31	108.38	109.55	120.90	112.94
1977-78	117.59	102.14	108.07	109.16	99.66	115.12
1978-79	119.06	102.77	109.22	110.13	100.88	115.85
1979-80	92.11	84.23	87.56	88.70	79.91	109.36
1980-81	93.27	81.90	86.47	87.79	98.99	113.88
1981-82	114.03	96.44	102.32	105.42	119.55	118.25
1982-83	153.09	125.99	133.22	139.71	131.86	121.51
1983-84	134.55	96.30	108.82	108.28	80.33	139.71
1984-85	138.59	92.83	107.91	107.11	99.08	149.29
1985-86	135.25	83.50	99.68	99.29	93.11	161.97
1986-87	149.89	87.35	104.45	106.63	107.10	171.60
1987-88	140.95	74.98	94.18	94.08	89.14	187.99
1988-89	151.02	79.54	97.41	100.28	106.52	189.88
1989-90	166.59	81.10	100.59	105.59	105.08	205.41
1990-91	184.28	86.23	104.95	114.14	107.83	213.71
1991-92	177.09	76.62	96.23	103.50	91.30	231.14
1992-93	172.39	70.41	89.82	96.83	93.84	244.83
1993-94	195.21	72.18	92.15	103.21	106.19	270.46
1994-95	225.02	85.55	106.80	120.83	117.44	263.03
1995-96	340.34	118.17	141.51	174.96	141.77	288.02
Annual Trend Rates (% Per Annum)						
1973-95	4.28	–0.87*	0.29+	0.89*	0.52+	5.19
	(9.221)	(1.996)	(.756)	(2.015)	(1.177)	(2.875)
1973-84	3.11*	0.28+	1.24+	1.36+	0.12+	2.82
	(2.720)	(.283)	(1.256)	(1.300)	(.090)	(5.885)
1985-95	7.10	1.13+	1.44+	3.25*	2.39*	5.90
	(5.406)	(.832)	(1.257)	(2.357)	(2.187)	(24.908)

Source : Data computed from appendix Tables A-5, A-11, A-17 and A-23 as per methodology explained in Chapter-2.

Notes : 1. The growth rates are calculated by fitting exponential function of the form $Y = ab^t$.

2. Figure in brackets are t-values of estimates and are significant at 1% level of significance unless otherwise specified.

3. * Insignificant at 5% level; ** Significant at 10% level; + Insignificant.

year for most of the period except for 1976-79 and for 1982-83 and 1995-96. Annual trend of the index has been negative and significant at 10 per cent level of significance, indicating that capital productivity was stagnant in industry. Total factor productivity in the industry was also stagnant in the industry as all three indexes of total factor productivity has increased at insignificant trend rate of 0.29 per cent, 0.89 per cent and 0.52 per cent respectively, for TFPK, TFPS and TFPT. Chart 4.9 shows that graph of labour productivity has been below the graph of capital intensity especially after 1983-84. It points towards the presence of excess capacity in the industry. Inter-temporal comparison in the industry shows that the performance of the industry, in terms of productivity, has been significant in later half (1985-95) as compared to the first half (1973-84). Labour productivity has increased significantly at trend rate of 7.10 per cent in later half as compared to 3.11 per cent increase in the first half. Chart 4.10 shows that the graphs of labour productivity by single deflation and double deflation have shown similar movements. Capital productivity has increased at insignificant trend rate of 0.28 per cent and 1.13 per cent for first half and second half respectively. Solow index and Translog index, in second half, increased at a significant (5 per cent level) annual trend rate of 3.25 per cent and 2.30 per cent respectively whereas, Kendrick index has increased at insignificant trend rate of 1.44 per cent. This difference in trend rates of Kendrick index may be due to the fact that the share of labour in value added had changed significantly and this index uses fixed base year weights for combining inputs. The analysis of productivity trends with double deflation and its comparison with single deflation shows increase in all productivity indexes especially during period 1985-95. This indicates that input prices had moved faster than output prices thereby suppressing real gross value added and productivity. Labour productivity with double deflation had increased at trend rate of 5.12 per cent, 3.12 per cent (significant at 10 per cent only) and 9.03 per cent respectively for entire period, first half and later half. The index of capital productivity has been stagnant using this method also. The increase in total factor productivity for whole period has been significant at trend rate 1.82 per cent, 1.77 per cent and 1.81 per cent for TFPK, TFPS and TFPT respectively. The increase in TFP has been insignificant for period 1973-84 and it has registered significant growth only during 1985-95. Analysis of trends in capital intensity show a significant increase in capital intensity and index has been above base year for entire period (column-7, Table 4.19). Capital intensity has increased more than 188 per cent, at average annual trend rate of 5.19 per cent. The increase in capital intensity has been more in later half (5.90 per cent) than in first half (2.82 per cent). Trends in capital intensity synchronized with trends in labour productivity. It seems that increased capital intensity has contributed to the increase in labour productivity, decomposition of labour productivity shows that labour productivity has increased from Rs. 0.1387 lakh in 1973-74 to Rs. 0.4719 lakh in 1995-96 showing a net gain of Rs. 0.3332 lakh. Out of this increase, 60.7 per cent is due to increase in productivity or technological progress and 39.3 per cent is attributable to increased capital intensity. But during first half most of increase in labour productivity is due to increase in capital intensity (76.2 per cent) and in later period most of the increase in labour productivity is result of increased productive efficiency (76.4 per cent). Trends in unit labour cost presented in Table 4.20 (column-7) shows that increased labour productivity has resulted in reduction of unit labour cost. Index of unit labour cost has decreased by 48.5 per cent, average annual decline being at trend rate of 1.75 per cent. Index of unit labour cost has been less than 100 throughout period. The rate of decline has been more in later half than in initial period. *Decline in unit labour cost along with increase in labour productivity indicates that wage increase has been less than increase in labour productivity.*

4.3.5b. Production Function Estimates

Estimates of restricted CD production function shows that coefficient of LnK/L is significant. When the assumption of constant return to scale are relaxed, coefficient of LnL is positive but not significantly different from zero indicating that assumption of constant returns to scale are not rejected. But, when time trend is introduced to capture the exponential growth rate of Hicks-neutral technical progress, estimates of CD function do not give satisfactory results. This may be due to presence of multicollinearity between LnK/L and time (r = 0.986). Estimates of CES production function with and without trend variable indicates that coefficients of wage rate are significant. *High elasticity of labour productivity with respect to wage rate implies that marginal productivity of labour is more than wage*

CHART-4.9

Movement of Indexes of Labour and Capital Productivity & TFP (Translog Index) and Capital Intensity : Motor Vehicles Industry

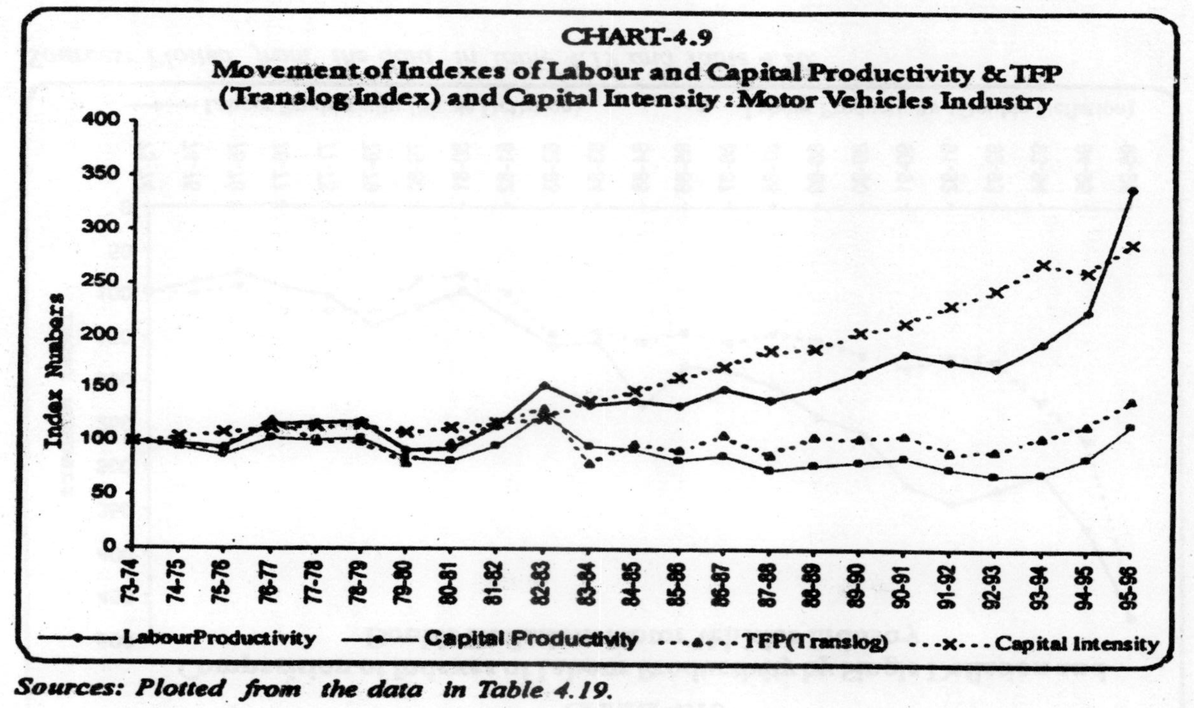

Sources: Plotted from the data in Table 4.19.

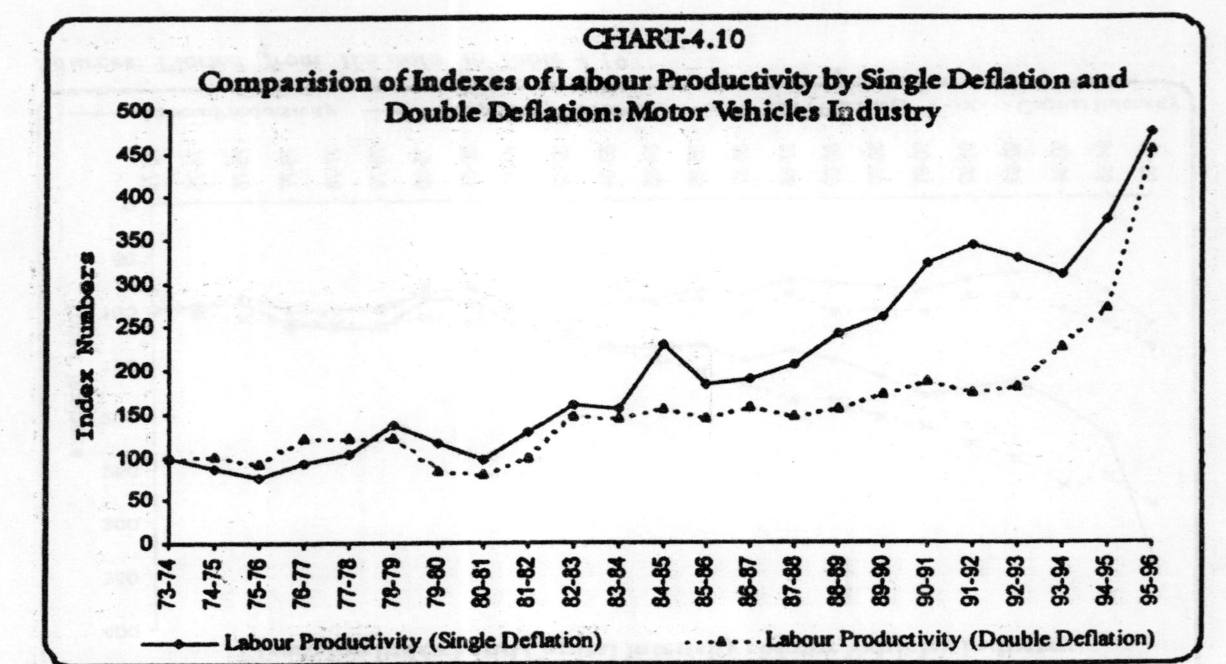

CHART-4.10

Comparision of Indexes of Labour Productivity by Single Deflation and Double Deflation: Motor Vehicles Industry

Sources: Plotted from the data in Table 4.19 and Table 4.20.

Table 4.20 : Estimates of Indexes of Factor Productivity (Double Deflation) and Unit Labour Cost: Motor Vehicles Industry

Year	Indexes of Partial Factor Productivity		Indexes of Total Factor Productivity			Unit Labour Cost
	Labour	Capital	Kendrick	Solow	Translog	W/V
1	2	3	4	5	6	7
1973-74	100.00	100.00	100.00	100.00	100.00	99.99
1974-75	100.74	96.77	98.68	98.65	98.64	97.48
1975-76	92.54	84.85	88.46	88.07	88.41	96.60
1976-77	122.29	108.27	114.72	114.78	114.55	83.36
1977-78	123.13	106.95	114.32	114.20	113.99	85.15
1978-79	122.16	105.45	113.03	112.86	112.67	88.02
1979-80	84.55	77.31	80.70	81.81	80.46	90.89
1980-81	80.31	70.52	75.00	76.01	74.93	88.47
1981-82	98.98	83.71	90.55	92.31	90.59	76.09
1982-83	147.72	121.57	133.12	136.36	132.97	62.58
1983-84	145.78	104.34	121.23	120.77	119.71	82.58
1984-85	155.87	104.41	124.56	123.83	122.66	86.32
1985-86	144.95	89.49	110.15	108.38	108.36	86.53
1986-87	157.56	91.82	115.43	113.84	113.61	80.04
1987-88	148.38	78.93	102.43	100.31	101.16	88.89
1988-89	156.66	82.50	107.43	105.31	106.15	79.07
1989-90	172.79	84.12	112.39	110.71	111.37	77.01
1990-91	187.70	87.83	118.82	117.40	117.88	68.39
1991-92	174.48	75.49	104.57	102.69	104.11	73.30
1992-93	181.33	74.07	104.31	102.87	104.25	74.51
1993-94	227.25	84.02	121.58	121.83	121.98	70.15
1994-95	272.78	103.71	148.96	148.65	149.46	65.49
1995-96	456.39	158.46	233.02	238.10	232.70	51.55
Annual Trend Rates (% Per Annum)						
1973-95	5.12	–0.07^{+}	1.82	1.77	1.81	–1.75
	(7.507)	(.124)	(3.011)	(2.852)	(2.984)	(5.424)
1973-84	3.12	0.29^{+}	1.53^{+}	1.62^{+}	1.44^{+}	–2.23*
	(1.810)	(.205)	(1.011)	(1.081)	(.947)	(2.761)
1985-95	9.03	2.96**	4.79*	5.09*	5.01*	–3.81
	(4.761)	(1.548)	(2.551)	(2.599)	(2.688)	(5.05)

Source: Data computed from Appendix Tables A-5, A-11, A-17 and A-23 as per methodology explained in Chapter-2.

Notes:
1. The growth rates are calculated by fitting exponential function of the form $Y = ab^t$.
2. Figure in brackets are t-values of estimates and are significant at 1% level of significance unless otherwise specified.
3. ** Significant at 5% level; ** Significant at 10% level; $^{+}$Insignificant.*

rate indicating underpayment to labour. Coefficient of LnL is positive and significantly different from zero indicating presence of increasing returns to scale in industry. Calculated value of TFP by CES-I is 15.7 per cent and by CES-II it is 6.13 per cent, VES production function gives TFP as 2.77 per cent. Elasticity of labour productivity, w.r.t. wage rate, is significant and close to unity.

Table 4.21: Production Function Estimates: Motor Vehicles Industry

Dependent variable—Ln V/L
Number of observation—23

Functional Forms	Constant	Coefficient of LnK/L	Lnw	LnL	Time	Adj. R^2	D-W Statistics	F/Rho
Estimates Without Trend Variable								
CD-I	.679⁺	.845	-	-	-	.7379	1.287	.2646⁺
	(1.266)	(7.996)						(1.227)
CD-II	–.821⁺	.598	-	.558**	-	.7375	1.281	.3178**
	(.763)	(3.091)		(1.584)				(1.460)
CES-I	–2.404	-	1.588	-	-	.7758	1.570	.4212*
	(2.881)		(8.838)					(2.077)
CES-II	–4.029	-	1.145	.725	-	.8510	1.604	.4842*
	(4.939)		(6.322)	(3.754)				(2.412)
VES	–1.889*	.254⁺	1.176	-	-	.7941	1.556	.3774*
	(2.096)	(1.228)	(3.320)					(1.776)
Estimates With Trend Variable								
CD-I	1.538⁺	.651**	-	-	.0103**	.7290	1.270	.2580⁺
	(.721)	(1.396)			(.414)			(1.164)
CD-II	–16.775	2.346	-	2.329	–.1358	.8085	1.586	.3011**
	(2.833)	(3.554)		(3.246)	()			(1.339)
CES-I	–.469⁺	-	1.106	-	.0166*	.8286	1.540	.3380**
	(.400)		(4.186)		(2.101)			(1.565)
CES-II	–8.766	-	1.484	1.433	–.0297	.8516	1.537	.5814
	(3.847)		(6.380)	(3.913)	()			(3.032)
VES	1.803⁺	–.967*	1.565	-	.0544*	.8288	1.609	.4134*
	(1.052)	(1.835)	(4.60)		(2.472)			(1.926)

Table 4.22 : Estimates of Function Explaining Sources of Productivity Change: Motor Vehicles Industry

Explanatory Variable	Constant	LnV	Coefficient of Lnw	LnK/L	Time	Adj. R^2	D-W Statistics	F/Rho Value
Ln V/L	−2.194	.779	.220*	.491	−.0410	.9902	1.383	.4281*
	(4.565)	(17.076)	(1.897)	(3.175)	(5.284)			(1.953)
Ln V/K	2.411	.779	.220*	−.510	−.0410	.9768	1.383	.4281*
	(5.015)	(17.076)	(1.897)	(3.293)	(5.284)			(1.953)
TFPK	2.471	.603	.416	−.543	−.0206	.9265	1.276	.4071*
	(3.951)	(9.990)	(2.721)	(2.688)	(2.024)			(1.838)
TFPS	.857**	.833	.126+	−.129+	−.0439	.9664	1.497	.4162*
	(1.628)	(16.525)	(.982)	(.762)	(5.142)			(1.887)
TFPT	.564+	.908	−.932*	.916*	−.0799	.6082	2.289	9.530
	(.427)	(5.599)	(2.442)	(2.065)	(3.505)			(3.19)

Source : Estimated using data in Table 4.19 and 6.9 and Aappendix Table A-11.

Notes:
1. The figure in parenthesis refers to the corresponding t-values.
2. All t-values are significant at 1% level of significance unless otherwise specified.
3. * Significant at 5% level; ** Significant at 10% level; + Insignificant.

4.3.5c. Sources of Productivity Change

Table 4.22 shows that labour productivity and all other measure of productivity are significantly related to value added thereby supporting Vedroon law. Labour productivity is significantly related to capital intensity but coefficient of wage rate is significant at 10 per cent only. Coefficient of time trend is significant and negative in all equations indicating deterioration in institutional factors. Coefficient of K/L is negatively related to capital productivity. The function for TFP has mixed sign for wage and capital intensity coefficients. This may be due to presence of multicollinearity among explanatory variables and estimates are not free from autocorrelation even after applying 'C-O' and 'P-W' corrections.

4.3.6 Watches and Clocks Industry

The gross value added by single deflation in the industry has increased at the rate of 12.38 per cent. Labour input in the industry has increased at trend rate of 5.70 per cent whereas capital input in the industry has increased at trend rate of 13.96 per cent. The average share of workers in total employment has been 75.7 per cent and the share of workers in employ-ment is decreasing from 78.2 per cent in base year to 74.5 per cent in the terminal year. The productivity estimates for the industry are analysed below.

4.3.6a. Estimates of Factor Productivity

In Table 4.23 are set out the data on the indexes of partial and total factor productivities based on real value added obtained by single deflation along with indexes of capital intensity in the industry (depicted in Chart 4.11). Column-2 of table shows that index of labour productivity has increased by 318.6 per cent at the average annual trend rate of 6.32 per cent. Index of capital productivity has shown increasing trend in initial period but declining trend in later period, overall trend rate being negative 1.39 per cent. Inter-temporal comparison of partial factor productivity indexes shows marked differences. Labour productivity increased at the trend rate of 8.28 per cent and 3.97 per cent for periods 1973-84 and 1985-95 respectively whereas, index of capital productivity has increased at the trend rate of 2.09 per cent for 1973-84 but for 1985-95 it has declined at the trend rate of 3.29 per cent. Index of total factor productivity has also shown similar trends. All indexes of TFP namely, TFPK, TFPS and TFPT has increased at the trend rates of 4.60 per cent, 4.05 per cent and 4.23 per cent respectively for period 1973-84 but during 1985-95 indexes declined at the trend rate of 1.61 per cent, 2.05 per cent and 0.50 per cent respectively. For entire period TFP in the industry has increased at the trend rate of 1.05 per cent, 0.66 per cent and 1.45 per cent for TFPK, TFPS and TFPT respectively.

Analysis so far has ignored the effect of input price on productivity indexes. Chart 4.12 shows that graph of labour productivity by double has been above the graph of labour productivity by single deflation. The index of labour productivity with double deflation shows that productivity in industry has increased at trend rate of 9.61 per cent for entire period and most of this increase has taken place in first half where labour productivity increased at significantly high trend rate of 13.21 per cent against the trend rate of 6.96 per cent in later half. Similarly, capital productivity index has moved at positive trend rate of 1.66 per cent. Index has increased at trend rate of 6.74% in first half but decreased at the trend rate of 0.5% in second half. TFP using double deflation has also increased at the trend rate of 4.18%, 2.55% and 3.11% for TFPK, TFPS and TFPT respectively. Most of

Table 4.23 : Estimates of Indexes of Factor Productivity (Single Deflation) and Capital Intensity: Watches and Clocks Industry

Year	Indexes of Partial Factor Productivity		Indexes of Total Factor Productivity			Capital Intensity
	Labour	Capital	Kendrick	Solow	Translog	K/L
1	2	3	4	5	6	7
1973-74	100.00	100.00	100.00	100.00	100.00	100.00
1974-75	115.91	131.69	123.65	122.17	124.19	88.02
1975-76	151.37	135.61	142.70	141.25	141.03	111.62
1976-77	169.10	152.15	159.79	158.17	157.98	111.14
1977-78	150.02	138.15	143.57	142.67	142.18	108.60
1978-79	156.98	150.02	153.26	152.34	152.12	104.64
1979-80	150.90	143.92	147.17	146.25	146.04	104.85
1980-81	194.70	140.85	162.27	159.31	157.04	138.24
1981-82	199.68	130.85	156.63	152.01	150.35	152.60
1982-83	288.00	200.90	234.80	225.74	226.78	143.36
1983-84	224.14	145.59	174.84	163.52	168.31	153.95
1984-85	265.60	131.40	173.17	162.89	169.13	202.13
1985-86	284.19	136.72	181.74	171.49	177.90	207.86
1986-87	292.04	134.80	181.44	171.77	178.25	216.64
1987-88	300.13	123.31	171.57	163.68	170.73	243.39
1988-89	306.64	115.14	164.05	157.91	165.21	266.32
1989-90	354.12	128.61	184.79	179.14	186.74	275.35
1990-91	352.84	100.99	153.19	145.50	159.99	349.38
1991-92	491.52	150.85	225.45	208.41	233.30	325.84
1992-93	306.95	87.12	132.38	117.83	138.63	352.32
1993-94	373.89	91.10	142.59	132.96	155.04	410.42
1994-95	410.43	96.23	151.66	142.96	166.48	426.50
1995-96	418.65	111.49	171.60	155.59	182.90	375.51
Annual Trend Rates (% Per Annum)						
1973-95	6.32	–1.39	1.05*	0.66	1.45	7.82
	(13.881)	(2.552)	(1.961)	(1.218)	(3.011)	(22.856)
1973-84	8.28	2.09*	4.60	4.05	4.23	6.06
	(7.355)	(1.709)	(4.134)	(3.586)	(3.854)	(6.251)
1985-95	3.97	–3.29*	–1.61⁺	–2.05	–0.50⁺	7.51
	(3.226)	(2.327)	(1.198)	(1.485)	(.385)	(9.719)

Source : Data computed from Appendix Tables A-6, A-12, A-18 and A-24 as per methodology explained in Chapter-2.

Notes:
1. The growth rates are calculated by fitting exponential function of the form $Y = ab^t$.
2. Figure in brackets are t-values of estimates and are significant at 1% level of significance unless otherwise specified.
3. * Significant at 5% level; ⁺ Insignificant.

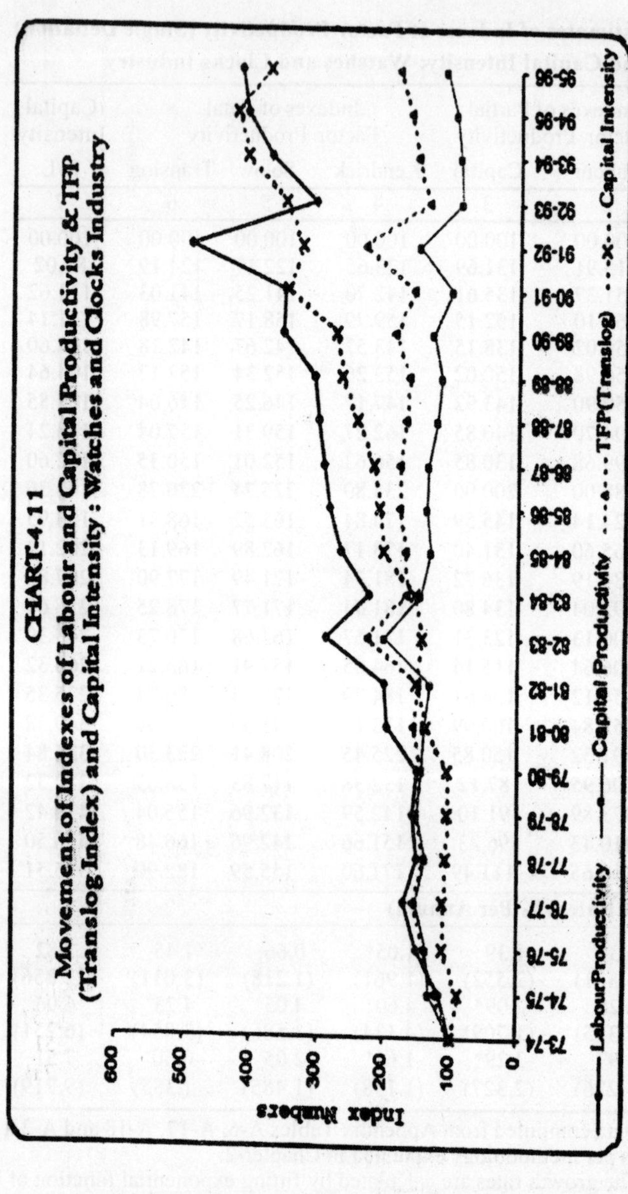

CHART-4.11

Movement of Indexes of Labour and Capital Productivity & TFP (Translog Index) and Capital Intensity : Watches and Clocks Industry

Sources: Plotted from the data in Table 4.23.

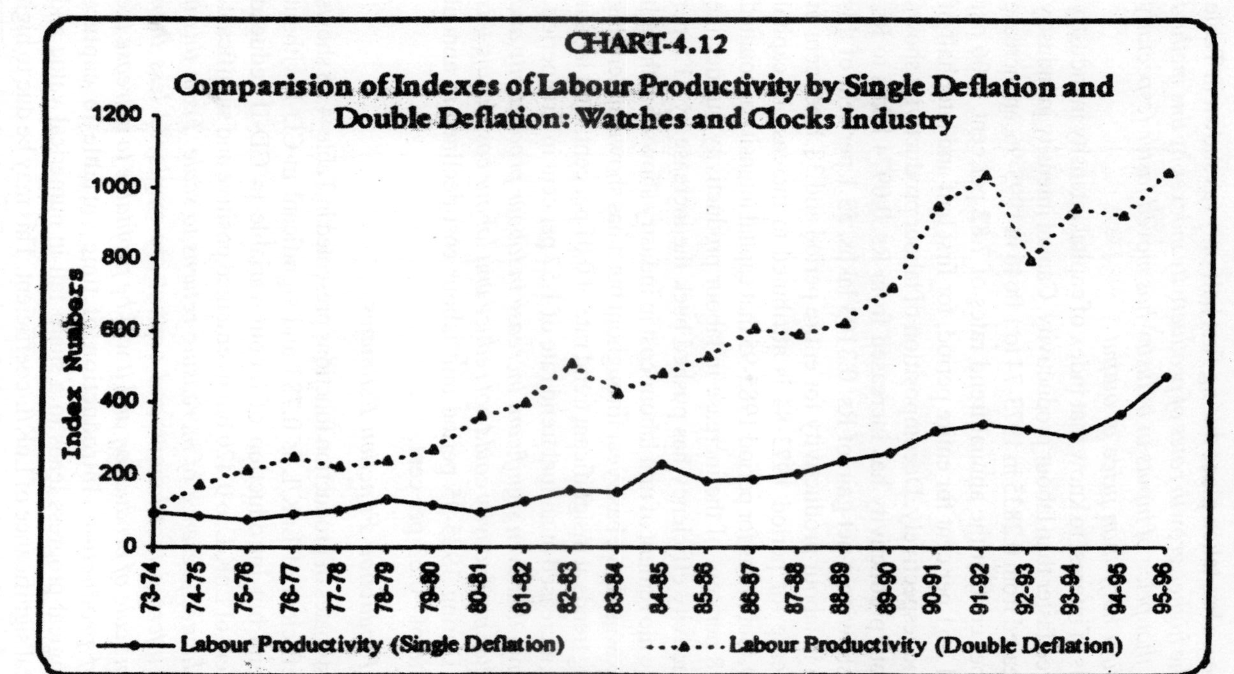

Sources: Plotted from the data in Table 4.22 and Table 4.24.

this increase has taken place during first half only (as shown in Table 4.24). *The higher growth rates of productivity indexes by this method indicate that price of inputs in industry has moved faster (especially during first half) than price of output.*

It is of interest to know that index of capital intensity in industry has moved faster than labour productivity. Capital intensity in industry has increased from 0.2835 in 1973-74 to 1.0646 in 1995-96, an increase of 376 per cent, at the annual trend rates of 7.82 per cent, 6.06 per cent and 7.51 per cent for entire period, for first half and later half of the period respectively. Decomposition of labour productivity shows that labour productivity has increased from Rs. 0.0974 lakhs to Rs. 0.4077 showing a net gain of Rs. 0.3103 lakhs. 53.1 per cent of this increase in labour productivity for entire period and 38.1 per cent of the increase for period 1973-84 is attributed to increase in capital intensity. But it was for period 1985-95 that capital intensity accounted for 131.8 per cent of the increase in labour productivity but decline in productivity efficiency has pushed back the increase by 31.8 per cent. The movement of unit labour cost in industry shows that though the index was above base year throughout but it has shown underlying declining trends at insignificant trend rate of 0.01 per cent. Unit labour cost has increased at annual trend rate of 1.57 per cent in first period. *This shows that even significant increase in labour productivity and total factor productivity could not reduce unit labour cost during this period.* During 1985-95 period unit labour cost declined at annual trend rate of –0.63 per cent.

4.3.6b. Production Function Estimates

Estimates of production functions presented in Table 4.25 shows that coefficient of LnK/L is 0.783 and significant in CD-I without time trend but introduction of labour variable in CD-II reduced coefficient of LnK/L to 0.420 but it remained positive and significant. *This indicates presence of increasing returns to scale. From this it can be inferred that labour and capital are employed less than optimum scale of production and it will be profitable to increase the scale of production.* Introduction of time variable to capture technological progress leads to a sharp fall in numerical value and statistical significance of LnK/L coefficient. This may be due to high degree of correlation between LnK/L and time. Estimated values TFP by CD functions are 6.01 per cent and negative 1.25 per cent which

Table 4.24 : Estimates of Indexes of Factor Productivity (Double Deflation) and Unit Labour Cost: Watches and Clocks Industry

Year	Indexes of Partial Factor Productivity		Indexes of Total Factor Productivity			Unit Labour Cost
	Labour	Capital	Kendrick	Solow	Translog	W/V
1	2	3	4	5	6	7
1973-74	100.00	100.00	100.00	100.00	100.00	100.00
1974-75	173.16	196.73	184.73	179.42	187.27	106.87
1975-76	214.16	191.86	201.90	188.01	195.32	118.22
1976-77	252.84	227.48	238.92	222.55	231.33	123.80
1977-78	225.54	207.69	215.84	202.42	209.95	112.40
1978-79	240.24	229.58	234.55	220.96	229.83	117.18
1979-80	275.49	262.76	268.69	253.06	263.15	120.76
1980-81	365.05	264.08	304.25	271.02	278.31	131.56
1981-82	399.71	261.94	313.53	273.29	280.37	134.98
1982-83	512.00	357.14	417.42	364.17	378.72	139.52
1983-84	429.05	278.69	334.68	282.36	299.33	115.43
1984-85	483.87	239.38	315.48	248.39	272.34	116.29
1985-86	528.47	254.24	337.97	265.76	290.96	117.64
1986-87	605.32	279.41	376.08	295.51	322.41	115.95
1987-88	591.07	242.85	337.88	259.00	286.66	115.66
1988-89	622.83	233.87	333.21	253.42	281.04	115.24
1989-90	722.18	262.28	376.85	286.93	317.03	131.06
1990-91	954.70	273.25	414.50	314.09	342.65	111.57
1991-92	1040.94	319.47	477.45	360.37	396.67	139.13
1992-93	800.41	227.18	345.21	251.58	285.45	104.08
1993-94	945.23	230.31	360.47	262.87	297.05	110.10
1994-95	928.21	217.64	342.99	249.57	282.64	109.39
1995-96	1047.1	278.93	429.31	305.80	354.23	113.71
Annual Trend Rates (% Per Annum)						
1973-95	9.61	1.66*	4.18	2.55	3.11	–0.01⁺
	(16.795)	(2.424)	(6.209)	(3.833)	(4.776)	(.041)
1973-84	13.21	6.74	9.36	7.53	7.93	1.57*
	(8.786)	(3.735)	(5.687)	(4.458)	(4.700)	(2.303)
1985-95	6.96	–0.50⁺	1.22⁺	0.26⁺	0.75⁺	–0.63⁺
	(5.888)	(.443)	(1.087)	(.221)	(.75)	(.783)

Source: *Data computed from Appendix Tables A-6, A-12, A-18 and A-24 as per methodology explained in Chapter-2.*

Notes: 1. *The growth rates are calculated by fitting exponential function of the form $Y = ab^t$.*

2. *Figure in brackets are t-values of estimates and are significant at 1% level of significance unless otherwise specified.*

3. **Significant at 5% level; ⁺ Insignificant.*

is not satisfactory. Estimates of CES production function show that coefficient of wage rate is not significantly different from zero except in CES-I without time trend. This indicates that prevailing wage rate in the industry is more than marginal productivity of labour and it is not possible to employ more labour by replacing capital. Computed value of technological progress by CES production function are 6.13 per cent and 4.29 per cent by CES-I and CES-II respectively, which is an over-estimation compared to the value given by non-parametric methods. Estimates of VES production function also shows that coefficient of wage rate is insignificant. But coefficient of LnK/L is significant when function is estimated without trend variable and introduction of time variable again reduced the coefficient of LnK/L. Here insignificant coefficient of LnK/L should not be construed as insignificance of capital in production.[13]

Table 4.25 : Production Function Estimates: Watches and Clocks Industry

Dependent Variable—V/L

Number of observation—23

Functional Forms	Coefficient of Constant	Ln K/L	Ln w	Ln L	Time	Adj. R^2	D-W Statistics	F/Rho
Estimates Without Trend Variable								
CD-I	1.377	.783	-	-	-	.8785	1.598	138.34
	(3.920)	(11.762)						(1.21)
CD-II	.427⁺	.420	-	.538	-	.9040	1.808	104.54
	(1.024)	(3.308)		(3.192)				(2.20)
CES-I	.479	-	.953	-	-	.8704	1.570	148.68
	(1.162)		(12.193)					(1,21)
CES-II	−0.51⁺	-	.531	.518	-	.9193	1.896	112.72
	(.133)		(3.627)	(3.222)				(2.20)
VES	−.791*	.331⁺	.565⁺	-	-	.8734	1.631	76.40
	(1.625)	(1.178)	(1.66)					(2.20)
Estimates With Trend Variable								
CD-I	4.684	.016⁺	-	-	.0601⁺	.8923	1.757	91.76
	(3.593)	(.052)			(2.612)			(2.20)
CD-II	−.418⁺	.520⁺	-	.626⁺	−.0125⁺	.8989	1.805	66.43
	(.120)	(1.201)		(1.566)	(.244)			(3.19)
CES-I	3.619	-	.251⁺	-	0.458	.8962	1.786	95.49
	(2.736)		(.857)		(2.472)			(2,20)
CES-II	−.204⁺.	-	.549**	.533⁺	−.0021⁺	.9064	1.895	71.41
	(.081)		(1.685)	(1.764)	(.062)			(3.19)
VES	3.909*	−.127*	.309*	-	.0518*	.8909	1.803	60.97
	(2.508)	(.374)	(.917)		(2.090)			(3.19)

Table 4.26 : Estimates of Function Explaining Sources of Productivity Change: Watches and Clocks Industry

Explanatory Variable	Coefficient of Constant	Ln V/L	Ln w	LnK/L	Time	Adj. R^2	D-W Statistics	F/Rho Value
Ln V/L	−2.032*	.701	.236*	.550	−.0778	.9788	1.658	.1551
	(2.700)	(11.988)	(1.888)	(3.988)	(5.573)			(.0769)
Ln V/K	2.573	.701	.236*	−.451	−.0778	.9263	1.494	.7005
	(4.259)	(11.067)	(1.868)	(3.259)	(5.573)			(3,19)
TFPK	.584⁺	.806	.279	−.176**	−.0872	.9240	1.738	.2207⁺
	(.799)	(13.650)	(2.267)	(1.416)	(6.509)			(1.018)
TFPS	.653*	.806	.237*	−.146⁺	−.0911	.9132	1.609	58.56
	(.833)	(13.092)	(1.998)	(1.123)	(6.581)			(3,19)
TFPT	.639⁺	.751	.301*	−.159⁺	−.0792	.9009	1.857	.3674⁺
	(1.172)	(11.480)	(2.083)	(1.151)	(5.277)			(1.531)

Source: Estimated using data in Tables 4.23 and 6.11 and Appendix Table A-12.

Notes: 1. The figure in parenthesis refers to the corresponding t-values.
2. All t-values are significant at 1% level of significance unless otherwise specified.
3. * Significant at 5% level; ** Significant at 10% level; ⁺ Insignificant.

4.3.6c. Sources of Productivity Change

Table 4.26 details the different regression functions explaining the changes in partial factor productivities and TFP indexes over time. It can be noticed from Table 4.26 that in the function of labour productivity, the coefficient of LnV, Lnw and LnK/L are positive and significant. *Thus, as scale, wage rate and capital per unit of labour expands, the productivity of labour increases.* Coefficient of wage rate is significant, not only for labour productivity but also for capital productivity and total factor productivity; this supports the efficiency wage hypothesis, i.e., higher wage rate tends to push up the level of productivity. All the measures of productivity show that coefficient of value added is significant, this shows that as the scale of output increases the level of productivity also increases. Capital intensity has positively and significantly related to labour productivity but it is negatively and significantly related to capital productivity. Contribution of capital intensity in explaining total factor productivity has been insignificant. Time variable have been negative and significant, thereby, indicating that the deterioration in institutional factors have been depressing labour productivity over time.

Table 4.27 : Decomposition of Labour Productivity for Different Industries Using Solow Method

Industry	Period	Labour productivity in base year (V/L0)	Labour productivity in terminal year (V/Lt)	Change in labour productivity over period (CV/L)	A(t) in terminal year (A(t)/A(o))	Labour productivity net of technical change	Change in labour productivity due capital intensity	Change in labour productivity technical progress
1	2	3	4	5	6	7	8	9
Organised Manufac Sector	73-95	9282	27714	18432	1.7158	16152	6870 (37.3)	11562 (62.7)
	73-84	9282	13644	4362	1.2034	11338	2056 (47.1)	2306 (52.9)
	85-86	14854	27714	12860	1.3881	19966	5112 (39.8)	7748 (60.2)
Sugar Industry	73-95	5604	19945	14341	1.2026	16586	10981 (76.6)	3360 (23.4)
	73-84	5604	11040	5436	0.9038	12215	6610 (121.6)	–1175 (–21.6)
	85-86	10789	19945	9156	1.4302	13946	3157 (34.5)	5999 (65.5)
Paper and Paperboard Industry	73-95	13678	29471	15793	1.1371	25917	12240 (77.5)	3554 (22.5)
	73-84	13678	13904	226	0.7492	18558	4880 (2159)	–4654 (–2059)
	85-86	12015	29471	17456	1.7361	16976	4960 (28.4)	12495 (71.6)

conti.

1	2	3	4	5	6	7	8	9
Fertiliser & Pesticide Industry	73-95	25364	120396	95032	2.0972	57409	32045 (33.7)	62987 (66.3)
	73-84	25364	58533	33169	1.4925	39219	13855 (41.8)	19314 (58.2)
	85-86	46540	120396	73857	1.6676	72199	25660 (34.7)	48197 (65.3)
Motor Vehicle Industry	73-95	13865	47187	33322	1.7496	26970	13105 (39.3)	20217 (60.7)
	73-84	13865	19215	5350	1.0711	17939	4074 (76.2)	1276 (23.9)
	85-86	18753	47187	28434	1.7622	26778	8025 (28.2)	20409 (71.8)
Watches & Clocks Industry	73-95	9737	40766	31029	1.5559	26201	16463 (53.1)	14565 (46.9)
	73-84	9737	25863	16125	1.6289	15877	6139 (38.1)	9986 (61.9)
	85-86	27673	40766	13094	0.9073	44932	17259 (131.8)	–4166 (–31.8)

Source : Calculated as per the methodology explained in chapter-2.
Note: Calculated as follows.
Col. 5 = Col. 4—Col. 3 Col. 7 = Col. 4/Col. 6
Col. 8 = Col. 7—Col. 3 Col. 5 = Col. 5 — Col. 8

4.4 Inter-Industry Differences in Productivity Growth

In last section, we have analysed the productivity trends in different industries. We have seen wide differences in growth rates of these industries. In this section, we will explore possible reason for difference in these divergent trends in different industries.

As already mentioned, we have used two measures of productivity, one based on concept of gross value added by single deflation and other on gross value added by double deflation. For a comparative study of physical efficiency, we outline the trends on productivity based on double deflation. Out of five industries studied, sugar industry recorded maximum increase in labour productivity at growth rate of 13.42 per cent followed by fertilisers and watches & clocks industries (growth rates are 11.68 per cent and 9.61 per cent respectively). Labour productivity has increased at the modest trend growth rates of 5.37 per cent and 5.12 per cent respectively, for motor vehicles and paper & paperboard industries. Labour productivity in organized manufacturing sector has increased at growth rate of 5.51 per cent. Capital productivity recorded the highest increase in fertilisers industry (6.31 per cent) followed by sugar industry (5.19 per cent) and watches & clocks industry (1.66 per cent). Capital productivity has decreased in paper & paperboard and motor vehicles industries although, the decline has been statistically insignificant. Capital productivity in aggregate of industries has increased but insignificantly at trend rate of 0.55 per cent. Total factor productivity growth (TFPT index), which summarises the overall efficiency in utilisation of inputs, is the highest in sugar industry (6.99 per cent) followed by fertilisers (6.57 per cent) and watches & clocks industry (3.11 per cent). In motor vehicles industry, TFP increase has been low at the trend rate of 1.81 per cent. Paper & paperboard industry recorded insignificant increase in TFP (1.10 per cent) and TFP in organised manufacturing industry has increased at trend rate of 1.67 per cent.

We now come to a comparative analysis of trends in productivity indexes, based on single deflation. Chart 4.13 depicts the trend growth rates of productivity indexes along with capital intensity. Labour productivity, here also, recorded maximum increase in sugar industry (10.9 per cent) followed by fertilisers (7.99 per cent) and watches and clocks (6.32 per cent) industries. Labour productivity in organised manufacturing sector as a whole has increased at the trend rate of

5.21 per cent. Whereas, motor vehicles and paper & paperboard industries recorded increase at the rate of 4.28 per cent and 2.96 per cent respectively. It may be noted that there is wide difference between labour productivity by single deflation and labour productivity by double deflation, except organised manufacturing sector and motor vehicles industries (where difference is not so significant). This means that the indexes based on single deflation are generally depressed by relative rise in the price enjoyed by supplier of raw materials. Same trend is observed in movement of capital and total factor productivity. *It may be seen that gross value added, distributable to labour and capital, has been significantly lower than what would it had been if the price of raw materials and other inputs have been stable. This means supplier of raw material have snatched the large slice in the form of higher price for their supplies.*

Capital intensity (capital-labour ratio) has increased maximum is sugar and watches & clocks industries (at growth rate of 7.82 per cent). The increase in rest of the industries has been similar at the growth rate of 5.74 per cent, 5.05 per cent and 5.19 per cent for paper & paperboard, fertilisers & pesticides and motor vehicles industries respectively. The increase in capital intensity in organised manufacturing industries has been 4.94 per cent. It has been generally argued that labour productivity is significantly increased with the increase in capital intensity due to '*more machines to work with effect*'. It is of interest to know the growth rate of pure labour productivity after separating the effect of capital intensity. Decomposition of labour productivity shows that pure labour productivity increased maximum in fertilisers & pesticides industry (5.30 per cent) followed by watches & clocks (2.96 per cent) and motor vehicles industry (2.60 per cent). Sugar industry, which had recorded maximum increase in labour productivity, shows that pure labour productivity in the industry has increased at trend rate of 2.55 per cent only. This indicates that most of the increase recorded in labout productivity in industry is due to increased capital intensity. It is the case with paper & paperboard industry also where labour productivity increase is insignificant, if we separate the effect of capital intensity. Pure labour productivity increase had been 3.21 per cent for whole manufacturing sector (aggregate of industries).

CHART-4.13

Comparative Growth Rates of Labour Productivity, Capital Productivityy, Total Factor Productivity(Translog) and Capital Intensity in Selected Industries

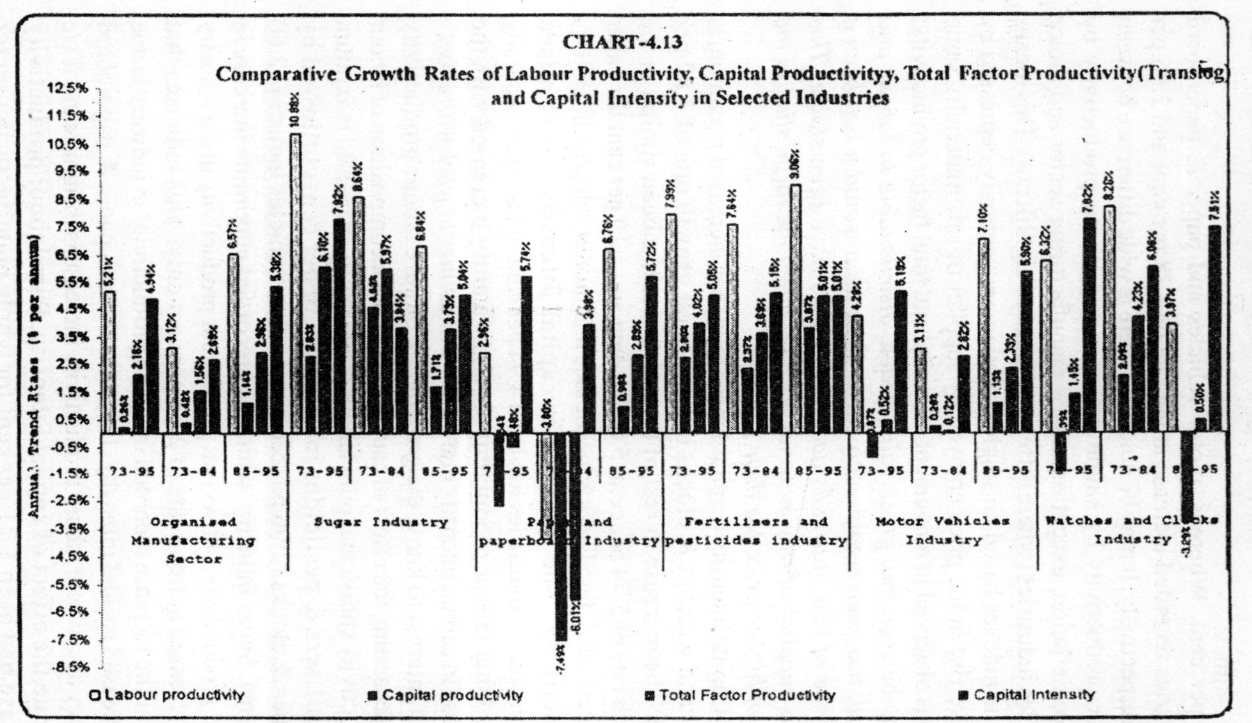

Estimates of production functions shows that constant return to scale exist in sugar, paper & paperboard and fertilisers & pesticides industries whereas, increasing returns to scale are present in motor vehicles and watches & clocks industries. Estimates of elasticity of substitution show that elasticity of substitution is low and not statistically different from zero. It is high and more than unity in motor vehicles industry. The hypothesis of unit elasticity of substitution is not outrightly rejected in rest of the industries.

So far, in comparing inter-industry differences in productivity, we have not taken the absolute value of different variables into analysis. Table 4.28 shows the range of the values of different variables used in the analysis. Table shows high absolute labour productivity in fertilisers & pesticides industry and low in sugar and paper & paperboard industry. It is moderate in motor vehicles and watches & clocks industries. Comparison of labour productivity shows that except sugar (low labour productivity associated with low capital intensity) and fertilisers & pesticides (high labour productivity associated with high capital intensity) all other industries do not show positive relationship. High capital intensity in paper & paperboard industry is associated with low labour productivity and low capital intensity in motor vehicles and watches & clocks industry is associated with moderate labour productivity. Thus, we do not find any conclusive evidence that high capital-intensive industries are high labour productivity industries. This seems to contradict theory because it is expected that high capital intensity should be associated with high labour productivity. However, as expected high capital-intensive industries has low capital productivity and vice-versa. Comparison of wages with labour productivity indicates that high wage industries have high labour productivity except paper & paperboard industry where moderate wage is associated with low labour productivity. One of the reasons of this positive relationship besides the efficiency wage hypothesis may be that wages form part of value added (our measure of output) and if share of wage in value added is more, high wage would automatically inflate value added.

Explanation of Inter-Industry Differences—Econometric Exploration : The inter-industry differences in productivity can be

Table 4.28 : Range of Values Different Variables Across Industries

Industry	Labour productivity	Capital productivity	Capital intensity	Real Wages	Unit Labour Cost
Manufac-turing sector	9282-27714 (15472)	0.1516-1.006	0.6123-1.585 (.9806)	3976-7151 (5524)	0.1613-0.4625 (.3768)
Sugar	4431-41892 (16220)	0.1147-0.2534	0.2425-1.271 (.66234)	1726-7915 (4836)	0.2675-0.5974 (.4637)
Paper & Paperboard	13678-29471 (16256)	0.0751-0.1252	0.7952-2.736 (1.453)	4838-7635 (6009)	0.2316-0.5525 (.3438)
Fertilisers & Pesticides	19084-120396 (52028)	0.0715-0.1732	2.342-6.930 (4.389)	7163-14887 (10493)	0.1409-0.2907 (.2270)
Motor Vehicles	13865-47187 (20552)	0.1907-0.3120	0.5120-1.475 (.8542)	6505-12744 (9111)	0.2527-0.4902 (.3948)
Watches & Clocks	9737-40766 (25646)	0.2992-0.3829	0.2835-1.064 (.6124)	4183-7931 (6144)	0.2729-0.4774 (.3819)

Source : Computed from appendix tables

Note : The value in parenthesis is average over period for the respective variable.

explained by application of simple econometric model. In the analysis of function explaining sources of productivity change, we have found that labour productivity, for that matter, all the indexes of productivity are having strong association between changes in productivity and value added. Vedroon identified positive association of growth of value added and growth of labour productivity as early as 1949. It is argued that strong positive association between growth of value added to growth in productivity emanates from the fact that the faster an industry grow the more it has the opportunity to exploit the benefits of an expanding level of operations. The expansion allows the industry to exploit the economies of scale, both internal and external. An important source of scale economies is specialisation. The output growth is very important in determining the extent to which such specialisation can be attained.

Table 4.29 : Estimates of Function Explaining Inter-Industry Variation in Productivity

Explanatory Variable	Constant	LnV	Lnw	LnK/L	Adj. R^2	D-W Statistics	F/Rho
Ln V/L	−1.255**	.784*	.412*	.538*	.6495	2.399	8.588
	(1.832)	(2.266)	(1.952)	(1.791)			(3,7)
TFPK	−4.579	2.743	.908*	−1.252	.7561	2.814	11.332
	(4.259)	(5.049)	(2.741)	(2.659)			(3,7)
TFPS	−2.969⁺	1.855**	.805⁺	−.732⁺	.1107	2.493	1.415
	(1.337)	(1.652)	(1.175)	(.752)			(3,7)
TFPT	−6.459*	2.055⁺	1.092⁺	.871⁺	.2234	2.072	1.959
	(2.031)	(1.279)	(1.113)	(.625)			(3,7)

Source: Computed from tables as explained in Section 4.4.

Notes: 1. All t-values are significant at 1% level of significance unless otherwise specified.

2. * Significant at 5% level; ** Significant at 10% level; ⁺ Insignificant.

Technological progress, either exogenous or endogenous, is another reason for the positive association. Taking technical progress as exogenous, it is found that higher rate of growth in output leads to a higher rate of growth in productivity because of the following reasons: (a) faster output would permit greater addition of new and superior capacity, (b) rapid growth in output may shorten the lag in application of new knowledge because it attracts better managers, reduce the risk of uncertainty or forces quicker replacement or leads to lower labour resistance of technological change and (c) firms can employ optimum sized plant readily only in a growing industry rather than in the industry where output is stagnant. If technical progress is taken as endogenous then, following Arrow (1962), technological progress can be viewed as the process of learning and since learning is the result of experience arising out of attempts to solve a problem, therefore cumulative investment will determine the rate of improvement in the quality of machine and hence, in productivity. The state of technology or the level of productivity is therefore, is a function of cumulative gross investment, which over a reasonably long period of time will be mainly determined by increases in output. Accordingly, there is a fairly close association between long period rate of growth in output and productivity.

Another important factor affecting growth of productivity is capital intensity. It is possible to argue that industries with relatively high capital intensity will be the industries with more changes of embodied technical progress and more scope of learning by doing.[14] Salter (1969, p. 71) argued that increased capital intensity might raise the productivity of labour in two ways: the first is to employ more mechanised techniques; the second is to increase the volume of replacement expenditures and speed up the adjustment to new methods. Substitution via the degree of mechanisation raises labour productivity by providing each worker with a greater volume of capital equipment; substitution via the adjustment process gives each worker a more modern set of capital equipment. Thus, we expect capital intensity to capture the impact of technological progress and a positive relation between its growth and productivity growth.

The arguments advanced by 'efficiency wage hypothesis' make it imperative to include wage rate to find out its impact on productivity. The wage rate is expected to have a positive association with productivity.

As we have included only five industries along with manufacturing sector so inclusion of three variables in regression will leave us with two degree of freedom. Thus, for the purpose of further analysis we will take growth rates of sub-periods.

The regression functions giving us the determinants of productivity change in different industries presented in Table 4.29 is limited by the low value of R^2. The regression equation explaining growth of TFPS and TFPT are insignificant as indicated by low F value. This means that the included variable does not explain growth in these indexes. But the function explaining growth of labour productivity proves Vedroon Law that growth in output has positive relation with growth in labour productivity. Labour productivity is positively related to wage rate and capital intensity but their association is not significant. Coefficient of value added is positive and significant in explaining growth rate of TFPK across industries. Coefficient of wage rate is also positive and significant; this means that wage rate has positively affected growth of total factor productivity across industries as measured by TFPK. But coefficient of capital intensity is negative and significant in function explaining total factor productivity. It appears from the results that capital intensity has not helped in improving total factor productivity growth across industries.

4.5 Summing Up

In this chapter, productivity trends in different industries have been presented and analysed for the period 1973-74 to 1995-96. Both the production function approach and productivity approach have been adopted for analysis. Analysis of productivity in selected industries has also been done using double deflation approach. Attempts have been made to find out the sources of productivity growth in particular industry and factor responsible for the differences in growth of productivity across industries. The analysis in last chapter can be summed up as follows.

* Labour productivity has increased significantly in all the industries under study.
* Capital productivity has declined in paper & paperboard, watches & clocks and motor vehicles industries. It has increased significantly in fertiliser and pesticide industry and has been stagnate in manufacturing sector as a whole. Decline in capital productivity implies that capital requirement per unit of output has been increasing over time, i.e., more and more capital would be required for increasing output in these industries.
* Total factor productivity has increased in all the industries except in paper and paperboard industry. Increase in total factor

productivity implies that overall efficiency in the industries is increasing.

* Capital intensity has increased significantly in all the industries which imply that more and more capital is required for increasing employment in these industries. Considering the general character and the resources endowment of the country, this is not in desirable direction. The technological change should be in conformity with the resource endowments of the country.
* The prices of inputs in the industries have increased faster than that of the price of output. This implies that labour productivity and value added have been suppressed by the rise of prices of inputs. And, suppliers of raw materials have been profited, at the cost of labour and capital.
* Returns to scale have been found constant in all industries except increasing returns to scale in watches & clocks and motor vehicles industries. Increasing returns to scale in these industries implies that labour and capital were not employed to their optimum level, i.e., inputs remained underemployed.
* Elasticity of substitution has been low or unity in all industries except motor vehicles industries. This implies that capital in these industries cannot be replaced by labour.
* The estimates of TFP growth by production function approach and index number approach widely differ. At best, they are consistent in terms of direction only. This may be partly because of the presence of multicollinearity among explanatory variables and partly due to differences in assumptions underlying both approaches.
* Growth in value added has significantly and positively related to the productivity in all the industries. This is in agreement with other studies whereas time has negative and significant association with productivity.
* Productivity increase during 1985-96 has been more than that for period 1973-85 except for watches & clocks and sugar industries. This implies that productivity is picking up lately.
* Productivity growth across industries has been positively and significantly associated with the growth in wage rate. This means that increase in the level of wages can increase productivity in these industries.

However, it will be interesting to know that whether the wage increases itself is the result of increased productivity. A detailed analysis will be carried out in Chapter-7 to analyse two-way relation between wages and productivity.

References

1. The methods are explained in detail in Chapter-2 during the discussion on measurement of output.
2. See Bruno (1984), Balakrishnan and Pushpangadan (1998) and Rao (1996) for details.
3. B.N. Goldar (1986) *Productivity Growth in Indian Industry*. New Delhi: Allied Publishers Pvt. Ltd, pp. 34-39.
4. He demonstrated giving mathematical expressions that the measurement biases are less in this method.
5. Same result was reported by Banerjee (1975).
6. I.J. Ahluwalia (1991) *Productivity and Growth in Indian Manufacturing*. New Delhi: Oxford University Press, p. 197.
7. The separate production functions are not estimated for both sub-periods as this would have reduced number of observation significantly.
8. The trend rates have been calculated using the semi-log function of the form LnY = a + bt. The annual trend rate of growth is calculated as % growth = (Antilog of b – 1)* 100. Thus, the trend rate reported here and elsewhere denotes the exponential growth rate per annum.
9. This is precisely what we have discussed in last section, i.e., the turn around is not confirmed when double deflation method is used.
10. It is expected that the growth rate of at least one sub-period should be more than entire period but due to variance difference, such results can be obtained. For more details, see P. Apte (1988) Relationship between Sub-Period and Total Period Regression. Artha-Vijnana, Vol. 30, No. 3, pp. 277-86.
11. Such results are reported earlier. Elimination of time trend by including a separate time variable might led to an underestimation of capital coefficient and overestimation of time coefficient. See Asit Banerjee (1975), pp. 19-20 and Goldar (1985), p. 53.
12. Rajlaxmi (1985), p. 82 remarked that negative elasticity of capital might arise due to cumulative effect of the following factors. (i) Entry to large number of new industrial units, the full capacity utilisation of which is yet to be achieved. (ii) Existence of large number of uneconomic units, which are carrying on production with worn-out machinery.
13. It seems that due to high correlation between LnK/L and time (r = 0.980), time variable might have captured the effect of capital intensity on labour productivity.
14. I.J. Ahluwalia (1991) *Productivity and Growth in Indian Manufacturing*. New Delhi: Oxford University, Press, p 131.

5

Trends in Distribution of Productivity Gains

5.1 Introduction

All discussions about the measures to increase productivity, inevitably involve some considerations of the way in which the benefits would be distributed. This is quite natural as no group has any interest in increased productivity unless they are convinced that they will share the gains. So far, our main concern has been with productivity measurements and some of the problems confronting such efforts. In this chapter our attention will concentrate on the distributional aspect of the final product and productivity gains, for we must know how the various claimants share gains (or losses) from increment (or decrement) in productivity.

Distribution is certainly a very important aspect of any economy. In the absence of proper and equitable distribution of productivity gains, the very purpose of productivity increment efforts get defeated. In order to ensure that higher productivity, in fact, leads to higher standard of living, "it is of the utmost importance that the benefits of higher productivity should be equitably distributed among capital, labour and consumers; and that the demand for goods and services should be maintained at a sufficiently high level" as "failure to distribute widely the benefits... and to maintain demand and employment would mean that the conditions for continuous increase in productivity does not exist."[1] The growth must be integrated with redistributable justice. In view of increasing trends in labour productivity and pressure for increasing labour share in it on one hand, and needs for capital formation on the other; the problem of measurement of contribution of factors in net distribution has assumed special importance.

However, at the outset, it is very important to clarify that when we refer productivity gains, we are not concerned with the productivity gains obtained through incentive-based system of payment, but with the increase in productivity gains of an industry arising out of technological advancement. This chapter examines the results with following questions in mind: (i) how the productivity gains are distributed between labour and capital, (ii) by what method are they distributed and (iii) what are the factors responsible for their respective shares over time.

This chapter is divided in five sections. Section 5.2 deals with the normative approach to productivity gains. This section deals with the issues involved in the distribution of productivity gains. The methodology for measurement of productivity gains and mechanism of transfer of productivity gains is discussed in section 5.3. Section 5.4 deals with the analysis of productivity gains in different industries. Inter-industry differences in productivity gains are discussed in section 5.5 and findings of the chapter are summed up in section 5.6.

5.2 Normative Approach to Productivity Gains

The efforts have been made to provide some norms based on which the productivity gains should be distributed. These norms provide for how the gains should be distributed among major claimants. This requires that claimant to increased productivity should first be recognised and then their shares should be decided. The present section deals with these issues. This section is subdivided in three sub-sections. Section 5.2.1 discusses the claimants of productivity gains whereas, section 5.2.2 deals with norms and methods of productivity gains. Section 5.2.3 discusses briefly about the Indian efforts to evolve a formula for sharing the gains of productivity.

5.2.1 Claimants of Productivity Gains

The various claimants of productivity gains are capital, labour, consumers and government. It is widely accepted view that on technological productivity gains to which labour (for that matter, any single factor) has made no specific contribution, the consumers at large and the government (in the form of increased tax revenue) also have justifiable claims. There are various arguments in favour of reduction in prices to give consumers a share in productivity gains. Some economists even, hold the view, that in the gains of technological advance, to which labour makes no specific contribution, the claims of labour, over and above those of other, in same income group, are weak, if not altogether untenable.[2] ILO also supports the view when it observes, "...provided that workers are compensated for any increased effort or sacrifices which may sometimes be required, they appear to have, over and above this, no claims in equity to receive a large share of the benefits of higher productivity than other people in the same income group."[3] The wide sharing of productivity among consumers would lessen the adverse influences of the economic friction. Apart from this, several sections of the society adversely affected by the technological advance might need relief and by reduction in the prices they stand to gain as part of the community. Beckman (1959, p. 189) remarked that when increases in productivity are reflected in price reduction, all groups in the community benefit. When they are used to raise wages, only affected workers benefit.

Nevertheless, it is generally accepted that there is some justification for distributing part of productivity gains in the form of higher wages, on the grounds that if this method is not adopted, the full potentialities of technological gains may not be realised. ILO in this regard says, "Unless worker receive some increase in the money wages from time to time, it will be very difficult to convince them, that they are in fact sharing the gains of productivity."[4] While there are distinct advantages in keeping the wage level more or less steady and reducing prices out of gains of productivity, some economist argue that in order to give greater stimulus to new investment, it would be better to ensure stability of prices and simultaneously to raise money wages as productivity increases.[5] Reduction of prices, they argue, might discourage investment and employment. They further argue that if productivity gains are to be shared on the basis of the principle of equity and economic justice, among the major contributors to the rising productivity, the share of each claimant must be equitable and proportional to their respective contribution to the emergence of productivity gains. From this angle also, the share of consumers (in the forms of reduced prices) is not tenable since consumers does not make any direct effort for productivity improvement. Here, it should also be construed that price reduction should not be associated, at all, with rising productivity. In fact, the consumers as a class will generally benefit from increased productivity to the extent of reduction in the cost of production or improvement in the quality of product and higher tax receipts to the government (sizeable amount of which is spend on the welfare related scheme).

5.2.2 Norms and Methods

Once the question of identification of main claimants is decided, the next logical step is to evolve the methodology for equitable distribution of gains of productivity. So far, no operational formula has been evolved to apportion the gains of productivity. The apparent reason for this being that productivity gains are not the efforts of any group of factor of production, but the joint product of dynamic forces operating in the economy e.g., advanced research and improved technology, economies of scale, improvement in labour and management skills, capital accumulation and socio-political structure of the economy. Discussing on the principle of sharing the gains of higher productivity, ILO says, "these arguments, though may help to set the problem in perspective, do not answer the question: what is the labourer's reasonable share of benefits of higher productivity in a particular case? Nor do they settle the question of the form which these gains should take." Then it says, "These are clearly the questions to which there are no simple universal answers."[6]

5.2.3 Efforts for Evolving Formula for Sharing

The National Productivity Council (NPC) in India tried to evolve a formula for sharing the gains of increased productivity. The efforts in this direction were done in a conference on *'Co-Operation for Higher Productivity and Sharing the Gains of Productivity'* in year 1960. Pursuant to the recommendations of the conference, an expert committee of 13 members with an employer's representative, Shri Naval Tata as chairman, was appointed to examine the principles which should govern the distribution of gains of productivity. The committee presented its view in the form of a working paper. NPC appointed another committee in October 1963, under the chairmanship of another employer's representative Leslie Sawhney, to examine the report of Naval Tata Committee and to make specific recommendations, on how the gains should accrue to labour. The committee submitted its report in 1967 with dissenting notes from two of its members. To bridge the gap, the NPC chairman, Shri NN Wanchoo put forward his own compromise formula suggesting 20 per cent of the gains to reduction in the price, 40 per cent or more to labour and 40 per cent or less for capital, against the recommendation of 20 per cent for reduction in prices, 20 per cent for distribution as additional dividend on capital, and remaining 60 per cent for utilising between productivity bonus to labour and for re-investment for development. These reports or formula does not find unanimous acceptance in NPC, thereby ending the whole exercise futile. Dandekar (1967) also suggested a percentage formula by making some modification in the committee formula and suggested that 20 per cent can be set aside for lowering prices, 20 per cent for granting additional dividends to shareholder and out of remaining 30 per cent to be given to labour for plough back in the form of new shares in the firm. This formula was also not accepted unanimously. NPC, therefore, again set up a committee under the chairmanship of Kashinath Pandey. The Pandey committee submitted its report and *interalia* suggested that government of India should pass an appropriate legislation for establishing productivity norms and other related standards and for giving directions and awards for sharing the gains of productivity.

It may be noted that feasibility of sharing gains in the individual establishment is easy for the productivity gains obtained through incentive system because, here additional efforts of workers can be directly and correctly measured but in the case of technology productivity, to which workers make no immediately visible or measurable contribution, the problem of sharing assumes vagueness and uncertainty such as that have dogged the NPC committee.[7] The National Commission on Labour in this regard aptly remarked, "thus, on the questions of measurement of productivity and its allocation among different factor of production, no clear cut view emerges out of evidence... Any suggestion for sharing will be debatable ... the essence of the wisdom in such matter is to approach the matter pragmatically."[8]

Here, it is worthwhile to point out that the percentage formula as suggested by NPC for sharing gains are purely arbitrary and based on value judgement. Almost all the formulas have suggested 20 per cent of total productivity gains for price reduction, in this regard Subramanium rightly asks why 20 per cent is a suitable figure for price reduction, whether it is based on the rate of inflation in the recent years or to bring down the price by specific margin. Similarly, how one can say precisely that a particular factor say labour should get this much without knowing their contribution to productivity increment, it is very difficult to break productivity by individual factor of production.[9] The statistical problems of concretely measuring the gains of productivity are immense; the difficulties of isolating relative contribution of different factor of production no less so. Had the contribution of each factor to the productivity gains been known or measured separately and accurately, there would have been no problem in allocating such percentages to the factor of production. It is, therefore, necessary that further attempt should be made to find out the techniques of such measurement on the basis of which a scientific way of distributing the gains of productivity in a fair and equitable manner would be achieved.

5.3 Methodology for Present Study

In this chapter, we would make no such attempt to prescribe percentages, on a normative basis, to be given to factors out of increased productivity. Following Sinha and Sawhney[10] the chapter concern itself to the actual sharing of productivity gains by labour and capital in relations to their share in incremental input. It also examine annual variations in

(a) Factors shares in total input
(b) Factors share in net distributable output
(c) Relative factor prices

Here, it may be noted that if productivity is based on the gross output, the seller of raw material also share the benefits of increased productivity along with labour and capital. For convenience of analysis the share of raw materials has been eliminated for measuring the productivity gains. The value of raw materials, fuel and power (at current prices) has been deducted from gross output (at current prices) and the amount thus obtained is deflated by the index of output price to give the amount that is to be distributed among labour and capital only.[11]

The methodology for the measurement and distribution of productivity gain is same as followed by Sinha and Sawhney (1970). The total productivity gain between two periods is measured by the difference between the changes in the net distributable output and the changes in the total real input both at their respective base year prices. The total factor input (TFI) is obtained by assuming that labour and capital are compensated at their base year rate of reward. It implicitly assumed that base year prices of capital and labour are equal to their respective marginal productivity. Thus, total factor input (TFI) would measure the output that would be produced if there were no productivity change. Symbolically:

$$TFI_t = w_0 L_t + r_0 K_t \qquad ...(5.1)$$

Here, w_0 and r_0 are the base year prices of labour and capital and L_t and K_t are current year labour and capital inputs. Thus, total productivity gains have been measured as the difference between output actually produced and the output that would have been produced in the absence of productivity change. Total gains are shared between labour and capital. The gains accruing to labour (G_L) is measured by the difference between total labour compensation at constant price (total emoluments deflated by product price index) and change in the value of labour input (w_0L_t) if it is rewarded at base year rate. It is obtained by multiplying wage rate (earnings per employee) in the base year by corresponding labour input (total number of persons engaged). In fact, real labour input indicates what the real income of labour would have been if there had been no change in real compensation per employee over time. Similarly, gains accruing to capital may be measured by the difference between the change in total non-labour income at constant product prices and the change in the value of capital input if it is compensated at the rate of return at the base year rate. The real capital input represents the real income of capital that would have accrued if there had been no change in its base year rate of return. Base year rate of return may be calculated by dividing the non-labour income by the gross fixed capital in base year. Symbolically:

$$r_0 = (V_0 - w_0 L_0)/K_0. \qquad ...(5.2)$$

The share of labour in productivity gains is the excess of increment to real income accruing to labour over the increment to labour inputs and the residual is the share of capital in the productivity gains. The total productivity gains and gains accruing to labour and capital may be expressed symbolically in following identities:

$$G_T = [V_t - V_0] - [TFI_t - TFI_0] \quad ...(5.3)$$

$$G_L = [W_t - W_0] - [L_t - L_0] \quad ...(5.4)$$

$$G_K = [R_t - R_0] - [K_t - K_0] \quad ...(5.5)$$

Here, G_T is total productivity gain, G_L and G_K express gains accruing to labour and capital respectively, V is the net distributable output at constant product prices, W represents total wage bill (total emoluments) at constant product prices, R represents total non-labour income at constant product price, L represents real labour input in terms of value, i.e., base year wage rate multiplied by total number of employee, K represents capital input or income accruing to capital if compensated at base year rate of return, i.e., multiplied by base year rate of return, TFI is the sum of labour and capital input, subscript t and 0 are the terminal year and base year. Here, it may be pointed out that the income accruing to labour and capital at constant product prices, adds upto total divisible pool of output and respective gains of two factors adds up to the total productivity gains.[12]

It would also be of interest to analyse the trends in average share of labour and capital in net distributable output. The factors share in income could be directly obtained by dividing the respective money income of labour and capital by the gross value added at current prices. But here, we would analyse the factor share in output through a relatively complicated process of multiplying the relative share of each factor in total factor input by the respective index of relative factor prices (P_L/P_F or P_K/P_F). Both the method would give same result but the second method gives an additional information about the movement of relative factor prices in relation to change in relative factor inputs which may help us indirectly to infer with ease that which factor is substitutable with other. Factor's share in net distributable output may be obtained as follows:

$$S_L = W_t/V_t = (L_t/TFI_t).(P_L/P_F) \quad ...(5.6)$$

$$S_L = R_t/V_t = (K_t/TFI_t).(P_K/P_F) \quad ...(5.7)$$

Here, S_L and S_K are the shares of labour and capital in net distributable output respectively, P_L and P_K are the average price index of labour and capital at time t and P_F is the average factor price. The equations 5.6 and 5.7 indicate that share of each factor in total distributable output will vary in accordance with the net effect of change in quantity of factor employed relative to total factor input (given by L_t/TFI_t & K_t/TFI_t) and in relative factor prices to the average fixed prices (P_L/P_F & P_K/P_F).

It is imperative to mention here that some researchers[13] have used the following formulae for studying the pattern of productivity gains and their distribution. A CD function of the form $P = a\,L^{a}C^{b}$ was fitted and from them marginal product of labour (MPLi) and capital (MPCi), given by

$$MPLi = P/L^{a}$$
$$MPCi = P/C^{b}$$

for each year, are obtained. The relative contribution of labour (RDCLi) and capital in productivity gains (RDCCi) in total productivity gains are obtained by:

RDCLi = [(MPLi)(Li)*100]/[(MPLi) Li + (MPCi) Ci].

And RDCCi = [(MPCi)(Ci)*100]/[(MPLi) Li + (MPCi) Ci]

And their shares are obtained as

Labour's share = VAMi*RDCLi/100

and capital's share = VAMi*RDCCi/100

The study have preferred the formula provided by Sinha and Sawhney mainly for its simplicity and its ability to provide relative price movements of output, labour and capital for the study.

5.4 Distribution of Productivity Gains in Selected Industries

Distribution of productivity gains as presented in this section are derived by using the formula given by Sinha and Sawhney (1971). Due to fluctuant character of the variables, year-wise data are not of much help. It will be more revealing if whole period is divided in sub-periods. We have first divided entire period into two parts, i.e., period from 1973-74 to 1984-85 and 1985-86 to 1995-96. But, the trends in productivity gains are same for both the periods and to have more clear understanding of pattern of distribution we have also seen how the productivity gains are distributed in periods corresponding to plan periods. It was observed during the analysis of productivity trends that most of the industries have shown sharp increase in productivity in nineties, so we have also analysed the pattern of distribution for 1990-91 to 1995-96.

5.4.1 Organised Manufacturing Sector

The data on total productivity gains and their distribution between labour and capital are presented in Table 5.1. The productivity increment during the period has been Rs. 31,030 crore of which 88.9 per cent was shared by capital and labour shared only 11.1 per cent.

Table 5.1 : Factor's Share in Productivity Gains: Organised Manufacturing Sector

(Value in Rs. '0000000)

Period	Change in Income	Change in Factor Input	Productivity Gains (G_T)	Change in Labour Income	Change in Labour Input	Productivity Gains (G_L)	Change in Capital Income	Change in Capital Input	Productivity Gains (G_K)
1	2	3	4	5	6	7	8	9	10
73-95	43206	12176 (100)	31030 (*100*)	5341	1890 (15.5)	3451 (*11.1*)	37865	10286 (84.5)	27579 (**88.9**)
73-84	5488	3749 (100)	1739 (*100*)	2243	928 (24.8)	1315 (*75.6*)	3245	2821 (75.2)	424 (**24.4**)
85-95	37343	8304 (100)	29039 (*100*)	3328	1133 (13.6)	2195 (*7.6*)	34015	7174 (86.4)	26844 (**92.4**)
73-78	3162	1625 (100)	1537 (*100*)	1085	613 (37.7)	472 (*30.6*)	2076	1012 (62.3)	1064 (**69.4**)
80-84	3383	1384 (100)	1999 (*100*)	1436	55 (3.9)	1382 (*69.1*)	1947	1330 (96.1)	617 (**30.9**)
85-89	4447	2167 (100)	2280 (*100*)	1047	289 (13.3)	758 (*33.2*)	3400	1879 (86.7)	1522 (**66.8**)
90-95	31463	5354 (100)	26109 (*100*)	2108	834 (15.6)	1274 (*4.9*)	29355	4520 (84.4.)	24835 (**95.1**)
92-95	29302	3669 (100)	25633 (*100*)	1704	595 (16.2)	1109 (*4.3*)	27597	3073 (83.8)	24524 (**95.7**)

Source: Computed from Table 5.3 as explained in methodology.

Notes: 1. Col 4 = Col 3 – Col 2; Col 7 = Col 5 – Col 6; Col 10 = Col 9 – Col 8.
2. Figures in brackets are the percentage share of respective factors in productivity gains and incremental input.
3. The table may not be internally consistent due to rounding off of values.

Table 5.2 : Factor's Share in Total Input, Net Distributable Output and Relative Factor Prices: Organised Manufacturing Sector

Year	% Share in Input		Relative Factor Price		% Share in NDO	
	Labour (L/I)	Capital (K/I)	Labour (P_L/P_F)	Capital (P_K/P_F)	Labour (W/V)	Capital (R/V)
1	2	3	4	5	6	7
1973-74	46.3	53.7	100.0	100.0	46.3	53.7
1974-75	46.2	53.8	95.6	103.8	44.1	55.9
1975-76	41.0	59.0	97.5	101.7	40.0	60.0
1976-77	45.7	54.3	94.9	104.3	43.4	56.6
1977-78	45.5	54.5	98.8	101.0	44.9	55.1
1978-79	44.3	55.7	94.5	104.4	41.9	58.1
1979-80	44.1	55.9	97.1	102.3	42.8	57.2
1980-81	43.4	56.6	101.4	98.9	44.0	56.0
1981-82	42.1	57.9	96.3	102.7	40.5	59.5
1982-83	41.2	58.8	101.9	98.7	42.0	58.0
1983-84	39.0	61.0	100.6	90.6	43.5	56.5
1984-85	37.4	62.6	116.3	90.3	39.2	60.8
1985-86	35.1	64.9	114.1	92.4	40.1	59.9
1986-87	33.8	66.2	120.6	89.5	40.7	59.3
1987-88	33.1	66.9	122.8	88.7	40.7	59.3
1988-89	31.6	68.4	119.1	91.2	37.7	62.3
1989-90	31.0	69.0	114.2	93.6	35.4	64.6
1990-91	29.1	70.9	115.0	93.9	33.4	66.6
1991-92	27.9	72.1	113.4	94.8	31.7	68.3
1992-93	27.3	72.7	116.5	93.8	31.8	68.2
1993-94	25.9	74.1	105.7	98.0	27.3	72.7
1994-95	25.0	75.0	71.9	109.4	17.9	82.1
1995-96	25.0	75.0	64.6	111.8	16.1	83.9

Source: *Computed from Table 5.3 as follows:*

Col 2 = Col 8/Col 5; Col 3 = Col 11/Col 5;
Col 4 = Col 9/Col 6; Col 5 = Col 12/Col 6;
Col 6 = Col 2*Col 5/100; Col 7 = Col 3*Col 5/100

In first half, the productivity gains are only Rs. 1739 crore of which 75.6 per cent is availed by labour and in the second half, a period of rapid productivity rise, most of the increase in productivity gains are availed by capital (92.6 per cent). The trends during plan period show that except sixth five year plan (69.1 per cent) labour got less than capital in all plans. Labour availed only 4.3% of productivity gains in eighth five year plan (this again being the period of remarkable productivity growth). During 1990-95 also most of the increase in productivity is availed by capital (95.1 per cent). Thus, in the organised manufacturing sector capital enjoyed substantial share in productivity gains in the periods of rising productivity.

The data on factor prices presented in Table 5.3 shows that positive factor shares in productivity gains are reflected in the higher factor price relative to the product price. Total factor price, which is a weighted average of capital and labour prices moved up by 15.9 times whereas, labour price moved up by 10.28 times and capital price increased by 17.79 times. But product price has increased by 5.76 time only (column 4, Table 5.3). This clearly indicates that both labour and capital have positive share in productivity gains over the entire period; the relative share of capital in productivity gains is substantially higher than the share of labour. But a cursory look at the movement of prices of labour and capital indicates that price rise of capital has been more than that of the labour for last two years only. The analysis will be more revealing if we look at the share of labour and capital in incremental input. For entire period, labour's share in increased input is 15.5 per cent whereas its share in increased productivity is only 11.1 per cent. But in first sub-period and for all plan periods, except sixth and eighth five year plans, labour's share in productivity gain has been more than its share in increased input. It is only in nineties that labour's share in productivity gain is less than its share in increased input.

So far in our analysis, we have not seen that what is happening to the share of labour and capital in total input and total output. Data presented in columns 2 and 3 of Table 5.2 shows that share of labour in total input is declining over time and that of capital is rising over time. Share of labour in total input has decreased from 46.3 per cent in 1973-74 to 25.0 per cent in 1995-96 on the other hand share of capital has increased from 53.7% in 1973-74 to 75.0 per cent in 1995-96. This indicates

Table 5.3 : Net Distributable Output (NDO), Factor Input, Product Price and Factor Prices: Organised Manufacturing Sector

Value in Rs. '0000000)

Year	NDO Current Prices	NDO Constant Prices	Product Price Index	Total Factor Input	Factor Price Index (P_T)	Labour Income Current Prices	Labour Income at base rate	Labour Price Index (P_L)	Capital Income Current Prices	Capital Income at base rate	Capital Price Index (P_K)
1	2	3	4	5	6	7	8	9	10	11	12
73-74	5402	5402	100.0	5402	100.0	2499	2499	100.0	2904	2904	100.0
74-75	6916	5715	121.0	5629	122.8	3052	2599	117.4	3864	3031	127.5
75-76	6641	5412	122.7	5431	122.3	2659	2229	119.3	3983	3202	124.4
76-77	8380	6672	125.6	6244	134.2	3637	2855	127.4	4743	3389	140.0
77-78	9339	7270	128.5	6694	139.5	4196	3045	137.8	5143	3649	141.0
78-79	11019	8564	128.7	7027	156.8	4612	3112	148.2	6408	3915	163.7
79-80	12542	8107	154.7	7477	167.7	5372	3297	163.0	7170	4180	171.5
80-81	13846	7507	184.4	7767	178.3	6097	3372	180.8	7749	4395	176.3
81-82	16723	8621	194.0	8057	207.6	6778	3389	200.0	9946	4668	213.1
82-83	19141	9813	195.1	8500	225.2	8046	3506	229.5	11095	4994	222.2
83-84	23520	11092	212.0	8812	266.9	9218	3432	268.6	14302	5379	265.9
84-85	24942	10890	229.0	9151	272.6	10860	3427	316.9	14081	5724	246.0
85-86	27667	11265	245.6	9274	298.3	11081	3256	340.3	16586	6018	275.6
86-87	30199	11735	257.3	9600	314.6	12299	3241	379.5	17900	6359	281.5
87-88	34586	12499	276.7	10238	337.8	14081	3393	415.0	20505	6845	299.6
88-89	41760	13937	299.6	10667	391.5	15728	3373	466.2	26032	7293	356.9

conti

89-90	52037	15712	331.2	11442	454.8	18409	3545	519.3	33628	7897	425.8
90-91	61578	17146	359.1	12224	503.7	20586	3555	579.1	40991	8670	472.8
91-92	66168	16542	400.0	12780	517.8	20970	3572	587.1	45197	9208	490.9
92-93	85671	19307	443.7	13910	615.9	27226	3794	717.7	58445	10116	577.7
93-94	104801	21919	478.1	14674	714.2	28639	3794	754.8	76162	10880	700.0
94-95	197132	37313	528.3	15877	1241.6	35342	3961	892.1	161790	11916	1357.8
95-96	279720	48609	575.5	17578	1591.3	45116	4389	1028.0	234603	13190	1778.7

Source: 1. Computed from Appendix tables.
2. Col 4 = Col 3/Col 2;Col 6 = Col 2/Col 5;
Col 9 = Col 7/Col 8;Col 12 = Col 10/Col 11.

that importance of capital as an input is increasing over time in organised manufacturing sector, i.e., Indian manufacturing sector is getting more capital intensive. Last two column of Table 5.2 (depicted in Chart 5.1) shows that share of labour and capital in net distributable output (GVA). It shows that share of labour in net distributable output has been less than its share in input up to 1979-80. But for the period 1982-83 to 1993-94 share of labour has been more than its share in input. This indicates that for this period labour appropriated more than capital in productivity gains. Chart 5.1 clearly shows that in last two years, share of labour has been considerably less than its share in total input. The average share of labour in total output (37.6%) for entire period is also more than its average share in total input (36.6%).

5.4.2 Sugar Industry

Total productivity gains and their relative shares between labour and capital in sugar industry are presented in Table 5.4. Table shows that gains resulting from productivity amounts to Rs. 44,335 lakh and out of which 48.9 per cent (Rs. 21,667 lakh) was shared by labour and remaining 51.1 per cent (Rs. 22,658 lakh) by capital. In the first sub-period however, labour gets more than capital, their respective share being 65.8 per cent and 34.2 per cent. In the period 1985-95 labour get 48 per cent of the increment in productivity and rest 52 per cent went to capital. It will be worthwhile to compare the share of labour and capital in incremental input with their share in incremental productivity. Over the entire period, the share of labour in productivity increments (48.9 per cent) is higher than its share in incremental input (21.4 per cent). In first sub-period labour gets 65.8 per cent in productivity gains against accounting for only 34.6 per cent of the increase in input. The same trend holds in second sub-period where share of labour is 48.0 per cent of productivity gains against 17.4 per cent in increment inputs. The pattern of sharing during plan period shows that in fifth plan period, a period of stagnant labour productivity, capital gets increment of Rs. 1439 lakhs which is more than the total gains enjoyed by the industry (Rs. 489 lakhs) and consequently labour has to suffer a loss of Rs. 950 lakhs. But during sixth five year plan, labour has enjoyed 69.9 per cent of productivity gains with its share in increment input decreasing. The same pattern holds good for other plans also where share of labour in productivity gains is more than its share in incremental input.

CHART-5.1

Labour's Share in Input (L/I) and Net Distributable Output (W/V) : Organised Manufacturing Sector

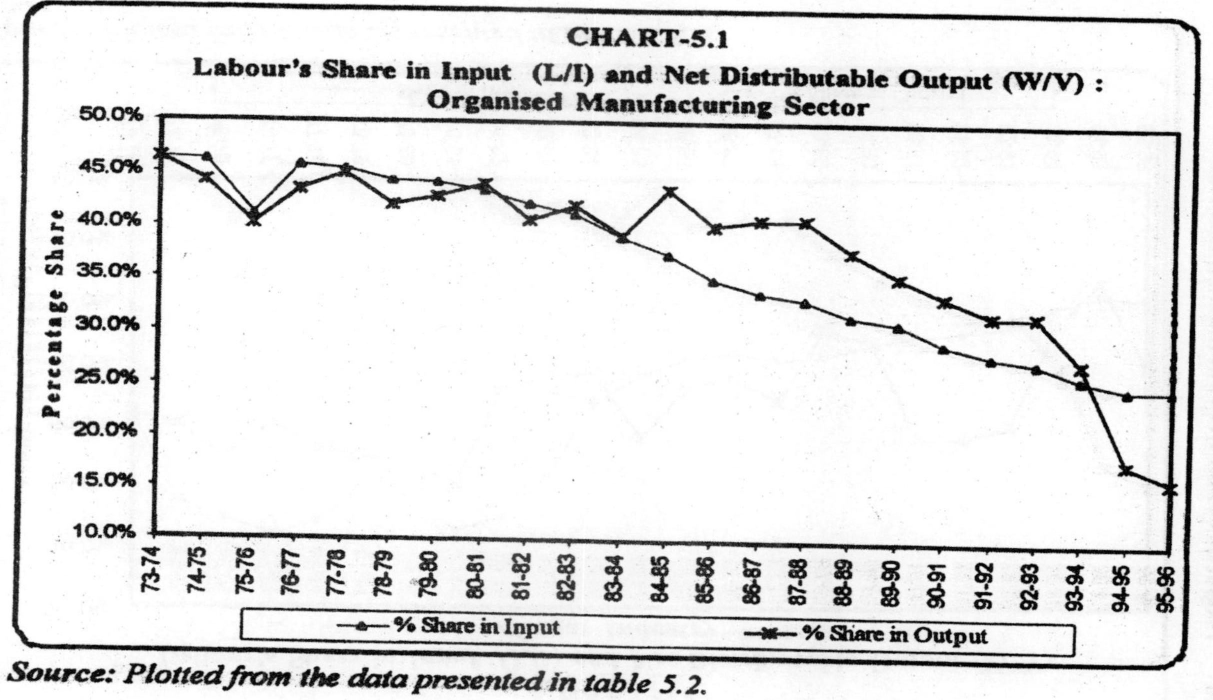

Source: Plotted from the data presented in table 5.2.

CHART-5.2

Labour's Share in Input (L/I) and Net Distributable Output (W/V) : Sugar Industry

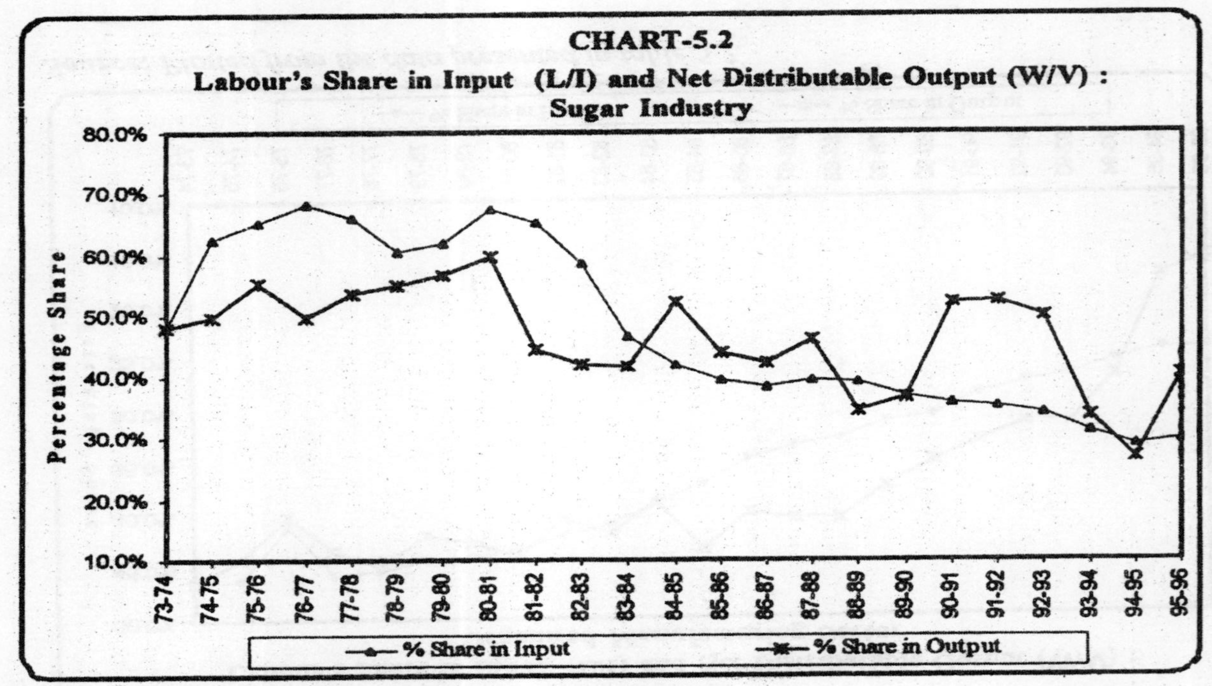

Source: Plotted from the data presented in table 5.5.

Table 5.4: Factor's Share in Productivity Gains: Sugar Industry

(Value in Rs. '00000)

Period	Change in Income	Change in Factor Input	Productivity Gains (G_T)	Change in Labour Income	Change in Labour Input	Productivity Gains (G_L)	Change in Capital Income	Change in Capital Input	Productivity Gains (G_K)
1	2	3	4	5	6	7	8	9	10
73-95	69202	24867 (100)	44335 (*100*)	26987	5310 (21.4)	21677 (***48.9***)	42215	19557 (78.7)	22658 (*51.1*)
73-84	24375	9207 (100)	15167 (*100*)	13168	3185 (34.6)	9983 (***65.8***)	11207	6022 (65.4)	5184 (***34.2***)
85-95	48265	15986 (100)	32280 (*100*)	18273	2778 (17.4)	15495 (***48.0***)	29992	13208 (82.6)	16784 (*52.0*)
73-78	10892	10402 (100)	489 (*100*)	6808	7758 (74.6)	-950 (*-194*)	4084	2645 (25.4)	1439 (*294*)
80-84	22339	-8641 (100)	30980 (*100*)	10579	-11079 (128.2)	21658 (*69.9*)	11760	2439 (-28.2)	9322 (***30.1***)
85-89	30366	6138 (100)	24228 (*100*)	8786	1784 (29.1)	7002 (***28.9***)	21580	4354 (70.9)	17226 (***71.1***)
90-95	2975	717 (100)	2257 (*100*)	1686	106 (6.1)	1580 (***24.0***)	1289	611 (93.9)	678 (***76.0***)
92-95	29379	7492 (100)	21888 (*100*)	5713	456 (2.7)	5257 (*17.2*)	23666	7036 (97.4)	16631 (***82.8***)

Source: Computed from Table 5.3 as explained in methodology.

Notes: 1. Col 4 = Col 3 – Col 2; Col 7 = Col 5 – Col 6; Col 10 = Col 9 – Col 8.
2. Figures in brackets are the percentage share of respective factors in productivity gains and incremental input.
3. The table may not be internally consistent due to rounding off of values.

The mechanism of sharing productivity gains between labour and capital may be clearly illustrated with the help of variations in factor prices in relation to product prices. The distribution of productivity gains between labour and capital is reflected in the corresponding rise in wages and rate of return to capital in relation to product prices. Where productivity gains are positive and both labour and capital share gains then wages and capital returns necessarily rise in relation to product prices since this is the means whereby the productivity gains are distributed to workers and investors by the market mechanism.[14] Data on average product price and factor prices presented in Table 5.6 show that over the entire period both labour and capital had positive share in productivity gains; since labour and capital price increased by 11.6 times and 7.3 times while product price increased only by 3.87 times. But the rise in labour price in fifth plan period has been less than that of product price that is why labour has to suffer a loss during fifth plan period when price of labour decreased whereas price of capital increased.

Table 5.5 : Factor's Share in Total Input, Net Distributable Output and Relative Factor Prices: Sugar Industry

Year	% Share in Input		Relative Factor Price		% Share in NDO	
	Labour (L/I)	Capital (K/I)	Labour (P_L/P_F)	Capital (P_L/P_F)	Labour (L/I)	Capital (K/I)
1	2	3	4	5	6	7
1973-74	47.94	52.06	100.00	100.00	47.94	52.06
1974-75	62.27	37.73	79.68	133.53	49.61	50.39
1975-76	65.03	34.97	84.69	128.47	55.07	44.93
1976-77	68.26	31.74	72.68	158.75	49.62	50.38
1977-78	65.97	34.03	81.31	136.23	53.64	46.36
1978-79	60.51	39.49	90.86	114.00	54.98	45.02
1979-80	61.71	38.29	91.75	113.29	56.62	43.38
1980-81	67.30	32.70	88.77	123.12	59.74	40.26
1981-82	65.04	34.96	68.53	158.55	44.57	55.43
1982-83	58.52	41.48	71.79	139.81	42.01	57.99
1983-84	46.62	53.38	89.67	109.02	41.80	58.20
1984-85	42.04	57.96	123.82	82.72	52.06	47.94
1985-86	39.53	60.47	111.00	92.81	43.88	56.12
1986-87	38.32	61.68	110.27	93.62	42.26	57.74
1987-88	39.38	60.62	117.17	88.84	46.14	53.86
1988-89	39.13	60.87	88.14	107.63	34.49	65.51
1989-90	37.12	62.88	98.78	100.72	36.67	63.33
1990-91	35.96	64.04	145.11	74.67	52.18	47.82
1991-92	35.45	64.55	147.90	73.70	52.43	47.57
1992-93	34.12	65.88	146.67	75.83	50.04	49.96
1993-94	31.10	68.90	108.30	96.25	33.68	66.32
1994-95	29.09	70.91	91.96	103.30	26.75	73.25
1995-96	29.83	70.17	135.05	85.10	40.28	59.72

***Source:** Computed from Table 5.6 as follows:*

Col 2 = Col 8/Col 5; Col 3 = Col 11/Col 5;
Col 4 = Col 9/Col 6; Col 5 = Col 12/Col 6;
Col 6 = Col 2*Col 5/100; Col 7 = Col 3*Col 5/100

Table 5.6: Net Distributable Output (NDO), Factor Inputs, Product and Factor Prices in Sugar Industry

(Value in Rs.'00000)

Year	NDO Current Prices	NDO Constant Prices	Product Price Index	Total Factor Input	Factor Price Index (P_T)	Labour Income Current Prices	Labour Income at base rate	Labour Price Index (P_L)	Capital Income Current Prices	Capital Income at base rate	Capital Price Index (P_K)
1	2	3	4	5	6	7	8	9	10	11	12
73-74	11638	11638	100.0	11638	100.0	5579	5579	100.0	6059	6059	100.0
74-75	12630	11692	108.0	17088	73.9	6266	10640	58.9	6364	6448	98.7
75-76	16288	15150	107.5	19567	83.2	8970	12724	70.5	7318	6843	106.9
76-77	18065	16395	110.2	22880	79.0	8963	15618	57.4	9102	7262	125.3
77-78	18062	17801	101.5	23521	76.8	9688	15516	62.4	8374	8005	104.6
78-79	21024	22530	93.3	22040	95.4	11559	13337	86.7	9465	8704	108.7
79-80	22222	19690	112.9	24171	91.9	12583	14917	84.4	9639	9254	104.2
80-81	21794	13673	159.4	29486	73.9	13019	19843	65.6	8775	9643	91.0
81-82	35972	21862	164.5	28765	125.1	16032	18708	85.7	19940	10056	198.3
82-83	54387	37360	145.6	25528	213.0	22850	14940	152.9	31537	10588	297.9
83-84	61585	41956	146.8	20877	295.0	25743	9732	264.5	35842	11144	321.6
84-85	55887	36013	155.2	20845	268.1	29093	8764	332.0	26794	12081	221.8
85-86	60152	32575	184.7	20520	293.1	26393	8111	325.4	33759	12408	272.1
86-87	70453	36361	193.8	21233	331.8	29770	8136	365.9	40683	13097	310.6

conti.

1	2	3	4	5	6	7	8	9	10	11	12
87-88	81809	41022	199.4	23147	353.4	37750	9116	414.1	44059	14031	314.0
88-89	130249	60539	215.2	24453	532.6	44920	9569	469.5	85329	14885	573.3
89-90	153044	62940	243.2	26658	574.1	56117	9895	567.1	96927	16763	578.2
90-91	125130	51461	243.2	29014	431.3	65295	10433	625.9	59835	18580	322.0
91-92	146223	54435	268.6	29731	491.8	76660	10539	727.4	69563	19192	362.5
92-93	179585	59023	304.3	31527	569.6	89869	10757	835.5	89716	20770	432.0
93-94	266991	75169	355.2	32552	820.2	89922	10123	888.3	177069	22429	789.5
94-95	397221	100489	395.3	34806	1141.3	106252	10124	1049.5	290969	24682	1178.9
95-96	312861	80840	387.0	36505	857.0	126034	10889	1157.5	186827	25616	729.3

Notes: 1. Computed from Appendix tables.

2. Col 4 = Col 3/Col 2; Col 6 = Col 2/Col 5;
Col 9 = Col 7/.Col 8; Col 12 = Col 10/Col 11.

We may now analyse the trends in average factor shares in total factor input and gross value added. The ratios of each factor input to total factor input are presented in column 2 and 3 of Table 5.5 which shows that in initial years (up to 1982-83) labour accounted for around 60 per cent of total factor input. However, after 1982-83 its share has been continuously found declining so that, in 1995-96 its share was only 29.9 per cent. On the other hand, share of capital has increased to 70.1 per cent. The relative factor price of labour and capital has moved inversely with the trends in their respective share in factor input. Relative labour price index has been less than 100 up to year 1983-84 and for this period share of labour in output has been less than its share in input. But, thereafter the share of labour in output (46.3%) has been more than its share in input (47.8%) with minor exceptions. Chart 5.2 shows that share of labour in total input has been more than its share in total output for most of the years. As an average also, share of labour in total input has been more than its share in net distributable output. In fact, this is the only industry where average share of labour in input is more than average share in total output for the period. In last few years, particularly after 1990-91, the share of capital in net distributable output has been much less than its share in total input. *Such a trend would obviously imply, diminishing capacity of the industry to expand through the re-investment of internal funds.*

5.4.3 Paper and Paperboard Industry

Data on productivity gains and their sharing between labour and capital are presented in Table 5.7 which shows that the industry has suffered a loss of Rs. 1823 lakh in the sense that the increment in total product fell short of the increase in input. *The whole loss on the account for productivity decrement had to be suffered by capital alone, in fact, capital has suffered a loss of Rs. 4344 lakh and the gains of labour Rs. 2521 lakh are at the expense of the capital.*

The industry shows negative productivity gains in fifth and sixth five year plans and positive gains in next two five year plans. In fifth and sixth five year plan periods of negative productivity gains (i.e., productivity decrement), capital suffered the decrement in its income, which is large than the total productivity decrement of the industry. This implies that labour enjoyed significant positive gain during the periods, at the expense of the capital. In the periods of positive productivity gains capital appropriated the major part of productivity gain (around 80%) as shown in the Table 5.7 (seventh and eighth five year plan period). Here , it is worthwhile to note that the capital contributed a large part of incremental input over the entire period as well as in each of the plans but, as observed earlier, it had a positive share in productivity gains during seventh and eighth five years plan period. Here also, share of capital in productivity gain is less than its share in incremental input as shown in Table 5.7.

Table 5.7 : Factor's Share in Productivity Gains: Paper and Paperboard Industry

(Value in Rs.'00000)

Period	Change in Income	Change in Facor Input	Productivity Gains (G_T)	Change in Labour Income	Change in Labour Input	Productivity Gains (G_L)	Change in Capital Income	Change in Capital Input	Productivity Gains (G_K)
1	2	3	4	5	6	7	8	9	10
73-95	29057	30880 (100)	-1823 *(100)*	5466	2946 (9.5)	2521 *(138.3)*	23591	27934 (90.5)	–4344 *(–238.3)*
73-84	5591	12717 (100)	-7125 *(100)*	1570	1920 (15.1)	–350 *(4.9)*	4021	10797 (84.9)	–6776 *(95.1)*
85-95	26572	20100 (100)	6472 *(100)*	3821	1437 (7.2)	2384 *(36.8)*	22751	18663 (92.9)	4088 *(63.2)*
73-78	1970	3305 (100)	-1335 *(100)*	1006	809 (24.5)	197 *(-14.8)*	963	2495 (75.5)	-1532 *(114.8)*
80-84	3026	6345 (100)	-3319 *(100)*	418	302 (4.8)	116 *(–3.5)*	2607	6042 (95.2)	–3435 *(103.5)*
85-89	12256	5631 (100)	6625 *(100)*	1493	199 (3.5)	1293 *(19.5)*	10763	5432 (96.5)	5332 *(80.5)*
90-95	10556	11823 (100)	-1267 *(100)*	1745	895 (7.6)	850 *(–67.1)*	8811	10928 (92.4)	–2117 *(167.1)*
92-95	17103	8740 (100)	8363 *(100)*	2145	525 (6.0)	1620 *(19.4)*	14958	8215 (94.0)	6744 *(80.6)*

Source : Computed from Table 5.9 as explained in methodology.

Notes: 1. Col 4 = Col 3 – Col 2;
Col 7 = Col 5 – Col 6;
Col 10 = Col 9 – Col 8.

2. Figures in brackets are the percentage share of respective factors in productivity gains and incremental input.

3. The table may not be internally consistent due to rounding off of values.

Table 5.8 : Factor's Share in Total Input, Net Distributable Output and Relative Factor Prices: Paper and Paperboard Industry

Year	% Share in Input		Relative Factor Price		% Share in NDO	
	Labour (L/I)	Capital (K/I)	Labour (P_L/P_F)	Capital (P_K/P_F)	Labour (W/V)	Capital (R/V)
1	2	3	4	5	6	7
1973-74	35.96	64.04	100.00	100.00	35.96	64.04
1974-75	34.76	65.24	69.72	116.13	24.23	75.77
1975-76	33.90	66.10	85.15	107.62	28.87	71.13
1976-77	33.07	66.93	102.65	98.69	33.94	66.06
1977-78	34.75	65.25	106.32	96.64	36.95	63.05
1978-79	33.08	66.92	116.30	91.94	38.47	61.53
1979-80	33.90	66.10	109.16	95.30	37.01	62.99
1980-81	31.81	68.19	118.82	91.22	37.80	62.20
1981-82	31.14	68.86	124.10	89.10	38.64	61.36
1982-83	30.92	69.08	178.61	64.81	55.23	44.77
1983-84	27.16	72.84	163.45	76.34	44.40	55.60
1984-85	24.22	75.78	136.72	88.26	33.11	66.89
1985-86	24.50	75.50	171.60	76.77	42.04	57.96
1986-87	22.62	77.38	152.07	84.78	34.40	65.60
1987-88	22.56	77.44	184.23	75.46	41.56	58.44
1988-89	19.32	80.68	169.42	83.38	32.73	67.27
1989-90	20.01	79.99	135.81	91.04	27.17	72.83
1990-91	19.36	80.64	132.36	92.23	25.63	74.37
1991-92	18.93	81.07	152.49	87.74	28.87	71.13
1992-93	18.65	81.35	168.78	84.23	31.48	68.52
1993-94	17.52	82.48	183.12	82.35	32.08	67.92
1994-95	14.03	85.97	193.14	84.80	27.10	72.90
1995-96	15.94	84.06	145.29	91.41	23.16	76.84

Source: Computed from Table 5.9 as follows:

Col 2 = Col 8/Col 5; Col 3 = Col 11/Col 5;

Col 4 = Col 9/Col 6; Col 5 = Col 12/Col 6;

Col 6 = Col 2*Col 5/100; Col 7 = Col 3*Col 5/100

The mechanism of transfer of productivity increment may be clearly illustrated from the data on variations in prices of labour and capital relative to the price of product presented in Table 5.9. It may be noted that the total factor price moved faster than product price in

Table 5.9: Net Distributable Output (NDO), Factor Input, Product Prices and Factor Prices: Paper and Paperboard Industry

(Value in Rs.'00000)

Year	NDO Current Prices	NDO Constant Prices	Product Price Index	Total Factor Input	Factor Price Index (P_T)	Labour Income Current Prices	Labour Income at base rate	Labour Price Index (P_L)	Capital Income Current Prices	Capital Income at base rate	Capital Price Index (P_K)
1	2	3	4	5	6	7	8	9	10	11	12
73-74	9878	9878	100.0	9878	100.0	3552	3552	100	6326	6326	100.0
74-75	19028	13303	143.0	10637	178.9	4611	3697	124.7	14417	6940	207.7
75-76	17099	12020	142.3	11113	153.9	4936	3767	131.0	12163	7346	165.6
76-77	15084	10821	139.4	11734	128.6	5120	3880	132.0	9964	7854	126.9
77-78	17079	11960	142.8	12957	131.8	6310	4503	140.1	10769	8455	127.4
78-79	17973	11848	151.7	13183	136.3	6915	4361	158.6	11058	8821	125.4
79-80	22714	12362	183.8	14488	156.8	8406	4912	171.1	14308	9576	149.4
80-81	25253	12444	202.9	16250	155.4	9546	5170	184.7	15707	11080	141.8
81-82	28425	13014	218.4	17451	162.9	10983	5434	202.1	17442	12018	145.1
82-83	21155	9120	232.0	19190	110.2	11684	5934	196.9	9471	13256	71.4
83-84	28879	11452	252.2	20483	141.0	12822	5564	230.4	16057	14919	107.6
84-85	43522	15469	281.4	22595	192.6	14411	5472	263.4	29111	17123	170.0
85-86	36200	12363	292.8	20659	175.2	15218	5061	300.7	20982	15598	134.5

conti.

1	2	3	4	5	6	7	8	9	10	11	12
86-87	49363	16245	303.9	22824	216.3	16981	5163	328.9	32382	17661	183.4
87-88	48188	15342	314.1	23916	201.5	20028	5396	371.2	28160	18520	152.1
88-89	59665	17927	332.8	25903	230.3	19528	5004	390.3	40137	20899	192.1
89-90	94705	24619	384.7	26290	360.2	25735	5260	489.2	68970	21029	328.0
90-91	116415	28379	410.2	28935	402.5	29835	5603	532.5	86580	23332	371.1
91-92	118748	24626	482.2	30269	392.3	34283	5731	598.2	84465	24538	344.2
92-93	125380	21832	574.3	32018	391.6	39474	5972	661.0	85906	26046	329.8
93-94	135098	22321	605.3	33566	402.5	43333	5879	737.0	91765	27686	331.4
94-95	188268	30908	609.1	43672	431.1	51013	6127	832.6	137255	37545	365.6
95-96	268807	38935	690.4	40758	659.5	62262	6498	958.2	206545	34260	602.9

Notes: 1. Compared from Appendix tables
2. Col 4 = Col 3/Col 2; Col 6 = Col 2/Col 5; Col 9 = Col 7/Col 8; Col 12 = Col 10/Col 11.

last two plan periods whereas, in rest of the period and entire first sub-period total factor price moved slower than product price which correspond to the periods of productivity decrement. Labour price moved faster than the price of product over the entire period and in each of plan periods, this is clearly reflected in positive productivity gains accruing to labour in each period. The price of capital moved slower than the product price up to 1987-88 but rather that P_k moved faster than product price so as to enable it to appropriate nearly all the productivity gains of the period.

The trends in average share of labour and capital in the divisible pool of output as well as in total factor input shows that the share of labour in input basket is continuously declining. The data set out in Table 5.8 indicates that labour is much less important than capital as an input in the industry. Its share in base year in combined factor input was 35.96 per cent and steadily declined over the period so that it was only 14.03 per cent in 1994-95. Share of capital on the other hand increased from 64.04 per cent to 85.97 per cent in 1994-95. The trends in relative factor price shows that relative price of labour has been rising and its share in the input has been declining whereas, the relative price of capital has been declining and its share in input basket has been increasing. This conforms to a pattern expected on the basis of a competitive model.[15] The factor's share in divisible output shows that except the first three years the share of labour has been more than its share in total input. This can be clearly seen from the Chart 5.3. Average share of capital in net distributable output has been around 66 per cent that is significantly lower than its average share in total factor input (around 73 per cent). Such a trend would obviously prejudice the step up in the rate of investment in the industry through the plough back of internal funds.

5.4.4 Fertilisers and Pesticides Industry

Data on productivity gains and their sharing between labour and capital in fertilisers and pesticides industry are presented in Table 5.10. The total gains for period 1973-74 to 1995-96 amounted to Rs. 62629 lakh out of which about 83.9 per cent are appropriated by capital alone and labour got only 16.1 per cent. For both sub-periods also capital appropriated most of the increase in productivity (81.5 per cent and 87.2 per cent respectively for the first and second half). This has been a general trend in all the plan periods. In period 1990-91 to 1995-96, out of total productivity gains of Rs. 35,345 lakh capital has got Rs. 35,786

CHART-5.3

Labour's Share in Input (L/I) and Net Distributable Output (W/V) : Paper and Paperboard Industry

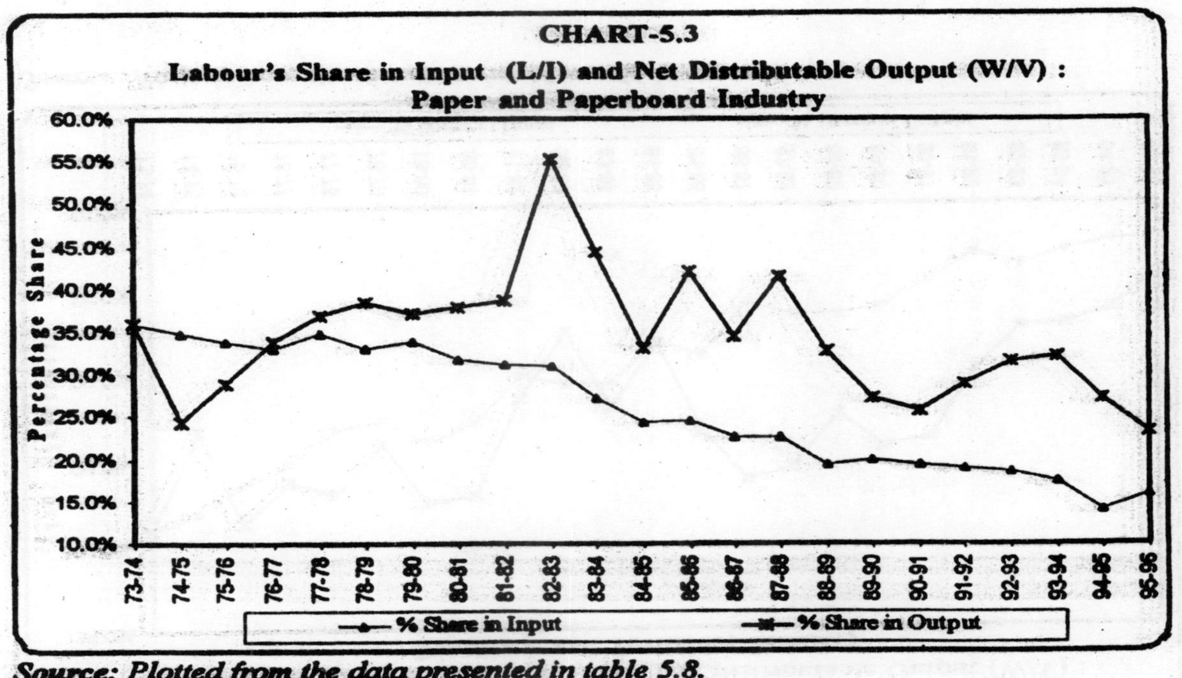

Source: Plotted from the data presented in table 5.8.

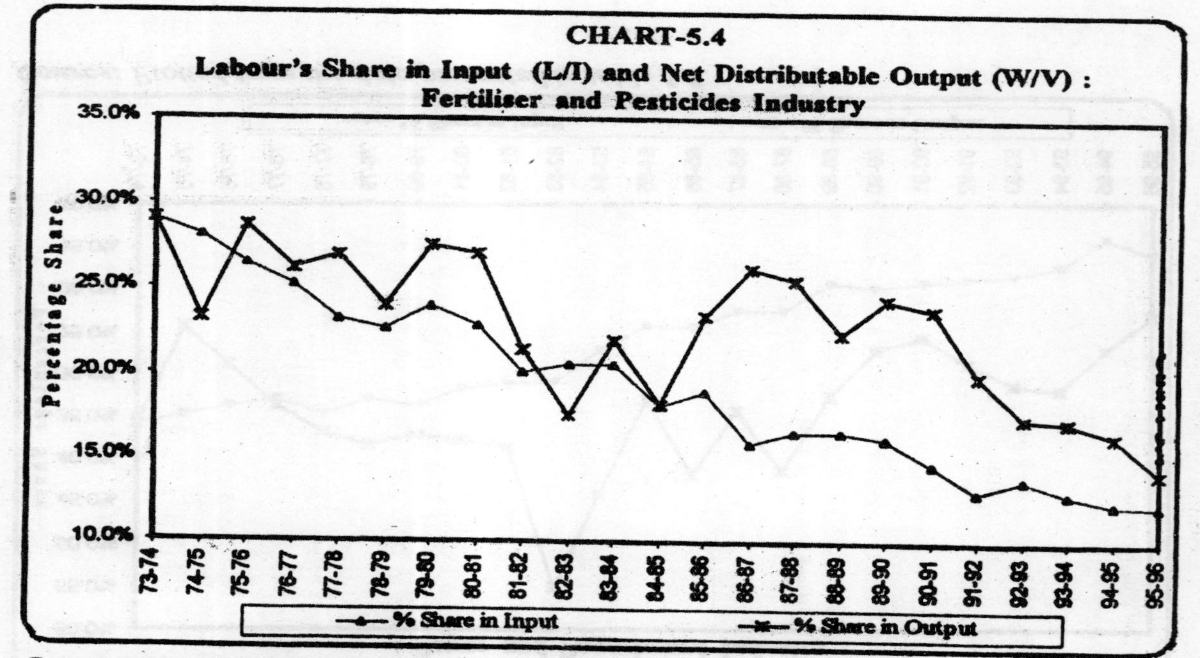

CHART-5.4

Labour's Share in Input (L/I) and Net Distributable Output (W/V) : Fertiliser and Pesticides Industry

Source: Plotted from the data presented in table 5.11.

lakh, this means that labour has to suffer a loss of Rs. 440 lakh. This is the case when worker have failed to secure a positive share in productivity gains. However, when we look at the respective share of factor input in incremental input, we find that share of labour in productivity gains has been more than its share in incremental input. For the entire period labour accounted for only 7.9% of the incremental input whereas, it has obtained 16.1% of productivity gains. Same trend is

Table 5.10 : Factor's Share in Productivity Gains: Fertilisers and Pesticides Industry

(Value in Rs.'00000)

Period	Change in Income	Change in Factor Input	Productivity Gains (G_T)	Change in Labour Income	Change in Labour Input	Productivity Gains (G_L)	Change in Capital Income	Change in Capital Input	Productivity Gains (G_K)
1	2	3	4	5	6	7	8	9	10
73-95	113287	50658 (100)	62629 *(100)*	14043	3994 (7.9)	10049 *(16.1)*	99244	46664 (92.1)	52580 *(83.9)*
73-84	27760	15506 (100)	12254 *(100)*	3645	1383 (8.9)	2261 *(18.5)*	24115	14123 (91.1)	9993 *(81.5)*
85-95	88895	32363 (100)	56532 *(100)*	9054	1826 (5.6)	7228 *(12.8)*	79841	30537 (94.4)	49304 *(87.2)*
73-78	9148	7886 (100)	1262 *(100)*	1535	963 (12.2)	572 *(45.3)*	7613	6923 (87.8)	690 *(54.7)*
80-84	21222	2866 (100)	18356 *(100)*	2131	-705 (-24.6)	2836 *(15.5)*	19091	3571 (124.6)	15520 *(82.6)*
85-89	25162	11913 (100)	13249 *(100)*	6464	1059 (8.9)	5405 *(40.8)*	18698	10854 (91.1)	7844 *(59.2)*
90-95	55153	19808 (100)	35345 *(100)*	888	1328 (6.7)	-440 *(-1.3)*	54265	18480 (93.3)	35786 *(101.3)*
92-95	42251	9640 (100)	32612 *(100)*	3243	325 (3.4)	2918 *(9.0)*	39008	9315 (96.6)	29693 *(91.1)*
92-95	17103	8740 (100)	8363 *(100)*	2145	525 (6.0)	1620 *(19.4)*	14958	8215 (94.0)	6744 *(80.6)*

Source: Computed from Table 5.3 as explained in methodology.

Notes: 1. Col 4 = Col 3 – Col 2;
Col 7 = Col 5 – Col 6;
Col 10 = Col 9 – Col 8.

2. Figures in brackets are the percentage share of respective factors in productivity gains and incremental input.
3. The table may not be internally consistent due to rounding off of values.

Table 5.11 : Factor's Share in Total Input, Net Distributable Out-put and Relative Factor Prices: Fertilisers and Pesticides Industry

Year	% Share in Input		Relative Factor Price		% Share in NDO	
	Labour (L/I)	Capital (K/I)	Labour (P_L/P_F)	Capital (P_K/P_F)	Labour (W/V)	Capital (R/V)
1	2	3	4	5	6	7
1973-74	29.07	70.93	100.00	100.00	29.07	70.93
1974-75	28.09	71.91	82.61	106.79	23.20	76.80
1975-76	26.45	73.55	108.32	97.01	28.65	71.35
1976-77	25.19	74.81	103.90	98.69	26.17	73.83
1977-78	23.19	76.81	116.28	95.08	26.97	73.03
1978-79	22.66	77.34	105.74	98.32	23.96	76.04
1979-80	24.02	75.98	114.72	95.35	27.56	72.44
1980-81	22.85	77.15	118.52	94.52	27.08	72.92
1981-82	20.02	79.98	106.72	98.32	21.36	78.64
1982-83	20.49	79.51	85.30	103.79	17.48	82.52
1983-84	20.50	79.50	107.26	98.13	21.98	78.02
1984-85	18.05	81.95	100.68	99.85	18.17	81.83
1985-86	18.95	81.05	123.62	94.48	23.42	76.58
1986-87	15.89	84.11	165.08	87.71	26.22	73.78
1987-88	16.48	83.52	154.58	89.23	25.48	74.52
1988-89	16.50	83.50	135.67	92.95	22.38	77.62
1989-90	16.16	83.84	150.56	90.25	24.34	75.66
1990-91	14.64	85.36	162.49	89.28	23.79	76.21
1991-92	12.97	87.03	152.86	92.12	19.83	80.17
1992-93	13.74	86.26	126.08	95.85	17.33	82.67
1993-94	12.84	87.16	133.71	95.03	17.17	82.83
1994-95	12.30	87.70	132.73	95.41	16.33	83.67
1995-96	12.17	87.83	115.83	97.81	14.09	85.91

Source : Computed from Table 5.12 as follows:

Col 2 = Col 8/Col 5; Col 3 = Col 11/Col 5;

Col 4 = Col 9/Col 6; Col 5 = Col 12/Col 6;

Col 6 = Col 2*Col 5/100; Col 7 = Col 3*Col 5/100

Table 5.12 : Net Distributable Output (NDO), Factor Input, Product Prices and Factor Prices: Fertilisers and Pesticides Industry

(Value in Rs.'00000)

Year	NDO Current Prices	NDO Constant Prices	Product Price Index	Total Factor Input	Factor Price Index (P_T)	Labour Income Current Prices	Labour Income at base rate	Labour Price Index (P_L)	Capital Income Current Prices	Capital Income at base rate	Capital Price Index (P_K)
1	2	3	4	5	6	7	8	9	10	11	12
73-74	12833	12833	100.00	128333	100.00	3731	3731	100.00	9102	9102	100.00
74-75	21755	12206	178.23	14591	149.10	5048	4098	123.17	16707	10493	159.22
75-76	21541	11428	188.50	16694	129.03	6172	4416	139.77	15369	12278	125.17
76-77	22703	13865	163.74	17204	131.96	5941	4333	137.11	16762	12871	130.23
77-78	24465	15708	155.75	19192	127.48	6598	4451	148.24	17867	14741	121.21
78-79	33811	21981	153.82	20719	163.19	8100	4694	172.56	25711	16025	160.44
79-80	35943	24485	146.80	25516	140.86	9905	6130	161.59	26038	19387	134.31
80-81	41276	19371	213.08	25473	162.04	11176	5819	192.05	30100	19653	153.15
81-82	56988	23724	240.21	26620	214.08	12173	5328	228.47	44815	21292	210.48
82-83	73054	29963	243.81	26584	274.8	12768	5447	234.41	60286	21137	285.21
83-84	76981	32778	234.86	29885	257.59	16924	6125	276.29	60057	23760	252.76
84-85	93552	40593	230.47	28339	330.12	16998	5114	332.38	76554	23225	329.62

conti.

1	2	3	4	5	6	7	8	9	10	11	12
85-86	87229	37225	234.33	31128	280.23	20432	5898	346.4	66797	25230	264.75
86-87	86676	34184	253.56	32774	264.47	22730	5206	436.58	63946	27568	231.96
87-88	108306	40713	266.02	34889	310.43	27597	5751	479.87	80709	29138	276.99
88-89	132042	52040	253.73	37881	348.57	29555	6250	472.91	102487	31632	324.01
89-90	158844	62387	254.61	43041	369.05	38659	6958	555.64	120185	36084	333.07
90-91	180688	70967	254.61	43683	413.63	42993	6397	672.13	137695	37287	369.29
91-92	231959	72783	318.7	47435	489.00	45999	6154	747.51	185960	41282	450.46
92-93	346815	83869	413.52	53852	644.02	60086	7400	811.99	286729	46452	617.26
93-94	341200	72913	467.95	53387	639.1	58575	6854	854.57	282625	46533	607.37
94-95	483350	96080	503.07	60925	793.35	78913	7494	1052.97	404437	53431	756.93
95-96	683033	126120	541.57	63491	1075.79	96258	7725	1246.09	586775	55766	1052.2

Notes:
1. Computed from Appendix tables
2. Col 4 = Col 3/Col 2; Col 6 = Col 2/Col 5;
   Col 9 = Col 7/Col 8; Col 12 = Col 10/Col 11.

observed in both sub-periods and plan periods except for period 1990-91 to 1995-96, where labour, in spite of accounting for more than 6.7 per cent of increase in incremental input, has to suffer loss. But during seventh five year plan period labour has enjoyed 15.5 per cent of productivity gains even when its share in incremental input was negative.

The trends in relative sharing of productivity gains can also be understood with the help of indexes of product and factor prices given in Table 5.12. The index of product price has increased faster than the index of total factor price (column 4 and 6 of Table 5.12). The labour price index has moved faster than capital price index for the whole period. The data on average factor share in total factor input and net distributable output presented in Table 5.11 shows, that the share of labour in input basket was 29.07 per cent in the base year, which by continuous decline fell to 12.17 per cent in 1995-96. *This falling trend in the share of labour in total factor input indicates that importance of labour as an input in the industry is decreasing over time, i.e., the industry is getting more and more capital intensive.* The share of capital has steadily increased from 70.93 per cent in the base year to 87.83 per cent in terminal year. Average share of labour in net distributable output (22.7 per cent) has been more than its average share in total input (19.3 per cent). The movement of relative factor price shows that relative price of labour has been above 100 throughout, except in the years of 1973-74 and 1982-83. *This implies that share of labour in net distributable output has been more than its share in total factor input, i.e., sharing of output on the whole was relatively favourable to wage income.* This can also be seen from the comparison of labour's share in input with its share in net distributable output, depicted in Chart 6.4, where except few exceptions, the share of labour in output has been more than its share in input.

5.4.5 Motor Vehicles Industry

The total productivity gains and their distribution among labour and capital in the industry are given in Table 5.13. Table 5.13 shows that labour gained, over the entire period, 25.6 per cent of productivity gains and the share of capital was remaining 74.4 per cent. But, the gains accruing to labour has been very high in the first half as labour appropriated 71.6 per cent of productivity gains whereas, in the second half gains accruing to labour has been only 21.8 per cent of productivity gains. The pattern of distribution of gains during plan period shows that during fifth and eighth five year plan period, the share of labour at 21.4 per cent and 17.6 per cent was less than the share of capital whereas, during sixth and seventh plan labour gained more (66.9 per cent and 61.4 per cent of total gains) than capital. The situation will be more clear when we look at the share of labour and capital in incremental input. The share of labour in incremental input over the entire period was 16.8 per cent and it gained 25.6 per cent of incremental productivity whereas, capital, which accounted for the 83.2 per cent of increased input, got only 74.4 per cent of productivity gains.

Table 5.13 : Factor's Share in Productivity Gains: Motor Vehicles Industry

(Value in Rs.'00000)

Period	Change in Income	Change in Facor Input	Productivity Gains (G_T)	Change in Labour Income	Change in Labour Input	Productivity Gains (G_L)	Change in Capital Income	Change in Capital Input	Productivity Gains (G_K)
1	2	3	4	5	6	7	8	9	10
73-95	98094	49265 (100)	48828 (*100*)	20767	8269 (16.8)	12498 (*25.6*)	77326	40997 (83.2)	36330 (*74.4*)
73-84	16474	13231 (100)	3243 (*100*)	5837	3516 (26.6)	2320 (*71.6*)	10637	9715 (73.4)	923 (*28.5*)
85-95	81466	33545 (100)	47921 (*100*)	14832	4405 (13.1)	10426 (*21.8*)	66634	29140 (86.9)	37494 (*78.2*)
73-78	6312	4168 (100)	2143 (*100*)	1730	1270 (30.5)	460 (*21.4*)	4582	2898 (69.5)	1684 (*78.6*)
80-84	11975	5560 (100)	6415 (*100*)	4842	553 (10.0)	4289 (*66.9*)	7133	5007 (90.1)	2126 (*33.2*)
85-89	8597	6252 (100)	2345 (*100*)	1681	242 (3.9)	1439 (*61.4*)	6916	6010 (96.1)	905 (*38.6*)
90-95	66190	24333 (100)	41858 (*100*)	12693	3577 (14.7)	9116 (*21.8*)	53497	20755 (85.3)	32741 (*78.2*)
92-95	67319	18089 (100)	49229 (*100*)	11642	3002 (16.6)	8639 (*17.6*)	55677	15087 (83.4)	40590 (*82.5*)

Source: Computed from table 5.15 as explained in methodology.

Notes: 1. Col 4 = Col 3 – Col 2;
Col 7 = Col 5 – Col 6;
Col 10 = Col 9 – Col 8.

2. *Figures in brackets are the percentage share of respective factors in productivity gains and incremental input.*

3. *The table may not be internally consistent due to rounding off of values.*

Table 5.14 : Factor's Share in Total Input, Net Distributable Output and Relative Factor Prices: Motor Vehicles Industry

Year	% Share in Input		Relative Factor Price		% Share in NDO	
	Labour (L/I)	Capital (K/I)	Labour (P_L/P_F)	Capital (P_K/P_F)	Labour (W/V)	Capital (R/V)
1	2	3	4	5	6	7
1973-74	49.02	50.98	100.00	100.00	49.02	50.98
1974-75	48.01	51.99	99.53	100.44	47.78	52.22
1975-76	46.85	53.15	101.08	99.05	47.36	52.64
1976-77	45.98	54.02	88.86	109.48	40.86	59.14
1977-78	45.51	54.49	91.72	106.92	41.74	58.26
1978-79	45.35	54.65	95.14	104.03	43.15	56.85
1979-80	46.78	53.22	95.23	104.19	44.55	55.45
1980-81	45.78	54.22	94.74	104.44	43.37	56.63
1981-82	44.84	55.16	83.18	113.68	37.30	62.70
1982-83	44.17	55.83	69.44	124.18	30.67	69.33
1983-84	40.76	59.24	99.31	100.48	40.48	59.52
1984-85	39.17	60.83	108.03	94.83	42.32	57.68
1985-86	37.25	62.75	113.87	91.76	42.42	57.58
1986-87	35.91	64.09	109.27	94.81	39.24	60.76
1987-88	33.84	66.16	128.77	85.29	43.57	56.43
1988-89	33.61	66.39	115.31	92.25	38.76	61.24
1989-90	31.88	68.12	118.41	91.38	37.75	62.25
1990-91	31.03	68.97	108.05	96.38	33.53	66.47
1991-92	29.38	70.62	122.32	90.72	35.93	64.07
1992-93	28.20	71.80	129.53	88.40	36.52	63.48
1993-94	26.22	73.78	131.33	88.93	34.39	65.61
1994-95	26.77	73.23	119.93	92.72	32.10	67.90
1995-96	25.03	74.97	100.97	99.68	25.27	74.73

Source : *Computed from Table 5.15 as follows:*

Col 2 = Col 8/Col 5; *Col 3 = Col 11/Col 5;*

Col 4 = Col 9/Col 6; *Col 5 = Col 12/Col 6;*

*Col 6 = Col 2*Col 5/100;* *Col 7 = Col 3*Col 5/100*

The data presented in Table 5.13 shows that the sharing of productivity gains is relatively favourable to labour over the entire period (i.e., labour got more than its share in input) except in the fifth plan period where labour's share in productivity gains (21.4%) is less than its share in incremental input (30.5%). Capital has to suffer in sixth and seventh five year plan period, as despite of accounting for most of the increase in input (90.1% and 96.1%) it has obtained only 33.2% and 38.6% of the productivity gains. The respective share of labour and capital in productivity gains can also be explained with the help of change in factor and product prices. Table 5.15 shows labour and capital prices have increased by more than 11.6 and 10.6 times whereas, product price have increased by 6.6 times only. This indicates positive share of labour and capital in productivity gains. As far as, distribution of gains among labour and capital is concerned, a rise in the price of one factor, relative to the other, means relatively more share in productivity gains. As in fifth and eighth five year plans, the price of capital risen faster than labour and the share of labour was less than capital for the period.

Table 5.14 shows the actual share of labour and capital in total input & output and their annual movements. The share of labour in total input has been gradually declining from 49.02 per cent to 25.03 per cent in 1995-96 while, that of capital has risen from 50.98 per cent to 74.97 per cent. *It indicates that the importance of labour in total input to the industry has been continuously decreasing.* Chart 5.5 shows that share of labour in input has been more than its share in output up to 1983-84 but thereafter the trend has reversed. The relative factor price does not show any consistent trend over the period. The labour price index has been less than capital price index up to 1983-84, except 1975-76 and thereafter, the price of labour has been more than the price of capital. The last two columns of the table shows that the share of labour in total output has decline from 49.02 per cent to 25.27 per cent while share of capital has increased from 50.98 per cent to 74.73 per cent. *The sharing of net distributable output between labour and capital has its obvious significance for capital accumulation in the industry. Evidently, if it is desired to accelerate the expansion of the industry through plough back of internal funds, the share of capital in net distributable has to be higher than its share in total factor input.* Such a situation prevailed in the industry up to 1983-84 but thereafter the share of capital in net distributable output found to be lower than its share in total input.

Table 5.15: Net Distributable Output (NDO), Factor Input, Product Prices and Factor Prices: Motor Vehicles Industry

(Value in Rs.'00000)

Year	NDO Current Prices	NDO Constant Prices	Product Price Index	Total Factor Input	Factor Price Index (P_T)	Labour Income Current Prices	Labour Income at base rate	Labour Price Index (P_L)	Capital Income Current Prices	Capital Income at base rate	Capital Price Index (P_K)
1	2	3	4	5	6	7	8	9	10	11	12
73-74	16927	16927	100	16927	100.00	8297	8297	100	8630	8630	100.00
74-75	21578	16950	127.3	17694	122.0	10311	8495	121.38	11267	9198	122.49
75-76	23465	16821	139.5	18595	126.2	11112	8712	127.55	12353	9883	124.99
76-77	28651	21001	136.43	19187	149.3	11707	8823	132.69	16944	10364	163.48
77-78	30212	21646	139.58	19827	152.4	12610	9023	139.76	17602	10804	162.92
78-79	35324	23239	152.01	21095	167.5	15241	9567	159.31	20083	11528	174.21
79-80	39332	20804	189.06	23664	166.2	17524	11071	158.29	21808	12593	173.18
80-81	46881	21426	218.8	24598	190.6	20331	11260	180.56	26550	13338	199.06
81-82	68562	27533	249.02	26392	259.8	25574	11835	216.08	42988	14556	295.32
82-83	101648	39533	257.12	28656	354.7	31180	12658	246.33	70468	15998	440.99
83-84	81276	31952	254.37	28556	284.6	32902	11640	282.65	48374	16916	285.97
84-85	89088	33401	266.72	30158	295.4	37698	11813	319.11	51390	18345	280.14

conti.

1	2	3	4	5	6	7	8	9	10	11	12
85-86	103331	33555	307.95	32647	316.5	43828	12160	360.42	59503	20487	290.44
86-87	122883	38075	322.74	34674	354.4	48215	12451	387.23	74668	22223	335.99
87-88	116095	33750	343.98	34687	334.7	50586	11737	430.98	65509	22950	285.44
88-89	151597	39277	385.97	37924	399.7	58761	12748	460.95	92836	25177	368.74
89-90	181500	42152	430.59	38900	466.6	68521	12402	552.49	112979	26498	426.38
90-91	228675	48830	468.3	41860	546.3	76665	12988	590.25	152010	28871	526.51
91-92	243604	46630	522.42	43936	554.5	87532	12906	678.2	156072	31030	502.98
92-93	267970	47702	561.76	48103	557.1	97873	13563	721.6	170097	34539	492.47
93-94	307066	53536	573.56	51260	599.0	105599	13443	785.55	201467	37817	532.74
94-95	415725	67655	614.48	55057	755.1	133455	14737	905.56	282270	40320	700.08
95-96	758788	115021	659.7	66192	1146.3	191735	16566	1157.42	567053	49627	1142.64

Notes: 1. Computed from Appendix tables

2. Col 4 = Col 3/Col 2; Col 6 = Col 2/Col 5;
Col 9 = Col 7/Col 8; Col 12 = Col 10/Col 11.

CHART-5.5

Labour's Share in Input (L/I) and Net Distributable Output (W/V) : Motor Vehicles Industry

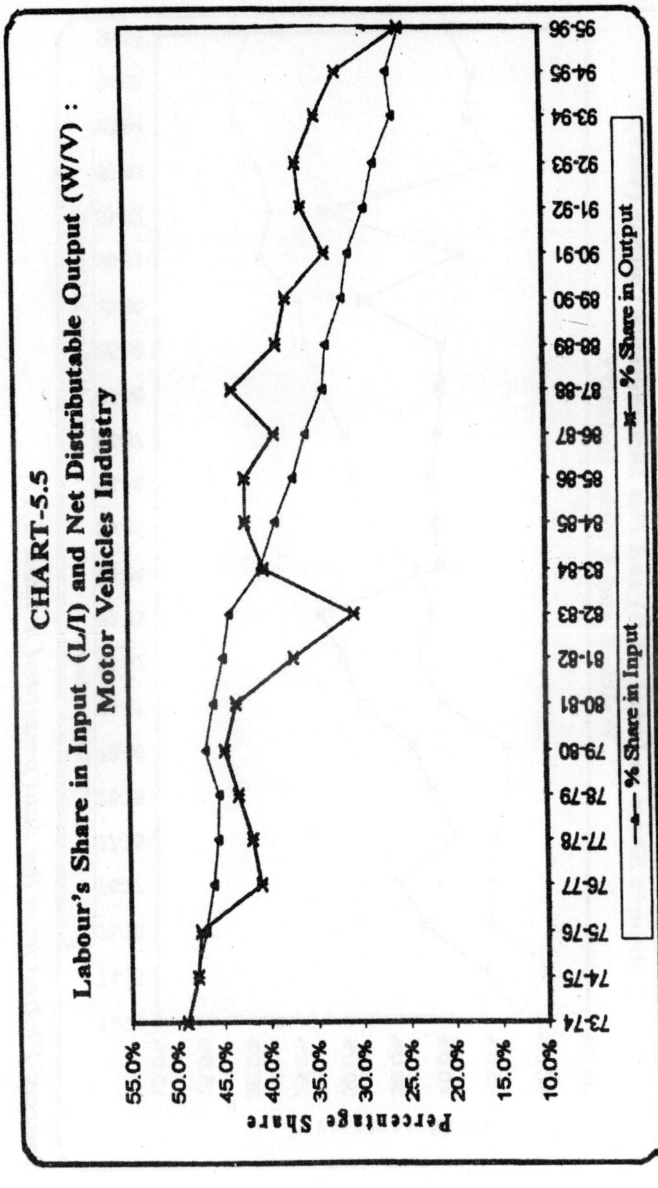

Source: Plotted from the data presented in table 5.14.

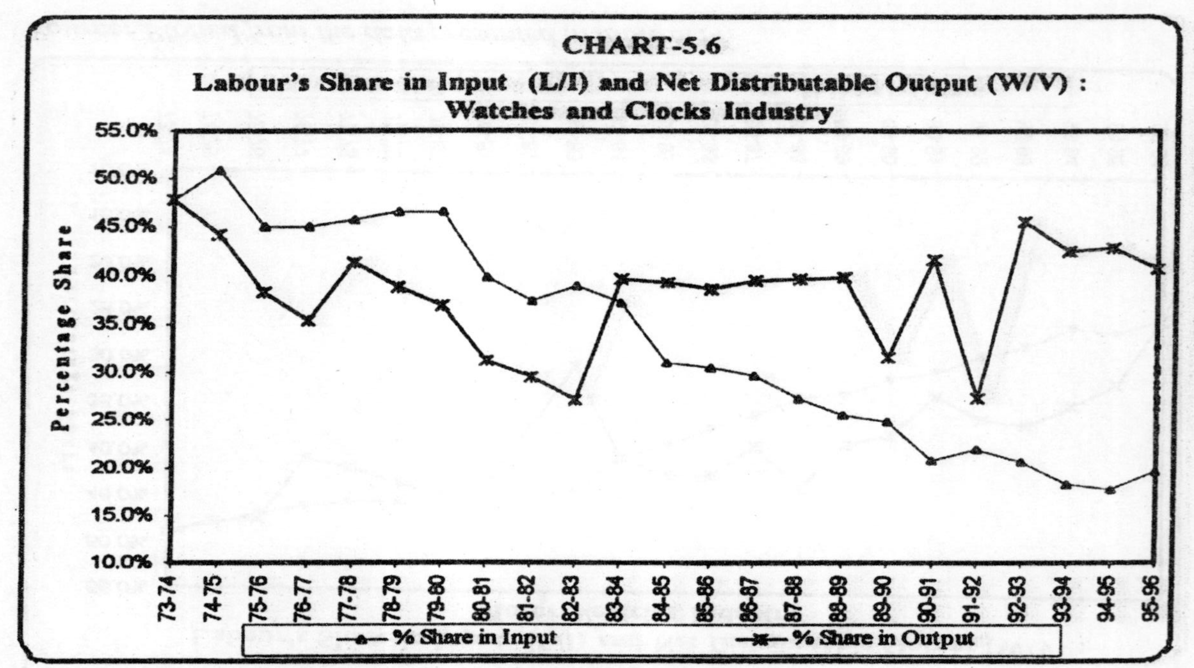

Source: Plotted from the data presented in table 5.17.

5.4.6 Watches and Clocks Industry

The total productivity gains and their distribution among labour and capital in the industry are set out in Table 5.16. Table shows that labour gained, over entire period, 69.9 per cent of productivity gains and the remaining 30.1% went to capital. The share of capital in gains has been more than that of labour in all plan periods, except sixth five year plan period. During sixth five year plan capital has suffered a loss (-6.3%) whereas, labour has gained more than the total gains. The analysis will be more meaningful when their (labour and capital) respective share in incremental productivity is compared with their share in incremental

Table 5.16 : Factor's Share in Productivity Gains: Watches and Clocks Industry

(Value in Rs.'00000)

Period	Change in Income	Change in Facor Input	Productivity Gains (G_T)	Change in Labour Income	Change in Labour Input	Productivity Gains (G_L)	Change in Capital Income	Change in Capital Input	Productivity Gains (G_K)
1	2	3	4	5	6	7	8	9	10
73-95	10221	5679 (100)	4542 *(100)*	4100	924 (16.3)	3175 *(69.9)*	6121	4755 (83.7)	1366 *(30.1)*
73-84	2911	1400 (100)	1510 *(100)*	1085	326 (23.3)	760 *(50.3)*	1825	1075 (76.8)	751 *(49.7)*
85-95	6784	4087 (100)	2697 *(100)*	2837	552 (13.5)	2284 *(84.7)*	3947	3535 (86.5)	413 *(15.3)*
73-78	944	385 (100)	559 *(100)*	306	172 (44.7)	134 *(24.0)*	638	213 (55.3)	425 *(76.0)*
80-84	1092	534 (100)	558 *(100)*	626	34 (6.3)	593 *(106.3)*	465	500 (93.7)	-35 *(-6.3)*
85-89	3134	1659 (100)	1475 *(100)*	700	286 (17.3)	413 *(28.0)*	2434	1372 (82.7)	1062 *(72.0)*
90-95	5092	2562 (100)	2530 *(100)*	2001	457 (17.9)	1544 *(61.0)*	3091	2105 (82.1)	966 *(39.0)*
92-95	4537	1548 (100)	2989 *(100)*	1521	254 (16.4)	1267 *(42.4)*	3016	1294 (83.6)	1721 *(57.6)*

Source: Computed from Table 5.18 as explained in methodology.

Notes: 1. Col 4 = Col 3 – Col 2;
Col 7 = Col 5 – Col 6;
Col 10 = Col 9 – Col 8.

2. Figures in brackets are the percentage share of respective factors in productivity gains and incremental input.

3. *The table may not be internally consistent due to rounding off of values.*

Table 5.17 : Factor's Share in Total Input, Net Distributable Output and Relative Factor Prices: Watches and Cocks Industry

Year	% Share in Input		Relative Factor Price		% Share in NDO	
	Labour (L/I)	Capital (K/I)	Labour (P_L/P_F)	Capital (P_K/P_F)	Labour (W/V)	Capital (R/V)
1	2	3	4	5	6	7
1973-74	47.74	52.26	100	100	47.74	52.26
1974-75	50.93	49.07	86.68	113.82	44.15	55.85
1975-76	45.01	54.99	84.91	112.35	38.22	61.78
1976-77	45.11	54.89	78.26	117.87	35.31	64.69
1977-78	45.69	54.31	90.31	108.15	41.26	58.74
1978-79	46.61	53.39	83.16	114.7	38.76	61.24
1979-80	46.56	53.44	79.24	118.09	36.89	63.11
1980-81	39.79	60.21	78.54	114.18	31.25	68.75
1981-82	37.45	62.55	78.67	112.27	29.46	70.54
1982-83	38.92	61.08	69.6	119.37	27.09	72.91
1983-84	37.24	62.76	106.54	96.12	39.68	60.32
1984-85	31.13	68.87	126.03	88.24	39.23	60.77
1985-86	30.53	69.47	126.18	88.5	38.52	61.48
1986-87	29.66	70.34	132.85	86.15	39.41	60.59
1987-88	27.29	72.71	144.95	83.13	39.56	60.44
1988-89	25.54	74.46	155.74	80.88	39.78	60.22
1989-90	24.91	75.09	126.48	91.22	31.51	68.49
1990-91	20.73	79.27	201.15	73.55	41.69	58.31
1991-92	21.9	78.1	124.65	93.09	27.29	72.71
1992-93	20.59	79.41	221.50	68.5	45.61	54.39
1993-94	18.21	81.79	233.22	70.35	42.46	57.54
1994-95	17.64	82.36	242.82	69.41	42.84	57.16
1995-96	19.57	80.43	207.35	73.88	40.57	59.43

Source: Computed from Table 5.18 as follows:

Col 2 = Col 8/Col 5; Col 3 = Col 11/Col 5;
Col 4 = Col 9/Col 6; Col 5 = Col 12/Col 6;
Col 6 = Col 2*Col 5/100; Col 7 = Col 3*Col 5/100

input. The share of labour in incremental input was only 16.3 per cent whereas, its share in productivity gains was 69.9 per cent. This implies that labour enjoyed higher gains at the cost of capital. The capital which has accounted for 83.7 per cent of the increased input, had to satisfy itself with 30.1 per cent of increased productivity. This shows that cost of labour in the industry is increasing faster than the cost of capital, as reflected in their prices (P_L and P_K in Table 5.17). The sharing of productivity gains has been relatively favourable to labour over the entire period, except during fifth five year plan period where, share of labour in produc-tivity gains (24.6 per cent) has been less than its share in incremental input (44.7 per cent). Capital has suffered most in the sixth five year plan where in spite of, accounted for most of the increased input (93.7 per cent), it had suffered a loss (-6.3 per cent). The labour had taken more than the total productivity gains (106.3 per cent). During seventh and eighth five year plan capital got more than labour in productivity gains but its share has been less than its share in total increased input.

The trends in relative sharing of productivity gains may be clearly understood with the help of product and factor prices indexes given in Table 5.18. The relatively higher index of total factor price compared with product price, throughout the period, shows that combined income of labour and capital at constant product prices have been more than, what actually would have been at base year's rate of reward (means positive productivity gains).

The data on average factor shares in net distributable output as well as in total input are presented in Table 5.17. Table shows that in initial years the share of labour in total input was almost half (47.7 per cent). During the whole period and particularly after the year 1979-80 the share of labour in total factor input has gradually decline so that, in 1994-95 it was only 17.6 per cent; and the share of capital has increased conversely. *Thus, importance of labour in the industry as an input has been continuously decreasing. This points to the rising capital intensity in the industry. It is interesting to note that while the share of labour in total input has declined significantly, the relative rise in its price enable it to maintain a nearly constant share in net distributable output.* Comparison of share of labour in input with its share in output in Chart 6.2 shows that share of labour in input has been more than its share in output in first half but thereafter share of labour in output is more than its share in input and the gap between both graphs is widening. The share of capital in net distributable output after 1982-83 has been significantly lower than its share in total factor input. The average share of capital in total input has been

Table 5.18: Net Distributable Output (NDO), Factor Input, Product Prices and Factor Prices: Watches and Clock Industry

(Value in Rs.'00000)

Year	NDO Current Prices	NDO Constant Prices	Product Price Index	Total Factor Input	Factor Price Index (P_T)	Labour Income Current Prices	Labour Income at base rate	Labour Price Index (P_L)	Capital Income Current Prices	Capital Income at base rate	Capital Price Index (P_K)
1	2	3	4	5	6	7	8	9	10	11	12
73-74	664	664	100	664	100.00	317	317	100	347	347	100
74-75	863	811	106.45	656	131.6	381	334	114.1	482	322	149.82
75-76	1201	1054	113.98	738	162.7	459	332	138.11	742	406	182.73
76-77	1504	1289	116.67	807	186.4	531	364	145.9	973	443	219.74
77-78	1602	1317	121.68	917	174.7	661	419	157.78	941	498	188.95
78-79	2020	1608	125.63	1049	192.5	783	489	160.12	1237	560	220.84
79-80	2556	1877	136.2	1275	200.4	943	594	158.82	1613	681	236.71
80-81	3504	2483	141.13	1530	229.0	1095	609	179.86	2409	921	261.5
81-82	3296	2285	144.27	1459	226.0	971	546	177.76	2325	912	254.82
82-83	5807	3976	146.06	1693	342.9	1573	659	238.67	4234	1034	409.39
83-84	4683	3131	149.55	1791	261.5	1858	667	278.58	2825	1124	251.34
84-85	5455	3575	152.6	2064	264.3	2140	643	333.05	3315	1422	233.17

conti.

85-86	6435	4101	156.9	2257	285.2	2479	689	359.18	3956	1568	252.35
86-87	7476	4648	160.84	2562	291.68	2946	760	387.71	4530	1802	251.4
87-88	8484	4942	171.68	2880	294.6	3356	786	426.94	5128	2094	244.86
88-89	9666	5224	185.04	3184	303.6	3845	813	472.76	5821	2371	245.51
89-90	14393	7235	198.92	3916	367.6	4535	975	464.91	9858	2940	335.3
90-91	11575	5793	199.82	3781	306.1	4826	784	615.73	6749	2998	225.15
91-92	22433	10218	219.53	4533	494.9	6123	993	616.92	16310	3540	460.73
92-93	15642	6348	246.42	4795	326.2	7134	987	722.57	8508	3808	223.44
93-94	17164	7016	244.62	4921	348.8	7288	896	813.47	9876	4025	245.37
94-95	20681	7971	259.45	5256	393.5	8859	927	955.46	11822	4329	273.11
95-96	28863	10885	265.16	6343	455.0	11711	1241	943.47	17152	5102	336.17

Notes:

1. Computed from Appendix tables
2. Col 4 = Col 3/Col 2; Col 6 = Col 2/Col 5;
   Col 9 = Col 7/Col 8; Col 12 = Col 10/Col 11.

66.6 per cent and it has gained only 61.8 per cent of the total productivity gains. Such trends obviously show that the capacity of the industry to expand through the re-investment of its internal funds, is decreasing.

5.5 Inter-Industry Differences in Productivity Gains

The pattern of distribution of gains shows that share of labour in total incremental productivity gains has been more than its share in total incremental input in all the industries under study except organised manufacturing sector. It is argued that wages are ordinary sticky and slow to respond to productivity changes, resulting in an inverse relationship between rate of productivity advance and the share of labour in productivity gains. Such a trend is observed in watches and clocks and paper & paperboard industries. In sugar industry, where rate of productivity advance has been the maximum, the share of labour which was expected to be lower, was unexpectedly close to half (48.9 per cent). Similarly, in motor vehicles industry where TFP increased at rate of 0.89 per cent, the share of labour in productivity gain is only 25.6 per cent. In sub-periods also, same trends are observed except for first sub-period in paper & paperboard and for second sub-period in organised manufacturing sector where share of labour in productivity gains are less than its share in incremental input. It will be of interest to know what happens to the share of labour in input and output basket when there are decrements in productivity. The period of negative productivity gains are observed in paper & paperboard industry only. In all such periods, share of labour has been mostly positive, but, when recorded negative, it was only a small part of total productivity decrements.

Share of labour and capital in total factor input and net distributable output shows that labour was an important component in input basket in base year except for paper & paperboard and fertilisers & pesticides industries. The share of labour in input is minimum in fertilisers & pesticides (29.07 per cent) followed by paper & paperboard industry (35.96 per cent). The share is maximum in motor vehicles (49.02 per cent) which are closely followed by sugar (49.94 per cent) and watches & clocks (49.74 per cent) industries and it was 46.3 per cent in organised manufacturing sector. Overtime trend shows that the share of labour in input has been steadily declining in all industries (except sugar industry where share of labour has increased initially) and decline is sharp after 1983-84 or 1984-85. Comparative analysis shows that the share of labour recorded maximum and sharp decline in watches and clocks (decline by 59 per cent) followed by fertilisers & pesticides (58.1 per cent) and paper & paperboard industries (55.6 per cent). This points towards capital substitution in all the industries. The hypothesis of constancy of labour's share in total output states that relative price of labour should rise so that it can maintain constant share. Such a trend was confirmed in watches & clocks industries only with few reservations.[16] The trends in relative price show that relative price of labour has been consistently higher than that of capital in paper & paperboard and fertilisers & pesticides industries. And, the trends also show that in watches & clocks and motor vehicles industries the relative price of labour has been consistently higher only after year 1983-84 and 1984-85 respectively. When we look at the share of labour in net distributable output the trends shows that labour has been able to maintain its share in net distributable output more than its share in total input for the period. In watches & clocks industry the average share of labour in output (38.2 per cent) has been more than the average share of labour in input (33.4 per cent) for the period. This trend was also found in other industries; only exception being sugar industry, whose average share in total input was more than its average share in total output.

5.6 Summing Up

In this chapter, we have highlighted the sharing of gains arising out of productivity increase in different industries. We have already eliminated the share of raw material by considering productivity in terms of value added. Labour and capital, thus, remained as the claimants of productivity gains. The trends of sharing of productivity gains, share of factor in input and output in industries, and relative prices of labour and capital for the years 1973-74 to 1995-96 are analysed. The results of analysis of productivity gains and pattern of their sharing can be summed up as follows:

* Labour enjoyed positive gains not only in the periods of productivity increment but also in the periods of productivity

decrement except few exceptions. This confirms the downward rigidity of wages.

* Labour gets more than capital in the periods of relatively slow productivity growth. In the periods of rapid rising productivity gains, capital tends to get more than labour. This again confirms the sticky behaviour of wages because, as a residual claimant, share of capital would increase in the periods of large productivity increments (because wages would not increase).

* The share of labour in total factor input has been declining in all five industries studied, along with manufacturing sector as a whole. This indicates a trend of more mechanization and capital-labour substitution in the industries.

* In all the industries under study, the relative factor price of labour has increased in the periods where its share in total input has decreased, but this trend is not confirmed by manufacturing sector as a whole.

References

1. S.N. Mehrotra (1967) "Sharing Gains in Productivity". *The Indian Journal of Labour Economics*, Vol. 9, No. 4, p. 391.
2. K.N. Subramanium (1977) *Wages in India*. New Delhi: Tata McGraw Hill Publishing Co. Ltd, p. 392.
3. ILO (1954) *Higher Productivity in Manufacturing Industries*. (Geneva: International Labour Organisation), p. 25.
4. Ibid., p. 24.
5. K. Mohanty (1993) *Wages and Productivity in a Developing Economy*. New Delhi: Discovery Publishing House, p. 129.
6. ILO (1954), op. cit., p. 30.
7. Subramanium (1977), op. cit., p. 397.
8. Government of India (1969) *Report of the National Commission on Labour. Ministry of Labour, Employment and Rehabilitation*, p. 267.
9. Subramanium (1977), op. cit., p. 397.
10. J.N. Sinha and P.K. Sawhney (1970) *Wages and Productivity in Selected Indian Industries*. New Delhi: Vikas Publishing House, pp. 134-135.
11. This is what we have referred as gross value added single deflation in the earlier sections.
12. It is for this very reason that wage and non-wage income are deflated by

product price index. It may be noted that wage and non-wage income at constant product prices are different from real wage (wages deflated by CPIIW) and real non-wage income (deflated by constant capital prices). However, if we use separate deflator the total would not add up to total distributable output and their respective gains would not adds up to total productivity gains.

13. R.M. Tiwari, (1971) *Labour Productivity in Indian Cotton Textile Industry* With Special Reference to Kanpur. Ph. D Thesis Submitted to Lucknow University, p. 134.
14. Sinha and Sawhney (1970), op. cit., p. 68.
15. Ibid., p. 78.
16. Relative price recorded decline in initial period.

6

Trends in Wages and Earning

6.1 Introduction

Wages and earnings (earnings are of greater importance than wages) of labour play a vital role not only in the field of industrial production and prices, but also in regulating the economy of the country as well. For labour particularly, wages are the largest and most important source of living, and hence, any change in wage income, will affect not only the socio-economic status of labour in the society, but also their effectiveness in industrial activities. The analysis of trends in wages is of special importance because besides welfare function, wages performs several other important functions in the economy. They are reward for work as a factor of production and they provide an instrument for reallocating manpower between skill, occupations, industries and regions. Output related earnings tend to improve workers efficiency and serve as an incentive to further effort. Variances in the share of wages in total income also affect the size of other factor's income. Beckman remarked that what happens to wages is of crucial concern to everyone. To the workers, wages represent income; to the businessmen, they represent costs; and to the government they represent potential taxes. Wages are largest source of purchasing power; hence, changes in labour income have an important bearing on the level of economic activity (1959, p. 3). All of them (businessmen, workers and government) influence wages in one way or other. Workers may influence wages by devoting more time, more efforts or more money on improvement of quality of labour services or by collective bargaining through trade unions. Businessmen influences wages by activities aimed at making profits for themselves. Government influences wages by intervening in the process of wage determination.

Even apart from broader economic consideration, an industry-wide study of real wages is of greater significance from the standpoint of planning. A rise or fall in the wages is an important factor in the choice of production techniques and this choice, in the final analysis, determines the rate of surplus emerging out of the industrial sector and ultimately the rate of capital formation for the economy as a whole (Palekar, 1974, p. 2). The present chapter shall examine the trends in wages and earnings in the selected industries.

The chapter is further divided in eight sections. Section 6.2 relates to the concepts and definitions of various variables used in study. The methodology for measurement of factor compensation forms the part of section 6.3 whereas section 6.4 describes the effects of techniques on wages. In section 6.5 the results of estimates of wages and earnings are analysed. The estimates of wage function and employment function are also presented in this section. Section 6.6 deals with the analysis of inter-industry differences in wages and earnings whereas, section 6.7 deals with the inter-plan differences in wages and earnings. The findings of this chapter are summed up in section 6.8.

6.2 Concepts and Definitions

Before analysing trends in wages it is desired to know the concepts and definitions of various variables involved in the analysis. ASI defines wages to include all remuneration capable of being expressed in monetary terms and also payable more or less regularly in each pay period to workers as compensation for work done during the accounting year. It includes (a) direct wages and salary (i.e., basic wages/salaries, payments for overtime, dearness, compensatory, and other allowances including house rent), (b) remuneration for period not worked (i.e., basic wages, salaries and allowances payable for leave period, paid holiday, lay-off payments and compensation for unemployment, if not paid from sources other than employers), (c) bonuses and ex-gratia payment paid both at regular and less frequent intervals (i.e., incentive bonuses, good attendance bonuses, productive bonuses, profit sharing bonuses, festival or year-end bonuses etc.). It excludes lay-off payments which are made from trust or other special funds set up expressly for this purpose, i.e., payments not made by employer. It also excludes imputed value of benefits in kind, employer's contribution to old age benefits and other social security charges, direct expenditure on maternity benefits, creches and other group benefits. Travelling and other expenses incurred for business purposes and reimbursed by employers are excluded. The wages are expressed in terms of gross value, i.e., before deduction for fines, damages, taxes, provident fund, employer's insurance contribution etc.

The distinction is sometime made between wages and earnings. The earnings are different from wages because besides wages it also includes imputed value of benefit in kind. For the present study, ASI gives data on wages to worker and total emoluments. Total emoluments are defined in same way as wages (defined above) but paid to all employees, plus imputed value of benefits in kind, i.e., the net cost to the employer on those goods and services provided to employees free of charge or at markedly reduced cost which are clearly and primarily of benefits to the employees as consumers. Hence, we get two values of remuneration (1) wages to workers and (2) earnings to employees. Here, it may be noted that wages to worker does not include fringe benefits whereas, earnings per employee includes them.

The fringe benefits may be defined as the non-wage cost incurred by employers on the employees and not related to the efforts to employees. Only those payments should fall in the category of 'fringe benefits' which are, in first place, computable in terms of money and in second place, the amount of which is not predetermined and, lastly, for which no contract indicating when the sum is payable, exists. The purpose of fringe benefits is to supplement money wages of workers, filling up the gap left between the money wages and the cost of living index. The fringe benefits are very important in the promotion of economic welfare of the workers on one hand and in raising labour productivity and improving labour welfare on other hand. The share of fringe benefits in total wage cost has been increasing overtime due to reasons such as government policies, court rulings, union effects and voluntarily by employers (to increase productivity).

6.3 Measurement of Factor Compensation

The money income and money wages are of special interest because in business world all payments are made in money terms only. The study prepares two values of labour compensation at current prices namely,

(1) Earnings per employee (EE_m)
(2) Wages per worker (WW_m).

But the money values do not indicate the state of labour welfare; only the real earnings can be of help in analysing labour welfare. The real earnings can be obtained by deflating the money values by consumer price index for industrial workers (CPIIW) because this indicates the purchasing power of industrial worker in real terms. *Changes in real wages provide for the fundamental test to decide whether or not a worker is improving his economic well being. Increases in his wages which in turn are offset by rises in prices do not enable him to advance his level of living. It is only when wages rise in relation to the prices of goods and services that real wages rise.* Therefore, this study prepares two indexes of labour compensation to analyse labour welfare, namely

(1) Real consumption earnings per employee (EE_r)
(2) Real consumption wages per worker (WW_r).

While the analysis of real consumption earnings are significant for worker welfare though they do not represent real wage burder/cost to the industry. It is quit possible that while money/real consumption wages may increase but the real wage cost to the industry may decline and vice-versa. What is relevant for the analysis of real wage burden to the industry is the money wages/earnings deflated by product price index termed henceforth as 'product wages/earnings'. Therefore, we accordingly deflate the respective indexes of labour compensation by the product price index and prepare two indexes, namely

(1) Product earning per employee (EE_P)
(2) Product wage per worker (WW_P).

These indexes are required to study the real wage burden to the industry. *The relation between the trends in product wages and that in labour productivity would measure the real burdens of wage payment on the industry. A rise in product wage faster than labour productivity would imply rising real wage burdens on the industry.* Here, it may be observed that concept of product earning/wages is very important for productivity analysis. The index of product earnings/wages above 100 indicates that the labour enjoys a positive share in the productivity gains. Since additional divisible pool of output is created by either a rise in the price of product or by productivity increase or by both. If money wages are increasing at a faster rate than the price of product, it means a rising part of money wages is being paid out of that part of additional divisible pool of output, which has been created by productivity increase, indicating that labour is enjoying positive gains.

For understanding wage-productivity relationship in industry, an index is prepared which indicates the wage-productivity movement. This index is obtained by dividing the index of productivity earnings per employee by the index of labour productivity (gross value added per employee at constant product price). *A rise in this index indicates that wages/earnings surpassed labour productivity which in turn results in an increase in labour cost per unit of output and a rise in the relative share of labour in output while the reverse means wages/earnings lags behind the labour productivity which results in declining unit labour cost and relative share of labour in output.* We have also prepared a series of ratio of the price relatives of wages and labour productivity to analyse and compare the year-to-year growths of wages and labour productivity. *The value of this ratio if more than one for a year, indicates that the rate of growth of wages surpasses the rate of growth of labour productivity in that year and vice-versa.*

To analyse how nominal wage rate in the industry adjusted in relation to the change in labour productivity and change in consumer price index, we have regressed money earnings per employee on labour productivity and consumer price index lagged by one period. To find out if the wage rate behaviour is different for the years in which labour productivity have recorded significant increase, a slope dummy (D*Ln (LP)) is introduced where D takes value 1 for the years in which labour productivity have significantly increased and 0 for others). We have also introduced an intercept dummy to find out whether wage rate behaviour is different in both sub-periods (IDMY, 1 for years after 1984-85 and 0 for others).

One line of thought is that labour in organised manufacturing industries are enjoying high wages and this results in the reduction of employment. A candid assertion of the above position comes in a World

Bank study by Fallen and Lucas (1991). They argue that industrial wages have grown significantly relative to consumer prices for industrial workers, and that the wage growth created by union-militancy and job security regulation prevalent in India have resulted in a long term reduction of employment by about 18 per cent in the industries. Similar argument can also be found in an earlier study Lucas (1988) where it is argued that real product wage in manufacturing steadily increased by some 86 per cent between 1960-61 to 1979-80 and much of the wage increase can be attributed to the prevalence of trade union militancy, minimum wage regulations and job security laws. The apparent rise in manufacturing wages remains a point of concern in several studies. Such an increase run contrary to the expectation of an economy undergoing structural adjustment programme. Ahluwalia (1991) also attributed the decline in employment to the sharp increase in the wages.

To test the hypothesis that an increase in wage rate results in reduction of employment, we have estimated following frequently used employment function in empirical analysis, specified as:

$$\text{Log}(L) = \lambda + \alpha \text{Ln}(EE_p) + \beta \text{Ln}(Y) + \gamma \text{Ln}(L_{-1}) + u$$

The coefficient of log (EE_p) is expected to be negative since, an increase in real wages (labour cost) should reduce employment. The coefficient of Ln(Y) is expected to be positive since, an increase in level of output should raise employment. The assumptions about lag structure underlying the model requires the coefficient of Ln(L_{-1}) to be a positive fraction. The short-run elasticity of employment with respect to real wage rate is given by α, and the long-run elasticity by $\alpha/(1-\gamma)$. Similarly, the short-run elasticity with respect to output is given by β and the long-run elasticity by $\beta/(1-\gamma)$. The coefficient of lagged employment $(1-\gamma)$ indicates the speed of adjustment to desired employment level.

While analysing labour rate of compensation, it is also worthwhile to see what happens to the rate of return on capital. The rate of return on capital can be computed by subtracting the labour compensation (total emoluments) from the gross value added and dividing the resultant by adjusted capital stock series in a year. It refers to earnings per unit of capital.

To obtain real rate of return a suitable deflator must deflate the non-wage income. The choice of deflator will depend on the purpose in view; if it is to examine the welfare implications of the rate of return, we would require a cost of living index based on prices of commodities on which investor spend their income; if it is desired to relate them to productivity (at constant product price), the non-wage income must be deflated by the index of output prices; if however, the purpose is to measure the re-investment potentialities of non-wage income, the index of machinery prices would be a more appropriate deflator. Since our interest lies in the last two, therefore, we prepares the following three indexes of rate of return on capital, namely,

(1) Rate of return on capital at current prices (RR_m)
(2) Rate of return on capital at constant machinery prices (RR_k)
(3) Rate of return on capital at constant product prices (RR_p).

6.4 Effect of Techniques on Wages

The type of technique, which is being used in the economy, generally affects wage share. In a developing economy, like India, with emphasis on industrialisation, capital-labour ratio is bound to change rapidly either through substitution of labour for capital or due to application of labour-saving techniques. This type of change will definitely affect the wage share over time.

Hicks, while analysing the 'effect of progress upon distribution', pointed out that technical progress can be of three types—*neutral, labour saving* and *capital saving.* For given capital-labour ratio and neutral technical progress, the ratio of marginal product of labour of marginal product of capital remains unchanged and, hence, the income distribution between labour and capital remain unaffected. On the other hand, if technical progress is 'labour saving' the ratio of the two marginal products will fall, since, the marginal product of capital is raised more than that of labour and hence, relative wage share will fall. At a given point of time this amounts to saying that between two industries, the higher capital-labour ratio in one industry would mean a lower ratio of the marginal product of labour to that of capital as compared to other industry where capital-labour ratio is lower. Thus, the labour share can be expected to be negatively related to the capital-labour ratio in different industries.

Hicks (1964), while discussing the improvement in technique on the distribution of income assumed that an invention could only be profitably adopted if its ultimate effect is to increase the 'national dividend'. On this assumption it was concluded that "Increasing capital accompanied by stagnate invention may very well raise labour's relative share in the dividend (because elasticity of substitution will ultimately falls as more and more advantageous applications are used up); but increasing capital, with active inventions, is very likely to do the contrary. And since the activity of invention is definitely favourable to the growth of the dividend...it is highly probable that periods of most rapidly rising real wages will also be the periods of a falling relative share of labour."[1] By combining the effects of technological change with the appropriate elasticity of substitution, constancy of labour share can be explained. The elasticity of substitution of labour for capital is unity, greater than unity or less than unity according to the total amount spend on labour remains unchanged, decrease or increases as wages rises respectively. With a secular rise in wages, a neutral invention would leave the labour share unchanged if only the elasticity of substitution is unity. Similarly, a labour saving invention could leave the labour share unchanged if the elasticity of substitution is less than unity, and a capital saving invention might do the same if elasticity of substitution is greater than unity. In a developing country like India, thus, the trends in factor share will be affected by the increase in the capital-labour ratio, caused by an improvement in technique, depending upon the elasticity of substitution between factors, i.e., labour and capital. If elasticity of substitution is greater than one then the share of faster growing factor would increase and vice-versa. In this case, it is argued "The wage rate and the relative wage share are therefore, to move in the opposite direction where the elasticity of substitution is greater than one. There is then an indication that wage share moves inversely with capital intensity and wage rate."[2]

6.5 Trends in Factor Compensation in Different Industries

In this section, the trends in factor compensation are analysed. Besides time series presentation of different variables such as rate of compensation for capital and labour at nominal, constant product, constant consumption and machinery prices; employment, gross value added, total emoluments and unit labour costs; the employment and wage functions are also presented in this section.

6.5.1 Organised Manufacturing Sector

6.5.1a. Trends in Wages and Earnings

Data on index of wages per worker and earnings per employee in the organised manufacturing sector are presented in Table 6.1. The share of fringe benefits in total emoluments has been steadily increasing from 12.41 per cent in 1979-80 to 23.23 per cent in 1995-96 (column 8 of Appendix Table A-19). The rising share of fringe benefits in total emoluments indicates increasing welfare activities in the organised manufacturing sector. The money earnings per employee (EE_m) has increased at trend rate of 11.36 per cent per annum whereas trend rate of money wages per worker (WW_m) being 11.23 per cent. In value terms the wages per worker has increased from Rs. 3364 in 1973-74 to Rs. 36647 in 1995-96 (data given in Appendix A-19). The growth rate for period 1985-86 to 1995-96 (11.10 per cent for EE_m and 11.25 per cent for WW_m) has been more than the period of 1973-74 to 1984-85 (10.60 per cent for EE_m and 10.24 per cent for WW_m) as shown in Table 6.1, columns 2 and 3. The increase in money wages per worker and nominal earnings per employee has been more than the consumer price index for the entire period. Chart 6.8(A) clearly shows that growth rate of money earnings per employee has been more than that of the consumer price index for most of the years except 1974-75, 1991-92 and 1993-94. The growth of money earnings has been same as that of per capita national income and in second half of the period the growth of money wages per worker and nominal earnings per employee has been even less than per capita national income for the period (13.25 per cent). This means that relative position of worker in organised manufacturing sector has not improved.

The real consumption earnings per employee have increased from Rs. 4293 in 1973-74 to Rs. 7151 in 1995-96: an increase of 67 per cent at the annual trend rate of 2.52 per cent. Real ages per worker has also significantly increased from Rs. 3364 to Rs. 5937 at annual trend rate of 2.65 per cent. The increase in the rate of real compensation in first half at the rate of 3.12 per cent and 2.78 per cent for WW_r and EE_r has been more than second half where WW_r and EE_r increased at the rate of only 1.28 per cent and 1.42 per cent respectively. This shows that the real consumption wages/ earnings moved slower after 1985-86 in comparison to the earlier period. It may be noted this period

Table 6.1 : Index No. of Wages and Earnings: Organised Manufac-turing Sector

Year	Earnings Per Employee at Current Prices (EE_m)	Wages Per Workers at Current Prices (WW_m)	Earnings Per Employee at Constant Consumer Prices (EE_r)	Wages Per Worker at Constant Consumer Prices (WW_r)	Earnings Per Employee at Constant Product Prices (EE_p)	Wages Per Worker at Constant Product Prices (WW_p)
1	2	3	4	5	6	7
1973-74	100.00	100.00	100.00	100.00	100.00	100.00
1974-75	117.43	113.79	92.61	89.74	97.05	94.04
1975-76	119.26	142.41	95.25	113.74	97.18	116.04
1976-77	127.39	129.51	105.81	107.57	101.43	103.12
1977-78	137.79	135.56	106.32	104.60	107.27	105.53
1978-79	148.20	159.17	111.93	120.22	115.17	123.70
1979-80	162.96	175.00	113.16	121.52	105.34	113.12
1980-81	180.80	193.92	112.72	120.90	98.02	105.14
1981-82	199.97	213.92	110.85	118.58	103.09	110.28
1982-83	229.50	242.42	118.05	124.70	117.66	124.28
1983-84	268.58	285.75	122.75	130.60	126.66	134.76
1984-85	316.94	329.74	136.14	141.64	138.38	143.97
1985-86	340.33	362.26	137.23	146.07	138.57	147.51
1986-87	379.50	401.85	140.76	149.05	147.47	156.15
1987-88	414.96	438.07	140.95	148.80	149.97	158.32
1988-89	466.19	507.65	148.28	161.47	155.58	169.42
1989-90	519.31	554.20	152.20	162.43	156.81	167.34
1990-91	579.15	621.72	152.25	163.44	161.26	173.11
1991-92	587.11	645.04	135.95	149.36	146.78	161.26
1992-93	717.70	744.78	151.64	157.37	161.74	167.85
1993-94	754.81	788.67	148.36	155.01	157.86	164.95
1994-95	892.13	939.03	159.30	167.67	168.86	177.74
1995-96	1028.01	1089.32	166.55	176.48	178.64	189.30
Annual Trend Rates (% Per Annum)						
1973-95	11.23 (58.39)	11.36 (59.8)	2.52 (13.933)	2.65 (16.115)	2.98 (13.710)	3.10 (14.031)
1973-84	10.24 (16.138)	10.60 (18.11)	2.78 (6.274)	3.12 (7.619)	2.49 (4.164)	2.82 (3.910)
1985-95	11.25 (32.42)	11.10 (30.16)	1.42 (3.090)	1.28 (3.346)	1.81 (4.349)	1.68 (4.763)

Source: Calculated from data given in Appendix Table A-19.

Notes:
1. Data computed from table as per the methodology explained.
2. The trend rates are calculated by fitting exponential function of type $Y = ab^t$.
3. Figure in brackets refers to the t-values of trend coefficient. All trend rates are significant at 1% level of significance.

coincides with the first phase of liberalisation in India. As mentioned earlier the real consumption wages does not indicate the real wage cost to the employers. Product earnings per employee have increased at trend rate of 2.98 per cent as against the trend rate of 2.52 per cent for consumption earnings per employee for the period under study. This indicates that wages as a cost component to industry/employer has increased at a rate more than the wages, as income component to workers. The trend rate of product earnings per employee has been 2.49 per cent and 1.81 per cent for first and second sub-period respectively. This means that in second sub-period the product earnings (wage cost) has been more than the real income in contrast to the first sub-period. However, it may be noted that the manufacturing sector has passed most of the increase in money wages on to the consumers through the rise in product price. The movement of wage-productivity index as shown in column 5 of Table 6.2 indicates that increase in the money wages has been less than the increase in labour productivity as compared to base year. This can also be seen from Chart 6.1 where the graph of product earnings is below the graph of labour productivity throughout the period. To compare the year-to-year movement of wages and productivity, we have taken the ratio to link relatives of wages and labour productivity indexes. The value of ratio greater than one in a year indicates that in that year increase in wages has been more than the increase in labour productivity and vice-versa. Column 6 of Table 6.2 shows that the ratio does not show any definite trend throughout the period but after year 1987-88 the ratio has been consistently less than one except for 1992-93 implying that in recent period the growth rate of wages on year to year basis has been less than the growth of labour productivity.

6.5.1b. Trends in Employment, Gross Value Added and Wage Share

The employment in the organised manufacturing sector, as shown in Appendix Table A-1, has increased from 58.201 lakh in 1973-74 to 102.222 lakh in 1995-96: an increase of 75.6 per cent at the trend rate of 1.95 per cent for the period under study. The increase has been more in the period up to 1984 and thereafter the employment has increased at a comparatively slow rate. On the other hand, total wage cost to the industry has increased from Rs. 249,874 lakh to Rs. 4,511,605 lakh, an increase of more than 18 times at the trend

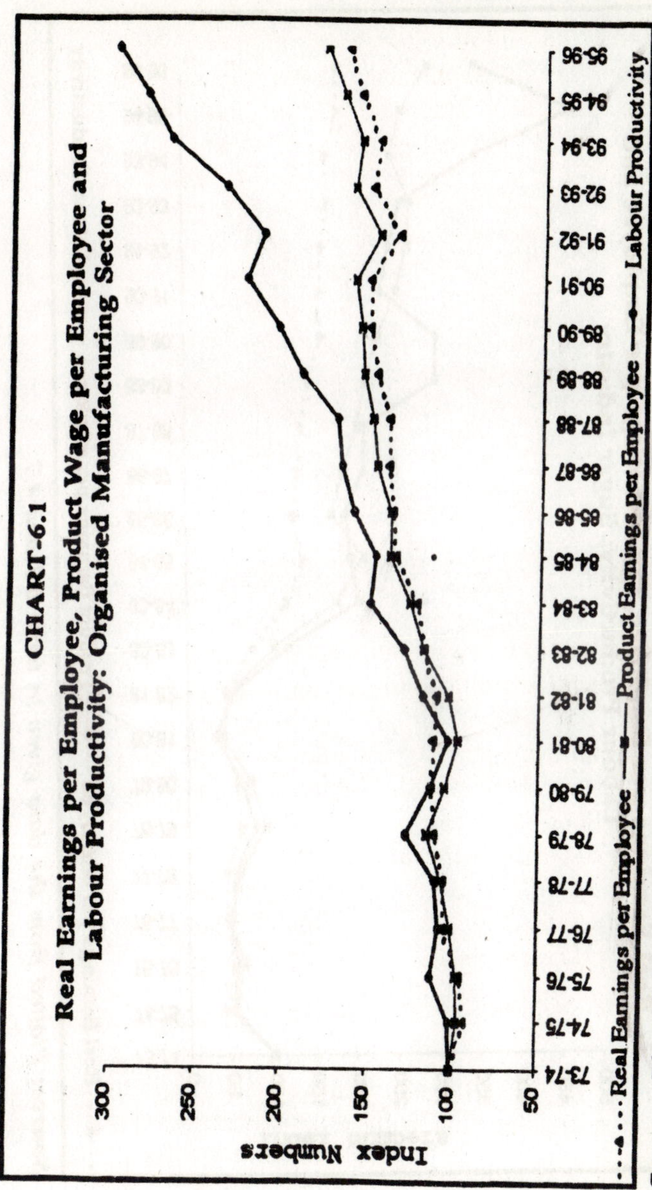

CHART-6.1

Real Earnings per Employee, Product Wage per Employee and Labour Productivity: Organised Manufacturing Sector

Source: Plotted from the data given in table 6.1 and 4.1.

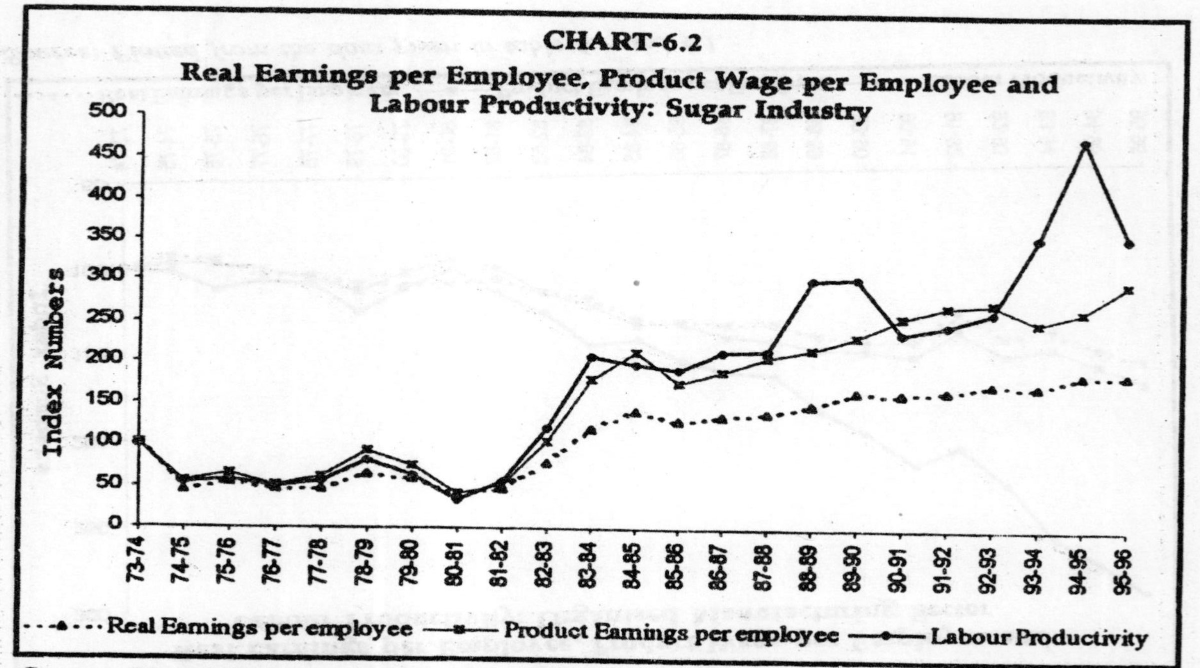

Source: Plotted from the data given in table 6.3 and 4.7.

Table 6.2 : Indexes of Rate of Returns and Wage-Productivity Movement: Organised Manufacturing Sector

Year	Rate of returns at Current Prices (RR_m)	Rate of returns at Constant Machinery Prices (RR_k)	Rate of returns at Constant Product Prices (RR_p)	Wage-Productivity Index (W-P)	Ratio of Growth Rates of Wages & Labour Productivity
1	2	3	4	5	6
1973-74	100.00	100.00	100.00	100.00	100.00
1974-75	127.49	99.74	105.36	95.40	0.954
1975-76	124.38	87.76	101.35	86.55	0.907
1976-77	139.96	100.13	111.44	93.82	1.084
1977-78	140.95	99.68	109.73	97.14	1.035
1978-79	163.65	109.34	127.18	90.48	0.931
1979-80	171.52	99.15	110.88	92.60	1.023
1980-81	176.34	93.04	95.61	95.20	1.028
1981-82	213.09	102.44	109.85	87.62	0.920
1982-83	222.17	101.46	113.91	90.88	1.037
1983-84	265.88	114.52	125.39	84.73	0.932
1984-85	245.99	101.25	107.41	94.14	1.111
1985-86	275.59	103.11	112.21	86.59	0.920
1986-87	281.48	99.85	109.38	88.05	1.017
1987-88	299.55	102.14	108.26	88.02	1.000
1988-89	356.93	110.65	119.12	81.43	0.925
1989-90	425.83	119.08	128.58	76.48	0.939
1990-91	472.81	121.94	131.65	72.28	0.945
1991-92	490.86	109.52	122.71	68.52	0.948
1992-93	577.73	116.31	130.21	68.71	1.003
1993-94	700.84	136.81	146.58	59.08	0.860
1994-95	770.84	136.32	145.90	38.76	0.656
1995-96	893.93	148.01	155.34	34.87	0.900
Annual Trend Rates (% Per Annum)					
1973-95	9.62 (30.753)	1.53 (6.203)	1.50 (5.899)	-3.11 (5.701)	-
1973-84	8.53 (16.137)	0.77+ (1.443)	1.89+ (1.312)	-0.62+ (1.611)	-
1985-95	13.13 (24.956)	3.65 (6.745)	3.53 (8.095)	-8.25 (6.023)	-

Source: *Calculated from data given in Appendix Table A-1, A-7, A-13 & A-19..*

Notes: *1. Data computed from tables as per the methodology explained..*

2. The trend rates are calculated by fitting exponential function of type $Y = ab^t$.

3. Figure in brackets refers to the t-values of trend coefficient. All trend rates are significant at 1% level of significance unless otherwise specified.

4. + Insignificant.

rate of 13.40 per cent per annum, considering that product price has increased at the rate of 8.01 per cent, the real wage cost has increased at the rate of 5.39 per cent. The data presented in appendix table A-7 shows that gross value added in the industry has increased at annual trend rate of 15.84 per cent real (GVA at the rate of 7.24 per cent). The rate of growth of GVA has been more in second sub-period (19.53 per cent) as against the first sub-period (15.2 per cent). Column 2 of Table 6.13 shows that the share of wages in gross value added declined from 0.4625 in 1973-74 to 0.1613 in 1995-96 with fluctuation in between, but since 1986-87 the wage share has been consistently declining. The increase in real wages per worker associated with a decline in the wage share supports the hypothesis that capital-labour ratio is negatively associated with wage share. This also confirms that technical progress is labour shaving. The invention is 'active' in 'Hicksian' sense as increase in GVA and real wages per worker is associated with the reduced relative share of labour.

6.5.1c. Trends in Rate of Return on Capital

The data on rate of return on capital in the organised manufacturing sector are presented in Table 6.2. The rate of return at current prices has been continuously increasing from 8.15 per cent to 73.83 per cent, at the exponential growth rate of 9.62 per cent per annum. The rate of return has picked up in second sub-period at the rate of 13.13 per cent against the growth rate of 8.52 per cent in first sub-period. When the rate of return on capital is deflated by product prices the range become narrow from 7.79 per cent to 12.66 per cent. Therefore, it is evident that part of higher rate of return, noted at current prices, is due to rising product prices. The RRp has increased at the rate of 1.50 per cent for the entire period but most of this increase has been recorded in second sub-period (at the rate of 3.53 per cent). The rate of return is comparatively higher in the years of rising productivity, i.e., in 1978-79, 1983-84, 1990-91 and 1993-94. The rate of return at constant machinery prices has ranged from 6.32 per cent to 12.06 per cent. Since, this rate includes taxes, depreciation etc., it indicates that the industry has been in unfavourable position from the point of re-investment of internal funds. The rate of return is picking up especially after year 1992-93 corresponding to eighth five-year plan period after the introduction of privatisation and liberalisation as new economic policy.

6.5.1d. Wage and Employment Functions

In principle, the nominal wage rate is expected to be positively related to lagged labour productivity and price level. The wage function shows that money wages in organised manufacturing sector does not fully adjust to the changes in labour productivity and changes in prices. Equation 6.1 shows that the elasticity of money wage rate with respect to the productivity of labour is 0.593 and is well below unity. This indicates that benefits of growth in labour productivity are not fully transformed to labour. But, the combined elasticity of labour productivity and price level is 0.956, which indicates that changes in money wage rates are explained by changes in labour productivity and price level.

$$\text{Ln}(EE_m) = \underset{(0.522)}{0.3282} + \underset{(2.645)}{0.593}\ \text{Ln}(LP_{-1}) + \underset{(1.040)}{0.363}\ \text{Ln}(CPIIW_{-1}) \quad ...(6.1)$$

Adj. $R^2 = 0.967$, *D-W* = 2.093, *Rho* = 0.551 (2.856)

Introduction of slope dummy for the years where productivity has increased significantly shows adjustment of wages to labour productivity is slowed down by 0.12 per cent in the periods of higher productivity growth. This supports the finding of last chapter that in the periods of rising productivity capital gets larger share in productivity gains than labour. The wage rate behaviour to the adjustment to productivity and prices is not different for two periods as coefficient of intercept dummy is insignificant.

$$\text{Ln}(EE_m) = \underset{(1.572)}{0.836} + \underset{(4.399)}{0.796}\ \text{Ln}(LP_{-1}) + \underset{(0.192)}{0.059}\ \text{Ln}(CPIIW_{-1})$$

$$- \underset{(3.038)}{0.012}\ D\ \text{Ln}(LP_{-1}) + \underset{(0.119)}{0.008}\ IDMY. \quad ...(6.2)$$

Adj. $R^2 = 0.944$, *D-W* = 1.784, *Rho* = 0.784 (5.483).

The estimates of employment function in organised manufacturing sector as shown by equation 6.3 indicates that the coefficients are of expected sign and the coefficient of product wage is significant at 5 per cent level of significance. The short run elasticity of employment w.r.t. product wage rate is 0.364 and long-run elasticity is 0.625. It appears from our result that with a 10 per cent increase in product wage rate, the employment will reduce by 3.6 per cent within one year and its cumulative effect over long period will be 6.25 per cent reduction in employment.

$$\text{Ln}(L) = 2.961 - 0.364\ \text{Ln}(EE_p) + 0.313\ \text{Ln}(V) + 0.417\ \text{Ln}(L_{-1}).$$
$$(3.530)\ (1.942) \qquad (3.149) \qquad (2.520)\ \ldots(6.3)$$

Adj. $R^2 = 0.837$; *D-H* $= 0.837$, $F_{3,\,18} = 37.05$.

The short-run elasticity of employment with respect to output is 0.313 and long-run elasticity is 0.537. These results are in conformity with the findings of Diwan & Gujrati (1968) and Goldar (1987). *The finding of a less than unitary elasticity of employment with respect to output indicates that even if product wages do not rise, increase in output will leads to a less than proportionate increase in employment.* The significant coefficient of lagged labour variable points to the significant lag in the adjustment of actual labour employment to the desired level. This may be due to the fact that organised sector employment is highly regulated. We have also introduced slope (for EE_p) and intercept dummy for period 1985-95 but all the coefficient of the dummy variables are numerically low and statistically insignificant (that is why results are not reported). This indicates that employment function for both sub-periods are not statistically different.

6.5.2 Trends in Factor Compensation in Sugar Industry

6.5.2a. Trends in Wages and Earnings

The data on index of rate of compensation in sugar industry are set out in Table 6.3. In absolute terms (Table A-20) money wages per worker in the industry has increased from Rs. 3335 to Rs. 44,536: an increase of more than 13.4 times at the trend rate of 17.16 per cent. Whereas, the money earnings per employee have increased from Rs. 4221 to Rs. 48,852: an increase of 11.5 times at trend rate of 16.33%. The annual trend rates during period 1973-74 to 1984-85 for EE_m and WW_m are 12.73 per cent and 13.71 per cent respectively while the trend rates during period 1985-86 to 1995-96 are 13.83% and 13.74% respectively. The increase in money wages per worker and nominal earnings per employee has been more than the increase in national per capita income throughout the period. The rising share of fringe benefits in total emoluments indicates that the expenditure on welfare related activities is increasing in industry. It may be noted that despite the fact that the share of fringe benefits in total emoluments have been steady or even increasing from 10 per cent in 1979-80 to 14 per cent in 1995-96 (column 8 of Table A-20), the rise in WW_m index has been more than the EE_m index throughout the period. This implies that the other components of earnings, salary per person in salaried class are moving slower than the WW_m. The money wages per worker and money earnings per employee has been less than the base year value up to 1981-82. Comparison of annual growth rates of EE_m and CPIIW in Chart 6.8(B) clearly shows that the growth rate of earnings has been consistently more than the growth of consumer price except for years 1974-75, 1979-80, 1980-81 and 1985-86. The analysis of real consumption wages shows that for the entire period, real consumption wages per worker/consumption earnings per employee have increased from Rs. 3335/4221 to Rs. 7215/7915: an increase of 116.4/87.5 per cent at the trend rate of 7.80/7.23 per cent per annum. This indicates the significant improvement in the position of labour in the industry. The rise in real wages per worker/ earnings per employee has been particularly high in years 1982-83 and 83-84. The real product earnings per employee in the industry have increased at a faster rate than real consumption earnings per employee at the trend rate of 9.02 per cent for the period. The increase has been much higher in first period (7.62 per cent) as compared to second period (4.82 per cent). The comparatively higher increase in the wages per worker/earnings per employee in the industry may be due to the 'catching up' effect because the wages/earnings has been low during the initial period. The rapidly rising index of product earnings clearly suggests that industry has failed to shift the burden of rising wage bill on to the customers. This is obvious as the price of sugar is controlled for most of the period. The trend in wage-productivity index shows that for most of the years the index has been above 100 implying that increase in earnings per employee has surpassed the increase in labour productivity. This is also depicted in Chart 6.2 where graph of product earnings is above the graph of labour productivity. The year-to-year comparison does not show any definite pattern but for most of the years, particularly after 1986-87 the value has been less than one, implying that the wage increase has been at a lower rate than labour productivity.

Table 6.3: Indexes of Wages and Earnings: Sugar Industry

Year	Earnings Per Employee at Current Prices (EE_m)	Wages Per Workers at Current Prices (WW_m)	Earnings Per Employee at Constant Consumer Prices (EE_r)	Wages Per Worker at Constant Consumer Prices (WW_r)	Earnings Per Employee at Constant Product Prices (EE_p)	Wages Per Worker at Constant Product Prices (WW_p)
1	2	3	4	5	6	7
1973-74	100.00	100.00	100.00	100.00	100.00	100.00
1974-75	58.89	58.99	46.44	46.52	54.52	54.61
1975-76	70.50	72.79	56.31	58.14	65.57	67.71
1976-77	57.39	60.73	47.66	50.54	52.08	55.11
1977-78	62.44	63.89	48.18	49.29	61.54	62.96
1978-79	86.67	97.84	65.46	73.90	92.78	104.85
1979-80	84.35	96.50	58.58	67.02	74.74	85.51
1980-81	65.61	73.94	40.90	46.10	41.16	46.39
1981-82	85.70	95.28	47.50	52.82	52.08	57.91
1982-83	152.94	168.77	78.67	86.82	105.06	115.94
1983-84	264.51	300.88	120.89	137.52	180.20	204.98
1984-85	331.98	341.84	142.60	146.84	213.92	220.27
1985-86	325.39	309.51	131.20	124.80	176.21	167.61
1986-87	365.89	423.18	135.71	156.97	188.83	218.40
1987-88	414.12	481.35	140.67	163.50	207.65	241.37
1988-89	469.45	540.77	149.32	172.00	218.20	251.35
1989-90	567.13	646.12	166.22	189.37	233.24	265.72
1990-91	625.85	728.30	164.52	191.46	257.38	299.52
1991-92	727.40	846.92	168.43	196.11	270.79	315.29
1992-93	835.46	928.42	176.52	196.17	274.58	305.14
1993-94	888.27	1021.48	174.59	200.77	250.08	287.59
1994-95	1049.50	1192.19	187.39	212.87	265.50	301.60
1995-96	1157.46	1335.55	187.52	216.38	299.07	345.09
Annual Trend Rates (% Per Annum)						
1973-95	16.33 (17.194)	17.16 (15.767)	7.23 (8.635)	7.8 (7.686)	9.02 (8.975)	9.6 (8.206)
1973-84	12.73 (3.934)	13.71 (3.481)	5.11* (1.882)	6.02⁺ (1.330)	7.62* (2.240)	8.56* (1.929)
1985-95	13.83 (24.374)	13.74 (51.571)	3.77 (6.859)	4.54 (12.241)	4.82 (5.709)	5.59 (7.725)

Source: Calculated from data given in Appendix Table A-20.

Notes:
1. Data computed from tables as per the methodology explained..
2. The growth rates are calculated by fitting exponential function of type $Y = ab^t$.
3. Figure in brackets refers to the t-values of trend coefficient. All trend rates are significant at 1% level of significance unless otherwise specified.
4. * Significant at 5% level; ⁺ Insignificant.

6.5.2b. Trends in Employment, Gross Value Added and Wage Share

The data on employment presented in Table A-2 (column 5) shows that employment in the industry has continuously increased up to 1980-81 from 132.2 thousands to 470.1 thousands in 1980-81, but thereafter it decreased continuously up to 1986-87 when it reached 192.8 thousands. After this, the employment has shown a rising trend and it became 258 thousands in 1995-96. On the other hand, total wage bill in the industry (column 7) has continuously increased from Rs. 5579 lakh in base year to Rs. 126,034 lakh in 1995-96: an increase of more than 22 times at the trend rate of 15.09 per cent per annum. Most of this increase has been due to the increase in consumer price index, which increased at the rate of 8.49 per cent per annum. Gross value added (Table A-8) at current prices in the industry has increased by 26.88 times at the trend rate of 17.05 per cent. The Real GVA in the industry has increased at the rate of 9.70 per cent per annum. The wage share in the industry has been fluctuating over the period from a peak of 0.5974 in 1980-81, when real earnings per worker were the lowest, to a bottom of 0.2675 in 1994-95.

6.5.2c. Trends in Rate of Return on Capital

Data on rate of return on capital, presented in Table 6.4, reveals that the rate of return on capital at current prices has increased at trend rate of 11.15 per cent, ranging from 7.36 per cent in 1980-81 to 95.39 per cent in 1994-95. The rate of return at constant machinery prices increased at the rate of 2.95 per cent, ranging from 3.89 per cent to 16.87 per cent with a mean of 8.62 per cent. The low value of RR_p particularly during initial periods indicates that the re-investment potential of the industry has been low. It may be noted that RR_p has moved upward in harmony with capital productivity. The rate of return at constant machinery prices increased at a healthier rate of 4.16 per cent per annum ranging from 4.62 per cent to 24.13 per cent.

The money wage rate in the industry is positively related to both lagged labour productivity (LP) and consumer price index (CPIIW). The results presented in equation 6.4 suggest that money wages in sugar industry are fully adjusted in relation to the change in consumer price (elasticity being more than unity) but are partially adjusted to the change in labour productivity.

Table 6.4 : Indexes of Rate of Returns and Wage-Productivity Movement: Sugar Industry

Year	Rate of returns at Current Prices (RR_m)	Rate of returns at Constant Machinery Prices (RR_k)	Rate of returns at Constant Product Prices (RR_p)	Wage-Productivity Index (W-P)	Ratio of Growth Rates of Wages & Labour Productivity
1	2	3	4	5	6
1973-74	100.00	100.00	100.00	100.00	100.00
1974-75	98.70	77.21	91.37	103.49	0.958
1975-76	106.94	75.45	99.47	114.88	1.115
1976-77	125.34	89.67	113.75	103.50	0.879
1977-78	104.62	73.98	103.11	111.89	1.174
1978-79	108.74	72.65	116.53	114.69	1.115
1979-80	104.16	60.21	92.29	118.12	0.852
1980-81	91.00	48.01	57.09	124.61	0.747
1981-82	198.28	95.32	120.50	92.97	0.723
1982-83	297.85	136.01	204.60	87.64	1.066
1983-84	321.61	138.53	219.10	87.20	0.987
1984-85	221.78	91.28	142.91	108.59	1.178
1985-86	272.07	101.80	147.33	91.53	0.708
1986-87	310.63	110.19	160.31	88.15	0.918
1987-88	314.00	107.06	157.45	96.26	1.061
1988-89	573.27	177.71	266.45	71.94	0.693
1989-90	578.23	161.69	237.80	76.49	0.941
1990-91	322.03	83.06	132.44	108.85	1.423
1991-92	362.46	80.87	134.94	109.36	0.909
1992-93	431.95	86.96	141.96	104.39	0.843
1993-94	789.48	154.11	222.27	70.26	0.577
1994-95	1178.88	208.48	298.23	55.80	0.714
1995-96	729.33	120.75	188.45	84.03	1.538
Annual Trend Rate (% Per Annum)					
1973-95	11.15	2.95+	4.16+	–1.68+	-
	(3.429)	(.935)	(1.753)	(1.258)	-
1973-84	10.44	2.55+	5.43+	–0.94+	-
	(3.900)	(.998)	(1.961)	(.972)	
1985-95	11.52	2.18+	2.69+	–1.89+	-
	(3.562).	(.679)	(.960)	(.968)	

Source: Calculated from data given in Appendix Table A-2, A-8, A-14 & A-20.

Notes: 1. Data computed from tables as per the methodology explained..

2. The trend rates are calculated by fitting exponential function of type $Y = ab^t$.

3. Figure in brackets refers to the t-values of trend coefficient. All trend rates are significant at 1% level of significance unless otherwise specified..

4. * Significant at 5% level; + Insignificant.

6.5.2d. Wage and Employment Functions

$$\text{Ln}(EE_m) = -3.371 + 0.291\,\text{Ln}(LP_{-1}) + 1.342\,\text{Ln}(CPIIW_{-1})$$
$$(3.803)\quad(2.628)\quad(5.412) \qquad ...(6.4)$$
Adj. $R^2 = 0.917$, $DW = 1.374$, $Rho = 0.5735\ (2.984)$

A slope dummy for years of significantly rising labour productivity is introduced to see the wage rate adjustment behaviour in these years, and an intercept dummy is introduced to see that whether the wage rate adjustment process is different in both sub-periods. The results show that both coefficients are insignificant; this means that neither wages respond differently to the rising productivity nor the wage adjustment in relation to productivity and price, is different in the later half of period.

$$\text{Ln}(EE_m) = 3.204 + 0.276\,\text{Ln}(LP_{-1}) + 1.139\,\text{Ln}(CPIIW_{-1})$$
$$(3.117)\quad(1.986)\qquad(4.905)$$
$$+\,0.001\,D^*\,\text{Ln}(LP_{-1}) + 0.068\,IDMY. \qquad ...(6.5)$$
$$(0.062)\qquad(0.334)$$
Adj. $R^2 = 0.916$, $DW = 1.405$, $Rho = 0.537\ (2.548)$.

The estimates of employment function for sugar industry shows that short run elasticity of employment with respect to wage rate is 0.355 and long-run elasticity is 0.529. This indicates that a rise in product wage results in the reduction in employment. The elasticity of employment with respect to output is very low (0.118) and is statistically insignificant. This indicates the low labour absorption in the industry. Statistical results show that a 10 per cent increase in output increased the employment only by 1.1 per cent in short-run and 1.8 per cent in long run.

$$\text{Ln}(L) = 4.666 - 0.355\,\text{Ln}(EE_p) + 0.118\,\text{Ln}(V) + 0.3291\,\text{Ln}(L_{-1}).$$
$$(8.278)\quad(3.215)\qquad(1.008)\qquad(3.253) \quad ...(6.6)$$
Adj. $R^2 = 0.716$, $D\text{-}H = 0.745$, $Rho = 0.513\ (2.485)$.

6.5.3 Paper and Paperboard

6.5.3a. Trends in Wages and Earnings

The share of fringe benefit in total emoluments has been increasing in the industry steadily, rising from 12.8 per cent in 1979-80 to 20.7 per cent in 1994-95. In Table 6.5 the data on indexes of wages per worker and earnings per employee in the industry (absolute values are in Table A-21) are shown. The earnings per employee has increased from Rs. 4918 in the base year to Rs. 47,128 in 1995-96: an increase by 9.58 times at the trend rate of 10.50 per cent per annum. Whereas, the wages per worker has increased from Rs. 3700 to Rs. 41,838: an increase of 11.3 times at the growth rate of 11.46 per cent per annum. The rise in EE_m and WW_m for first half of the period has been at the trend rate of 8.02 per cent and 9.88 per cent respectively. The period from 1985-86 to 1995-96 shows a more rapid rise in the nominal rate of compensation at the trend rate of 12.36 per cent and 12.92 per cent for EE_m and WW_m respectively. However, it may be noted that the growth of earnings in the industry has been less than the national per capita income for the entire period (11.16 per cent) and for both the sub-periods (9.6 per cent & 13.15 per cent respectively). Comparatively slow growth in EE_m indicates that wages per worker has been increasing faster than salary per person in salaried class. The graph (chart-6.3) of money wages and inflation shows that the rise in money wages has been more than the rise in CPIIW. The money wages and earnings, discussed above, convey no idea about the change in the standard of living. When the money values are deflated by CPIIW, the real consumption earnings per employee increased by 55 per cent from Rs. 4918 to Rs. 7635, at the trend rate of 1.86 per cent per annum. Whereas, real wages increased by 83 per cent from Rs. 3700 to Rs. 6778, at annual trend rate of 2.74 per cent. Like money wages or earnings, the increase has been more in second sub-period (2.43 per cent and 2.94 per cent for EE_r and WW_r respectively) than first sub-period (0.71 per cent and 2.45 per cent for EE_r and WW_r respectively). It may be noted that the index of real earnings has been more than 100, even in the periods of downward movement of productivity. Chart 6.3 also shows that the graph of real earnings is above the graph of labour productivity and product earnings for the period when labour productivity was below base year. The product earnings per employee have increased at a trend rate of 1.97 per cent. The growth rates of product wages per worker and product earnings per employee are significantly lower than the growth rate of money wages per worker and earnings per employee, indicating that the industry has successfully shifted the rising wage burden on to the consumers through a rise in product price. The annual trend rate of product earnings has been negative in the first sub-period (–0.46 per cent). Most of the rise in product earnings took place during the second period at the trend rate of 2.27%. The comparison of labour productivity with earnings shows that there are several periods where productivity lags behind earnings. The wage-productivity index has been more than 100 for most of the times. This implies that earnings surpassed labour productivity, which in turn results in an increase in net labour cost per unit of output and a rise in relative share of labour in output. This may be seen from the graph (Chart 6.3) where product earnings per employee, lies above the value added per employee from 1977-78 to 1983-84, 1985-86 and 1987-88. This implies that earnings increased faster than output. This trend is a very disturbing; it puts the industry in unfavourable position by suppressing the rate of return on capital. The comparisons of growth rate of earnings per employee and labour productivity show that increase in earnings has been more than the increase in labour productivity for the period 1975-76 to 1982-83 except the year 1979-80 and again from the year 1991-92 to 1993-94.

Table 6.5: Indexes of Wages and Earnings: Paper and Paperboard Industry

Year	Earnings Per Employee at Current Prices (EE_m)	Wages Per Workers at Current Prices (WW_m)	Earnings Per Employee at Constant Consumer Prices (EE_r)	Wages Per Worker at Constant Consumer Prices (WW_r)	Earnings Per Employee at Constant Product Prices (EE_p)	Wages Per Worker at Constant Product Prices (WW_p)
1	2	3	4	5	6	7
1973-74	100.00	100.00	100.00	100.00	100.00	100.00
1974-75	124.72	118.29	98.36	93.29	87.19	82.70
1975-76	131.02	122.61	104.65	97.93	92.10	86.19
1976-77	131.96	128.49	109.60	106.72	94.66	92.18
1977-78	140.13	135.63	108.13	104.65	98.13	94.98
1978-79	158.56	172.58	119.76	130.35	104.52	113.76
1979-80	171.14	182.58	118.84	126.79	93.14	99.36
1980-81	184.66	206.12	115.12	128.51	90.99	101.57
1981-82	202.13	223.33	112.05	123.80	92.54	102.25
1982-83	196.90	215.87	101.29	111.05	84.88	93.06
1983-84	230.44	259.53	105.32	118.62	91.38	102.92
1984-85	263.36	293.37	113.13	126.02	93.61	104.27
1985-86	300.70	329.29	121.25	132.78	102.70	112.46
1986-87	328.90	370.44	122.00	137.41	108.24	121.91
1987-88	371.20	400.94	126.09	136.19	118.18	127.65
1988-89	390.25	444.96	124.13	141.53	117.26	133.70

conti.

1989-90	489.23	570.06	143.39	167.08	127.18	148.19
1990-91	532.52	620.86	139.99	163.21	129.81	151.35
1991-92	598.24	684.94	138.52	158.60	124.06	142.05
1992-93	660.95	775.95	139.65	163.95	115.09	135.11
1993-94	737.03	805.65	144.86	158.35	121.77	133.11
1994-95	832.64	959.44	148.67	171.31	136.69	157.51
1995-96	958.22	1130.76	155.24	183.20	138.79	163.78
Annual Trend Rates (% Per Annum)						
1973-95	10.50 (39.948)	11.46 (51.15)	1.86 (9.928)	2.74 (12.856)	1.90 (6.996)	2.78 (10.471)
1973-84	8.02 (18.439)	9.88 (20.42)	0.71+ (1.339)	2.45 (3.439)	–0.46+ (.981)	1.25* (1.878)
1985-95	12.36 (42.149)	12.92 (29.374)	2.43 (7.733)	2.94 (6.204)	2.27 (4.093)	2.77 (4.055)

Source: Calculated from data given in Appendix Table A-21.

Notes: 1. Data computed from tables as per the methodology explained..

2. The trend rates are calculated by fitting exponential function of type $Y = ab^t$.
3. Figure in brackets refers to the t-values of trend coefficient. All trend rates are significant at 1% level of significance unless otherwise specified.
4. * Significant at 5% level; + Insignificant.

6.5.3b. Trends in Employment, Gross Value Added and Wage Share

The employment in the industry was 72.2 thousands in 1973-74. It has continuously increased up to year 1982-83 (120.6 thousands) except for year 1978-79 (Appendix Table A-3). The employment fluctuated up to year 1988-89 (101.7 thousands) after this it has continuously increased up to 1995-96 (132.1 thousands). Employment increased at the annual trend rate of 2.21 per cent for entire period, the increase has been more in first sub-period (4.94 per cent) than in second sub-period (2.42 per cent). On the other hand, the gross value added in the industry has increased from Rs. 9878 lakhs to Rs. 268,807 lakhs: an increase of more than 27 times at the trend rate of 14.12 per cent. Most of this increase has taken place in second sub-period only (20.17 per cent). In real terms, this increase has been at the trend rate of 5.23 per cent and here also most of the increase has taken place in second sub-period (9.35 per cent). Total wage cost to the industry has increased by 17.5 times at the trend rate of 12.9 per cent (13.4 per cent and 15.2 per cent for both sub-periods).

CHART-6.3

Real Earnings per Employee, Product Wage per Employee and Labour Productivity: Paper and Paperboard Industry

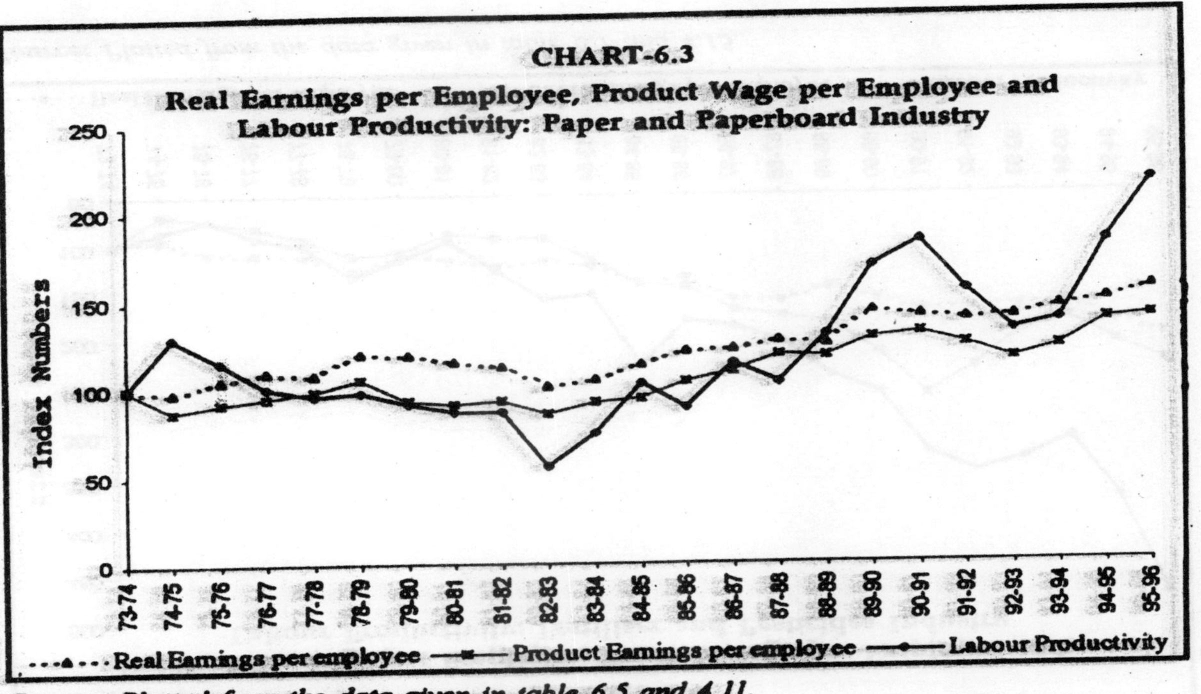

Source: Plotted from the data given in table 6.5 and 4.11.

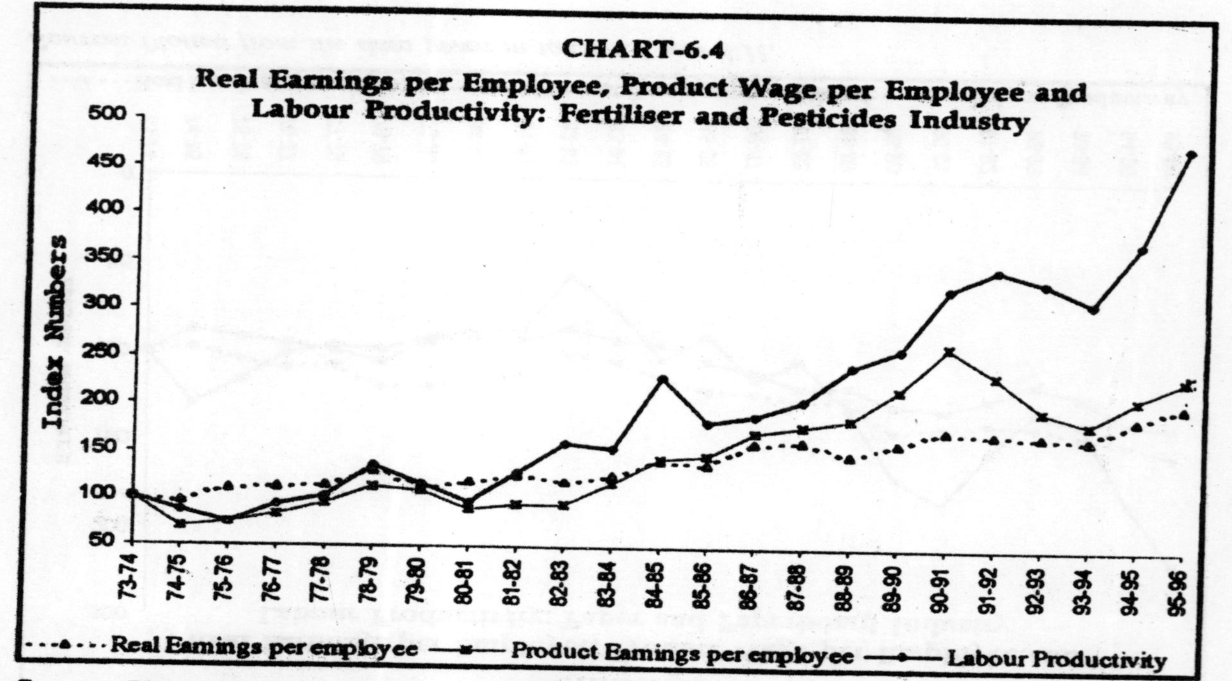

Source: Plotted from the data given in table 6.7 and 4.15.

It may be noted that the increase in wage cost to the industry has been less than the increase in gross value added. Share of wages in value added was 0.3596 in 1973-74 and it has increased from 0.2423 in 1974-75 to 0.5523 in 1982-83. It has been showing a downward trend from year 1987-88 (0.4156). It was as low as 0.2316 in 1995-96. It is interesting to note that wage share and employment have moved in same direction for the period up to 1982-83. Thus, it may be said that the paper and paperboard industry has been changing in character from first sub-period to second sub-period. The first sub-period shows an increase in wage rate associated with the rising wage share, indicating that this was the period when technical progress was capital saving, elasticity of substitution was low and 'invention' was 'stagnate' in Hick's terminology. But in the second period, the fall in wage share has been associated with increasing wage rate indicating the increase in capital intensity. This shows that labour was being substituted by the capital for the period. The invention has been 'active' in Hicksian sense.

6.5.3c. Trends in Rate of Return on Capital

Data on rate of return presented in the Table 6.6 (absolute value in Table A-15) reveals that industry has been in unfavourable position for most of the years under study. The nominal rate of return on capital ranged from 7.9 per cent to 66.4 per cent. The rate of return at constant product prices has ranged from 3.39 per cent to 16.00 per cent and for most of the years it has been less than the base year's rate of return (11.02 per cent). The trend rate at current prices has been 6.13 per cent but for period 1973-74 to 1984-85 the trend rate being negative 1.66 per cent. It is interesting to note that this was the period when wage-productivity index has increased at the positive rate of 3.47 per cent. In the period of 1985-86 to 1995-96 the RR_m increased at the rate of 13.29 per cent where corresponding wage-productivity index decreased at the rate of 4.21 per cent. The rate of return at constant product prices (RR_p) has shown a declining trend at the rate of 2.14 per cent per annum. The first sub-period was a steep decline (9.39 per cent per annum) against an increase in second sub-period (3.11per cent per annum). It may be noted that in general the rate of return has moved up with upward movement in capital productivity. The rate of return at constant machinery prices ranged from 3.59 per cent to 17.9 per cent with the mean value of 8.62 per cent. This is low and does not show a healthy state for re-investment in the industry.

Table 6.6 : Indexes of Rate of Returns and Wage-Productivity Movement: Paper and Paperboard Industry

Year	Rate of returns at Current Prices (RR_m)	Rate of returns at Constant Machinery Prices (RR_k)	Rate of returns at Constant Product Prices (RR_p)	Wage-Productivity Index (W-P)	Ratio of Growth Rates of Wges & Labour Productivity
1	2	3	4	5	6
1973-74	100.00	100.00	100.00	100.00	100.00
1974-75	207.73	162.51	145.23	67.39	0.674
1975-76	165.58	116.82	116.39	80.28	1.191
1976-77	126.87	90.77	91.01	94.40	1.176
1977-78	127.37	90.08	89.20	102.75	1.088
1978-79	125.35	83.75	82.63	107.00	1.041
1979-80	149.42	86.37	81.32	102.92	0.962
1980-81	141.76	74.80	69.85	105.12	1.021
1981-82	145.14	69.77	66.45	107.45	1.022
1982-83	71.45	32.63	30.80	153.59	1.429
1983-84	107.63	46.36	42.68	123.47	0.804
1984-85	170.01	69.98	60.43	92.08	0.746
1985-86	134.52	50.33	45.94	116.91	1.270
1986-87	183.86	65.04	60.34	95.67	0.818
1987-88	152.05	51.84	48.41	115.58	1.208
1988-89	192.05	59.54	57.70	91.02	0.787
1989-90	327.97	91.71	85.26	75.57	0.830
1990-91	371.08	95.71	90.46	71.27	0.943
1991-92	344.22	76.80	71.39	80.29	1.127
1992-93	329.83	66.40	57.43	87.55	1.091
1993-94	331.44	64.70	54.76	89.20	1.019
1994-95	365.58	64.65	60.02	75.35	0.845
1995-96	602.87	99.82	87.32	64.41	0.855
Annual Trend Rates (% Per Annum)					
1973-95	6.13 (5.473)	−1.71⁺ (1.683)	−2.14* (2.117)	−1.03⁺ (1.631)	-
1973-84	−1.66⁺ (.704)	−8.69 (4.121)	−9.39 (4.884)	3.47* (2.402)	-
1985-95	13.29 (6.384)	3.8* (1.862)	3.11⁺ (1.440)	−4.21 (3.467)	-

Source: *Calculated from data given in Appendix Tables A-3, A-9, A-15 and A-21.*

Notes: *1. Data computed from tables as per the methodology explained..*

2. The trend rates are calculated by fitting exponential function of type $Y = ab^t$.

3. Figure in brackets refers to the t-values of trend coefficient. All trend rates are significant at 1% level of significance unless otherwise specified..

*4. * Significant at 5% level; ⁺ Insignificant.*

6.5.2d. Wage and Employment Function

The money wage rate in the industry is positively and significantly related to lagged consumer price index (CPIIW). It is also positively related to lagged labour productivity (LP) but the coefficient is small and insignificant. This indicates that money wages in the industry are more responsive to consumer prices than labour productivity and wages are fully adjusted to the change in consumer prices. Here, it may be noted that due to high correlation among explanatory variables effect of labour productivity may have been captured by consumer prices. Introduction of slope dummy for rising productivity years and intercept dummy from the year 1984-85 shows that both the coefficients are insignificant.

$$\text{Ln}(EE_m) = -0.845 + 0.109\,\text{Ln}(LP_{-1}) + 1.095\,\text{Ln}(CPIIW_{-1}).$$
$$(4.258)\quad(1.492)\qquad\qquad(10.82)\qquad\qquad\ldots(6.7)$$
$$Adj.\ R^2 = 0.988,\ DW = 1.625, F_{2,\,19} = 843.7$$

$$\text{Ln}(EE_m) = -0.837 + 0.087\,\text{Ln}(LP_{-1}) + 1.114\,\text{Ln}(CPIIW_{-1})$$
$$(2.147)\quad(1.052)\qquad\qquad(8.529)$$
$$+\,0.005\,D^*\,\text{Ln}(LP_{-1}) - 0.006\,IDMY.\qquad\qquad\ldots(6.8)$$
$$(0.759)\qquad\qquad(0.034)$$
$$Adj.\ R^2 = 0.987,\ DW = 1.697,\ F_{4,\,1^-} = 393.5$$

The estimates of employment functions (6.9) show that coefficients of product wage (EE_p) and output are insignificant. This indicates that employment in the industry is not affected by increase in wages and output. The coefficient of adjustment is also very low (1–0.836 = 0.164) implying that only about 16.4 per cent discrepancy between actual and desired employment is eliminated during a year.[3] The long-run elasticity of employment with respect to wage rate 0.999 is substantially greater than corresponding short-run elasticity 0.164.

$$\text{Ln}(L) = 1.087 - 0.164\,\text{Ln}(EE_p) + 0.118\,\text{Ln}(V) + 0.836\,\text{Ln}(L_{-1})$$
$$(1.717)\quad(0.829)\qquad\qquad(1.296)\qquad\qquad(9.648)\ldots(6.9)$$
$$Adj.\ R^2 = 0.876,\ D\text{-}H = -0.431;\ F_{(3,\,18)} = 50.41$$

6.5.4 Fertilisers and Pesticides Industry

6.5.4a. Trends in Wages and Earnings

The data on wages and earnings in the industry are presented in Table 6.7. Both money wages and money earnings show a significantly rising trend. The money wages per worker in the industry are increased by 13.79 times from Rs. 5324 in 1973-74 to Rs. 73,513 in 1995-96, at the trend rate of 12.08 per cent. The money earnings per employee in the industry increased by 12.46 times from Rs. 7374 to Rs. 91,890, at the trend rate of 11.78 per cent. The share of fringe benefits in total emoluments is also increasing overtime rising steadily from 15.0 per cent in 1979-80 to 30 per cent in 1995-96 (column 8 of table A-22). This suggests that the welfare activities in the industry are increasing. The increase in money earnings in the industry has been more than national per capita income indicating relative improvement in the position of the workers in the industry. In absolute term also the real wages per worker increased to Rs. 11,910, at the 1973-74 prices showing an increase of 124 per cent at the trend rate of 3.31 per cent. Whereas, the real earnings have increased to Rs. 14,887 at constant price: an increase of 102 per cent at the trend rate of 3.03 per cent was noted. This indicates the significant improvement in the position of workers in the industry. The EE_p (real wage cost to the industry per employee) has increased at the trend rate of 5.72 per cent, which is significantly less than the increase in EE_m indicating that the industry has shifted a part of increased wage cost on to the consumer through rise in product prices. But, the EE_p has increased at a much higher rate than the EE_r; this implies that the wages, as a cost component to the industry, increased at a rate greater than the wages, as income component to the industry. This points to the presence of wage good constraint. The comparison of movements of product earnings with labour productivity shows that the former has lagged behind the later over the period (This can also be seen from Chart 6.4). The year-to-year comparison of growth rates of EE_p and labour productivity reveal that for most of the years particularly after 1986-87 the growth rate of labour productivity has been more than the growth rate of product earnings. This suggests the possibility of rising rate of return in the industry.

Table 6.7 : Indexes of Wages and Earnings: Fertilizers and Pesticides Industry

Year	Earnings Per Employee at Current Prices (EE_m)	Wages Per Workers at Current Prices (WW_m)	Earnings Per Employee at Constant Consumer Prices (EE_r)	Wages Per Worker at Constant Consumer Prices (WW_r)	Earnings Per Employee at Constant Product Prices (EE_p)	Wages Per Worker at Constant Product Prices (WW_p)
1	2	3	4	5	6	7
1973-74	100.00	100.00	100.00	100.00	100.00	100.00
1974-75	123.17	113.24	97.14	89.31	69.11	63.54
1975-76	139.77	143.57	111.64	114.67	74.15	76.16
1976-77	137.11	140.77	113.88	116.91	83.74	85.97
1977-78	148.24	144.41	114.38	111.43	95.17	92.72
1978-79	172.56	192.04	130.33	145.05	112.18	124.85
1979-80	161.59	202.72	112.22	140.77	110.08	138.09
1980-81	192.05	202.72	119.73	126.39	90.13	95.14
1981-82	228.47	256.46	126.65	142.16	95.11	106.77
1982-83	234.41	266.02	120.58	136.84	96.14	109.11
1983-84	276.29	340.60	126.28	155.67	117.64	145.03
1984-85	332.38	371.82	142.77	159.71	144.22	161.33
1985-86	346.40	379.22	139.68	152.91	147.83	161.83
1986-87	436.58	473.65	161.94	175.69	172.18	186.80
1987-88	479.87	535.93	163.00	182.04	180.39	201.46
1988-89	472.91	547.38	150.42	174.10	186.38	215.73
1989-90	555.64	616.82	162.85	180.78	218.23	242.26
1990-91	672.13	792.48	176.69	208.33	263.98	311.25
1991-92	747.51	877.88	173.09	203.27	234.55	275.46
1992-93	811.99	914.43	171.57	193.21	196.36	221.13
1993-94	854.57	987.67	167.96	194.13	182.62	211.06
1994-95	1052.97	1147.77	188.01	204.94	209.31	228.15
1995-96	1246.09	1379.66	201.88	223.52	230.09	254.75
Annual Trend Rates (% Per Annum)						
1973-95	11.78 (16.02)	12.08 (45.26)	3.03 (4.401)	3.31 (16.88)	5.72 (7.323)	6.01 (10.80)
1973-84	10.04 (5.046)	14.15 (18.190)	2.60* (2.280)	6.42 (6.185)	3.95 (3.149)	7.83 (3.941)
1985-95	12.58 (19.22)	12.76 (17.86)	2.63 (4.199)	2.8 (3.911)	2.96+ (1.159)	3.13+ (1.299)

Source : Calculated from data given in Appendix Table A-22.

Notes : 1. Data computed from tables as per the methodology explained..

2. The trend rates are calculated by fitting exponential function of type $Y = ab^t$.

3. Figure in brackets refers to the t-values of trend coefficient. All trend rates are significant at 1% level of significance unless otherwise specified..

4. * Significant at 5% level; + Insignificant.

6.5.4b. Trends in Employment, Gross Value Added and Wage Share

The employment in the industry has increased from 50.6 thousands to 104.8 thousands: an increase of 107 per cent at the trend rate of 2.75 per cent. The increase in employment in the industry has fluctuated over the period. The gross value added at current prices in the industry has increased from Rs. 12,833 lakhs to Rs. 683,033 lakhs: a remarkable increase by more then 53 times at the significant growth rate of 17.32 per cent. In real terms also gross value added has increased at the trend rate of 10.96 per cent. It is interesting to note that employment elasticity of output in the industry is very low (0.2509). The total wage bill to the industry has increased from Rs. 3731 lakhs to Rs. 96,258 lakhs: an increase by 25.8 times at trend rate of 14.85 per cent. The wage cost at constant product price has also increased to Rs. 17,774 lakhs: an increase by 476 per cent at the trend rate of 8.62 per cent. The higher growth rate of gross value added than the wage bill have resulted in the falling share of wages in value added in the industry over time: from 0.2907 to 0.1409, almost half of the base year. The increasing real wages/earnings along with falling wage share in GVA demonstrates that capital intensity has increased and technical progress has been capital using, in the industry. Thus, labour has been substituted by the capital in the industry and the invention of capital has been 'active' in Hick's terminology.

6.5.4c. Trends in Rate of Return on Capital

The data on rate of return in the industry presented in Table 6.8 shows that at current prices the value of RR_m has ranged from 7.68 per cent to 80.82 per cent: an increase of more than 10.5 times at the trend rate of 9.34 per cent. The rate of return at constant capital prices (RR_k) has ranged from 5.96 per cent (1979-80) to 13.38 per cent (1995-96) with a mean of 8.18 per cent and at trend rate of 1.27 per cent. The RR_k has been low, despite a significant rise in gross value added, because capital in the industry has risen at significantly high rate. The RR_p in the industry has increased at the rate of 3.41 per cent ranging from 5.52 per cent (1980-81) to 14.92 per cent (1995-96) with a mean of 8.72 per cent. The increase in RR_p has been more in the periods of increasing capital productivity.

Table 6.8 : Indexes of Rate of Returns and Wage-Productivity Movement: Fertilisers and Pesticides Industry

Year	Rate of returns at Current Prices (RR_m)	Rate of returns at Constant Machinery Prices (RR_k)	Rate of returns at Constant product Prices (RR_p)	Wage-Productivity Index (W-P)	Ratio of Growth Rates of Wages & Labour Productivity
1	2	3	4	5	6
1973-74	100.00	100.00	100.00	100.00	100.00
1974-75	159.22	124.56	89.34	79.81	0.881
1975-76	125.17	88.31	66.41	98.55	0.906
1976-77	130.23	93.17	79.54	90.01	0.915
1977-78	121.21	85.72	77.82	92.76	1.190
1978-79	160.44	107.2	104.31	82.40	1.025
1979-80	134.31	77.64	91.49	94.79	0.947
1980-81	153.15	80.81	71.88	93.13	0.840
1981-82	210.48	101.18	87.62	73.47	0.919
1982-83	285.21	130.24	116.98	60.11	0.962
1983-84	252.76	108.87	107.63	75.62	1.444
1984-85	329.62	135.67	143.03	62.50	1.031
1985-86	264.75	99.06	112.98	80.57	0.902
1986-87	231.96	82.28	91.48	90.20	1.059
1987-88	276.99	94.44	104.12	87.64	1.034
1988-89	324.00	100.44	127.69	76.99	1.004
1989-90	333.07	93.14	130.82	83.71	0.696
1990-91	369.29	95.24	145.04	81.84	1.456
1991-92	450.46	100.51	141.34	68.21	0.644
1992-93	617.26	124.27	149.27	59.59	1.720
1993-94	607.37	118.56	129.79	59.05	0.914
1994-95	756.93	133.86	150.46	56.16	1.045
1995-96	1052.2	174.21	194.29	48.47	0.992
Annual Trend Rates (% Per Annum)					
1973-95	9.34	1.27*	3.41	–2.11	-
	(14.05)	(2.020)	(6.836)	(4.682)	
1973-84	9.51	1.68⁺	3.45*	–3.43	-
	(5.163)	(1.020)	(2.151)	(3.415)	
1985-95	15.21	5.56	5.37	–5.60	-
	(11.70)	(4.252)	(4.944)	(6.709)	

Source: Calculated from data given in Appendix Tables A-4, A-10, A-16 & A-22.

Notes: 1. Data computed from tables as per the methodology explained.

2. The trend rates are calculated by fitting exponential function of type $Y = ab^t$.

3. Figure in brackets refers to the t-values of trend coefficient. All trend rates are significant at 1% level of significance unless otherwise specified..

4. * Significant at 5% level; ⁺ Insignificant.

6.5.4d. Wage and Employment Functions

Wage behaviour in fertilisers and pesticides industry shows that the coefficient of lagged labour productivity in equation 6.10 is negative which is not conceivable. So when we exclude lagged consumer price from model, we find that wages in industry are positively related to lagged labour productivity (equation 6.11) and a negative sign of lagged labour productivity in subsequent models may be due to the high correlation between $CPIIW_{-1}$ and LP_{-1} ($r = 0.990$). However, in this case also, coefficient of wages is less than unity indicating that wage rate in industry does not fully adjust to change in productivity, i.e., 10 per cent increase in labour productivity leads to an increase of only 8.45 per cent in wages.

$$\text{Ln}(EE_m) = -2.221 - 0.228\,\text{Ln}(LP_{-1}) + 1.740\,\text{Ln}(CPIIW_{-1}) \qquad \text{..(6.10)}$$
$$(6.147) \qquad (1.832) \qquad (8.715)$$
$$Adj.\ R^2 = 0.992,\ DW = 1.654,\ F_{2,\,19} = 1244$$

$$\text{Ln}(EE_m) = 0.795 + 0.845\,\text{Ln}(LP_{-1}) \qquad \text{...(6.11)}$$
$$(3.509) \qquad (22.55)$$
$$Adj.\ R^2 = 0.960,\ DW = 1.881,\ F_{1,\,20} = 508.3$$

It is found that the wage rate behaviour in the industry is different for the years of significantly rising productivity, as the coefficient of slope dummy is positive and significant in equation 6.12. The wage rate adjustment to labour productivity has accelerated in periods of rising productivity. However, the wage behaviour in relation to adjustment to labour productivity and prices is same for both sub-periods.

$$\text{Ln}(EE_m) = -1.359 + 0.043\,\text{Ln}(LP_{-1}) + 1.362\,\text{Ln}(CPIIW_{-1})$$
$$(2.147)\ (0.319) \qquad (5.752)$$
$$+\,0.0128\,D^*\,\text{Ln}(LP_{-1}) + 0.0626\,IDMY. \qquad \text{...(6.12)}$$
$$(2.354) \qquad (1.174)$$
$$Adj\ R^2 = 0.993,\ DW = 2.324,\ F_{4,\,1^-} = 770.4.$$

It may be noted that wage rate is more responsive to consumer price index than to change in labour productivity and labour productivity along with consumer price index explain most of the variation in wage rate.

The employment function for the industry shows that all the coefficients are of expected sign, but the coefficient of wage rate is not statistically significant and is having low numerical value. The short-run employment elasticity for wage rate is 0.178 and long-run elasticity is 0.207. This implies that an increase in wage rate has not resulted in significant reduction in employment. The employment is significantly related to change in output, the elasticities being 0.301 and 0.355 for short-run and long-run, respectively. This implies that even if wages do not rise, a 10 per cent increase in output will increase the employment only by 3.01 per cent in short-run and 3.55 per cent in long-run.

$$\text{Ln (L)} = 3.494 - 0.178 \text{ Ln } (EE_p) + 0.306 \text{ Ln (V)} + 0.139 \text{ Ln}(LP_{-1}).$$
$$(4.706)\ (1.501) \qquad (3.469) \qquad (.752) \qquad ...(6.13)$$
$$Adj.\ R^2 = 0.825;\ D\text{-}H = -1.292;\ F_{(1,\ 18)} = 34.07.$$

6.5.5 Motor Vehicles Industry

6.5.5a. Trends in Wages and Earnings

The Table 6.9 (absolute values in Table A-23) shows a significantly rising trends in earnings per employee and wages per worker. The wages per worker at current prices (WW_m) have increased by 12.96 times from Rs. 5254 in 1973-74 to Rs. 68,096 in 1995-96, at the trend rate of 12.16 per cent per annum whereas, the earnings per employee at current prices (EE_m) have increased by 11.38 times from Rs. 6796 to Rs. 78,660, at the trend rate of 11.57 per cent. The increase in earnings has been close to the increase in national per capita income at current prices for the whole period. Thus, the relative position of the employees of the industry is more or less stagnant. The comparison of growth rates of EE_m and CPIIW in Chart 6.8(E) shows that growth rate of EEm is generally more than the growth rate of CPIIW. The growth rate of WW_m has been more than EE_m despite the increase in share of fringe benefits in total wage bill, this implies that the earnings per person in salaried class have increased slower than wages per worker in the industry. The welfare of workers and employees is indicated not by money earnings but by real earnings. When money wages and earnings are deflated by CPIIW, the earnings per employee at constant consumption price (EE_r) show an increase of 87 per cent, at the trend rate of 2.67 per cent per annum. Whereas, the wages per worker have more than doubled to Rs. 11,032 at the trend rate of 3.38 per cent, indicating a significant improvement in the position of workers. The increase in

Table 6.9 : Indexes of Wages and Earnings: Motor Vehicles Industry

Year	Earnings Per Employee at Current Prices (EE_m)	Wages Per Workers at Current Prices (WW_m)	Earnings Per Employee at Constant Consumer Prices (EE_r)	Wages Per Worker at Constant Consumer Prices (WW_r)	Earnings Per Employee at Constant Product Prices (EE_p)	Wages Per Worker at Constant Product Prices (WW_p)
1	2	3	4	5	6	7
1973-74	100.00	100.00	100.00	100.00	100.00	100.00
1974-75	121.38	116.96	95.72	92.24	95.35	91.88
1975-76	127.55	126.46	101.88	101.00	91.43	90.65
1976-77	132.69	133.68	110.21	111.03	97.26	97.98
1977-78	139.76	136.46	107.84	105.29	100.13	97.77
1978-79	159.31	169.09	120.32	127.71	104.80	111.24
1979-80	158.69	165.27	109.92	114.77	83.72	87.41
1980-81	180.56	192.41	112.57	119.96	82.52	87.94
1981-82	216.08	232.95	119.78	129.13	86.77	93.55
1982-83	246.33	265.30	126.71	136.47	95.80	103.18
1983-84	282.65	303.79	129.18	138.84	111.12	119.43
1984-85	319.11	338.93	137.07	145.59	119.64	127.07
1985-86	360.42	388.19	145.33	156.53	117.04	126.06
1986-87	387.23	413.29	143.63	153.30	119.98	128.06
1987-88	430.98	470.70	146.39	159.88	125.29	136.84
1988-89	460.95	525.37	146.61	167.10	119.43	136.12
1989-90	552.49	633.52	161.93	185.67	128.31	147.13
1990-91	590.25	672.50	155.17	176.79	126.04	143.60
1991-92	678.20	775.68	157.04	179.61	129.82	148.48
1992-93	721.60	806.31	152.47	170.37	128.45	143.53
1993-94	785.55	880.57	154.40	173.08	136.96	153.53
1994-95	905.56	1021.33	101.69	182.36	147.37	166.21
1995-96	1157.42	1296.11	187.52	209.99	175.45	196.47
Annual Trend Rates (% Per Annum)						
1973-95	11.38	12.16	2.67	3.38	2.45	3.17
	(51.96)	(61.47)	(17.66)	(18.22)	(7.767)	(10.97)
1973-84	10.35	11.44	2.89	3.91	0.81⁺	1.81*
	(16.38)	(16.38)	(8.518)	(9.022)	(.866)	(2.016)
1985-95	11.66	12.12	1.79	2.21	3.02	3.44
	(21.35)	(23.46)	(3.776)	(4.210)	(4.852)	(6.413)

Source : Calculated from data given in Appendix Table A-23.

Notes: 1. Data computed from tables as per the methodology explained.

2. The trend rates are calculated by fitting exponential function of type $Y = ab^t$.
3. Figure in brackets refers to the t-values of trend coefficient. All trend rates are significant at 1% level of significance unless otherwise specified.
4. * Significant at 5% level; $^+$ Insignificant.

wages and earnings has been more in first sub-period (3.91 per cent and 2.89 per cent) than in second sub-period (1.79 per cent and 2.21 per cent). The real earnings analysed above are significant for the welfare of workers, but they do not represent real wage cost to the industry. The relevant variable for the analysis of wage cost to the industry is money values deflated by product prices. The product earnings per employee have increased by 75 per cent at the trend rate of 2.46 per cent. The most of this increase took place in second sub-period (3.02 per cent). In first sub-period the EE_p has increased at insignificant trend rate of 0.81%. However, significantly lower growth rate of product earnings than money earnings indicates, that the industry has successfully transferred the increased wage cost to the customers. Contrary to other industries, here the EE_r increased faster than EE_p implying that wages as an income component to workers have increased faster than the wages as a cost component to employers. The movement of wage-productivity index, which never crossed 100, shows that the increase in wages has been less than the increase in labour productivity throughout the period, compared to the base year rates. This can also be seen from Chart 6.5 where the graph of labour productivity is above the graph of product earnings. If we compare year-to-year growth rates, no definite patterns emerges but the periods of higher growth rates of wages are discernable from 1977-79, 1983-85, 1987-88 and 1991-93.

b. Trends in Employment, Gross Value Added and Wage Share

The employment in the industry has increased from 122.1 thousands to 243.8 thousands, at the growth rate of 2.59 per cent per annum. The employment has continuously increased up to 1982-83 (186.3 thousands) and then it has shown fluctuations up to 1993-94. Again in last two years 1994-95 and 1995-96 employment recorded a significant rise (9.6 per cent and 12.4 per cent). On the other hand, the total wage cost to the industry has been continuously increasing from Rs. 8297 lakhs to Rs. 191,735 lakhs: an increase of more than 23 times at the trend rate of 14.26 per cent per annum. But, as product price has increased at the trend rate of 8.49 per cent, the real wage cost has increased at the trend rate of 5.77 per cent. The gross value added in the industry has increased from Rs. 416,927 lakh to Rs. 758,788 lakh: a remarkable increase by 44.8 times at the annual trend rate of 16.30 per cent. In real terms also the gross value

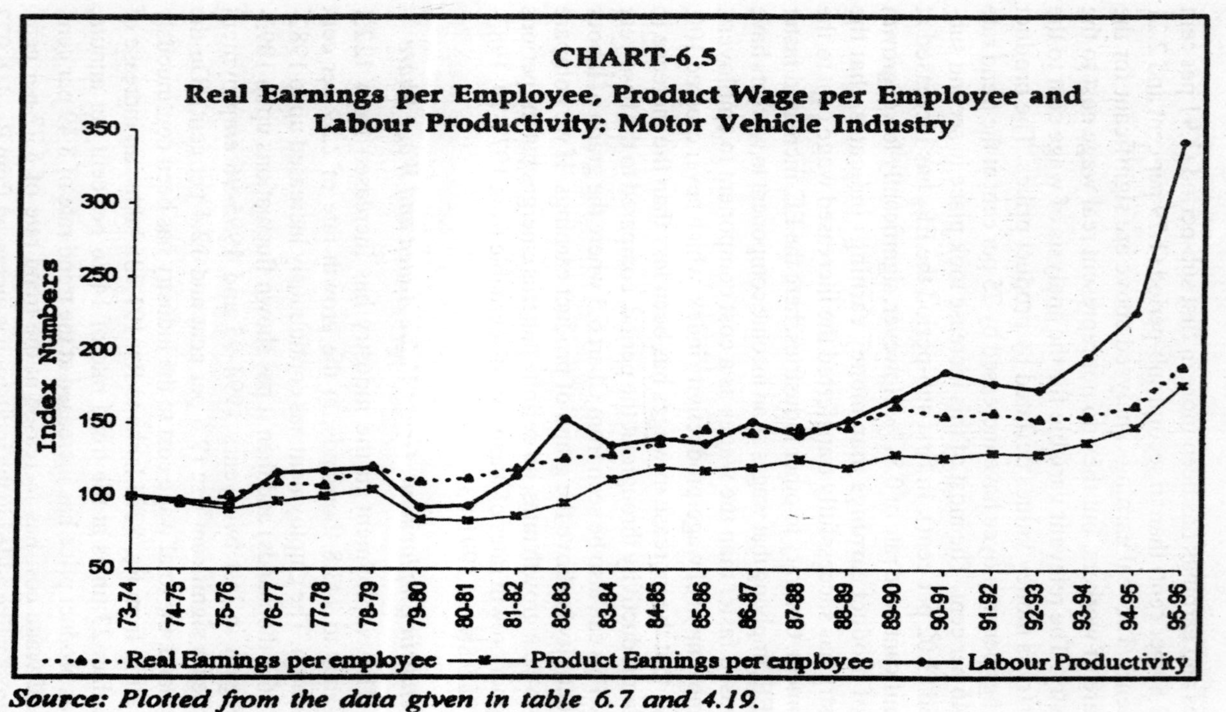

CHART-6.5

Real Earnings per Employee, Product Wage per Employee and Labour Productivity: Motor Vehicle Industry

Source: Plotted from the data given in table 6.7 and 4.19.

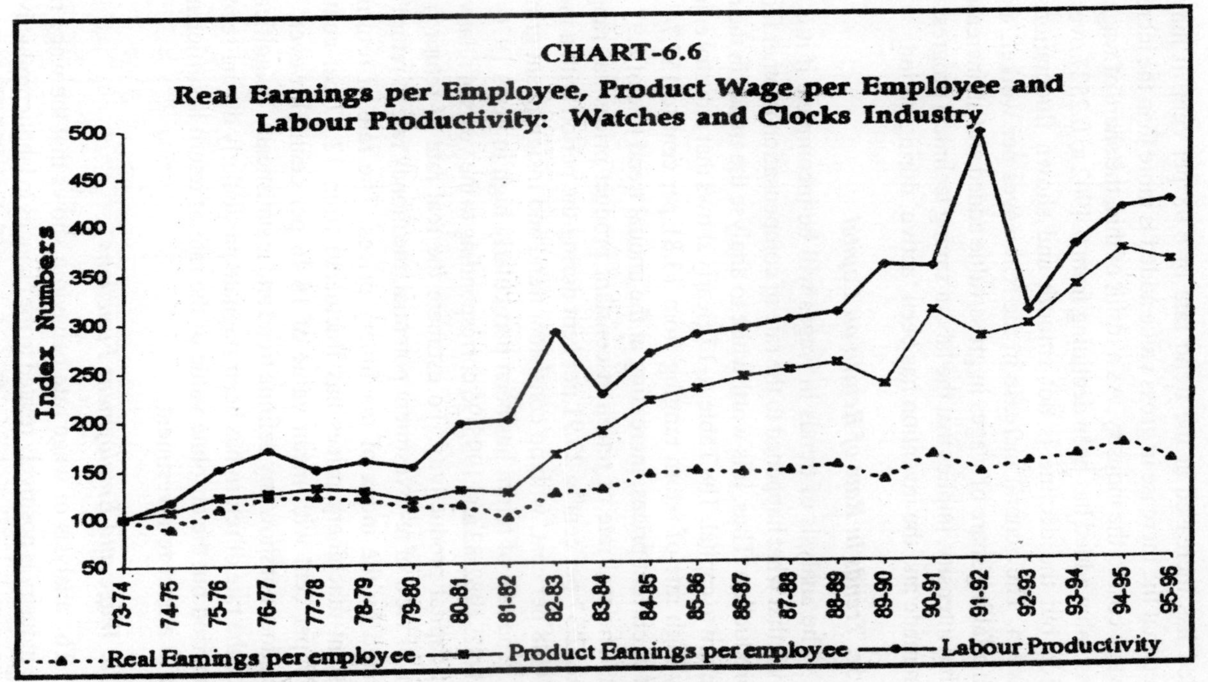

CHART-6.6

Real Earnings per Employee, Product Wage per Employee and Labour Productivity: Watches and Clocks Industry

Source: Plotted from the data given in table 6.9 and 4.23.

added has increased at the trend rate of 6.98 per cent. It may be noted that the increase in gross value added is more than the increase in wage cost to the industry. As a result of this, the share of wages in gross value added has been declining from 0.4902 to 0.2527 over the period but the decline is not smooth and shown fluctuations in between. The general increase in the real wages per worker, along with a falling share of wages in gross value added and an increase in capital intensity, implies that the labour saving technical progress has been made and the invention has been 'active' during period.

6.5.5c. Trends in Rate of Return on Capital

The analysis of trends in wages will be incomplete if it is not known that what happened to the rate of compensation to other factor of production. Thus, it is worthwhile to analyse the trends in the rate of return to capital. The Table A-17 clearly shows that industry enjoys very high rate of return ranging from 13.81 per cent to 157.74 per cent at current prices, increasing at the annual trend rate of 8.97 per cent. The real rate of return at constant product prices has ranged from 12.37 per cent to 23.91 per cent during the period with a mean of 14.88 per cent, with no consistent trend and insignificant growth rate. The rate of return has been particularly high in years 1976-77, 1981-82, 1982-83 and 1995-96 corresponding to the years of relatively high capital productivity. To estimate the real rate of return from point of view of re-investment potential, the money rate of return are deflated by the index of machinery prices. The rate of return at constant machinery prices has fluctuated from 12.17 per cent to 27.77 per cent with mean value of 16.46 per cent. However, the index does not show any definite trend and is statistically insignificant. Thus, the rate of return has been stagnate particularly during second sub-period but the absolute value of the rate of return is sufficiently high to attract re-investment.

6.5.5d. Wage and Employment Functions

The analysis of wege rate behaviour shows that the wage rate in the industry is positively related to the changes in labour productivity and consumer price indexes. But, the coefficient of lagged labour productivity is low indicating that wage rate in the industry is not fully adjusted in relation to changes in labour productivity.

Table 6.10 : Indexes of Rate of Returns and Wage-Productivity Movement: Motor Vehicles Industry

Year	Rate of returns at Current Prices (RR_m)	Rate of returns at Constant Machinery Prices (RR_k)	Rate of returns at Constant product Prices (RR_p)	Wage-Productivity Index (W-P)	Ratio of Growth Rates of Wges & Labour Productivity
1	2	3	4	5	6
1973-74	100.00	100.00	100.00	100.00	100.00
1974-75	122.49	95.83	96.22	97.49	0.975
1975-76	124.99	88.19	89.60	96.61	0.991
1976-77	163.48	116.97	119.83	83.36	0.863
1977-78	162.92	115.21	116.73	85.15	1.021
1978-79	174.21	116.39	114.61	88.02	1.034
1979-80	173.18	100.11	91.60	90.90	1.033
1980-81	199.06	105.03	90.98	88.48	0.973
1981-82	295.32	141.97	118.60	76.10	0.860
1982-83	440.49	201.15	171.32	62.58	0.822
1983-84	285.97	123.18	112.42	82.59	1.320
1984-85	280.14	115.30	105.03	86.33	1.045
1985-86	290.44	108.67	94.32	86.53	1.002
1986-87	335.99	119.18	104.11	80.05	0.925
1987-88	285.44	97.32	82.98	88.89	1.111
1988-89	368.74	114.31	95.54	79.08	0.890
1989-90	426.38	119.23	99.02	77.02	0.974
1990-91	526.51	135.79	112.43	68.40	0.888
1991-92	502.98	112.22	96.28	73.31	1.072
1992-93	492.47	99.14	87.67	74.51	1.016
1993-94	532.74	104.00	92.88	70.16	0.942
1994-95	700.08	123.81	113.93	65.49	0.933
1995-96	1142.64	189.19	173.21	51.55	0.787
Annual Trend Rates (% Per Annum)					
1973-95	8.97 (13.97)	0.93+ (1.543)	0.24+ (.403)	–1.75 (5.424)	-
1973-84	11.58 (7.041)	3.61* (2.323)	1.93+ (1.311)	–2.23* (2.670)	-
1985-95	11.93 (7.141)	2.56+ (1.534)	3.27* (1.922)	–3.81 (5.054)	-

Source: Calculated from data given in Appendix Tables A-5, A-11, A-17 & A-23.

Notes:
1. Data computed from table as per the methodology explained.
2. The trend rates are calculated by fitting exponential function of type $Y = ab^t$.
3. Figure in brackets refers to the t-values of trend coefficient. All trend rates are significant at 1% level of significance unless otherwise specified.
4. * Significant at 5% level; + Insignificant.

$$\text{Ln}(EE_m) = -1.087 + 0.313\ \text{Ln}(LP_{-1}) + 0.943\ \text{Ln}(CPIIW_{-1})$$
$$(2.796) \quad (2.131) \quad (4.628) \quad ...(6.14)$$
$$Adj.\ R^2 = 0.981,\ DW = 1.881,\ Rho = .3727\ (1.489)$$

It is found that wage rate behaviour in the industry was not different for the years to significantly rising productivity. Similarly, wage behaviour, in relation to adjustment to labour productivity and prices, is same for both sub-periods, as the coefficient of slope dummy and intercept dummy are statistically insignificant.

$$\text{Ln}(EE_m) = -0.634 + 0.383\ \text{Ln}(LP_{-1}) + 0.778\ \text{Ln}(CPIIW_{-1})$$
$$(1.237) \quad (2.247) \quad (2.986)$$
$$-0.0036\ D^*\ \text{Ln}(LP_{-1}) + 0.086\ IDMY. \quad ..(6.15)$$
$$(0.669) \quad (1.186)$$
$$Adj.\ R^2 = 0.981,\ DW = 1.797,\ Rho = 0.3692\ (1.463).$$

It may be noted that labour productivity and consumer price index explain most of the variation in wage rate and that nominal wage rate is more responsive to the consumer price index than to the change in labour productivity. The estimates of employment function (equation 6.16) show a good fit to the data. The coefficients are of expected to sign and, are statistically significant. The short-run elasticity of employment with respect to product wage is 0.348 and long-run elasticity is 0.735. This implies that an increase in product wage by 10 per cent will reduce employment by 3.5 per cent in one year and its compound effect over long time will reduce the employment by 7.4 per cent. This shows that labour absorption in the industry is quite sensitive to increase in the wage burden. The wage rate being stable, a 10 per cent increase in value added will increase employment by 3.0 per cent and its cumulative effect over long time will be to increase employment by 6.4 per cent.

$$\text{Ln}(L) = 2.401 - 0.348\ \text{Ln}(EE_p) + 0.301\ \text{Ln}(V) + 0.527\ \text{Ln}(L_{-1})$$
$$(5.227) \quad (3.892) \quad (5.580) \quad (5.186) \quad ...(6.16)$$
$$Adj.\ R^2 = 0.961;\ D\text{-}H = .694,\ F_{(3,18)} = 174.5.$$

6.5.6 Watches and Clocks Industry

6.5.6a. Trends in Wages and Earnings

The data on rates of labour compensation are presented in Table 6.11 (absolute values in Table A-24). The table reveals that money earnings per employee increased by 9.43 times from Rs. 4649 to Rs. 43,860, at the trend rate of 10.98 per cent per annum whereas, the wages per workers have increased by 10.91 times from Rs. 3580 to Rs. 39,064, at the trend rate of 11.44 per cent. The share of fringe benefit, in the industry, has been increasing over time from 17.2 per cent in 1979-80 to 22.0 per cent in 1995-96. This indicates increasing welfare activities in the industry. The increase in earnings per employee in the industry has been less than the increase in per capita income implying that the relative position of the employees in the industry declined during period. But, the increase in the earnings per employee has been more than the rise in consumer price index for industrial workers implying the absolute improvement in the standard of living of workers. Chart 6.8(F) shows that growth rate of earnings per employee has been more than the growth rates of consumer price index for most of the years. This is also shown by the rising index of real rate of compensation. The EE_r and WW_r increased at the trend rate of 2.29 per cent and 2.72 per cent. Most of the increase in real consumption earnings per employee took place in the first sub-period when EE_r and WW_r increased at the rate of 2.28 per cent and 3.66 per cent respectively. In second sub-period, the real earnings increased at the trend rare of 1.22 per cent and 1.72 per cent respectively for the EE_r and WW_r. Real wage cost per employee to the industry shows a much higher increase (at the rate of 7.32 per cent) than in real consumption earnings per employee. This means that wages as a cost component to the industry has increased at a much higher rate than wages as an income component to the workers. This points to the wage goods constraint in the industry. This shows that industry has failed to shift the rising wage cost on to the consumers. The wage-productivity index in the industry has been less than 100 indicating that the rise in labour productivity (GVA per employee) has been more than the rise in earnings per employee. This is also shown in Chart 6.6 where graph of product earnings per employees lie below the graph of labour productivity. However, the year-to-year growth rates of both does not show any such consistent trends. The growth rates of earnings have been less than the growth rates of labour productivity for the years up to 1982-83 except for the years 1978-79 and 1979-80. For the period 1983-84 to 1988-89, except year 1985-86, the growth of earnings has been more than the growth of labour productivity; thereafter no definite pattern is observed.

Table 6.11: Indexes of Wages and Earnings: Watches and Clocks Industry

Year	Earnings Per Employee at Current Prices (EE_m)	Wages Per Workers at Current Prices (WW_m)	Earnings Per Employee at Constant Consumer Prices (EE_r)	Wages Per Worker at Constant Consumer Prices (WW_r)	Earnings Per Employee at Constant Product Prices (EE_p)	Wages Per Worker at Constant Product Prices (WW_p)
1	2	3	4	5	6	7
1973-74	100.00	100.00	100.00	100.00	100.00	100.00
1974-75	114.10	108.76	89.98	85.77	107.18	102.17
1975-76	138.11	137.74	110.31	110.01	121.17	120.84
1976-77	145.90	144.06	121.18	119.65	125.06	123.48
1977-78	157.78	158.61	121.74	122.38	129.66	130.34
1978-79	160.12	175.63	120.94	132.65	127.46	139.81
1979-80	158.82	173.33	110.29	120.37	116.61	127.26
1980-81	179.86	194.67	112.13	121.36	127.44	137.93
1981-82	177.76	187.59	98.54	103.99	123.22	130.03
1982-83	238.67	263.39	122.77	135.49	163.41	180.33
1983-84	278.58	302.98	127.32	138.47	186.27	202.59
1984-85	333.05	377.77	143.06	162.27	218.25	247.56
1985-86	359.8	374.79	145.08	151.13	229.32	238.88
1986-87	387.71	418.02	143.81	155.05	241.05	259.89
1987-88	426.94	474.09	145.02	161.04	248.68	276.14
1988-89	472.96	524.26	150.37	166.75	255.5	283.33
1989-90	464.91	452.88	136.26	132.73	233.71	227.66
1990-91	615.73	659.95	161.86	173.49	308.14	330.27
1991-92	616.92	650.71	142.85	150.67	281.01	296.41
1992-93	722.57	784.57	152.67	165.77	293.23	318.39
1993-94	813.47	867.52	159.89	170.51	332.54	354.63
1994-95	955.46	1055.4	170.6	188.45	368.27	406.8
1995-96	943.47	1091.1	152.85	176.78	355.81	411.49
Annual Trend Rates (% Per Annum)						
1973-95	10.98 (37.71)	11.44 (37.52)	2.29 (8.57)	2.72 (8.64)	7.32 (18.89)	7.77 (18.59)
1973-84	9.7 (12.25)	11.18 (10.49)	2.28 (3.821)	3.66* (2.626)	3.03 (6.663)	4.42 (52.36)
1985-95	11.01 (12.24)	11.56 (19.07)	1.22* (2.298)	1.72* (2.298)	4.86 (5.526)	5.38 (7.287)

Source : Calculated from data given in Appendix Table A-24.

Notes: 1. Data computed from tables as per the methodology explained.

2. The trend rates are calculated by fitting exponential function of type $Y=ab^t$.
3. Figure in brackets refers to the t-values of trend coefficient. All trend rates are significant at 1% level of significance unless otherwise specified.
4. * Significant at 5% level.

Table 6.12 : Indexes of Rate of Returns and Wage Productivity Movement: Watches and Clocks Industry

Year	Rate of returns at Current Prices (RR_m)	Rate of returns at Constant Machinery Prices (RR_k)	Rate of returns at Constant Product Prices (RR_p)	Wage Productivity Index (W-P)	Ratio of Growth Rates of Wages & Labour Productivity
1	2	3	4	5	6
1973-74	100.00	100.00	100.00	100.00	0.3745
1974-75	149.82	117.21	140.74	92.47	0.6690
1975-76	182.73	128.92	160.32	80.05	0.3200
1976-77	219.74	157.21	188.35	73.95	–1.3520
1977-78	188.95	133.62	155.28	86.43	1.3373
1978-79	220.84	147.55	175.79	81.19	–0.3115
1979-80	236.71	136.83	173.79	77.28	0.3654
1980-81	261.50	137.98	185.29	6.55	–0.7510
1981-82	254.82	122.50	176.63	61.71	0.8780
1982-83	409.39	186.95	280.29	56.74	–0.7400
1983-84	251.34	108.26	168.06	83.11	1.1805
1984-85	233.17	95.97	152.80	82.17	–0.0786
1985-86	252.35	94.42	160.84	80.69	2.1577
1986-87	251.40	89.18	156.30	82.54	1.3832
1987-88	244.86	83.49	142.62	82.86	1.0462
1988-89	245.51	76.11	132.68	83.32	–0.5638
1989-90	335.30	93.76	168.56	66.00	52.776
1990-91	225.15	58.07	112.68	87.33	–0.0264
1991-92	460.73	102.80	209.87	57.17	–0.6879
1992-93	223.44	44.98	90.68	95.53	0.5053
1993-94	245.37	47.90	100.30	88.94	1.3188
1994-95	273.11	48.30	105.26	89.73	0.7957
1995-96	336.17	55.66	126.78	84.99	0.3745
Annual Trend Rates (% Per Annum)					
1973-95	2.89 (3.661)	–4.7 (6.246)	–1.42* (1.770)	0.94⁺ (.538)	-
1973-84	7.77 (4.075)	0.07⁺ (.403)	3.69* (2.115)	–4.85⁺ (.796)	-
1985-95	1.74⁺ (.810)	–6.78 (3.328)	–3.89⁺ (1.826)	–0.85⁺ (.582)	-

Source: Calculated from data given in Appendix Table A-5, A-12, A-18 & A-24.

Notes: 1. Data computed from tables as per the methodology explained..

2. The trend rates are calculated by fitting exponential function of type $Y = ab^t$.
3. Figure in brackets refers to the t-values of trend coefficient. All trend rates are significant at 1% level of significance unless otherwise specified.
4. * Significant at 5% level; ⁺ Insignificant.

6.5.6b. Trends in Employment, Gross Value Added and Wage Share

The employment in the industry has increased from 6.8 thousands in 1973-74 to 26.7 thousands at trend rate of 5.70 per cent resulting to an increase of more than 395 per cent. The gross value added in the industry has increased from Rs. 664 lakh to Rs. 28,863 lakh: a remarkable increase by more than 43 times at the trend rate of 17.27 per cent. In real terms also, the gross value added has increased at the trend rate of 12.38 per cent. The real gross value added has increased more in the first sub-period (17.0 per cent) than in the second sub-period (8.35 per cent). The employment elasticity in the industry has been less than unity (0.4604) indicating that 10 per cent increase in GVA brought about only 4.6 per cent increase in employment. This indicates that growth in the industry has not created proportionate increase in employment. The total wage bill in the industry has increased from Rs. 317 lakh to Rs. 11,711 lakh: an increase of more than 36.9 times at the trend rate of 16.25 per cent. In real terms also, the wage bill to the industry has increased at the rate of 12.40 per cent per annum. The share of wages in value added in the industry has been fluctuating with no definite pattern: shown in column 7 of Table 6.13. However, the underlying trend is that of decline in the wage share over the whole period (from 0.4774 to 0.4057).

6.5.6c. Trends in Rate of Return on Capital

The data on rate of return at constant price shows a rising trend ranging from 17.95 per cent to 82.7 per cent at the annual trend rate of 2.89 per cent per annum. But most of the increase in the RR_m is during the first period at the annual trend rate of 7.77 per cent. During the second period the trend rate is 1.74 per cent, which is statistically insignificant. The annual trend rate at constant output price has shown decreasing return to capital (–1.4 per cent) but during first period the RR_p increased at the rate of 3.69 per cent. One interesting point to note is that when we look at the graph of product earnings and labour productivity, there is a sharp increase in labour productivity in years 1976-77, 1982-83 and 1991-92; these years also corresponds with sharp increase in the rate of return. In year 1989-90 when product earnings shows a sharp decline corresponding to an increase in labour productivity the rate of return shows a sharp increase. The rate of return at constant capital price has shown a declining trend particularly in second sub-period when it declined at the rate of –7.08 per cent. The RR_k has been considerably high up to year 1982-83 to provide re-investment opportunity but after that RR_k is decreasing with minor exceptions. The low rate of return especially during second period shows that the capacity of the industry to give fair return has been declining and this inhibits the expansion of the industry through plough back.

6.5.6d. Wage and Employment Functions

The wage rate function shows that nominal wages in industry fully adjusted to change in consumer price index. But coefficient of labour productivity, though positive, is not statistically significant. It may not be construed that wages in the industry does not respond to changes in labour productivity because negative index of labour productivity may be due to collinearity problem as partial correlation between $CPIIW_{-1}$ and LP_{-1} is 0.985. To remove the collinearity when we estimated equation by removing CPIIW we find that coefficient of lagged labour productivity is not only statistically significant but is close to unity.

$$Ln(EE_m) = -0.063 + 0.097 \, Ln\,(LP_{-1}) + 1.049 \, Ln\,(CPIIW_{-1})$$
$$(1.174) \quad (.629) \quad (4.923) \qquad ...(6.17)$$
$$Adj.\ R^2 = 0.893,\ DW = 1.721,\ Rho = .6126\ (3.486)$$

$$Ln\,(EE_m) = -0.097 + 0.967 \, Ln\,(LP_{-1}).$$
$$(.337) \quad (19.875) \qquad ...(6.18)$$
$$Adj.\ R^2 = 0.949,\ DW = 1.636,\ F_{1,\,20} = 393.4.$$

We find that wage rate behaviour is not different for the years of significantly rising productivity, as the coefficient of slope dummy is insignificant. However, wage rate behaviour in second half is different than in first half as coefficient of intercept dummy is statistically significant.

$$Ln\,(EE_m) = -0.139 + 0.222 \, Ln\,(LP_{-1}) + 0.816 \, Ln\,(CPIIW_{-1})$$
$$(0.246) \quad (1.013) \quad (2.957)$$
$$-0.009\, D^* \, Ln\,(LP_{-1}) + 0.1651 \qquad ...(6.19)$$
$$(1.026) \quad (2.563)$$
$$Adj.\ R^2 = 0.932,\ DW = 1.814,\ Rho = 0.4719\ (2.208)$$

It can be seen from equation 6.20 that the estimated equation of employment function gives a good fit to data. The estimates of employment function for the industry shows that short-run elasticity of employment with respect to wage rate is 0.211 and long-run elasticity is 0.300. This indicates that a rise in product wage results in the reduction in employment. The elasticity of employment with respect to output is quite high at 0.447 which is statistically significant. This indicates that a 10 per cent increase in output resulted in 4.5 per cent increase in employment in short-run and 6.4 per cent in long-run.

$$\text{Ln}(L) = 2.088 - 0.211\,\text{Ln}(EE_p) + 0.447\,\text{Ln}(V) + 0.297\,\text{Ln}(L_{-1}) \quad \ldots(6.20)$$
$$(6.025)\quad(2.069)\quad(6.245)\qquad\qquad(3.253)$$
$$Adj.\ R^2 = 0.964,\ D\text{-}H = 1.245,\ F_{(3,\,18)} = 187.3.$$

6.6 Inter-Industry Variations in Wage Rate

The trends in wages, earnings, employment, gross value added, wage share and rate of return on capital in different industries differ widely. The employment growth in the industries varies from a very high growth rate of 5.7 per cent in watches & clocks to a negative growth rate of –1.07 per cent in sugar industry.[4] The employment in organised manufacturing sector has increased at a trend rate of 1.95 per cent. The employment in paper & paperboard, fertilisers & pesticides and motor vehicles industries recorded a moderate growth rate of 2.21 per cent, 2.75 per cent and 2.59 per cent respectively. As a general trend, the employment growth in the first half of period is significantly higher than in the second half implying that employment generation in the industries and organised manufacturing sector as a whole is declining. This will be clearer when we look at the growth rates of gross value added in the industries. In three industries sugar, fertilisers & pesticides and watches & clocks along with organised manufacturing sector, gross value added increased at the trend rate of more than 17 per cent. Even in paper & paperboard and motor vehicles industries, it has increased at the annual trend rate of 14.12 per cent and 16.3 per cent. The real gross value added has also increased at significantly high growth rate in the industries. But, the employment elasticity of value added[5] has been less than unity in all industries; it has been highest in watches & clocks (0.460) closely followed by paper & paperboard (0.423) and negative for sugar industry (–0.110). It has been low in fertilisers & pesticides (0.257) and motor vehicles (0.371) industries. The employment elasticity for organised manufacturing sector is very low (0.233) thus, inhibiting the growth of employment and substitution of labour by capital. The total wage bill to the industries has increased at low rate of 12.9 per cent in paper & paperboard industry to a high 17.3 per cent in watches & clocks industry. The wage bill in the organised manufacturing sector has increased at the growth rate of 13.4 per cent whereas in sugar, fertilisers & pesticides and motor vehicles industries wage bill increased at the growth rate of 15.1 per cent, 14.85 per cent, and 14.3 per cent respectively. But, the earnings per employee have increased faster in sugar industry at the rate of 16.33 per cent (17.66 per cent)[6] whereas, the increase has been moderate in fertilisers & pesticides and motor vehicles at the rate of 11.78 per cent (12.08 per cent) and 11.38 per cent (12.16 per cent). The growth of earnings per employee at the rate of 10.98 per cent (11.44 per cent) and 10.50 per cent (11.46 per cent) in watches & clocks and paper & paperboard industries has been less than the growth rate of per capita national income (11.23 per cent). The trend growth rate of earnings per employee in organised manufacturing sector has been same as that of per capita national income. Growth rate in real earnings per employee has not been significantly different from the growth rate of real national per capita income, the only exception being sugar industry where real earnings has increased at the growth rate of 7.23 per cent per annum. This may be due to the fact that the initial wages in this industry were considerably lower than other industries and the 'catch up' affect might have lead to the acceleration in wages particularly in second half. The comparison of growth rates of real consumption earnings per employee and real wage cost per employee reveals that latter has increased faster than former except motor vehicle industry. The real wage cost increase has been maximum in sugar industry (9.02 per cent) followed by watches & clocks industry (7.32 per cent). It has been low in motor vehicle (2.45 per cent) and paper & paperboard industry (1.9 per cent). For aggregate manufacturing sector it increased at the rate of 3.0 per cent). The trends of wage share in the industries reveals that the wage share has been low in fertilisers and pesticides (0.2907) and paper & paperboards (0.3596) industries indicating relatively high capital intensity. And wage share is high in industries like watches & clocks (0.4774), motor vehicles (0.4901) and sugar (0.4794) in 1973-74. The wage share was 0.4625 in entire organised manufacturing sector. The wage share has not behaved uniformly over the period in all

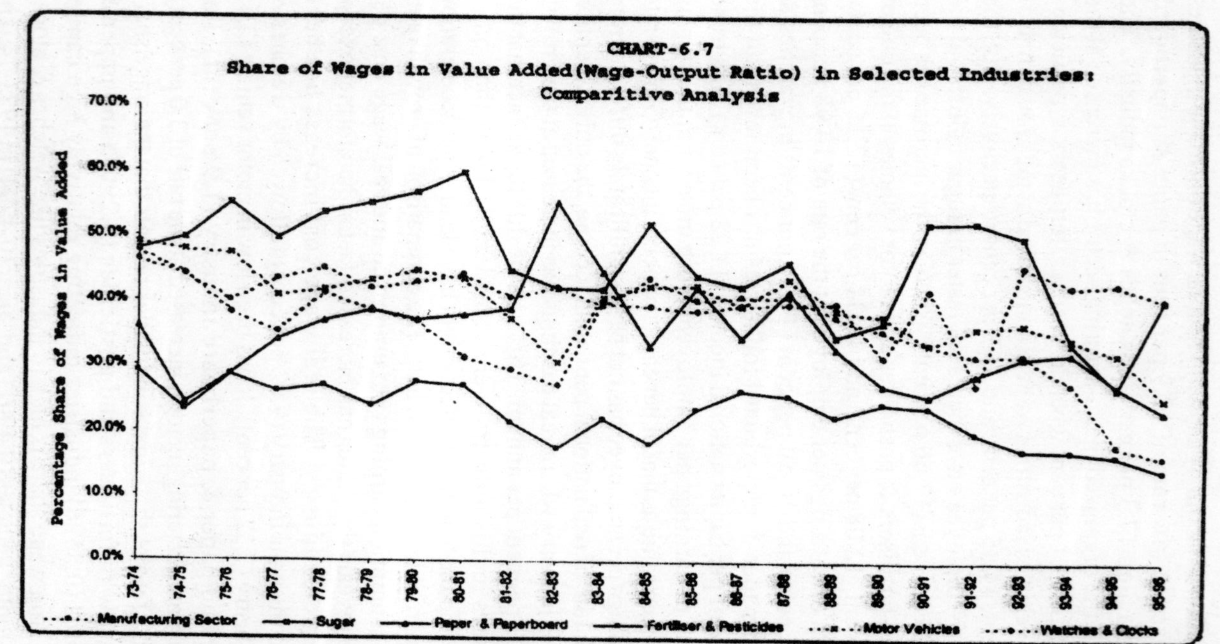

Sources: Plotted from the data given in Table 6.13

CHART: 6.8

Comparision of Growth Rates of Consumer Price Index and Nominal Earnings per Employee (EEm) in Different Industries

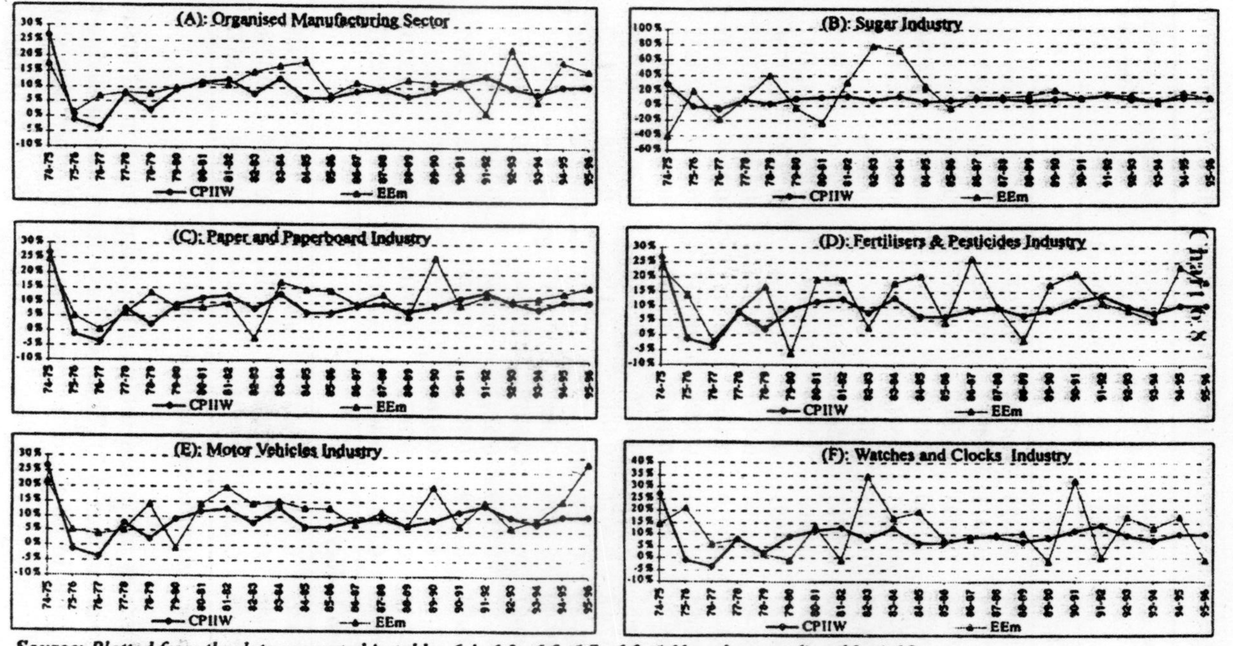

Source: Plotted from the data presented in tables 6.1, 6.3, 6.5, 6.7, 6.9, 6.11 and appendix table A-19.

Table 6.13: Share of Wages in Gross Value Added in Different Industries.

Year	Manufacturing Sector	Sugar	Paper & Paperboard	Fertilisers & Pesticides	Motor Vehicles	Watches & Clocks
1	2	3	4	5	6	7
1973-74	0.4625	0.4794	0.3596	0.2907	0.4902	0.4774
1974-75	0.4413	0.4961	0.2423	0.2320	0.4778	0.4415
1975-76	0.4003	0.5507	0.2887	0.2865	0.4736	0.3822
1976-77	0.4340	0.4962	0.3394	0.2617	0.4086	0.3531
1977-78	0.4493	0.5364	0.3695	0.2697	0.4174	0.4126
1978-79	0.4185	0.5498	0.3847	0.2396	0.4315	0.3876
1979-80	0.4283	0.5662	0.3701	0.2756	0.4455	0.3689
1980-81	0.4403	0.5974	0.3780	0.2708	0.4337	0.3125
1981-82	0.4053	0.4457	0.3864	0.2136	0.3730	0.2946
1982-83	0.4204	0.4201	0.5523	0.1748	0.3067	0.2709
1983-84	0.3919	0.4180	0.4440	0.2198	0.4048	0.3968
1984-85	0.4354	0.5206	0.3311	0.1817	0.4232	0.3923
1985-86	0.4005	0.4388	0.4204	0.2342	0.4242	0.3852
1986-87	0.4073	0.4226	0.3440	0.2622	0.3924	0.3941
1987-88	0.4071	0.4614	0.4156	0.2548	0.4357	0.3956
1988-89	0.3766	0.3449	0.3273	0.2238	0.3876	0.3978
1989-90	0.3538	0.3667	0.2717	0.2434	0.3775	0.3151
1990-91	0.3343	0.5218	0.2563	0.2379	0.3353	0.4169
1991-92	0.3169	0.5243	0.2887	0.1983	0.3593	0.2729
1992-93	0.3178	0.5004	0.3148	0.1733	0.3652	0.4561
1993-94	0.2733	0.3368	0.3208	0.1717	0.3439	0.4246
1994-95	0.1793	0.2675	0.2710	0.1633	0.3210	0.4284
1995-96	0.1613	0.4028	0.2316	0.1409	0.2527	0.4057
Mean Values						
1973-95	0.3763	0.4637	0.3438	0.2270	0.3948	0.3819
1973-84	0.4273	0.5064	0.3705	0.2430	0.4238	0.3742
1985-95	0.3207	0.4171	0.3147	0.2094	0.3632	0.3902

Source: Calculated from appendix tables.

industries but it has shown a declining trend in all industries (as shown in Chart 6.7). Thus, we have found labour saving technical progress in all the industries. The rate of return also shows wide differences amongst industries and it has been low for most of the industries. Except sugar industry (2.95%) other industries does not give fair return on capital, thus, inhibiting the plough back potential of the industries for expansion.

6.7 Inter-Plan Variations in Wage Rate

The inter-plan comparison is carried out in order to analyse the changes in wage rates during plan periods and to compare wage rate in industries with changes in per capita national income. In fifth plan period all the industries experienced an increase in money earnings more than the increase in consumer price index. The growth in real consumption earnings per employee during this plan period has also been higher than per capita national income for the plan (2.6%). Money earnings have recorded maximum growth in sixth five-year plan. It has been more than consumer's price index (increased at the rate of 9.83%) in all industries except paper & paperboard industry where growth in money earnings has been less than the growth in consumer prices. This resulted in negative growth of real earnings in the industry (– 0.96%). In other industries, earnings per employee have increased more than the increase in per capita national income (3.2%). In seventh five-year plan also earnings per employee have increased faster than consumer price index except watches & clocks industry. Real earnings per employee in this plan have increased less than per capita national income (3.6%) except sugar industry. The growth rate of earnings per employee in watches & clocks (– 0.81%), motor vehicles (2.40%), fertilisers & pesticides (2.36%) industries and organised manufacturing sector (2.63%), have been less than per capita national income. This means that relative position of employees in organised manufacturing sector has not improved. Same is the trend in eighth five-year plan where in organised manufacturing sector (3.59%), sugar industry (2.55%), paper & paperboard industry (3.49%) and watches & clocks industry (0.69%) real earnings per employee increased at a rate lower than national per capita income. However, increase in money earnings per employee has been more than increase in consumer price index. The inter-plan comparison of wage rate does not show any consistent trend but the growth of real earnings per employee has been generally lower than the growth rate of national per capita income in seventh and eighth five year plans.

The inter-plan variation in employment shows that in fifth plan period employment has increased in all industries. The employment in the manufacturing sector as a whole has increased at a trend rate of 6.95 per cent which is highest for the all plan periods. Watch industry recorded maximum increase at the trend rate of 10.46 per cent. The employment in the sixth five year plan has been either stagnate or decreasing (in sugar and fertilisers & pesticides industries). The employment in seventh five-year plan has started picking up at the trend rate of 2.12 per cent for organised manufacturing sector and except paper & paperboard industry the growth has been significant. The growth in employment in first four years to eighth five-year plan shows a remarkable increase in the employment at the trend rate of 4.92 per cent in organised manufacturing sector and significant increase in motor vehicles and watches & clocks industry at the rate of 7.18 per cent and 7.48 per cent respectively. Only exception being sugar industry where employment has been stagnant. The trend in GVA does not shows any consistent trends during plan period but eighth five-year plan period shows a notable increase in GVA for all the industries and organised manufacturing sector. The GVA increased significantly in all industries during fifth five-year plan except paper industry where it has declined at the rate of 2.34 per cent; watches & clocks, sugar and fertilisers & pesticides industry recorded very high growth rates. The seventh five-year plan also shows a significant growth rate of GVA for all industries except paper and paperboard. *The comparison of growth rates of employment and GVA shows that rising output in the industries does not provide the corresponding increase in employment.*

6.8 Summing Up

In this chapter, we have analysed the wage trends for the selected industries and organised manufacturing sector as a whole for the period 1973-74 to 1995-96. The trends in rate of return to capital; the employment, wage cost to industries, gross value added and share of wages in gross value added are also presented. By simple econometric exercise, we have also seen how nominal wage rate have adjusted to change in labour productivity and consumer prices. Following conclusions emerge from the analysis of wage trends in this chapter:

- The intensity and dimension of labour welfare activities in all industries has been increasing as shown by rising share of fringe benefits in total emoluments.

- Wages per worker in all industries have increased faster than the earnings per employee despite the rise in share of fringe benefits in total emoluments. This means that the rate of remuneration to workers (i.e., wages per workers) have increased more than the rate of remuneration to non-workers (i.e., salaries per person in salaried class).
- The money earnings per employee have increased faster than consumer price index in all industries and for all the plan periods. The only instances when earnings per employee have increased slower than consumer price index are paper & paperboard industry in sixth plan and watches & clocks industry in seventh plan. This means that workers in these industries have been able to protect themselves from price rise.
- The real earnings per employee have increased almost at the rate of increase of real per capita national income. This means that relative position of workers have not improved significantly.
- The employment elasticity of output (value added) is low. It indicates that less labour is required to increase output in these industries. This means that employment has not increased corresponding to increase in output. It shows the low absorption power to the industries in organised manufacturing sector.
- The regression analysis shows that nominal wage rate in all industries have not fully adjusted to change in labour productivity. This means that benefits of growth in labour productivity are not fully transferred to labour. This was also confirmed by the movements of wage-productivity index, which have been more than 100 for most of the periods in all industries. The nominal wage rate is more responsive to consumer prices than labour productivity.
- The estimates of employment function shows that increase in product wages have adversely affected the employment in all the industries but the affect is not significant. The increase in output has not resulted in corresponding increase in employment. There is a significant lag in the adjustment of actual labour employment to its desired level. This is not an

unexpected result considering the fact that labour market in India is highly regulated.

- The share of wages in value added is decreasing over time in all the industries. This points to a trend towards mechanisation and capital labour substitution in industries and rejects the constancy of wage share hypothesis.
- The wages as a cost component to employers have increased faster than the wages as an income component to workers in all industries except sugar industry. This indicates the problem of wage goods constraint in the economy.

References

1. J.R. Hicks (1964) *The Theory of Wages.* Landon: Macmillan and Company Limited, p 130. Bracket added.
2. S.C. Agarwal, (1998a) *Human Resources in Public Enterprises : A wage-Productivity Approach.* New Delhi: Anmol Publishing Pvt. Ltd, pp. 172-173.
3. This is expected for developing countries where there are large search, hiring and training costs associated with short term labour adjustments. Moreover due to stringent labour laws it is not easy to adjust employment especially in downward direction.
4. It may be noted that employment has increased in initial years.
5. The elasticity is calculated by dividing the growth rates of real gross value added by rate of growth of employment.
6. Figures in brackets refers to the corresponding value of wages per worker.

7

Wage-Productivity Relationship

An Empirical Analysis

7.1 Introduction

Productivity plays a very crucial role in the process of economic development and ultimately determines the standard of living of the people in a country. The changes in wage rates due to changes in productivity govern the growth of productivity itself and economy of a nation. An increase in productivity facilitates the increase in wage rate and an increase in wage rate leads to an increase in productivity. Present chapter will try to explore the relationship between wages and labour productivity using Granger type test of causal relationship. The causal relationship between wages and labour productivity has been earlier tested by Aggarwal (1998[b]) for Indian public sector enterprises, for the period 1974-75 to 1995-96. His estimates reveals a feedback relationship between two, establishing that the wages are both cause and affect of productivity. However, a study by Ghuman and Singh (1998) of nine PSEs for period 1977-78 to 1995-96 does not find the feedback relationship. The study concludes that causality is clearly one way and that is, from wage rate to labour productivity. They observed that the rise in wage rate has a much larger impact on labour productivity than that of labour productivity on wages.[1] But during the process of discussion on wage-productivity relationship, it may be remembered that productivity is not the sole criterion in wage determination. In fact, wage determination is one field where theory is not of much help because theorist generally explains wages in relation to a single factor: the subsistence theory of wages in term of the needs of workers; marginal productivity theory in terms of productivity of workers; demand-supply theory in terms of role of market forces; bargaining theory in terms of bargaining power of trade unions.[2]

Wage determination is a complex phenomenon depending on various socio-economic and political factors. Present chapter attempts to an empirical analysis of wage determination with special emphasis to investigate whether wages have any link with the labour productivity, with a view that it may be helpful in analysing factor affecting wages and their relative importance. The factor affecting wage determination (termed as criterion of wage determination) may be too numerous to be numerically handled. The various criterions may be productivity, need of workers, capacity to pay, capital intensity of technology, price of product, demand for labour, general economic environment etc.

The present chapter is divided in five sections, section 7.2 deals with the test of causality between wages and labour productivity using Granger type causality tests. Section 7.3 deals with the exploration of wage-productivity relationship by including other explanatory variables in models. In section 7.4 we will discuss the factor responsible for inter-industry wage differentials.

7.2 Causality Test: Wages and Productivity

In previous chapters, we have explored the productivity trends and wage trends in selected industries and it emerged that some relationship between both does exit. But it is not clear whether wages cause productivity increase or productivity causes wage increase. So, it is pertinent to test whether this relationship is one-way (if so, which way?) or two-way. The following section will specifically attempt to know the observed causal relationship between wages and productivity in selected industries.

7.2.1 Methodology

Numerous testing procedures exist for establishing the direction of inter-relationship in bivariate analysis. Many tests of Granger-type causality have been derived, including Granger (1969), Sim (1972) and Geweke et al. (1983) to test the direction of causality. These tests are all based upon the estimation of auto-regressive or vector auto-regression (VAR) models. Although it is common to test for the direction of causality, the conclusions drawn are sometimes fragile for two important reasons.[3] First, the choices of lag lengths in the autoregressive or VAR models are often arbitrary, although the length of lag chosen will critically affect results. Secondly, in the absence of evidence on cointegression 'spurious' causality may be identified. We will test the causal relationship using following approach. The standard Granger causality test (1969) is first used. Test assumes that the information relevant to the prediction of respective variables (here, wages and labour productivity) is contained solely in the time series. The test involves estimation of following equations:

$$W_t = \alpha_0 + \sum_{i=1}^{m} \alpha_i W_{t-1} + \sum_{j=1}^{n} \delta_i P_{t-1} + \mu_t \qquad ...(7.1)$$

$$W_t = \alpha_0 + \sum_{i=1}^{m} \alpha_i W_{t-1} + \mu_t \qquad ...(7.2)$$

$$P_t = \beta_0 + \sum_{i=1}^{q} \beta_i P_{t-1} + \sum_{j=1}^{r} \lambda_j W_{t-1} + v_t \qquad ...(7.3)$$

$$P_t = \beta_0 + \sum_{i=1}^{q} \beta_i P_{t-1} + v_t \qquad ...(7.4)$$

Where W is the real earnings per employee, P is the labour productivity obtained as real value added per employee and α, β, δ, λ, are the coefficients. It is assumed that μ_t and v_t are zero-mean, serially uncorrelated random disturbances and lag langths m, n, q, r are equal and finite due to finite length of data. We have run the regressions using four lags on the lagged dependent variable and the independent explanatory variables.

As discussed earlier, the arbitrary selection of lags in Granger test may give different results for different lag section. To solve this problem, we have assigned the lag lengths m, n, q, r on the basis of minimising Akaike's Final Prediction Error (FPE) criterion. Akaike FPE (Y (m), X (n)) can be defined as follows:

FPEy (m, n) = T + m + n + 1/T – m – n – 1*Qy (m, n)/T ...(7.5)

Where, T refers to the number of observations, m and n are the number of lags on W and P variables respectively; and Qy is the sum of square of the residuals.

The Granger causality test here based upon equation 7.1 and 7.3 involves following:

Productivity Granger causes, wages if, $H_0 : \delta_1 = \delta_2 = \delta_3 + = ... = \delta_n = 0$ is rejected against the alternative H_1 = at least one $\delta_1 \neq 0, j = 1...n$. This denotes unidirectional causality from productivity to wages. Wages Granger causes productivity if, $H_0 : \lambda_1 = \lambda_2 = \lambda_3 = ... = \lambda_r = 0$ is rejected against the alternative H_1 = at least one $\lambda_1 \neq 0, j = 1...r$. This denotes unidirectional causality from wages to productivity. Feedback or bilateral causality, is suggested when the set of W and P are statistically different from zero in both regressions (7.1 and 7.3). Conversely, independence is suggested when the set of W and P are not statistically different from zero in both regressions.

More generally, since the future cannot predict the past, if variable X causes variable Y, then changes in X should *precede* changes in Y. Therefore in regression of Y on other variables (including its own past values) if we include past or lagged values of X and it significantly improves the prediction of Y, then we can say that X (Granger) causes Y.[4] Based on above reasoning our test for Granger causality test will contain following steps.

1. Regress current W on all lagged terms of W but lagged P terms are not included (equation 7.2). From this regression, the restricted residual sum of square (RSS_R) is obtained.
2. Now equation is again run including the lagged P terms (equation 7.1) and from this regression, the restricted residual sum on square (RSS_{UR}) is obtained.
3. To test the hypothesis, we apply F test given by:

$$F = \frac{\left(RSS_R - RSS_{UR}\right)_{/m}}{\left(RSS_{UR}\right)_{/(n-k)}} \quad ...(7.6)$$

   Which follows F distribution with m and (n-k) degree of freedom. Here, m is the number of lagged P terms and k is the number of parameters estimated in the unrestricted regression.
4. If the computed F value exceeds the critical value, we reject the null hypothesis. This is another way to say that productivity causes the wages.

5. Steps 1 to 4 can be repeated to test whether wages causes productivity.

7.2.2 Empirical Results

The results of causality analysis are presented in Tables 7.1 and 7.2. From Table 7.1 it can be seen that no causal relationship exists between wages and productivity in the organised manufacturing sector and paper & paperboard industry. One way causal relationship from wages to productivity exists in sugar, fertilisers & pesticides

Table 7.1 : Granger Test of Casual Relationship between Wage Rate and Labour Productivity

Industry	Direction of causality	RSS_R	RSS_{UR}	F Value	Decision
Organised Manufacturing	W → P	.1517	.1253	$.5791^{+}$	Reject
Sector	P → W	.0132	.0116	$.3839^{+}$	Reject
Sugar	W → P	1.361	0.512	4.560^{*}	Don't Reject
Industry	P → W	0.044	0.0254	1.977^{+}	Reject
Paper and	W → P	1.464	1.140	0.782^{+}	Reject
Paperboard	P → W	0.018	0.014	0.870^{+}	Reject
Fertilisers & Pesticides	W → P	10.11	3.708	4.748^{*}	Don't Reject
Industry	P → W	0.088	0.049	2.138^{+}	Reject
Motor Vehicles	W → P	1.496	0.610	3.994^{*}	Don't Reject
Industry	P → W	0.050	0.041	0.622^{+}	Reject
Watches &	W → P	3.636	2.230	1.734^{+}	Reject
Chock industry	P → W	0.049	0.024	2.902^{**}	Don't Reject

Notes: 1. W→ P denotes the test whether wages causes productivity.
P→ W denotes the test whether productivity causes wages.

2. *denotes significant at 5% level; ** denotes significant at 10% level; + denotes not significant.

Table 7.2 : Granger Test of Casual Relationship between Wage Rate and Labour Productivity by Applying Akaike Information Criterion (FPE)

Industry	Direction of causality	RSS_R	RSS_{UR}	F Value	Decision
Organised Manufacturing	W → P	0.154	0.123 (3, 5)	0.504+	Reject
Sector	P → W	0.020	0.017 (1, 1)	2.693+	Reject
Sugar	W → P	0.943	0.299 (5, 4)	5.385**	Don't Reject
Industry	P → W	0.126	0.113 (1, 1)	2.301+	Reject
Paper and	W → P	1.937	1.720 (1, 1)	2.523+	Reject
Paperboard	P → W	0.021	0.020 (1, 1)	0.851+	Reject
Fertilisers & Pesticides	W → P	7.760	2.040 (5, 4)	7.010*	Don't Reject
Industry	P → W	0.093	0.041 (3, 4)	3.763**	Don't Reject
Motor Vehicles	W → P	2.256	1.095 (1, 4)	3.711**	Don't Reject
Industry	P → W	0.064	0.052 (1, 1)	4.786**	Don't Reject
Watches &	W → P	4.660	2.247 (2, 4)	3.490**	Don't Reject
Clock industry	P → W	0.059	0.036 (2, 3)	3.138***	Don't Reject

Notes: 1. W→ P denotes the test whether wages causes productivity. P→ W denotes the test whether productivity causes wages.

2. Figures in parenthesis are the optimum lags applied and are obtained by Akaike maximum information criterion.

3. *denotes significance at 1% level; ** denotes significance at 5% level; ***denotes significance at 10% level; + denotes not significant.

and motor vehicles industries. From this it can be inferred that wage increase in these industries have resulted in the increase in productivity. In watches & clocks industry, it is productivity increase that resulted in wage increase. But as discussed earlier, here (for results in table

7.1), we have taken four lags for both variables and this arbitrary selection of lags might have affected the results. So when lags are selected by applying *Akaike Final Information Criterion* by minimising FPE, we find that feedback or bilateral causal relationship exists in fertilisers & pesticides, motor vehicles and watches & clocks industries (Table 7.2.). But for other industries, results have been same. The absence of causal relationship in organised manufacturing sector and paper & paperboard industry indicates that wages does not increase productivity and vice versa. This means that there are the factors other than productivity, which explain the wage determination in industries.

7.3 Wage-Productivity Relationship: An Econometric Analysis

In order to clearly understand the links between wages and productivity in selected industries, this study has taken a simple econometric analysis. In the first place, different econometric models, depending upon the number of variables included in the exercise are selected.

7.3.1 Selection of Variables and Models

7.3.1a. Selection of Variables

In accordance with our major hypothesis, we sought to explain movement in real wages based on the movement in labour productivity. Therefore, labour productivity is the first variable considered. And, we expect a positive relationship between wage rate and labour productivity.

Second variable is consumer price index of industrial workers (CPIIW). Since, there are certain universally accepted requirements which must be fulfilled to a human being or a worker to live in a civilised community, they are: food, clothing & bedding and a shelter for self and family. So there can be a standard budget that is sufficient to satisfy the above-mentioned minimum need of workers. However, when this standard budget in terms of need-based minimum wage is determined, then the question of maintaining the same purchasing power arises. The system generally prevailed in India for the adjustment of wages against fluctuation in the value of money is that of paying dearness allowance over and above the basic wage. The cost of living index, therefore, can be taken as measure of workers needs. The justification of this criterion is that the real wages of workers should not be allowed to whittle down by price increase. The correction method adopted to neutralise the fall in value of money, so as to keep the workers real wages constant at a given level is based on consumer price index. But in the absence of automatic indexation of wages and periodic nature of dearness allowances, some degree of money illusion may creep in. Generally, any increase in price of consumer goods has a tendency to depress real wages. In this context, we expect a negative relationship between consumer price index and change in real earnings.

The capital intensity is another variable, which is theoretically and empirically taken to be a factor, determining wages. We take capital-labour ratio as a measure of capital intensity. It is argued that availability of higher per capita capital requires more skilled manpower, therefore, is paid higher wages. Moreover, capital intensity may also affect wages via productivity route, i.e., rising capital intensity which increases labour productivity leads to higher wages. And, higher wages may induce a substitution of capital for labour. Therefore, a positive relationship is expected between changes in capital-labour ratio and changes in wages. Sattinger (1980), while discussing effects of capital intensity on income inequality observed that, on the average, more capital-intensive industries employ fewer low earning workers and more high earning workers.

The capacity to pay may be one more variable as a factor determining wages. It is generally believed that capacity of the industry, to pay, should be taken into account while fixing the wages, other than minimum wages. The capacity of the industry to pay is one of the essential circumstances, to be taken into consideration except in the cases of bare subsistence or minimum wage which employer is bound to pay irrespective of the capacity to pay. There are various views and counter views on the capacity to pay as a criterion in wage determination process and the measure of the capacity to pay. Expansion in output (value added) may be taken as the measure of the industry's capacity to pay and a positive relationship between earnings and value added is expected. The rate of productivity advance as measured by total factor productivity can also be taken as the proxy of capacity to pay in the industry.[5]

The wage rate is also affected by conditions prevailing in product market. The most important factor in product market are the prices and demand for product as it is out of revenues received from the sale of product, an entrepreneur is supposed to pay. The product price index may be used as a proxy for the conditions prevailing in product market. The selection of PPI is further justified as it also reflects the demand for product in the market. The PPI also affects the capacity of the industry to pay. Thus, a positive relationship between movement of product price index and wage rate.

Trade union strength and activities play a very important role in determination of money wages. Union activities strengthen workers and help them in striking favourable wage deals. Unions may help workers in wage increases. The empirical analysis does not support the direct affect of unions in increasing money earnings. Unions fight for wage increases, might have adverse effects such as retrenchment, closures, lockout etc. Also, an increase in degree of unionisation might be accompanied by rivalry and factionalism, thus neutralising the effect which higher degree of unionisation might have exercised. Therefore, a priory relationship between the wage rate and union activities cannot be set out. The union activities may be measured as total mandays lost due to strikes divided by number of workers involved in the strikes. This measure represents the staying power of unionised labour and the ability of unionised labour, to withstand a strike. It takes into account both breadth and duration of union activities. It is also assumed that strike variable represents the union behaviour. It also looks pertinent that all other aspects of union behaviour are relatively unimportant, in the absence of strike weapon.

7.3.1b. Selection of Models

The models are selected so as to give us relation between wages and productivity. Various measures of productivity may affect wages differently, so our models are so designed to include one or more measures of productivity.

The analysis is based on the wages (EEr) as the dependent variables and labour productivity (LP), capital intensity (K/L), consumer price index (CPIIW), gross value added (V), total factor productivity (TFPT) and trend variable (t) as explanatory variables. As there was problem of multicollinearity, to reduce the effect of multicollinearity some of the variables are dropped. The variables trade union activities and product price index are dropped from the regression analysis. Unionisation has not been considered significant, as a number of empirical studies in India like Johri (1966), Suri (1976), Sen (1985) and Ramjas (1992) have found no positive influence of trade unions on the money earnings of workers in selected manufacturing industries in India. Moreover, it is argued that effect of trade union is limited only to for neutralise the adverse effect on real wages due to increase in consumer price index. Product price index is dropped because its effect is captured by labour productivity and value added variables. The effect of paying capacity is captured by the labour productivity variable. Even after dropping the above variables, the problem of multicollinearity is not completely solved.

The variables included and the models estimated for the analysis, using real variables, are given below.

Model I : $EE_r = Ae^{u} (LP)^{\alpha}$

Model II : $EE_r = Ae^{\lambda t+u} (LP)^{\alpha}$

Model III : $EE_r = Ae^{\lambda t+u} (LP)^{\alpha} (V)^{\beta}$

Model IV : $EE_r = Ae^{\lambda t+u} (LP)^{\alpha} (V)^{\beta} (k/L)^{\delta}$

Model V : $EE_r = Ae^{\lambda t+u} (LP)^{\alpha} (V)^{\beta} (K/L)^{\delta} (CPIIW)^{\lambda}$

Model VI : $EE_r = Ae^{\lambda t+u} (LP)^{\alpha} (TFPT)^{\beta} (K/L)^{\delta} (CPIIW)^{\wedge}$

Model VII : $EE_r = Ae^{u} (LP)^{\alpha} (V)^{\beta}$

Model VIII : $EE_r = Ae^{u} (LP)^{\alpha} (V)^{\beta} (K/L)^{\delta}$

Model IX : $EE_r = Ae^{u} (LP)^{\alpha} (TFPT)^{\beta} (K/L)^{\delta}$

7.3.2 Wage-Productivity Relationship in Different Industries

7.3.2a. Organised Manufacturing Sector

The results of regression analysis for functions explaining wage-productivity relationship are presented in Table 7.3. Model-1 shows that when real wage rate is regressed on labour productivity, the relationship is positive and statistically significant but model has low R^2 (0.657). Introduction of time variable in model-II significantly improves the explanatory power of model. Value and statistical significance of coefficient of labour productivity improves but trend coefficient becomes negative and insignificant. Introduction of value added in model-III improves value of R^2 and coefficient of labour productivity turns insignificant but coefficient of newly introduced

Table 7.3: Wage-Productivity Relationship: Organised Manufacturing Sector

Model No.	Const	LP	V	K/L	CPIIW	TFPT	Time	R2	DW	F/Rho
				Explanatory Variables						
1.	3.027	0.328	-	-	-	-	-	.6573	1.798	.2732^{+}
	(12.084)	(6.648)								(1.270)
2.	1.715*	0.627	-	-	-	-	-.0162**	.6880	1.886	.2786^{+}
	(2.198)	(3.577)					(1.765)			(1.265)
3.	0.169^{+}	0.166**	0.801	-	-		-0.493	.9410	1.808	118.1
	(.404)	(1.812)	(7.574)				(7.996)			(3,19)
4.	-0.955^{+}	-0.231^{+}	1.087	0.361^{+}	-		-.0666	.9420	2.119	90.26
	(.855)	(.642)	(4.012)	(1.144)			(3.518)			(5,18)
5.	-0.755	-0.069^{+}	0.953	0.141^{+}	0.151^{+}	-	-.0671	.9423	2.103	71.92
	(.172)	(.175)	(3.111)	(.359)	(.941)		(4.103)			(6,17)
6.	14.055	4.778	-	-3.140	0.152^{+}	-3.350	-.0061^{+}	.9412	1.838	70.87
	(3.604)	(3.968)		(8.218)	(.936)	(4.656)	(.563)			(6,17)
7.	3.324	0.037^{+}	0.221^{+}	-	-	-	-	.6539	1.796	.3149^{+}
	(9.368)	(.164)	(1.350)							(1.462)
8.	3.426	1.039	0.048^{+}	-0.845	-	-	-	.7481	2.111	.5757
	(14.612)	4.436)	(.434)	(5.554)						(2.988)
9.	15.024	5.092	-	-3.212	-	-4.151	-	.9421	1.725	122.4
	(5.206)	(5.145)		(5.399)		(4.052)				(3,19)

Notes: 1. The value in parenthesis indicates respective t-values of estimates or degree of freedom.
2. All value are significant at 1% level of significance unless otherwise specified.
3. *Significant at 5% level of significance;
** Significant at 10% level of significance;
+ Insignificant.

variable value added is positive and significant. Introduction of capital-labour ratio in model-IV turns the sign of labour productivity coefficient to negative but insignificant. Sign of value added coefficient remain positive and significant but the sign of capital intensity coefficient is positive and insignificant. Introduction of consumer price index in model-V shows that coefficient of CPIIW takes positive sign and is statistically insignificant indicating that increase in consumer price has not reduced real earnings of workers. Introduction of total factor productivity index in pace of value added in model-VI changes the coefficient of labour productivity into positive and significant; and coefficient of TFPT is negative & significant at 1% level; and coefficient of capital intensity is also negative. When we estimated the models excluding trend variables, no significant improvements were obtained in results.

The model that seems to be best fit to describe the relationship between real wage rate and other variable is given by following relationship:

$$\begin{aligned} \text{Ln (EEr)} &= 0.169 + 0.166 \text{ Ln (LP)} + 0.801 \text{ Ln (K/L)} - 0.0493t. \\ &\quad (0.404) \quad (1.812) \qquad\qquad (7.574) \qquad\qquad (7.996) \end{aligned}$$

Adj. $R^2 = 0.941$; *D-W* = 1.808; $F_{6,\,1^-} = 188.1$

The model though does not have highest explanatory power but has expected positive sign for labour productivity and value added. This indicates positive association of value added and real wages in manufacturing sector. But association of labour productivity with real wage rate is though positive, but not significant. *The negative sign for trend variable indicates that real wages are suppressed due to ineffectiveness of institutional factor. Thus, screening of various models show that there are no strong and conclusive evidence supporting strong association between real wage rate and productivity but on the whole, it can be said that wage rate in manufacturing sector is positively related to productivity (but not necessarily labour productivity).* However, it may be borne in mind that all the explanatory variable are having high correlation among themselves and problem of multicollinearity has made the separation of their effects difficult. Introduction of TFPT in models along with labour productivity shows that the coefficient of TFPT is negative and that of labour productivity is positive. And the value of labour productivity coefficient is more than that of TFPT. This indicates that labour productivity variable might have captured the effect of TFPT on real wage rate.

7.3.2b. Sugar Industry

The outcomes of regression analysis of functions exploring relationship between wages and productivity in sugar industry are presented in Table 7.4. The analysis of the models shows a strong association of wage rate and labour productivity in this industry. The coefficient of labour productivity is positive and statistically significant consistently in most of the equations. Model-I reveals that when labour productivity is taken, as sole factor to explain the relationship, the coefficient of labour productivity is positive & significant. Elasticity of real wage rate to labour productivity is equal to 0.681 and explaining power of relation is also high (R^2 = 0.958). Introduction of trend coefficient in model-II slightly reduces the explaining power of the model and numerical value of coefficient of labour productivity. In model-III when value added is included, the coefficient of value added comes to negative & significant at 1% level of significance. It seems that the influence of value added on wages is captured by trend variable, as numerical value and statistical significance of trend coefficient is increased after the introduction of value added. Model-IV seems to be suffering from multicollinearity as in spite of high explaining power of the model none of the coefficient is significant. Here also, coefficients of labour productivity and other variables, along with coefficient of newly introduced variable capital intensity, are positive. Model-V also seems to suffer from multicollinearity though the sign of CPIIW in the model is expected negative. In model-VI introduction of total factor productivity shows that TFPT coefficient takes negative sign but, numerical value of labour productivity coefficient improves, and their combined elasticity is positive (i.e., 0.290). *Screening of other models also shows that coefficient of labour productivity is mostly positive and when negative (last equation) the coefficient of TFPT is positive and their joint elasticity is also positive.* The model that seems to best describe the relationship between real wages and explanatory variable is given by following regression equation:

Table 7.4: Wage-Productivity Relationship: Sugar Industry

Model No.	Const	V/L	V	K/L	CPIW	TFPT	Time	R2	DW	F/Rho
					Explanatory Variables					
1.	1.239	0.681	-	-	-	-	-	.9584	1.556	507.8
	(8.181)	(22.54)								(1,21)
2.	1.181	0.698	-	-	-	-	-0.002+	.9572	1.585	243.9
	(4.741)	(10.614)					(.296)			(2,20)
3.	3.082	0.889	-0.576	-	-	-	0.031+	.9787	1.890	340.2
	(7.001)	(14.501)	(4.701)				(3.499)			(3,19)
4.	2.076+	0.678+	-0.362+	0.221+	-	-	0.017+	.9782	1.858	243.9
	(.810)	(1.270)	(.656)	(.232)			(.440)			(4,18)
5.	3.408+	0.507+	-0.213+	0.435+	-0.482+	-	0.044+	.9796	1.724	215.4
	(1.327)	(.977)	(.401)	(.801)	(1.679)		(1.108)			(5,17)
6.	5.013+	1.258+	-	0.141	-0.531**	-0.968+	0.029+	.9802	1.744	216.8
	(1.015)	(.690)		(.145)	(1.844)	(.525)	(1.327)			(5,17)
7.	1.665	0.902	-0.107+	-	-	-	-	.9291	1.704	.2580+
	(7.721)	(7.239)	(.715)							(1.139)
8.	0.955	0.451	-0.122+	0.458	-	-	-	.9792	1.805	339.5
	(3.581)	(3.410)	(1.518)	(3.491)						(3,19)
9.	-2.425+	-0.865+	-	1.185+	-	1.194	-	.9768	1.693	316.1
	(.731)	(.686)		(.743)		(0.927)				(3,19)

Notes: 1. The value in parenthesis indicates respective t-values of estimates or degree of freedom.
2. All value are significant at 1% level of significance unless otherwise specified.
3. *Significant at 5% level of significance;
** Significant at 10% level of significance;
+ Insignificant.

$$\text{Ln(EEr)} = 5.013 + 1.258\,\text{Ln(LP)} + 0.141\,\text{Ln(K/L)} - 0.531\,\text{Ln(CPIIW)}$$
$$(1.015)\ (0.690)\qquad (0.145)\qquad (1.844)$$
$$-0.968\ \text{Ln (TFP)} + \ 0.0689t$$
$$(0.525)\qquad (1.327)$$
$$R^2 = 9802 \qquad DW = 1.744\ F_{(5,\,1^-)} = 216.8$$

The model shows that wage rate is positively related to labour productivity and capital intensity but association is not statistically significant. The consumer price index is negatively related to real wages and institutional factors, represented by trend variables, are positively related to real wage rate. Negative sign of TFPT in this equation may be due to the fact that effect of productivity on real wage rate is already captured by labour productivity.

7.3.2c. Paper and Paperboard Industry

The result of regression functions for paper & paperboard industry are presented in Table 7.5. The estimates of different models reveals the positive association of labour productivity with the real wage rate in a more consistent manner in first few equation, as all models show that the coefficient of labour productivity is positive and in most of cases statistically significant. The trend coefficient also shows the presence of positive association of institutional factors with real wage rate. Model-I is having low explanation power along with low elasticity of labour productivity. Introduction of trend coefficient significantly improves the explaining power of model-II. Coefficient of value added in model-III is negative but it should not be construed as the negative association between value added and real wages. Careful examination of model shows that introduction of value added as an explanatory variable has significantly improved not only the coefficient of trend variable but also the coefficient of labour productivity, with value of R^2 decreasing. This may be due to the fact that the effect of value added is picked up by trend and labour productivity coefficients. It is the case with model-IV also where newly introduced variable, capital intensity (K/L), takes negative sign and improves the numerical value of coefficients of trend and labour productivity coefficients. In next model, CPIIW takes expected negative sign. Introduction of TFPT in model-VI shows that introduced variable takes negative sign but labour productivity retains positive sign. In view of this, we have chosen model-V as the best

Table 7.5: Wage-Productivity Relationship: Paper and Paperboard Industry.

Model	Explanatory Variables								
No.	Const	V/L	RGVA	K/L	CPIW	TFPT	Time	R2	DW	F/Rho
1.	3.962 (13.415)	0.176 (2.876)	-	-	-	-	-	.2219	1.691	.7644 (5.283)
2.	4.016 (19.527)	0.127 (2.745)	-	-	-	-	0.015 (5.791)	.7850	2.003	.4221* (2.143)
3.	4.170 (16.196)	.266+ (1.654)	-0.171+ (.934)	-	-	-	0.021 (3.381)	.7442	1.976	.4982* (2.426)
4.	6.029 (8.715)	0.501 (3.105)	-0.335** (1.831)	-0.484 (3.245)	-	-	0.048 (4.151)	.9208	1.600	65.03 (4,18)
5.	7.401 (12.342)	0.488 (4.171)	-0.271 (2.023)	-0.365 (3.266)	-0.475 (4.163)	-	0.077 (7.068)	.9587	1.714	102.8 (5,17)
6.	9.904 (5.474)	1.384* (2.262)	-	-0.889* (2.516)	-0.526* (2.130)	-1.136** (1.856)	0.065 (7.138)	.9572	2.259	99.12 (5,17)
7.	3.342 (20.02)	0.154 (1.839)	0.430 (6.348)	-	-	-	-	.8523	1.644	64.51 (2,20)
8.	3.248 (12.286)	0.066+ (.527)	0.233+ (1.623)	0.132+ (1.511)	-	-	-	.7386	2.012	.3431+ (1.483)
9.	2.129+ (.514)	-0.227+ (.155)	-	0.441+ (.490)	-	0.336+ (.230)	-	.6164	1.915	.4738* (2.285)

Notes : 1. The value in parenthesis indicates respective t-values of estimates or degree of freedom

2. All value are significant at 1% level of significance unless otherwise specified.

3. *Significant at 5% level of significance;

** Significant at 10% level of significance;

+ Insignificant.

fit to explain the relationship of wages with productivity. This model is free from autocorrelation as value of DW statistic indicating nearly no autocorrelation. It gives us the following relationship :

$$\begin{aligned}
Ln(EEr) &= 7.401 + 0.488\, Ln(LP) - 0.271\, Ln(V) - 0.365\, Ln(K/L) - 0.475\, Ln(CPIIW) \\
&\quad (12.342)(4.171) \qquad (2.023) \qquad (3.266) \qquad (4.163) \\
&\quad + .0771\, t \\
&\quad (7.068)
\end{aligned}$$

$$Adj.\ R^2 = 0.9587;\ DW = 1.714;\ F_{(5,17)} = 102.8$$

The equation depicts a relationship that shows that wage rate in paper and paperboard industry is significantly related to labour productivity. The elasticity of wage rate to labour productivity is 0.488 implying that 10% increase in labour productivity, increases the wage rate by 4.48%. However, it may be remembered that labour productivity coefficient seems to have captured the effect of capital intensity, i.e., capital intensity has affected wages through the route; higher capital intensity → higher labour productivity → higher wages. Similarly, it seems that the effect of value added is picked up by trend and labour productivity coefficients. This explains negative sign of capital intensity and value added in model. Model also reveals that an increase in consumer price index suppressed the real wages of the workers in the industry.

The examination of models without trend coefficient also brings about the positive association of wage rate with labour productivity. Thus, the analysis clearly brings out the positive association between wages and productivity in the industry.

7.3.2d. Fertilisers and Pesticides Industry

The analysis of different models presented in Table 7.6 confirmed the hypothesis that labour productivity has positively influenced the real wage rate. The coefficient of labour productivity in first five models is positive. The coefficient of labour productivity besides being positive is also statistically significant in first three models and models have high explanatory power. Introduction of value added in model-III shows that value added has taken a negative sign, and the coefficient of labour productivity and trend variable have increased in their numeric value and statistical significance. Introduction of capital intensity and consumer price index in next two models shows that both the new variables take expected positive and negative signs, respectively and all the coefficients became

Table 7.6: Wage-Productivity Relationship: Fertilisers and Pesticides Industry

Model No.	Const	V/L	V	K/L	CPIW	TFPT	Time	R2	DW	F/Rho
				Explanatory Variable						
1.	3.015	0.371	-	-	-	-	-	.9002	1.502	138.2
	(21.975)	(14.078)								(1,21)
2.	4.137	0.104+	-	-	-	-	0.022	.9287	1.785	145.7
	(11.01)	(1.185)					(3.136)			(2,20)
3.	4.512	0.316*	-0.294**	-	-	-	0.036	.9384	1.812	112.9
	(11.34)	(2.347)	(1.992)				(3.736)			(3,19)
4.	2.194+	0.128+	-0.079+	0.475+	-	-	0.005+	.9442	1.885	94.37
	(1.580)	(.766)	(.268)	(.765)			(.236)			(4,18)
5.	3.725**	0.220+	-0.183+	0.353+	-0.202+	-	0.031+	.9451	1.942	76.29
	(1.867)	(1.181)	(.867)	(1.192)	(1.065)		(.974)			(5,17)
6.	11.678+	2.711+	-	-1.408+	-0.188+	-2.649+	0.010+	.9413	1.846	74.02
	(1.301)	(1.082)		(.759)	(1.017)	(1.056)	(.560)			(5,17)
7.	3.153	0.221+	0.114+	-	-	-	-	.8994	1.547	98.53
	(15.221)	(1.304)	(.892)							(2,20)
8.	1.877	0.103+	-0.042+	0.533	-	-	-	.9472	1.877	132.4
	(5.748)	(.823)	(.421)	(4.398)						(3,19)
9.	7.102+	1.510+	-	-0.584+	-	-1.465+	-	.9456	1.889	128.5
	(.923)	(.690)		(.691)		(.667)				(3,19)

Notes: 1. The value in parenthesis indicates respective t-values of estimates or degree of freedom.
2. All value are significant at 1% level of significance unless otherwise specified.
3. *Significant at 5% level of significance;
** Significant at 10% level of significance;
+ Insignificant.

statistically insignifcant.[6] The increased coefficient of labour productivity, after the inclusion of TFPT in model-VI, shows that labour productivity has captured the effects of total factor productivity on wage rates. This model also seems to suffer from multicollinearity. Same results follows when equations are estimated without trend coefficient. The best model that seems to explain the relationship between real wage rate and explanatory variables gives following relationship:

$$\text{Ln (EEr)} = 4.512 + .316^{*} \text{ Ln (LP)} - 0.294 \text{ Ln (V)} + 0.0362 \text{ t}$$

$$(11.34) \quad (2.347) \qquad (1.992) \qquad (3.736)$$

Adj. R^2 *= 0.9384; DW = 1.812; Rho = 112.9 (3,19)*

The relationship shows that labour productivity have positive & significant effects on real wage rate in fertilisers and pesticides industry. The institutional factors have helped in increasing real wages in the industry. As discussed earlier that negative sign should not construed as negative association between value added and real wages.

7.3.2e. Motor Vehicles Industry

The results of regression function for different models of wage-productivity relationship are presented in Table 7.7. The analysis of the models shows a positive association between wage rate and labour productivity in the industry. The coefficient of labour productivity is positive and statistically significant but model suffers from low explaining power, indicating that there are factors other than labour productivity that influences real wages. Introduction of trend variable in model-II has increased the R^2 considerably, but has reduced the value and significance of labour productivity coefficient. Inclusion of value added in model-III has not increased the R^2. Introduction of capital-labour ratio in next model also does not improve the explanatory power of model and the coefficient of capital is negative & significant at 10% level only. Model-V shows that wage rate is negatively related to consumer price index (CPIIW). When value added in model-VI is replaced by its proxy variable TFPT, the best results are obtained. The model provides the following estimates.

Table 7.7: Wage-Productivity Relationship: Motor Vehicles Industry

Model No.	Const	V/L	RGVA	K/L	Explanatory Variables CPIW	TFPT	Time	R2	DW	F/Rho
1.	3.050	0.379	-	-	-	-	-	.4143	2.169	.8358
	(6.609)	(4.190)								(6.872)
2.	3.912	0.145+	-	-	-	-	0.027	.8807	2.158	.3615**
	(9.506)	(1.562)					(5.607)			(1.749)
3.	3.934	1.113+	0.026+	-	-	-	0.027	.8783	2.153	.3456+
	(9.236)	(.418)	(.112)				(3.540)			(1.138)
4.	6.851	0.779+	-0.574+	-0.179+	-	-	0.078	.8381	1.489	.6513
	(4.610)	(1.521)	(1.317)	(1.814)			(2.735)			(3.539)
5.	6.563	0.267+	-0.086+	0.027+	-0.653*	-	0.079	.8303	1.501	.6457
	(4.567)	(.536)	(.2032)	(.061)	(2.684)		(3.017)			(3.383)
6.	6.478	0.191+	-	0.088+	-0.674	-0.030+	0.076	.9279	2.075	.2643+
	(6.101)	(1.551)		(.406)	(2.961)	(.266)	(4.735)			(1.116)
7.	3.223	-0.117+	0.436**	-	-	-	-	.6118	2.396	.6580
	(6.221)	(.367)	(1.905)							(3.864)
8.	2.411	-0.222+	0.351	0.353+	-	-	-	.8228	2.183	.4573*
	(4.581)	(.854)	(2.846)	(1.770)						(2.256)
9.	1.473*	0.171+	-	0.463	-	-0.061	-	.6685	2.102	.6912
	(2.164)	(1.092)		(2.845)		(.472)				(4.190)

Notes: 1. The value in parenthesis indicates respective t-values of estimates or degree of freedom.
2. All value are significant at 1% level of significance unless otherwise specified.
3. *Significant at 5% level of significance;
** Significant at 10% level of significance;
+ Insignificant.

$$Ln(Wr) = 6.478 + 0.191\,Ln(LP) - 0.088\,Ln(K/L)$$
$$(6.101)\ (1.551)\qquad (0.406)$$
$$-0.674Ln(CPIIW) - 0.030\,Ln(TFPT)$$
$$(2.961)\qquad (0.266)$$
$$+0.0759\,t$$
$$= .2643\ (1.116)$$
$$Adj.\ R^2 = 0.9279;\ DW=2.075;\ Rho\ (4.735)$$

The function shows that wage rate in motor vehicle industry is positively related to labour productivity. The increase in consumer prices significantly reduces the real wages. Screening of models without trend variable also supports the hypothesis of positive association between wage rate and labour productivity.

7.3.2f. Watches and Clocks Industry

The results of regression analysis showing wage rate functions in watches and clocks industry are presented in Table 7.6. The results of statistical analysis show exceptionally high value of coefficients of estimates (specially constant) along with high standard error (i.e., low t-statistic), which is not conceivable. In such a situation, the results are to be interpreted with caution. The coefficient of labour productivity in model-I is positive and statistically significant. The introduction of trend variable also does not improve the explaining power of the model, and it has turned labour productivity coefficient insignificant. It seems that trend coefficient has captured the effect of labour productivity on real wage rate (r_{KL} = 0.950). Introduction of real gross value added has improved the numeric value and statistical significance of labour productivity and trend coefficients, but the coefficient of value added is negative. As explained earlier, it cannot be taken as negative association between value added and wage rate. Same trend continues with the introduction of capital intensity in next model. The coefficient of capital intensity is positive. Screening of other models shows that labour productivity coefficient is mostly positive and is negative only when total factor productivity is introduced with labour productivity. We get best result in term of R^2 by model-V that gives us following relationship:

Table 7.8: Wage-Productivity Relationship: Watches and Clocks Industry

No.	Const	V/L	RGVA	K/L	CPIW	TFPT	Time	R2	DW	F/Rho
				Explanatory Variables						
1.	2.978	0.345	-	-	-	-	-	.7512	1.674	63.32
	(12.492)	(7.958)								(1,21)
2.	4.065	0.112^{+}	-	-	-	-	0.016^{**}	.7883	1.566	37.227
	(6.542)	(.025)					(1.877)			(2,20)
3.	3.970	0.436^{**}	-0.301^{**}	-	-	-	0.031^{*}	.6701	1.943	$.2785^{+}$
	(6.687)	(1.882)	(1.755)				(2.678)			(1.246)
4.	3.324	0.291^{+}	-0.181^{+}	0.173^{+}	-	-	0.013^{+}	.6267	1.893	$.3336^{+}$
	(2.765)	(.873)	(.669)	(.637)			(.405)			(1.547)
5.	8.528	0.730	-0.606	-0.088^{+}	-0.916	-	0.130	.8472	1.615	25.39
	(4.755)	(2.520)	(2.529)	(.395)	(3.158)		(3.094)			(5,17)
6.	8.547^{+}	-4.868^{+}	-	3.364^{+}	-0.580^{**}	4.945^{+}	0.044^{+}	.7396	1.983	$.2776^{+}$
	(.945)	(1.581)		(1.769)	(1.981)	(1.596)	(1.630)			(1.235)
7.	3.026	0.322^{+}	0.012^{+}	-	-	-	-	.7263	1.670	3.172
	(5.529)	(1.282)	(.058)							(2,20)
8.	2.885	0.193^{+}	-0.087^{+}	0.278	-	-	-	.6326	1.858	.3541
	(5.469)	(.866)	(.682)	(2.809)						(1.549)
9.	-13.273^{+}	-5.499^{**}	-	3.692^{*}	-	5.699^{**}	-	.8092	1.552	32.12
	(1.529)	(1.856)		(2.007)		(1.894)				(3,19)

Notes: 1. The value in parenthesis indicates respective t-values of estimates or degree of freedom.
2. All value are significant at 1% level of significance unless otherwise specified.
3. * Significant at 5% level of significance;
** Significant at 10% level of significance;
+ Insignificant.

$$\text{Ln (EEr)} = 8.528 + 0.730 \text{ Ln (LP)} - 0.606 \text{ Ln(V)} - 0.088 \text{ Ln (K/L)} + 0.131 t$$
$$(4.755) \quad (2.520) \quad (2.529) \quad (0.395) \quad (3.094)$$

Adj. R^2 = .8472; *DW* = 1.615; $F_{(4, 18)}$= 25.39)

The relationship shows that real wage rate is statistically related to labour productivity. But model has low value of adj R^2, it shows that there are factors other than considered by us that have influenced real wage rates in this industry.

7.4 Explanation for Growth Rate Differentials in Wage Rates

Variety of factors such as productivity of labour, capital intensity, average size of the firm, profitability of industry, degree of unionisation, condition of economy etc. have been considered in empirical studies for explaining inter-industry wage differentials. Several studies[7] have been conducted in India to examine the inter-industry wage differentials in India manufacturing sector. These studies have used standard statistical techniques of multiple regression and correlation to show the significance of different variables in explaining the variations in wage rates. The basic theoretical frame adopted for explaining the inter-industry wage structure seems to be the one, provided by Brown,[8] who advanced the basic hypothesis that wage-level differences among manufacturing industries result from industry to industry differences in the employer's estimates of their future ability to pay. The experience of Indian manufacturing sector relating to wage fixation mechanism, such as adjudication, wage boards etc. indicates that they have operated on welfare criterion rather than market mechanism.[9]

In accordance with our main hypothesis that the inter-industry wage differentials exists due to difference in the labour productivity, we have taken labour productivity as an explanatory variable. It is argued that inter-industry wage differentials also results from the differences in technological levels of different industries, accordingly we have taken capital intensity as explaining variable for wage differentials among industries. We have also taken gross value added as it represents average size of the industry. Aggarwal (1998[a]) have also taken above variables for explaining the wage rate differentials among different public sector industries. His regression analysis does not provide any statistical evidence to support the hypothesis that inter-industry wage differences can be explained with the help of differences in labour productivity.

Following Aggarwal (1998) we have hypothesised the following functional relationship.

W = f (LP, V, K/L)

In explaining inter-industry wage differentials, an important factor influencing the wage levels, is expected to be the corresponding levels of labour productivity. Since income generated is the source out of which workers are paid, it is expected that the industries with higher productivity would have better capacity to pay higher wages, as compared to those have low productivity. This does not seem to be exaggeration of reality.

The hypothesised relationship is tested on the basis of observation obtained from five industries and organised manufacturing sector. For the purpose of analysis, we have taken growth rates of different variables. Thus, we could get only six observations and with three variables to estimate in equation, we left with only two degree of freedom. The regression obtained with the postulated relationship is:

$$EE_R = \underset{(0.472)}{0.557} + \underset{(5.239)}{0.716\ LP} + \underset{(2.286)}{0.501\ K/L} - \underset{(3.838)}{0.502\ V}$$

Adj. $R^2 = 0.913$; *D-W* $= 1.878$; $F_{3,2} = 18.45$

The results of regression reveals that labour productivity coefficient is positive and statistically significant at 5% level of significance. This indicates that wage rate growth differences are explained by the differences in the growth of labour productivity. This result is contrary to the finding of Aggarwal (1998[a]). The coefficient of capital intensity is also positive but statistically significant at 10% level only. This indicates that capital intensity differences in industries may result in different growth rates of wages among industries. The coefficient of value added is negative and significant at 5% level. This indicates that increase in average size of the industry negatively affects the wage rate. This result is not conceivable, a possible explanation of this may be that effect of size is already captured by labour productivity coefficient and hence, due to multicollinearity, we may get negative sign of value added.

7.5 Summing Up

In this chapter, we have examined the relationship between the real wage rate and labour productivity in selected industries. We have applied Granger causality test to establish link between wage rate and labour productivity. The study also attempted to find out the relationship of real wage rate with labour productivity, total factor productivity, capital intensity, price of consumer goods for industrial workers and time trend variable in a multiple regression framework. The study, however, started with a two variable relationship, i.e., between the real wage rate and the labour productivity but extended it to include other variables gradually. The results of analysis in this chapter can be summed up as follows:

* The bilateral causality between real wage rate and labour productivity exist in motor vehicles, fertilisers & pesticides and watches & clocks industries. In sugar industry, only unidirectional causality from wages to productivity exists. No causal relationship between wages and productivity exists in organised manufacturing sector and paper & paperboard industry.
* The inter-industry differences in the growth rates of real wage rates is explained by inter-industry difference in labour productivity and capital intensity. However, it may be noted that the number of observations are less and accordingly the results are to be interpreted with caution.
* The real wage rates in the industries are positively and significantly related to labour productivity when other variables are excluded. However, the changes in real wage rates are also explained by other factors such as capital intensity, value added and consumer price index.
* In spite the presence of linkage of money wages with inflation, the real wages of the workers tends to reduce with the increase in inflation. This result is confirmed by the negative sign of consumer price index in regression for all industries.

The results in this chapter show that the available statistical evidence supports the positive relationship between the real wage rate and labour productivity in these industries. However, the causal relationship between wages and labour productivity does not exists in organised manufacturing sector and paper & paperboard industry.

References

1. It may be noted that they have used fixed effect model whereas, Aggarwal used different methodology based on Granger type tests.
2. Papola, T.S. (1970) *Principle of Wage Determination: An Empirical Study Bombay*: Somaiya Publications Pvt. Ltd., p. 142.
3. L. Oxley and D. Greasly (1998) *Vector Autoregression*, Cointegration and Causality: Testing for Causes of the British Industrial Revolution. Applied Economics, Vol. 30, pp. 1387-97.
4. For details, see D.N. Gujrati (1995) *Basic Econometrics* (Third Edn.). Singapore: McGraw-Hill Book Company, pp. 620-623.
5. It may be noted that some researcher have taken profitability of industry as measure of capacity to pay e.g. Papola (1970).
6. This points towards multicollinearity problem in models.
7. Studies by Verma (1971), Papola (1972), Dholakia (1976), Suri (1976), Aggarwal (1998) etc. are discussed in section 3.4.
8. D.G. Brown (1962) Expected ability to pay and Inter-Industry Wage Structure in Manufacturing. Industrial and Labour Relation Review, Vol. XII, No. 1, October, p. 45.
9. S.C. Aggarwal (1998a) *Human Resources in Public Enterprises: A Wage-Productivity Approach.* New Delhi: Anmol Publishing Pvt. Ltd, p. 326.

8

Summary and Conclusion

8.1 Summary

In this study, we have analysed the trends in labour productivity and wages in selected Indian manufacturing industries for the period 1973-74 to 1995-96. The industries selected for study are sugar, paper & paperboard, fertilisers & pesticides, motor vehicles and watches & clocks. The industries are selected on the basis of their different characteristics representing various aspects of manufacturing sector. We have also compared the results with organised manufacturing sector as a whole (aggregate all ASI industries). The period of study was selected on the basis of availability and comparability of data.

Time series data on capital employed, labour employed, total emoluments paid and values added in industries are obtained from various issues of the ASI (Annual Survey of Industries). The figures reported by ASI are adjusted, according to the need, for present study. The study has taken gross fixed capital as the measure of capital. Working capital is excluded on the grounds that, firstly, the relationship between working capital and output is less influenced by technical factors, and secondly, the composition of working capital is such that it is difficult to make a suitable price index. The real gross value added is taken as the measure of output and total number of persons employed is taken as labour input.

The study while analysing labour productivity trends also examines the trends in capital productivity, total factor productivity (both by parametric and non-parametric method), capital intensity and unit labour cost to clearly understand the productive efficiency of industries (Chapter-IV). The labour productivity shows rising trends in all industries at varying paces. Labour productivity index has increased at an average growth rate of 5.21 per cent in organised manufactu-ring sector. The average growth rate of labour productivity comes to around 10.88 per cent, 2.96 per cent, 7.99 per cent, 4.28 percent and 6.32 per cent is sugar, paper & paperboard, fertilisers & pesticides, motor vehicles and watches & clocks industries respectively. The labour productivity has increased at a uniformly higher rate, when the input price is considered in double deflation method. The labour productivity has increased at average annual growth rate of 5.51 per cent, 13.42 per cent, 5.37 per cent, 11.68 per cent, 5.12 per cent and 9.61 per cent respectively, in aggregate manufacturing sector, sugar, paper & paperboard, fertilisers & pesticides, motor vehicles and watches & clocks industries. However, capital productivity has only increased in sugar (2.83%) and fertilisers & pesticides (2.80%) industries. In rest of the industries capital productivity has declined and in organised manufacturing sector it has been stagnate (0.26%).

The capital intensity in all industries has shown rising trends at an average annual growth rate of 4.94 per cent, 7.82 per cent, 5.74 per cent, 5.05 per cent, 5.19 per cent and 7.82 per cent respectively, in aggregate manufacturing sector, sugar, paper & paperboard, fertilisers & pesticides, motor vehicles and watches & clocks industries. The increase observed in labour productivity seems to be the result of increase in capital intensity. The decomposition shows that capital intensity accounted for 37.3 per cent of increase in labour productivity in registered manufacturing sector. For sugar, paper & paperboard, fertilisers & pesticides, motor vehicles and watches & clocks industries increased capital intensity accounted for 76.6 percent, 77.5 per cent, 33.7 per cent, 39.3 per cent and 53.1 per cent of increase in labour productivity respectively.

The total factor productivity, a measure of overall productivity efficiency of the industry, has shown declining trends in paper & paperboard industry. It has stagnated in watches & clocks and motor vehicles industries. The TFP has significantly increased in organised manufacturing sector, sugar and fertilisers & pesticides industries. The unit labour cost has significantly declined in all industries except watches & clocks industry. The hypothesised negative relationship between labour productivity and unit labour cost is observed for most of the periods but there are few periods where increase in labour productivity has not resulted in the reduction of unit labour cost.

The inter-temporal comparison shows that the growth in productivity has been more in second half of the period (1985-95) than in the first half (1973-85) except in watches & clocks and sugar industries. However, when double deflation was used we find that for organised manufacturing sector the growth of productivity (all indexes) in the second half is more than the growth of productivity in the first half. This result again confirms the findings of earlier studies that turnaround in productivity is only confirmed when single deflation is used. Same trend is observed for watches and clocks industry also.

The analysis of productivity by parametric method has confirmed the findings of non-parametric method in terms of direction only. Estimates of production function shows mixed trends. Increasing returns to scale are present in motor vehicles and watches & clocks industries, contrary to the assumption of constant return to scale implicit in TFP indices. Constant returns to scale exists in sugar, paper & paperboard and fertilisers & pesticides industries. The CES function reveals that the hypothesis of unit elasticity of substitution is not outrightly rejected in industries except motor vehicles.

The regression analysis for variations in labour productivity, capital productivity and total factor productivity pointed to a significant positive relationship with value added for all industries. The capital intensity has been positively related to labour productivity and negatively related to capital productivity. This finding supports the hypothesis that capital deepening would lead to an increase in labour productivity. Wage rate is generally positively related to labour productivity and total factor productivity in all industries except sugar industry. The analysis also discloses a significant but negative relationship between time variable and indexes of productivity.

The total productivity gains and their distribution between labour and capital are examined, using the framework provided by Sinha and Sawhney (Chapter-V). The labour enjoyed 11.1 per cent of total productivity gains in organised manufacturing sector though it has accounted for 15.5 per cent of the increased input. However, the share of labour in productivity gains in all industries has been more than its share in increased input. Labour enjoyed 48.9 per cent, 138.3

per cent, 16.1 per cent, 25.6 per cent and 69.9 per cent of total productivity gains in sugar, paper & paperboard, fertilisers & pesticides, motor vehicles and watches & clocks industries respectively. Whereas, their corresponding contribution in incremental inputs has been 21.4 per cent, 9.5 per cent, 7.9 per cent, 16.8 per cent and 16.3 per cent respectively. The share of labour in productivity gains has been more than that of capital in the periods of downward movements of productivity and in the periods of slow productivity growths. Capital enjoyed larger share in productivity gains during the periods of rapidly rising productivity.

The share of labour in total input has been declining in all industries. It has declined from 46.4 per cent to 25.0 per cent in organised manufacturing sector; 47.94 per cent to 29.83 per cent in sugar industry; 35.96 per cent to 14.03 per cent in paper & paperboard industry; 29.07 per cent to 12.17 per cent in fertilisers & pesticides industry, 49.02 per cent to 25.03 per cent in motor vehicles industry and 47.74 per cent to 14.57 per cent in watches & clocks industry. The decline in share of labour in gross value added has been comparatively low. It has declined to 16.1 per cent, 26.75 per cent, 23.16 per cent, 14.09 per cent, 25.27 per cent and 40.57 per cent respectively in aggregate manufacturing sector, sugar, paper & paperboard, fertilisers & pesticides, motor vehicles and watches & clocks industries. The relative price of labour has been generally higher than the relative price of capital.

The trends in wages and earnings of workers in the industries are analysed using various indexes of labour compensation. The trend in employment, wage share, total wage cost, gross value added and rate of return have also been examined during the analysis of wage trends (Chapter-VI). There has been a continuously rising trend in money wages of industrial workers. The rate has been different for different industries. Index of money wage rate (EE_m) increased from 100 in 1973-74 to 1028.1 in 1995-96, in organised manufacturing sector. In selected industries, the index increased from 100 in 1973-74 to 1157.5, 832.64, 1246.1, 1157.4 and 943.5 in 1995-96 for sugar, paper & paperboard, fertilisers & pesticides, motor vehicles and watches & clocks industries, respectively. The average annual growth rate in money wage rate comes to around 11.23 per cent, 16.33 per cent, 10.5 per cent. 11.78 per cent, 11.38 per cent, 10.98 per cent for organised manufacturing sector, sugar, paper & paperboard, fertilisers & pesticides, motor vehicles and watches & clocks industries respectively. The average growth rate of real consumption earnings per employee (money values deflated by CPI for industrial workers) works out to be only 2.52 per cent, 7.23 per cent, 1.86 per cent, 3.03 per cent, 2.67 per cent and 2.29 per cent for organised manufacturing sector, sugar, paper & paperboard, fertilisers & pesticides, motor vehicles and watches & clocks industries respectively. Continuous inflationary pressures in the economy wiped out the substantial amount of money wages of workers. Similarly, real product wage rate (money values deflated by product price index) in the industries works out to only 2.98 per cent, 9.02 per cent, 1.91 percent, 5.72 per cent, 2.45 per cent and 7.32 per cent for organised manufacturing sector, sugar, paper & paperboard, fertilisers & pesticides, motor vehicles and watches & clocks industries respectively. This means that industries have shifted rising wage cost on to the consumers. The employment in the industries has increased at an average growth rate of 1.95 per cent, -1.07 per cent, 2.21 per cent, 2.75 per cent, 2.59 per cent and 5.7 per cent for organised manufacturing sector, sugar, paper & paperboard, fertilisers & pesticides, motor vehicles and watches & clocks industries respectively.

The inter-temporal comparison shows that wages have increased at higher rate in the first half of the period (1973-74 to 1984-85) than in the second half of the period (1985-86 to 1995-96). Real consumption wage rate in organised manufacturing sector has increased at an average growth rate of 2.78 per cent in the first half whereas, in the second half it has increased at an average growth rate of 1.42 per cent. Same trends are observed in all selected industries except paper & paperboard. Employment growth in the first half of the period is significantly higher than in the second period.

The regression of money wage rate on lagged labour productivity and consumer price index shows that wage rate does not fully adjust to labour productivity. Same trend was shown by wage-productivity index, which shows that increase in labour productivity has been generally higher than the increase in wage rate. The money wage rate in the industries has been more responsive to consumer price index than labour productivity. The estimates of employment functions indicates that elasticity of employment to the output is low. This points to the low absorption of labour in relation to output. Though the increase in product wage has negatively affected the employment yet the relationship is not so strong to argue that increased wages have resulted in the adoption of capital-intensive techniques. The hypothesis that increase in wage cost to the industries does not have any effect on the level of employment is rejected for motor vehicles and sugar industries.

The casual relationship between real wage and labour productivity was examined by using conventional Granger causality test. The hypothesis of no casual relation between wage rate and labour productivity is accepted only in paper & paperboard industry and organised manufacturing sector. Bilateral causality found to exist in motor vehicles, fertilisers & pesticides and watches & clocks industries. Unidirectional causality from wages to labour productivity was found in sugar industry. The wage-productivity relationship was also examined in a multiple regression framework by including other relevant variables. The variables value added, capital intensity and consumer price index are included to capture the effect of size, technology level and inflation on real wage rate. The analysis shows that wage rate is positively related to labour productivity but the elasticity is low. The hypothesis of no association between wages and productivity is rejected in all the industries. The variation in wage rate is also explained by the factors other than labour productivity such as capital intensity and value added.

8.2 Conclusions and Suggestions

On the basis of the study the following conclusions emerge:

* Labour productivity has increased in all the industries. Labour productivity in an industry can be increased by a host of factors such as capital intensity, economies of scale, growth of industry, work environment etc. Capital intensity, which has increased significantly in all industries, seems to be the major factor behind the increase in labour productivity.
* Capital productivity has either declined or stagnated in most of the industries to mean that capital requirement per unit of output has increased and in future, increase in the output would require more and more increase in capital investment. This increase in capital intensity and decrease in capital productivity is not consistent with the resource endowment of the country. If such strains are not reversed or checked, they would put a

great strain on the economy in the form of lesser demand for workforce and greater demand for capital.

* The total factor productivity has increased significantly in all industries except that of paper & paperboard and watches & clock industries. In paper and paperboard industry the whole performance in terms of total factor productivity has been found sluggish. The main reason seems to be the decline in capital productivity and unwarranted increase in capital intensity. This points towards the over capitalisation and excess capacity in the industry. The performance of the industries in terms of total factor productivity was significantly better when input price was considered. It shows that the input price for these industries has increased faster than output price and the performance of the industries has been affected by the factors, well beyond its control.
* The labour productivity and total factor productivity are highly influenced by output. This means that as the output of the industry increases, the productivity also increase. It seems that rapid growth in output has induced technological progress and has generated economies of scale resulting in this strong association of productivity and output. The labour productivity is positively and significantly related with capital intensity, reflecting the influence of 'more machine to work with effect'. But negative association of capital intensity with total factor productivity in paper & paperboard, fertilisers & pesticides and watches & clocks industrious indicates the presence of over capitalisation and prevalence of excess capacity in these industries. The productivity is found to be positively related with labour productivity in all industries except paper & paperboard industry. This supports the efficiency wage hypothesis.
* The growth of output seems to be most important factor in explaining inter-industry differences in growth of labour and total factor productivity. Growth of wage rate is also significant in explaining the inter-industry differences in productivity. But capital intensity is not significant in explaining the inter-industry difference in productivity.
* Labour enjoyed positive productivity gains not only in the periods of positive productivity increments but also in the

periods of productivity decrements. This means a net transfer of income from capital to labour during such periods. The share of labour in increased inputs has been generally lower than the share of labour in increased productivity. It, thus, appears that labour did not participate in the productivity losses.

* The share of labour in productivity gains has been more than that of the capital in the periods of relatively slow productivity advance, and in the periods of rapid productivity advance, share of capital has been more than that of labour. This may be due to the sticky behaviour of wages, especially downward. This means that share of labour in productivity gains is inversely related to the rate of growth of productivity. Such a trend was observed in all industries. It indicates that wage burden on the industries will increase in the periods of adversity and productivity decrements.
* Another important finding emerging from analysis is that share of capital in total factor input has been increasing and that of labour is decreasing in all industries under study and in organised manufacturing sector over the period. This suggests that Indian manufacturing industries are moving towards mechanisation and substitution of capital for labour.
* The most of the increase in labour productivity is the result of increased capital intensity. This implies that the productivity of labour has increased due to increased inflow of investment in the industries. The share of pure labour productivity in the increase of total labour productivity has been quite low. This indicates that the demand for increased share of labour is not justifiable on sound economic considerations.
* The movement of wages is positively correlated with productivity. But the year-to-year comparisons do not show any consistent trend in wage-productivity movement. Wages and labour productivity seems to be related to trends and movements. But they are not related magnitude and level wise. However, the comparison of their trends shows that labour productivity has increased at a faster rate than that of product earnings per employee, implying a reduction in real wage burden on these industries. It also implies reduction in the unit labour cost and share of labour in output.

* It was found that factor's share in output (Gross Value Added) has been changing over time. This implies that hypothesis of constancy of share does not hold good in Indian manufacturing industries.
* The money rate of compensation has significantly increased in all industries. Wages per worker and earnings per employee have significantly increased but increases in price level have wiped out the most of the increase in wages and earnings of workers. The real consumption earnings have increased, at significantly lower rate, than money earnings. Product earnings have also increased significantly in these industries, this means that labour enjoyed positive share in productivity gains. The interesting finding that emerges from analysis is that increases in real consumption earnings have been generally less than the increase in real product wage. This means that wages as cost component to employer have increased faster than the wages as income component to employees. If this trend holds good for other industries also, then it points to a more basic constraint in industrialisation, i.e., the inability to increase real consumption of workers along with their increase in productivity.
* Money earnings per employee have been positively related to labour productivity and consumer price index. The earnings per employee are though, positively associated with labour productivity yet they generally do not fully adjust to labour productivity. It was found that money earnings are more responsive to changes in consumer prices than change in labour productivity. It seems that the industries are following some short of linkage between wages and inflation.
* Another important conclusion that emerges from analysis is that productivity of capital and total factor productivity may be taken into account along with labour productivity, while granting wage increases so that it may not be of inflationary character or depresses rate of return on capital. We found that in the periods of lower increase in wages, compared to corresponding increase in labour productivity also, capital could not be rewarded with higher or even stable rate of returns. This may be due to no corresponding increase in total factor productivity
* The other conclusion that emerges from analysis is that the input prices have considerable impact on the performance of

the industry. The increasing input prices specially fuels and electricity prices have affected industries adversely. The analysis based on double deflation have shown comparatively higher growth in productivity indexes than based on single deflation. It shows that supplier of raw materials have enjoyed considerable gains in productivity increments.

The system of neutralisation of a rise in the cost of living either through dearness allowance or periodic wage adjustment has not been successful in fully safeguarding the real wages in the periods of inflation. Wages and earnings are related to change in the consumer price index and are less influenced by the level of increase in productivity. This system would not be tenable and would be self-defeating in the long-run. This way of wage increase would introduce distortions in the cost-price structure of the economy and further fuel the forces of inflation. There is a need for evolving a system in which wages and salaries increases are related to changes in productivity. Along with it, the government efforts should be directed towards price stability by devising suitable income and price policy for the economy. The nationwide linking of wages with productivity may be the best option.

The study reconfirmed the finding that the existing system, through collective bargaining, adjudication etc., has ensured labour an adequate and sometime more than adequate share in productivity gains, flowing out of technological progress. If the same trend hold good for other industries also then specific formula for distribution of productivity gains may be necessary to safeguard the genuine returns to capital. The productivity of capital and total factor productivity may be taken into account along with labour productivity while granting wage increase so that wage increase is not of inflationary nature or depresses the rate of return on capital.

Effective utilisation of capital should be the correct criterion for a country where capital is a scarce factor. The emphasis should be put on maximizing capital productivity by checking underutilisation of capital. The capital deepening must reflect in capital efficiency. Some of the selected industries are characterised by declining or stable capital productivity, stable or declining rate of return on capital and increasing capital intensity. Such tendencies should be countered by devising suitable wage and price policy, better management, technology and technique selection.

Appendices

Appendix Table A-1: Basic Data for Organised Manufacturing Sector (Aggregate)

(Values are in lakhs except for column 2)

Year	No. of Factories	Fixed Capital	Workers	Total Employment	Wages to Workers	Total Emoluments	Fringe benefits	Total Input	Total Output	Depreciation
(1)	(2)	(3)	(4)	(5)	(6)	(7)	(8)	(9)	(10)	(11)
1973-74	64133	1075857	46.595	58.201	156758	249874	...	1416575	1956801	76940
1974-75	64217	1192240	47.621	60.528	182295	305167	...	1918348	2609901	83162
1975-76	71705	1402910	40.985	51.927	196358	165870	...	1836450	2500577	87184
1976-77	81277	1617056	52.103	66.493	227017	363670	...	2571063	3409065	106935
1977-78	84924	1946391	55.418	70.934	252736	419631	...	2952105	3886033	121334
1978-79	88077	2288593	56.665	72.481	303439	461172	...	3331245	4433179	147738
1979-80	95126	2682963	59.623	76.783	351016	537190	66650	3971612	5225785	167723
1980-81	96503	2990038	60.466	78.542	394470	609651	76571	4723833	6108413	191693
1981-82	105037	3470259	61.056	78.943	439417	677753	89949	5694900	7367247	216889
1982-83	93166	4100600	63.127	81.662	514828	804609	103545	6709650	8623768	246754
1983-84	96706	4860554	61.588	79.944	592078	921825	115821	7001692	9353741	338331
1984-85	96947	5484211	60.914	79.814	675730	1086021	140722	8062437	10556600	405440
1985-86	101016	6008524	58.192	75.840	709209	1108113	153120	9248839	12015540	440053
1986-87	97957	6723094	58.069	75.488	785043	1229918	168813	10284440	13304352	464637
1987-88	102596	7847463	60.618	79.038	893370	1408105	189157	11938728	15397307	625220
1988-89	104077	8909875	60.263	78.583	1029223	1572832	271161	14258830	18434878	712568
1989-90	107992	10692778	63.265	82.567	1179567	1840888	325353	17862255	23065940	866369
1990-91	110179	13364756	63.071	82.794	1319205	2058633	376556	20898600	27056353	1006294
1991-92	112286	15190240	62.590	83.196	1358263	2097048	421840	23302799	29919581	1134080
1992-93	119494	19287139	66.493	88.360	1666079	2722628	512513	28294279	36861377	1442279
1993-94	121594	22441333	66.323	88.377	1759741	2863947	566013	32085518	42574425	1645508
1994-95	123010	27764512	69.701	92.271	2201946	3534151	684052	39079472	51798701	1867530
1995-96	134571	34846773	76.323	102.222	2797035	4511605	1048027	50749118	67051423	2362586

Source : Obtained from various issues of 'Annual Survey of Industries (ASI)—Summary Results for Factory Sector' for years 1973-74 to 1995-96 from Central Statistical Organisation (CSO), Ministry of Planning, New Delhi.

Appendix Table A-2: Basic Data for Sugar Industry

(Values are in lakhs except for column 2)

Year	No. of Factories	Fixed Capital	Workers	Total Employment	Wages to Workers	Total Emoluments	Fringe Benefits	Total Input	Total Output	Depreciation
1	2	3	4	5	6	7	8	9	10	11
1973-74	261	19928	.95513	1.32185	3185	5579	-	59709	71347	2248
1974-75	251	23842	1.79048	2.52092	3522	6266	-	67509	80139	2328
1975-76	243	27831	2.09527	3.01475	5086	8970	-	92224	108512	2826
1976-77	261	31839	2.53087	3.70045	5125	8963	-	98368	96433	3224
1977-78	288	40509	2.49112	3.67625	5307	9688	-	89454	107516	4307
1978-79	286	47944	2.21667	3.15986	7232	11559	-	113553	134577	5502
1979-80	293	53241	2.42725	3.53433	7811	12583	1224	103080	125302	6467
1980-81	304	56283	3.15655	4.70148	7783	13019	1366	98854	120648	6062
1981-82	296	59801	3.00794	4.43259	9557	16032	1668	160710	196682	7113
1982-83	308	65785	2.45257	3.53983	13803	22850	2249	238942	293329	8407
1983-84	318	71568	1.60515	2.30592	16105	25743	2473	227876	289461	10175
1984-85	323	88522	1.38618	2.07639	15801	29093	2848	182734	238621	11180
1985-86	328	86790	1.52002	1.92182	15688	26393	3048	202347	262499	12527
1986-87	323	97557	1.26195	1.92778	17808	29770	3310	248043	618496	13226
1987-88	328	113131	1.44257	2.15982	23155	37750	4178	314614	396423	18294
1988-89	349	127114	1.52589	2.26713	27516	44920	5207	419740	549989	20031
1989-90	336	185413	1.57001	2.34443	33827	56117	7034	788439	641483	24701
1990-91	361	244776	1.68052	2.47193	40813	65295	8612	622947	748077	21771
1991-92	356	251652	1.67647	2.49702	47346	76660	9838	704980	851203	27003
1992-93	352	314789	1.71573	2.54866	53118	89869	11339	790354	969939	33659
1993-94	395	386048	1.56876	2.39855	53436	89922	12574	819429	1086420	23816
1994-95	399	506116	1.57105	2.39873	62457	106252	15211	1082322	1479543	37395
1995-96	394	530943	1.70897	2.57992	76110	126034	17193	1290648	1603509	45289

Source : Obtained from various issues of 'Annual Survey of Industries (ASI)—Summary Results for Factory Sector' for years 1973-74 to 1995-96 from Central Statistical Organisation (CSO), Ministry of Planning, New Delhi.

Appendix Table A-3: Basic Data for Paperboard Industry

(Values are in lakhs except for column 2)

Year	No. of Factories	Fixed Capital	Workers	Total Employment	Wages to workers	Total Emoluments	Fringe Benefits	Total Input	Total Output	Depreciation
1	2	3	4	5	6	7	8	9	10	11
1973-74	560	16709	0.56649	0.7222	2096	3552	-	17516	27394	1842
1974-75	490	21697	0.59106	0.75171	2587	4611	-	26128	45156	2139
1975-76	424	24470	0.59738	0.76601	2710	4936	-	25998	43097	2444
1976-77	449	28299	0.62304	0.7889	2962	5120	-	27798	42882	2617
1977-78	538	33144	0.7373	0.91552	3700	6310	-	33233	50312	2868
1978-79	500	35034	0.70443	0.88672	4498	6915	-	36974	54947	3094
1979-80	587	43066	0.78798	0.99870	5323	8406	1043	49953	72667	3818
1980-81	585	63634	0.81518	1.05109	6217	9546	1222	60258	85511	5313
1981-82	672	76618	0.84593	1.10477	6990	10983	1482	75105	103530	4717
1982-83	637	95705	0.92498	1.20652	7388	11684	1621	81596	102751	5535
1983-84	734	121148	0.84851	1.1313	8148	12822	1770	94158	123037	9601
1984-85	696	157600	0.83956	1.11257	9113	14411	2058	121371	164893	12147
1985-86	802	108212	0.78639	1.02897	9581	15218	2131	132158	168358	12389
1986-87	779	146739	0.80284	1.04973	11004	16981	2253	149641	199004	14266
1987-88	899	153518	0.8253	1.09703	12243	20028	2810	166881	215069	16111
1988-89	808	203601	0.77225	1.01741	12714	19528	3979	190612	250277	19574
1989-90	842	183713	0.81063	1.06953	17098	25735	4730	252833	347538	24113
1990-91	895	234667	0.87608	1.13914	20125	29835	5630	304148	420563	30104
1991-92	839	255313	0.90511	1.16517	22938	34283	6976	354381	473129	28407
1992-93	927	293871	0.93939	1.21431	26970	39474	7614	388061	513441	29426
1993-94	1005	349415	0.92372	1.19541	27535	43333	8330	436256	571354	20759
1994-95	953	828909	0.94732	1.24569	33629	51013	10558	540591	728859	26551
1995-96	989	612183	0.98487	1.32112	41205	62262	11690	692720	961527	36646

Source : Obtained from various issues of 'Annual Survey of Industries (ASI)—Summary Results for Factory Sector' for years 1973-74 to 1995-96 from Central Statistical Organisation (CSO), Ministry of Planning, New Delhi.

Appendix Table A-4: Basic Data for Fertiliser and Pesticides Industry *(values are in lakhs expect for column 2)*

Year	No. of Factories	Fixed Capital	Workers	Total Employment	Wages to workers	Total Emoluments	Fringe benefits	Total Input	Total Output	Depreciation
1	2	3	4	5	6	7	8	9	10	11
1973-74	335	58145	0.34795	0.50595	1854	3731	-	30535	43368	5215
1974-75	344	75148	0.3598	0.55575	2171	5048	-	54103	75858	6142
1975-76	378	101129	0.37687	0.59881	2883	6172	-	68024	89565	6962
1976-77	440	103537	0.38411	0.58758	2881	5941	-	75344	98047	8378
1977-78	469	128136	0.39924	0.60359	3072	6598	-	87532	111997	9822
1978-79	493	143012	0.41885	0.63654	4286	8100	-	102647	136458	10148
1979-80	503	204388	0.49003	0.83123	5293	9905	1512	134214	170157	14334
1980-81	447	191772	0.54195	0.78914	5854	11176	1598	159241	200517	19194
1981-82	618	215260	0.46951	0.72251	6416	12173	2286	223796	280784	20879
1982-83	442	189089	0.48269	0.73864	6842	12768	2448	250376	323430	21775
1983-84	495	239350	0.48489	0.83064	8800	16924	3194	276365	353346	29008
1984-85	469	195567	0.43853	0.6935	8688	16998	3196	282496	376048	26845
1985-86	546	237295	0.51741	0.79986	10455	20432	3963	306234	393463	28040
1986-87	474	292319	0.44342	0.70602	11191	22730	3896	394478	481154	30775
1987-88	515	312017	0.49387	0.77986	14103	27597	4437	417429	525735	40257
1988-89	594	372867	0.55773	0.84749	16267	29555	8306	453273	585315	43887
1989-90	556	518179	0.62535	0.94349	20553	38659	10567	671205	830049	61952
1990-91	569	516469	0.56903	0.86742	24028	42993	13023	713506	894194	62431
1991-92	509	669011	0.54335	0.83448	25416	45999	14997	972308	1204267	80568
1992-93	633	913632	0.64309	1.00347	31334	60086	18795	1084221	1431036	89701
1993-94	652	849813	0.60441	0.9295	31808	58575	20043	1087752	1428952	69231
1994-95	646	1265872	0.6482	1.01628	39642	78913	22677	1389494	1872844	91759
1995-96	753	1361664	0.66709	1.04754	49040	96258	28446	1689588	2372621	87827

Source : Obtained from various issues of 'Annual Survey of Industries (ASI)—Summary Results for Factory Sector' for years 1973-74 to 1995-96 from Central Statistical Organisation (CSO), Ministry of Planning, New Delhi.

Appendix Table A-5: Basic Data for Motor Vehicles Industry

(Values are in lakhs except for column 2)

Year	No. of Factories	Fixed Capital	Workers	Total Employment	Wages to Workers	Total Emoluments	Fringe Benefits	Total Input	Total Output	Depreciation
1	2	3	4	5	6	7	8	9	10	11
1973-74	523	16863	0.88468	1.22085	4648	8297	-	41168	58095	2444
1974-75	569	19066	0.90546	1.25000	5564	10311	-	52448	74026	3060
1975-76	990	23031	0.92190	1.28192	6125	11112	-	59934	83399	3062
1976-77	1021	24564	0.92493	1.29821	6496	11707	-	66728	95379	3342
1977-78	1023	25690	0.94763	1.32762	6794	12610	-	65564	95776	3378
1978-79	1113	29537	1.00622	1.40771	8939	15241	-	85811	121135	4004
1979-80	1267	38265	1.16226	1.62898	10092	17524	2532	109497	148829	4613
1980-81	1297	43005	1.18110	1.65687	11940	20331	3052	134985	181866	5484
1981-82	1565	54541	1.23777	1.74148	15149	25574	4172	171879	240441	6827
1982-83	1334	69017	1.30387	1.86254	18174	31180	5133	175756	277404	8390
1983-84	1302	75123	1.18378	1.71282	18894	32902	3702	183773	265049	9333
1984-85	1529	89602	1.22548	1.73828	21822	37698	7280	199372	288460	10666
1985-86	1594	118948	1.27630	1.78931	26030	43828	6778	265378	368709	12132
1986-87	1567	141843	1.27172	1.83211	27614	48215	7709	305630	428513	12556
1987-88	1463	143587	1.20288	1.72707	29747	50586	8107	336491	452586	13701
1988-89	1498	176173	1.31847	1.87574	36393	58761	12929	438734	590331	19438
1989-90	1569	187086	1.29449	1.82489	43086	68521	15477	579605	761105	23306
1990-91	1609	228227	1.35768	1.91117	47970	76665	17277	671972	900647	25528
1991-92	1586	267369	1.35845	1.89910	55361	87532	21550	600907	844511	30926
1992-93	1654	356783	1.40818	1.99577	59654	97873	24354	847836	1115806	36878
1993-94	1743	437107	1.39153	1.97801	64378	105599	25955	963873	1270939	41295
1994-95	1811	484919	1.52292	2.16849	81719	133455	35183	1416775	1832500	54695
1995-96	1793	815652	1.72296	2.43753	117327	191735	45661	2216885	2975673	76448

Source : Obtained from various issues of 'Annual Survey of Industries (ASI)—Summary Results for Factory Sector' for years 1973-74 to 1995-96 from Central Statistical Organisation (CSO), Ministry of Planning, New Delhi.

Appendix Table A-6: Basic Data for Watches and Clocks Industry

(Values are in lakhs except for column 2)

Year	No. of Factories	Fixed Capital	Workers	Total Employment	Wages to Workers	Total Emoluments	Fringe Benefits	Total Input	Total Output	Depreciation
1	2	3	4	5	6	7	8	9	10	11
1973-74	84	1021	0.05335	0.06819	191	317	-	862	1526	70
1974-75	92	763	0.05830	0.07183	227	381	-	1201	2064	78
1975-76	99	1291	0.05739	0.07149	283	459	-	1514	2715	138
1976-77	118	1414	0.06185	0.07829	319	531	-	2402	3906	163
1977-78	137	1673	0.07062	0.09012	401	661	-	2645	4247	176
1978-79	163	1952	0.08254	0.10519	519	783	-	3428	5448	239
1979-80	197	2648	0.09653	0.12772	599	943	162	4560	7116	473
1980-81	213	4633	0.10001	0.13096	697	1095	182	5232	8736	547
1981-82	299	4051	0.09053	0.11750	608	971	155	5467	8763	480
1982-83	209	4938	0.10679	0.14177	1007	1573	313	7610	13417	599
1983-84	237	5400	0.10860	0.14347	1178	1858	378	7494	12177	699
1984-85	196	8468	0.09479	0.13822	1282	2140	297	7712	13167	962
1985-86	223	9559	0.10769	0.14821	1445	2479	312	9408	15843	1082
1986-87	218	12024	0.11914	0.16345	1783	2946	487	13951	21427	1214
1987-88	225	15278	0.12567	0.16909	2133	3356	571	14818	23302	1523
1988-89	235	18630	0.12984	0.17495	2437	3845	834	18616	28282	1621
1989-90	219	27673	0.15931	0.20983	2583	4535	1093	28202	42595	2295
1990-91	161	26442	0.12511	0.16860	2956	4826	1025	34981	46556	2473
1991-92	242	36309	0.15878	0.21350	3699	6123	1374	44595	67028	3678
1992-93	211	39961	0.16067	0.21238	4513	7134	1492	45566	61208	3755
1993-94	192	41915	0.14344	0.19272	4455	7288	1720	43635	60799	4248
1994-95	197	47310	0.14688	0.19945	5550	8859	2127	42430	6311	4173
1995-96	220	69077	0.19888	0.26701	7769	11711	2680	67498	96361	4259

Source : Obtained from various issues of 'Annual Survey of Industries (ASI)—Summary Results for Factory Sector' for years 1973-74 to 1995-96 from Central Statistical Organisation (CSO), Ministry of Planning, New Delhi.

Appendix Table A-7: Price Indexes, Gross Value Added and Labour Productivity: Organised Manufacturing Sector

(Values in Rs '00000)

Year	Product Price index	Material Price index	Gross Value Added (GVA) At Current Prices	Gross Value Added (GVA) At Constant Prices Using SD	Gross Value Added (GVA) At Constant Prices Using DD	Labour Productivity Current Prices	Labour Productivity Constant Prices (DD)
1	2	3	4	5	6	7	8
1973-74	100.00	100.00	540226	540226	540226	0.09282	0.09282
1974-75	121.00	135.76	691553	571514	743852	0.11425	0.12289
1975-76	122.72	137.47	664127	541155	701626	0.12790	0.13512
1976-77	125.59	143.58	838002	667245	923774	0.12603	0.13893
1977-78	128.46	151.02	933928	727025	1070286	0.13166	0.15089
1978-79	128.67	157.34	1101934	856378	1328067	0.15203	0.18323
1979-80	154.70	198.95	1254173	810737	1381848	0.16334	0.17997
1980-81	184.44	242.74	1384580	750676	1365767	0.17628	0.17389
1981-82	193.98	268.03	1672347	862130	1673233	0.21184	0.21196
1982-83	195.05	277.50	1914118	981328	2003320	0.23440	0.24532
1983-84	212.04	287.14	2352049	1109232	1972859	0.29421	0.24678
1984-85	229.03	309.01	2494163	1089001	2000120	0.31250	025060
1985-86	245.59	320.44	2766701	1126546	2006185	0.36481	0.26453

conti.

1	2	3	4	5	6	7	8
1986-87	257.35	327.85	3019912	1173476	2032835	0.40005	0.26929
1987-88	276.70	335.91	3458579	1249927	2010438	0.43758	0.25436
1988-89	299.64	361.42	4176048	1393681	2207066	0.53142	0.28086
1989-90	331.18	383.35	5203685	1571243	2305161	0.63024	0.27919
1990-91	359.14	419.77	6157753	1714584	2555129	0.74374	0.30861
1991-92	400.00	462.78	6616782	1654196	2444460	0.79533	0.29382
1992-93	443.73	504.65	8567098	1930711	2700457	0.96957	0.30562
1993-94	478.14	554.00	10488907	2193707	3112673	1.18683	0.35220
1994-95	528.32	610.33	12719229	2407507	3401511	1.37846	0.36864
1995-96	575.45	658.52	16302305	2832960	3945461	1.59480	0.38597
Annual Trend Rate (% Per Annum)							
1973-95	8.01	8.02	15.84	7.26	7.57	13.63	5.51
1973-84	7.56	10.61	15.02	6.93	12.73	10.92	8.71
1985-95	9.27	7.98	19.53	9.39	6.78	16.45	4.03

Sources :

1. *Index Number of Wholesale Prices in India-A Time Series Presentation (1971-1986)*, Ministry of Industry, New Delhi and *'CIER Industrial Databook-98'* by SR Mahanot for price indexes for subsequent years. Base is shifted to 1973-74 = 100 for the purpose of study.
2. Col. 4 to Col. 8 are computed from Appendix Table A-1.

Notes:
1. SD and DD refers to Single Deflation and Double Deflation procedure Applied to derive Real Gross Value Added.
2. Input Price Index is weighted average of WPI of the various groups, weights taken from appendix Table A-25.
3. *Annual trend rates are computed using exponential growth model and values are significant at 1% level of significance.*
4. *Product Price Index is WPI for all commodities.*

Appendix Table A-8: Price Indexes, Gross Value Added and Labour Productivity: Sugar Industry

(Values in Rs '00000)

Year	Product Price index	Material Price index	Gross Value Added (GVA) Current Prices	GVA At Constant Prices Using SD	GVA At Constant Prices Using DD	Labour Productivity Current Prices	Labour Productivity Constant Prices (DD)
1	2	3	4	5	6	7	8
1973-74	100.00	100.00	11638	11638	11638	0.08804	0.08804
1974-75	108.02	106.71	12630	11692	10925	0.05010	0.04334
1975-76	107.51	110.65	16288	15150	17581	0.05403	0.05832
1976-77	110.18	112.10	18065	16395	17608	0.04882	0.04759
1977-78	101.46	112.95	18062	17801	26765	0.04913	0.07280
1978-79	93.32	121.99	21024	22530	51134	0.06654	0.16182
1979-80	112.86	148.60	22222	19690	41657	0.06288	0.11786
1980-81	159.39	169.14	21794	13673	17248	0.04636	0.03669
1981-82	164.54	173.43	35972	21862	26866	0.08115	0.06061
1982-83	145.58	176.37	54387	37360	66014	0.15364	0.18649
1983-84	146.79	187.50	61585	41956	75668	0.26707	0.32815
1984-85	155.19	198.46	55887	36013	61686	0.26916	0.29708
1985-86	184.66	214.83	60152	32575	47964	0.31300	0.24958
1986-87	193.76	229.56	70453	36361	56325	0.36546	0.29217
1987-88	199.43	245.25	81809	41022	70499	0.37878	0.32641
1988-89	215.15	262.17	130249	60539	95527	0.57451	0.42136
1989-90	243.16	287.95	153044	62940	94190	0.65280	0.40176

conti.

1	2	3	4	5	6	7	8
1990-91	243.16	313.60	125130	51461	109006	0.50620	0.44098
1991-92	268.62	337.22	146223	54435	107822	0.58559	0.43180
1992-93	304.26	378.20	179585	59023	109803	0.70463	0.43083
1993-94	355.19	447.84	266991	75169	122897	1.11314	0.51238
1994-95	395.29	493.66	397221	100489	155047	1.65596	0.64637
1995-96	387.01	566.38	312861	80840	186450	1.21268	0.72270
Annual Trend Rate (% Per Annum)							
1973-95	6.71	7.88	17.05	9.69	12.20	18.32	13.42
1973-84	4.75	7.04	16.64	11.35	17.29	13.80	14.44
1985-95	8.60	10.12	19.19	9.75	12.46	16.02	9.48

Sources : 1. Same as serial number 1. of Appendix Table A-7 for Column 2 and 3.
2. Col. 4 to Col. 8 are computed from Appendix Table A-2.

Notes: 1. Same as serial number 1, 2, 3 of Table A-7.
2. Product price index is the wholesale price index of sugar.

Appendix Table A-9: Price Indexes, Gross Value Added and Labour Productivity: Paper and Paperboard Industry

(Values in Rs '00000)

Year	Product Price index	Material Price index	Gross Value Added (GVA)			Labour Productivity	
			Current Prices	At Constant Prices Using SD	At Constant Prices Using DD	Current Prices	Constant Prices (DD)
1	2	3	4	5	6	7	8
1973-74	100.00	100.00	9878	9878	9878	0.13678	0.13678
1974-75	143.03	136.09	19028	13303	12371	0.25313	0.16457
1975-76	142.26	139.39	17099	12020	11644	0.22322	0.15201
1976-77	139.40	139.15	15084	10821	10786	0.1912	0.13672
1977-78	142.80	147.99	17079	11960	12776	0.18655	0.13955
1978-79	151.70	162.97	17973	11848	13532	0.20269	0.15261
1979-80	183.75	196.08	22714	12362	14072	0.22744	0.14090
1980-81	202.94	219.14	25253	12444	14638	0.24026	0.13927
1981-82	218.42	248.89	28425	13014	17224	0.25729	0.1559
1982-83	231.97	278.16	21155	9120	14962	0.17534	0.12401
1983-84	252.17	305.59	28879	11452	17980	0.25527	0.15893
1984-85	281.35	340.14	43522	15469	22926	0.39118	0.20606
1985-86	292.80	350.05	36200	12363	19745	0.35181	0.19190
1986-87	303.87	371.89	49363	16245	25252	0.47025	0.24055
1987-88	314.09	396.33	48188	15342	26368	0.43926	0.24036
1988-89	332.82	435.45	59665	17927	31425	0.58644	0.30888

conti.

1	2	3	4	5	6	7	8
1989-90	384.67	471.59	94705	24619	36733	0.88548	0.34345
1990-91	410.22	508.35	116415	28379	42691	1.02196	0.37477
1991-92	482.20	571.14	118748	24626	36071	1.01915	0.30958
1992-93	574.30	656.59	125380	21832	30300	1.03252	0.24952
1993-94	605.26	709.26	135098	22321	32889	1.13014	0.27513
1994-95	609.13	755.96	188268	30908	48144	1.51136	0.38649
1995-96	690.40	852.28	268807	38935	57992	2.03469	0.43896
Annual Trend Rate (% Per Annum)							
1973-95	8.44	9.66	14.12	5.23	7.70	11.65	5.37
1973-84	8.52	11.00	9.57	0.96	6.19	4.40	1.17
1985-95	9.87	9.56	20.14	9.35	8.07	17.30	5.52

Sources : 1. Same as serial number 1. of appendix table A-7 for Column 2 and 3.
2. Col. 4 to Col. 8 are computed from Appendix Table A-3.

Notes: 1. Same as serial number 1, 2, 3 of Table A-7.
2. Product price index is the wholesale price index of Paper and Paperboard.

Appendix Table A-10: Price Indexes, Gross Value Added and Labour Productivity: Fertilisers and Pesticides Industry

(Values in Rs '00000)

Year	Product Price index	Material Price index	Gross Value Added (GVA) Current Prices	GVA At Constant Prices Using SD	GVA At Constant Prices Using DD	Labour Productivity Current Prices	Labour Productivity Constant Prices (DD)
1	2	3	4	5	6	7	8
1973-74	100.00	100.00	12833	12833	12833	0.25364	0.25364
1974-75	178.23	165.03	21755	12206	9779	0.39145	0.17596
1975-76	188.50	169.88	21541	11428	7473	0.35973	0.12480
1976-77	163.74	169.09	22703	13865	15322	0.38638	0.26077
1977-78	155.75	175.05	24465	15708	21904	0.40533	0.36290
1978-79	153.82	182.74	33811	21981	32542	0.53117	0.51123
1979-80	146.80	253.55	35943	24485	62981	0.43241	0.75768
1980-81	213.08	340.87	41276	19371	47387	0.52305	0.60049
1981-82	240.21	364.24	56988	23724	55449	0.78875	0.76745
1982-83	243.81	359.29	73054	29963	62970	0.98903	0.85251
1983-84	234.86	348.84	76981	32778	71228	0.92677	0.85751
1984-85	230.47	364.45	93552	40593	85656	1.34898	1.23513
1985-86	234.33	380.78	87229	37225	87487	1.09055	1.09378
1986-87	253.56	378.33	86676	34184	85494	1.22767	1.21093
1987-88	266.02	385.83	108306	40713	89437	1.38879	1.14684
1988-89	253.73	398.27	132042	52040	116872	1.55804	1.37904
1989-90	254.61	423.65	158844	62387	167574	1.68358	1.77611

conti.

1	2	3	4	5	6	7	8
1990-91	254.61	458.76	180688	70967	195673	2.08305	2.25581
1991-92	318.70	501.56	231959	72783	184011	2.77968	2.20510
1992-93	413.52	549.88	346815	83869	148889	3.45616	1.48374
1993-94	467.95	613.22	341200	72913	127976	3.67079	1.37683
1994-95	503.07	673.71	483350	96080	166036	4.75607	1.63377
1995-96	541.57	741.12	683033	126120	210121	6.52035	2.00585
Annual Trend Rate (% Per Annum)							
1973-95	5.73	7.54	17.32	10.96	14.75	14.19	11.68
1973-84	5.86	11.98	18.28	11.73	24.68	13.95	20.12
1985-95	9.34	7.39	23.16	12.64	8.22	19.25	4.78

Sources : 1. Same as serial number 1 of Appendix Table A-7 for Column 2 and 3.
2. Col. 4 to Col. 8 are computed from Appendix Table A-4.

Notes: 1. Same as serial number 1, 2 and 3 of Table A-7.
2. Product price index is the wholesale price index of Fertilisers.

Appendix Table A-11: Price Indexes, Gross Value Added and Labour Productivity: Motor Vehicls Industry

(Values are in Rs. '00000)

Year	Product Price index	Material Price index	Gross Value Added (GVA) Current Prices	At Constant Prices Using SD	Using DD	Labour Productivity Current Prices	Constant Prices (DD)
1	2	3	4	5	6	7	8
1973-74	100.00	100.00	16927	16927	16927	0.13865	0.13865
1974-75	127.30	128.90	21578	16950	17460	0.17262	0.13968
1975-76	139.50	138.30	23465	16821	16448	0.18305	0.12831
1976-77	136.43	139.31	28651	21001	22011	0.22070	0.16955
1977-78	139.58	142.67	30212	21646	22665	0.22757	0.17072
1978-79	152.01	153.65	35324	23239	23843	0.25093	0.16937
1979-80	189.06	183.65	39332	20804	19096	0.24145	0.11723
1980-81	218.80	208.73	46881	21426	18449	0.28295	0.11135
1981-82	249.02	236.56	68562	27533	23899	0.39370	0.13723
1982-83	257.12	252.01	101648	39533	38146	0.54575	0.20481
1983-84	254.37	264.12	81276	31952	34619	0.47452	0.20212
1984-85	266.72	282.46	89088	33401	37566	0.51251	0.21611
1985-86	307.95	316.79	103331	33555	35961	0.57749	0.20098
1986-87	322.74	329.52	122883	38075	40024	0.67072	0.21846
1987-88	343.98	350.36	116095	33750	35530	0.67221	0.20573
1988-89	385.97	391.01	151597	39277	40742	0.80820	0.21720
1989-90	430.59	435.66	181500	42152	43718	0.99458	0.23957

conti.

1	2	3	4	5	6	7	8
1990-91	468.30	471.28	228675	48830	49736	1.19652	0.26024
1991-92	522.42	519.32	243604	46630	45942	1.28273	0.24192
1992-93	561.76	571.13	267970	47702	50177	1.34269	0.25141
1993-94	573.56	605.21	307066	53536	62324	1.55240	0.31508
1994-95	614.48	655.29	415725	67655	82015	1.91712	0.37821
1995-96	659.70	746.87	758788	115021	154244	3.11294	0.63279
Annual Trend Rate (% Per Annum)							
1973-95	8.71	9.03	16.30	6.98	7.84	13.37	5.12
1973-84	9.47	9.53	17.55	7.38	7.39	12.87	3.12
1985-95	8.39	9.13	19.07	9.85	11.83	16.08	9.03

Sources : 1. Same as serial number 1. of Appendix Table A-7 for Column 2 and 3.
2. Col. 4 to Col. 8 are computed from Appendix Table A-5.

Notes : 1. Same as serial number 1, 2 and 3 of Table A-7.
2. Product price index is the wholesale price index of motor vehicles.

Appendix Table A-12: Price Indexes, Gross Value Added and Labour Productivity: Watches and Clocks Industry

(Values are in Rs. '00000)

Year	Product Price index	Material Price index	Gross Value Added (GVA) Current Prices	Gross Value Added (GVA) At Constant Prices Using SD	Gross Value Added (GVA) At Constant Prices Using DD	Labour Productivity Current Prices	Labour Productivity Constant Prices (DD)
1	2	3	4	5	6	7	8
1973-74	100.00	100.00	664	664	664	0.09737	0.09737
1974-75	106.45	165.03	863	811	1211	0.12014	0.16862
1975-76	113.98	169.88	1201	1054	1491	0.16800	0.20854
1976-77	116.67	169.09	1504	1289	1927	0.19211	0.24620
1977-78	121.68	175.05	1602	1317	1979	0.17776	0.21962
1978-79	125.63	182.74	2020	1608	2461	0.19203	0.23393
1979-80	136.20	253.55	2556	1877	3426	0.20013	0.26826
1980-81	141.13	340.87	3504	2483	4655	0.26756	0.35547
1981-82	144.27	364.24	3296	2285	4573	0.28051	0.38922
1982-83	146.06	359.29	5807	3976	7068	0.40961	0.49856
1983-84	149.55	348.84	4683	3131	5994	0.32641	0.41779
1984-85	152.60	364.45	5455	3575	6512	0.39466	0.47117
1985-86	156.90	380.78	6435	4101	7627	0.43418	0.51459
1986-87	160.84	378.33	7476	4648	9634	0.45739	0.58943
1987-88	171.68	385.83	8484	4942	9732	0.50174	0.57555
1988-89	185.04	398.27	9666	5224	10610	0.55250	0.60648

conti.

1	2	3	4	5	6	7	8
1989-90	198.92	423.65	14393	7235	14756	0.68594	0.70322
1990-91	199.82	458.76	11575	5793	15674	0.68654	0.92964
1991-92	219.53	501.56	22433	10218	21641	1.05073	1.01362
1992-93	246.42	549.88	15642	6348	16553	0.73651	0.77940
1993-94	244.62	613.22	17164	7016	17738	0.89062	0.92042
1994-95	259.45	673.71	20681	7971	18027	1.03690	0.90384
1995-96	265.16	741.12	28863	10885	27233	1.08097	1.01992
Annual Trend Rate (% Per Annum)							
1973-95	4.36	7.54	17.27	12.38	15.85	10.95	9.61
1973-84	3.93	11.98	21.60	17.00	22.32	12.54	13.21
1985-95	5.87	7.39	14.71	8.35	11.47	10.07	6.96

Sources : 1. Same as serial number 1. of Appendix Table A-7 for Column 2 and 3.
2. Col. 4 to Col. 8 are computed from Appendix Table A-6.

Notes: 1. Same as serial number 1, 2 and 3 of Table A-7.
2. Product price index is the wholesale price index of watches and clocks.

Appendix Table A-13 : Capital Stock, Gross Investment, Reward to Capital and Capital Productivity: Organised Manufacturing Sector

Year	Adjusted Capital Stock Series (Rs '00000)	Capital Goods Price Index	Real Gross Investment (Rs'00000)	Income Accruing to Capital (Rs '00000)	Rate of Return Current Price (%)	Rate of Return Constant Product Price (%)	Capital Productivity (GVA per Unit of Capital
1	2	3	4	5	6	7	8
1973-74	3563867	100.00	...	290352	8.15	8.15	0.15158
1974-75	3719977	127.82	156110	386386	10.39	8.13	0.18590
1975-76	3930126	141.73	210149	398257	10.13	7.15	0.16898
1976-77	4159846	139.77	229720	474332	11.40	8.16	0.20145
1977-78	4478548	141.41	318702	514297	11.48	8.12	0.20853
1978-79	4805889	149.67	327341	640762	13.33	8.91	0.22929
1979-80	5130807	173.00	324918	716983	13.97	8.08	0.24444
1980-81	5393974	189.53	263167	774929	14.37	7.58	0.25669
1981-82	5729092	208.02	335117	994594	17.36	8.35	0.29190
1982-83	6129619	218.99	400527	1109509	18.10	8.27	0.31227
1983-84	6602690	232.16	473072	1430224	21.66	9.33	0.35623
1984-85	7026253	242.96	423562	1408142	20.04	8.25	0.35498
1985-86	7387078	267.27	360825	1658588	22.45	8.40	0.37453
1986-87	7805363	281.91	418285	1789994	22.93	8.13	0.38690
1987-88	8401902	293.29	596540	2050474	24.40	8.32	0.41164
1988-89	8952137	322.59	550235	2603216	29.08	9.01	0.46649

conti.

1	2	3	4	5	6	7	8
1989-90	9692963	357.61	740826	3362797	34.69	9.70	0.53685
1990-91	10641644	387.73	948681	4099120	38.52	9.93	0.57865
1991-92	11301966	448.20	660323	4519734	39.99	8.92	0.58545
1992-93	12417102	496.73	1115136	5844470	47.07	9.48	0.68994
1993-94	13354041	512.27	936939	7624960	57.10	11.15	0.78545
1994-95	14625683	565.47	1271642	9185078	62.80	11.11	0.86965
1995-96	16189459	603.98	1563776	11790700	72.83	12.06	1.00697
Annual Trend Rate (% Per Annum)							
1973-95	6.98	7.97	9.48	17.28	9.62	1.53*	8.28
1973-84	6.48	7.69	9.30	15.56	8.52	0.77+	8.02
1985-95	8.16	9.14	14.02	22.36	13.13	3.65	10.51

Sources: 1. Gross Fixed Capital is calculated from Appendix Table as per methodology explained in Chapter-III.
2. Same as number one of Table A-7 for column 3.
3. Computed from data given in Appendix Table A-1 and A-7.

Notes: 1. Capital goods price index is the wholesale price index of machinery and machinery tools.
2. Annual trend rates are calculated by fitting exponential growth model. Growth rates are significant at 1% level until unless specified.
3. * Significant at 5% level, + Insignificant.

Appendix Table A-14: Capital Stock, Gross Investment, Reward to Capital and Capital Productivity: Sugar Industry

Year	Adjusted Capital Stock Series (Rs '00000)	Real Gross Investment (Rs '00000)	Income Accruing to Capital (Rs '00000)	Rate of Return: Current Price (%)	Rate of Return: Constant Machinery Price (%)	Rate of Return: Constant Product Price (%)	Capital Productivity (GVA/Unit of Capital)
1	2	3	4	5	6	7	8
1973-74	74877	....	6059	8.09	8.09	8.09	0.15543
1974-75	79685	4808	6364	7.99	6.25	7.39	0.14673
1975-76	84569	4883	7318	8.65	6.11	8.05	0.17915
1976-77	89743	5174	9102	10.14	7.26	9.2	0.18269
1977-78	98920	9177	8374	8.47	5.99	8.34	0.17996
1978-79	107563	8644	9465	8.80	5.88	9.43	0.20946
1979-80	114363	6800	9639	8.43	4.87	7.47	0.17217
1980-81	119167	4804	8775	7.36	3.89	4.62	0.11474
1981-82	124278	5111	19940	16.04	7.71	9.75	0.17591
1982-83	130849	6572	31537	24.10	11.01	16.56	0.28552
1983-84	137723	6874	35842	26.02	11.21	17.73	0.30464
1984-85	149303	11580	26794	17.95	7.39	11.56	0.24120
1985-86	153342	4039	33759	22.02	8.24	11.92	0.21243
1986-87	161852	8511	40683	25.14	8.92	12.97	0.22465
1987-88	173400	11548	44059	25.41	8.66	12.74	0.23657
1988-89	183944	10544	85329	46.39	14.38	21.56	0.32912

conti

1	2	3	4	5	6	7	8
1989-90	207154	23210	96927	46.79	13.08	19.24	0.30383
1990-91	229617	22464	59835	26.06	6.72	10.72	0.22411
1991-92	237172	7555	69563	29.33	6.54	10.92	0.22952
1992-93	256677	19505	89716	34.95	7.04	11.49	0.22995
1993-94	277171	20494	177069	63.88	12.47	17.99	0.27120
1994-95	305017	27847	290969	95.39	16.87	24.13	0.32945
1995-96	316565	11547	186827	59.02	9.77	15.25	0.25536
Annual Trend Rate (% Per Annum)							
1973-95	6.66	6.82	18.56	11.15	2.95	4.16	2.84
1973-84	6.43	4.55	17.54	10.44	2.55	5.44	4.63
1985-95	7.90	11.35	20.34	11.52	2.18	2.69	1.71

Sources : 1. Gross Fixed Capital is calculated from Appendix Table as per methodology explained in Chapter-III.
2. Computed from data given in Appendix Table A-2 and A-8.

Notes: 1. Capital goods price index is the wholesale price index of machinery and machinery tools.
2. Annual trend rates are calculated by fitting exponential growth model.
3. Growth rates are significant at 1% level.

Appendix Table A-15 : Capital Stock, Gross Investment, Reward to Capital and Capital Productivity: Paper & Paperboard Industry

Year	Adjusted Capital Stock Series (Rs '00000)	Real Gross Investment (Rs '00000)	Income Accruing to Capital (Rs '00000)	Rate of Return: Current Price (%)	Rate of Return: Constant Machinery Prices (%)	Rate of Return: Constant Product Price (%)	Capital Productivity (GVA/Unit of Capital)
1	2	3	4	5	6	7	8
1973-74	57426	....	6326	11.02	11.02	11.02	0.17201
1974-75	63001	5576	14417	22.88	17.9	16.0	0.21116
1975-76	66682	3681	12163	18.24	12.87	12.82	0.18025
1976-77	71294	4612	9964	13.98	10.0	10.03	0.15178
1977-78	76748	5454	10769	14.03	9.92	9.83	0.15583
1978-79	80078	3330	11058	13.81	9.23	9.10	0.14795
1979-80	86928	6850	14308	16.46	9.51	8.96	0.14221
1980-81	100584	13656	15707	15.62	8.24	7.69	0.12371
1981-82	109093	8509	17442	15.99	7.69	7.32	0.11929
1982-83	120337	11244	9471	7.87	3.59	3.39	0.07579
1983-84	135432	15095	16057	11.86	5.11	4.70	0.08456
1984-85	155434	20003	29111	18.73	7.71	6.66	0.09952
1985-86	141591	–13843	20982	14.82	5.54	5.06	0.08732
1986-87	160317	18727	32382	20.2	7.16	6.65	0.10133
1987-88	168122	7805	28160	16.75	5.71	5.33	0.09126

conti.

1	2	3	4	5	6	7	8
1988-89	189715	21593	40137	21.16	6.56	6.36	0.09450
1989-90	190897	1181	68970	36.13	10.1	9.39	0.12897
1990-91	211803	20906	86580	40.88	10.54	9.96	0.13399
1991-92	222747	10944	84465	37.92	8.46	7.86	0.11056
1992-93	236434	13686	85906	36.33	7.31	6.33	0.09234
1993-94	251329	14895	91765	36.51	7.13	6.03	0.08881
1994-95	340820	89492	137255	40.27	7.12	6.61	0.09069
1995-96	311004	–29816	206545	66.41	11.0	9.62	0.12519
Annual Trend Rate (% Per Annum)							
1973-95	8.08	-	14.71	6.12	–1.71	–2.14	–2.64
1973-84	9.13	-	7.32	–1.66	–8.69	–9.39	–7.49
1985-95	8.28	-	22.67	13.29	3.81	3.11	0.98

Sources : 1. Gross Fixed Capital is calculated from Appendix Table as per methodology explained in Chapter-III.
2. Computed from data given in Appendix Table A-3 and A-9.

Note: Annual trend rates are calculated by fitting exponential growth model.

Appendix Table A-16 : Capital Stock, Gross Investment, Reward to Capital and Capital Productivity: Fertilisers and Pesticides Industry

Year	Adjusted Capital Stock series (Rs '00000)	Real Gross Investment (Rs '00000)	Income Accruing To Capital (Rs '00000)	Rate of Return: Current Price (%)	Rate of Return: Constant Machinery Prices (%)	Rate of Return: Constant Product Price (%)	Capital Productivity (GVA/Unit of Capital)
1	2	3	4	5	6	7	8
1973-74	118495	....	9102	7.68	7.68	7.68	0.10830
1974-75	136602	18107	16707	12.23	9.57	6.86	0.08936
1975-76	159844	23243	15369	9.61	6.78	5.10	0.07149
1976-77	167561	7717	16762	10.00	7.16	6.11	0.08275
1977-78	191903	24342	17867	9.31	6.58	5.98	0.08185
1978-79	208622	16719	25711	12.32	8.23	8.01	0.10536
1979-80	252386	43764	26038	10.32	5.96	7.03	0.09701
1980-81	255857	3471	30100	11.76	6.21	5.52	0.07571
1981-82	277185	21328	44815	16.17	7.77	6.73	0.08559
1982-83	275178	–2007	60286	21.91	10.00	8.99	0.10889
1983-84	309322	34144	60057	19.42	8.36	8.27	0.10597
1984-85	302351	–6971	76554	25.32	10.42	10.99	0.13426
1985-86	328455	26104	66797	20.34	7.61	8.68	0.11333
1986-87	358889	30434	63946	17.82	6.32	7.03	0.09525
1987-88	379332	20442	80709	21.28	7.25	8.00	0.10733
1988-89	411799	32468	102487	24.89	7.72	9.81	0.12637
1989-90	469758	57958	120185	25.58	7.15	10.05	0.13281

conti.

1	2	3	4	5	6	7	8
1990-91	485418	15661	137695	28.37	7.32	11.14	0.14620
1991-92	537429	52010	185960	34.60	7.72	10.86	0.13543
1992-93	604734	67305	286729	47.41	9.55	11.47	0.13869
1993-94	605790	1056	282625	46.65	9.11	9.97	0.12036
1994-95	695595	89805	404437	58.14	10.28	11.56	0.13813
1995-96	725997	30402	586775	80.82	13.38	14.92	0.17372
Annual Trend Rate (% Per Annum)							
1973-95	7.94	-	17.81	9.34	1.27	3.41	2.80
1973-84	9.15	-	18.75	9.51	1.68	3.45	2.37
1985-95	8.45	-2.20	24.94	15.21	5.56	5.36	3.87

Sources : 1. Gross Fixed Capital is calculated from appendix table as per methodology explained in chapter-III.
2. Computed from data given in appendix table A-4 and A-10.

Note: Annual trend rates are calculated by fitting exponential growth model.

Appendix Table A-17 : Capital Stock, Gross Investment, Reward to Capital and Capital Productivity: Motor Vehicles Industry

Year	Adjusted Capital Stock Series (Rs '00000)	Real Gross Investment (Rs '00000)	Income Accruing to Capital (Rs '00000)	Rate of Return: Current Price (%)	Rate of Return: Constant Machinery Price (%)	Rate of Return: Constant Product Price (%)	Capital Productivity (GVA/Unit of Capital)
1	2	3	4	5	6	7	8
1973-74	62512	....	8630	13.81	13.81	13.81	0.270778
1974-75	66630	4117	11267	16.91	13.23	13.28	0.254396
1975-76	71588	4958	12353	17.26	12.17	12.37	0.234974
1976-77	75075	3488	16944	22.57	16.15	16.54	0.279729
1977-78	78261	3185	17602	22.49	15.91	16.11	0.276585
1978-79	83506	5245	20083	24.05	16.07	15.82	0.278285
1979-80	91218	7712	21808	23.91	13.82	12.65	0.228065
1980-81	96612	5395	26550	27.48	14.50	12.56	0.221773
1981-82	105440	8828	42988	40.77	19.60	16.37	0.261126
1982-83	115882	10442	70468	60.81	27.77	23.65	0.341152
1983-84	122532	6650	48374	39.48	17.00	15.52	0.260767
1984-85	132881	10349	51390	38.67	15.92	14.50	0.251363
1985-86	148400	15519	59503	40.10	15.00	13.02	0.22611
1986-87	160976	12575	74668	46.38	16.45	14.37	0.236528

conti.

1	2	3	4	5	6	7	8
1987-88	166242	5266	65509	39.41	13.44	11.46	0.20302
1988-89	182369	16127	92836	50.91	15.78	13.19	0.215372
1989-90	191938	9569	112979	58.86	16.46	13.67	0.219611
1990-91	209133	17195	152010	72.69	18.75	15.52	0.23349
1991-92	224766	15633	156072	69.44	15.49	13.29	0.207459
1992-93	250191	25425	170097	67.99	13.69	12.10	0.190661
1993-94	273932	23741	201467	73.55	14.36	12.82	0.195437
1994-95	292059	18128	282270	96.65	17.09	15.73	0.231648
1995-96	359476	67417	567053	157.74	26.12	23.91	0.319967
Annual Trend Rate (% Per Annum)							
1973-95	7.92	10.27	17.48	8.97	0.93	0.24	–0.87
1973-84	7.08	9.62	19.28	11.58	3.61	1.93	0.28
1985-95	8.62	14.32	21.58	11.93	2.56	3.27	1.13

Sources : *1. Gross Fixed Capital is calculated from Appendix Table as per methodology explained in Chapter-III.*
2. Computed from data given in Appendix Table A-5 and A-11.

Note: *Annual trend rates are calculated by fitting exponential growth model.*

Appendix Table A-18 : Capital Stock, Gross Investment, Reward to Capital and Capital Productivity: Watches & Clock Industry

Year	Adjusted Capital Stock Series (Rs '00000)	Real Gross Investment (Rs '00000)	Income Accruing to Capital (Rs '00000)	Rate of Return: Current Price (%)	Rate of Return: Constant Machinery Prices (%)	Rate of Return: Constant Product Price (%)	Capital Productivity (GVA/Unit of Capital)
1	2	3	4	5	6	7	8
1973-74	1933	....	347	17.95	17.95	17.95	0.343473
1974-75	1792	–141	482	26.89	21.04	25.26	0.452304
1975-76	2262	470	742	32.80	23.14	28.78	0.465776
1976-77	2467	205	973	39.44	28.22	33.81	0.522579
1977-78	2775	308	941	33.92	23.98	27.87	0.474505
1978-79	3121	346	1237	39.64	26.48	31.55	0.515264
1979-80	3796	676	1613	42.49	24.56	31.20	0.49433
1980-81	5132	1336	2409	46.94	24.77	33.26	0.483766
1981-82	5083	–49	2325	45.74	21.99	31.70	0.449451
1982-83	5762	679	4234	73.48	33.56	50.31	0.690027
1983-84	6262	500	2825	45.11	19.43	30.17	0.500061
1984-85	7921	1659	3315	41.85	17.23	27.43	0.45132
1985-86	8734	813	3956	45.30	16.95	28.87	0.469601
1986-87	10039	1305	4530	45.13	16.01	28.06	0.463012
1987-88	11667	1629	5128	43.95	14.99	25.60	0.423539
1988-89	13209	1542	5821	44.07	13.66	23.82	0.395475

conti.

1	2	3	4	5	6	7	8
1989-90	16380	3170	9858	60.18	16.83	30.26	0.441734
1990-91	16700	320	6749	40.41	10.42	20.22	0.34687
1991-92	19722	3022	16310	82.70	18.45	37.67	0.518126
1992-93	21213	1491	8508	40.11	8.07	16.28	0.29924
1993-94	22424	1211	9876	44.04	8.60	18.00	0.312904
1994-95	24116	1692	11822	49.02	8.67	18.89	0.330535
1995-96	28425	4309	17152	60.34	9.99	22.76	0.382939
Annual Trend Rate (% Per Annum)							
1973-95	13.96	-	16.53	2.89	–4.70	–1.40	–1.39
1973-84	14.60	-	22.00	7.77	0.07	3.69	2.09
1985-95	12.03	7.91	13.99	1.74	–6.78	–3.89	–3.29

Sources : 1. Gross Fixed Capital is calculated from Appendix Table as per methodology explained in Chapter-III.
2. Computed from data given in Appendix Table A-6 and A-12.

Note: Annual trend rates are calculated by fitting exponential growth model.

Appendix Table A-19 : Labour Compensation at Current Prices, Constant Consumers Prices and Constant Product Prices: Organised Manufacturing Sector

(Wages and Earnings are in Rupees)

Year	Earnings per employee			Wages per Worker		Consumer Price Index Ind. Worker	Share of Fringe Benefit In Total Eml.
	At Current Prices (EE_M)	At Constant CPIIW (EE_R)	At Constant Product Price (EE_P)	At Current Prices (WW_M)	At Constant CPIIW (WW_R)	(CPIIW)	(S_{FB})
1	2	3	4	5	6	7	8
1973-74	4293	4293	4293	3364	3364	100.0	-
1974-75	5042	3976	4167	3828	3019	126.8	-
1975-76	5120	4090	4172	4791	3827	125.2	-
1976-77	5469	4543	4355	4357	3619	120.4	-
1977-78	5916	4565	4605	4561	3519	129.6	-
1978-79	6363	4806	4945	5355	4045	132.4	-
1979-80	6996	4858	4523	5887	4088	144.0	12.41
1980-81	7762	4839	4208	6524	4067	160.4	12.56
1981-82	8585	4759	4426	7197	3989	180.4	13.27
1982-83	9853	5068	5051	8155	4195	194.4	12.87
1983-84	11531	5270	5438	9613	4394	218.8	12.56
1984-85	13607	5845	5941	11093	4765	232.8	12.96
1985-86	14611	5892	5949	12187	4914	248.0	13.82
1986-87	16293	6043	6331	13519	5015	269.6	13.73
1987-88	17815	6051	6438	14738	5006	294.4	13.43

conti.

1	2	3	4	5	6	7	8
1988-89	20015	6366	6680	17079	5432	314.4	17.24
1989-90	22296	6534	6732	18645	5464	341.2	17.67
1990-91	24865	6536	6923	20916	5498	380.4	18.29
1991-92	25206	5837	6302	21701	5025	431.9	20.12
1992-93	30813	6511	6944	25056	5294	473.3	18.82
1993-94	32406	6369	6778	26533	5215	508.8	19.76
1994-95	38302	6839	7250	31591	5641	560.0	19.36
1995-96	44135	7151	7670	36647	5937	617.2	23.23

Sources: 1. Computed from data presented in appendix table A-1 and A-7.
2. Consumer price index is obtained from Indian Labour Statistics (various issues). The data is first converted to base1960 using linking factor and then base changed to 1973-74 = 100 for the purpose of study.

Note: Data for share of fringe benefits in total emoluments upto year 1979-80 are not available.

Appendix Table A-20 : Labour Compensation at Current Prices, Constant Consumers Prices and Constant Product Prices: Sugar Industry

(Wages and Earnings are in Rupees)

Year	Earnings per employee			Wages per Worker			Share of
	At Current Prices (EE_M)	At Constant CPIIW (EE_R)	At Constant Product Price (EE_P)	At Current Prices (WW_M)	At Constant CPIIW (WW_R)	At Constant Product Prices (WW_P)	Fringe Benefit In Total Eml. (S_{FB})
1	2	3	4	5	6	7	8
1973-74	4221	4221	4221	3335	3335	3335	-
1974-75	2486	1960	2301	1967	1551	1821	-
1975-76	2975	2376	2768	2427	1939	2258	-
1976-77	2422	2012	2198	2025	1682	1838	-
1977-78	2635	2033	2597	2130	1644	2100	-
1978-79	3658	2763	3920	3263	2464	3496	-
1979-80	3560	2472	3155	3218	2235	2851	9.73
1980-81	2769	1726	1737	2466	1537	1547	10.49
1981-82	3617	2005	2198	3177	1761	1931	10.4
1982-83	6455	3321	4434	5628	2895	3866	9.84
1983-84	11164	5102	7606	10033	4586	6835	9.61
1984-85	14011	6019	9029	11399	4896	7345	9.79
1985-86	13733	5538	7437	10321	4162	5589	11.55

conti.

1	2	3	4	5	6	7	8
1986-87	15443	5728	7970	14111	5234	7283	11.12
1987-88	17478	5937	8764	16051	5452	8049	11.07
1988-89	19814	6302	9209	18033	5736	8381	11.59
1989-90	23936	7015	9844	21546	6315	8861	12.53
1990-91	26415	6944	10863	24286	6384	9988	13.19
1991-92	30701	7109	11429	28241	6539	10514	12.83
1992-93	35261	7450	11589	30959	6541	10175	12.62
1993-94	37490	7369	10555	34063	6695	9590	13.98
1994-95	44295	7909	11206	39755	7098	10057	14.32
1995-96	48852	7915	12623	44536	7215	11507	13.64

Sources : Computed from data presented in Appendix Table A-2 and A-8.

Note: Data for share of fringe benefits in total emoluments upto year 1979-80 are not available.

Appendix Table A-21 : Labour Compensation at Current Prices, Constant Consumers Prices and Constant Product Prices: Paper and Paperboard Industry

(Wages and Earnings are in Rupees)

Year	Earnings per employee			Wages per Worker			Share of
	At Current Prices (EE_M)	At Constant CPIIW (EE_R)	At Constant Product Price (EE_P)	At Current Prices (WW_M)	At Constant CPIIW (WW_R)	At Constant Product Prices (WW_P)	Fringe Benefit In Total Eml. (S_{FB})
1	2	3	4	5	6	7	8
1973-74	4918	4918	4918	3700	3700	3700	-
1974-75	6134	4838	4288	4377	3452	3060	-
1975-76	6444	5147	4530	4536	3623	3189	-
1976-77	6490	5390	4656	4754	3949	3410	-
1977-78	6892	5318	4826	5018	3872	3514	-
1978-79	7798	5890	5141	6385	4823	4209	-
1979-80	8417	5845	4581	6755	4691	3676	12.41
1980-81	9082	5662	4475	7627	4755	3758	12.08
1981-82	9941	5511	4552	8263	4580	3783	13.49
1982-83	9684	4982	4175	7987	4109	3443	13.87
1983-84	11334	5180	4495	9603	4389	3808	13.80
1984-85	12953	5564	4604	10854	4663	3858	14.28
1985-86	14790	5964	5051	12184	4913	4161	14.00

conti.

1	2	3	4	5	6	7	8
1986-87	16177	6000	5324	13706	5084	4511	13.27
1987-88	18257	6201	5813	14835	5039	4723	14.03
1988-89	19194	6105	5767	16464	5237	4947	20.38
1989-90	24062	7052	6255	21092	6182	5483	18.38
1990-91	26191	6885	6385	22972	6039	5600	18.87
1991-92	29423	6813	6102	25343	5868	5256	20.35
1992-93	32507	6869	5660	28710	6066	4999	19.29
1993-94	36249	7125	5989	29809	5859	4925	19.22
1994-95	40952	7312	6723	35499	6339	5828	20.70
1995-96	47128	7635	6826	41838	6778	6060	18.78

Sources: Computed from data presented in Appendix Table A-3 and A-9.

Note: Data for share of fringe benefits in total emoluments upto year 1979-80 are not available.

Appendix Table A-22 : Labour Compensation at Current Prices, Constant Consumers Prices and Constant Product Prices: Fertilisers and Pesticides Industry

(Wages and Earnings are in Rupees)

Year	Earnings per employee			Wages per worker			Share of
	At Current Prices (EE_M)	At Constant CPIIW (EE_R)	At Constant Product Price (EE_P)	At Current Prices (WW_M)	At Constant CPIIW (WW_R)	At Constant Product Prices (WW_P)	Fringe Benefit in Total Eml. (S_{FB})
1	2	3	4	5	6	7	8
1973-74	7374	7374	7374	5328	5328	5328	-
1974-75	9083	7163	5096	6034	4759	3386	-
1975-76	10307	8233	5468	7650	6110	4058	-
1976-77	10111	8398	6175	7500	6230	4581	-
1977-78	10931	8435	7018	7695	5937	4940	-
1978-79	12725	9611	8273	10233	7729	6652	-
1979-80	11916	8275	8117	10801	7501	7358	15.27
1980-81	14162	8829	6646	10802	6734	5069	14..03
1981-82	16848	9339	7014	13365	7575	5689	18.78
1982-83	17286	8892	7090	14175	7292	5814	19.17
1983-84	20375	9312	8675	18148	8295	7728	18.87
1984-85	24510	10529	10635	19812	8510	8596	18.08
1985-86	25544	10300	10901	20206	8148	8623	19.04
1986-87	32195	11942	12697	25238	9361	9954	17.14
1987-88	35387	12020	13302	28556	9700	10734	16.08

conti.

1	2	3	4	5	6	7	8
1988-89	34874	11092	13744	29166	9277	11495	28.01
1989-90	40974	12009	16093	32866	9633	12909	27.33
1990-91	49564	13030	19467	42226	11100	16585	30.29
1991-92	55123	12764	17296	46776	10831	14677	32.06
1992-93	59878	12652	14480	48724	10295	11783	31.28
1993-94	63018	12386	13467	52627	10344	11246	34.22
1994-95	77649	13865	15435	61157	10920	12157	28.74
1995-96	91890	14887	16967	73513	11910	13574	29.55

Sources: Computed from data presented in Appendix Table A-4 and A-10.

Note: Data for share of fringe benefits in total emoluments upto year 1979-80 are not available.

Appendix Table A-23 : Labour Compensation at Current Prices, Constant Consumers Prices and Constant Product Prices: Motor Vehicles Industry

(Wages and Earnings are in Rupees)

Year	Earnings per employee			Wages per worker			Share of
	At Current Prices (EE_M)	At Constant CPIIW (EE_R)	At Constant Product Price (EE_P)	At Current Prices (WW_M)	At Constant CPIIW (WW_R)	At Constant Product Prices (WW_P)	Fringe Benefit in Total Eml. (S_{FB})
1	2	3	4	5	6	7	8
1973-74	6796	6796	6796	5254	5254	5254	-
1974-75	8249	6505	6480	6145	4846	4827	-
1975-76	8668	6924	6214	6644	5307	4763	-
1976-77	9018	7490	6610	7023	5833	5148	-
1977-78	9498	7329	6805	7169	5532	5137	-
1978-79	10827	8177	7123	8884	6710	5844	-
1979-80	10758	7471	5690	8683	6030	4593	14.45
1980-81	12271	7650	5608	10109	6303	4620	15.01
1981-82	14685	8140	5897	12239	6784	4915	16.31
1982-83	16741	8611	6511	13939	7170	5421	16.46
1983-84	19209	8779	7552	15961	7295	6275	11.25
1984-85	21687	9316	8131	17807	7649	6676	19.31
1985-86	24494	9877	7954	20395	8224	6623	15.46

conti.

1	2	3	4	5	6	7	8
1986-87	26317	9761	8154	21714	8054	6728	15.99
1987-88	29290	9949	8515	24730	8400	7189	16.03
1988-89	31327	9964	8116	27602	8779	7151	22.00
1989-90	37548	11005	8720	33284	9755	7730	22.59
1990-91	40114	10545	8566	35332	9288	7545	22.54
1991-92	46091	10673	8823	40753	9436	7801	24.62
1992-93	49040	10362	8730	42362	8951	7541	24.88
1993-94	53386	10493	9308	46264	9093	8066	24.58
1994-95	61543	10989	10015	53659	9581	8733	26.36
1995-96	78660	12744	11924	68096	11032	10322	23.81

Source: Computed from data presented in Appendix Table A-5 and A-11.

Note: Data for share of fringe benefits in total emoluments upto year 1979-80 are not available.

Appendix Table A-24 : Labour Compensation at Current Prices, Constant Consumers Prices and Constant Product Prices: Watches and Clocks Industry

(Wages and Earnings are in Rupees)

Year	Earnings per employee			Wages per worker			Share of
	At Current Prices (EE_M)	At Constant CPIIW (EE_R)	At Constant Product Price (EE_P)	At Current Prices (WW_M)	At Constant CPIIW (WW_R)	At Constant Product Series (WW_P)	Fringe Benefit in Total Eml. (S_{FB})
1	2	3	4	5	6	7	8
1973-74	4619	4649	4649	3580	3580	3580	-
1974-75	5304	4183	4983	3894	3071	3658	-
1975-76	6420	5128	5633	4931	3939	4326	-
1976-77	6782	5633	5814	5158	4284	4421	-
1977-78	7335	5659	6028	5678	4381	4666	-
1978-79	7444	5622	5925	6288	4749	5005	-
1979-80	7383	5127	5421	6205	4309	4556	17.18
1980-81	8361	5213	5924	6969	4345	494	16.62
1981-82	8264	4581	5728	6716	3723	4655	15.96
1982-83	11095	5708	7597	9430	4851	6456	19.91
1983-84	12950	5919	8659	10847	4958	7253	20.34
1984-85	15483	6651	10146	13525	5810	8863	13.88
1985-86	16726	6744	10660	13418	5411	8552	12.59
1986-87	18024	6685	11206	14966	5551	9305	16.53

conti.

1	2	3	4	5	6	7	8
1987-88	19847	6742	11560	16973	5765	9886	17.01
1988-89	21978	6990	11878	18769	5970	10144	21.69
1989-90	21613	6334	10865	16214	4752	8151	24.09
1990-91	28624	7525	14325	23627	6211	11824	21.24
1991-92	28679	6641	13064	23296	5394	10612	22.44
1992-93	33591	7097	13632	28089	5935	11399	20.91
1993-94	37817	7433	15459	31058	6105	12696	23.61
1994-95	44417	7931	17120	37786	6747	14564	24.01
1995-96	43860	7106	16541	39064	6329	14732	22.88

Source: Computed from data presented in Appendix Table A-6 and A-12.

Note: Data for share of fringe benefits in total emoluments upto year 1979-80 are not available.

Appendix Table A-25: Manday Lost and Number of Workers Involved in Different Industries

Year	Sugar		Paper and Paperboard		Fertiliser and Pesticide		Motor Vehicles		Watches and Clock	
	A	B	A	B	A	B	A	B	A	B
1	2	3	4	5	6	7	8	9	10	11
1973-74	11608	94	17456	448	3846	13	42045	596	-	-
1974-75	15861	90	11261	326	4159	124	4903	161	150	2
1975-76	12835	147	2721	109	1513	70	5876	67	-	-
1976-77	1886	3	15731	67	398	1	3301	8	245	2
1977-78	8241	38	18243	439	7421	78	13475	560	564	2
1978-79	14336	107	10260	180	11976	150	21076	853	226	3
1979-80	6261	80	19624	459	4218	62	38990	2562	477	3
1980-81	6608	36	16316	461	1598	43	21344	1293	2702	72
1981-82	1572	6	12988	301	2844	34	8500	303	2808	140
1982-83	6531	95	11675	525	3390	95	2097	188	665	45
1983-84	7307	72	16137	1809	2976	76	8998	438	44	3
1984-85	2613	24	12721	493	4807	89	13300	660	272	4
1985-86	2048	15	11983	479	1304	67	8577	235	10	1
1986-87	7774	139	17225	566	1141	34	2802	285	66	5
1987-88	14792	89	9334	831	1560	125	8544	603	516	19
1988-89	13070	35	4889	751	1080	23	6900	432	2267	57

conti.

1	2	3	4	5	6	7	8	9	10	11
1989-90	10104	145	7316	354	1271	37	3416	200	2393	36
1990-91	13088	192	8282	426	1373	28	4250	200	1851	21
1991-92	6733	139	5777	191	1323	32	540	50	624	25
1992-93	5466	58	2571	113	3826	126	917	131	111	5
1993-94	4148	15	5935	267	957	70	3990	243	383	3
1994-95	2590	8	3321	251	1026	57	1171	134	136	17
1995-96	474	8	5087	253	1573	41	3676	117	47	5

Source: 'Indian Labour Statistics—Various Issues' Ministry of Labour, Government of India, Labour Beuro, Shimla.

Note: A- Number of workers involved (numbers).

B- Number of mandays lost.

Appendix Table A-26: Distribution of Industrial Disputes by Causes and by Results

Year	Distribution by Causes					Distribution by Results			
	Wages & Allowances	Bonus	Personal & Retrenchment	Indiscipline	Leave & Others	Successful	Partial Successful	Unsuccessful	Indefinite
1	2	3	4	5	6	7	8	9	10
1973-74	34.1	10.3	24.3	5.7	25.6	36.6	20.8	33.1	9.5
1974-75	36.1	6.2	26.5	6.2	25.0	31.5	21.1	38.5	8.9
1975-76	32.0	7.9	29.9	8.9	21.3	23.7	26.1	40.8	9.4
1976-77	23.4	13.8	29.9	9.9	23.0	20.5	27.1	44.1	8.3
1977-78	31.2	15.2	23.0	8.8	21.8	29.7	27.6	33.0	9.7
1978-79	28.7	9.9	24.2	10.7	26.5	33.4	23.9	37.8	4.9
1979-80	31.9	8.8	21.7	9.1	28.5	28.1	23.7	44.3	3.9
1980-81	28.4	7.3	24.4	8.9	31.0	27.7	23.2	44.6	4.5
1981-82	29.7	8.4	22.4	9.9	29.6	28.4	26.8	40.5	4.3
1982-83	30.0	5.8	21.6	11.8	30.8	18.5	17.5	35.9	28.1
1983-84	27.7	6.0	21.4	13.3	31.6	17.4	15.3	35.3	32.0
1984-85	26.6	7.7	18.8	13.4	33.5	20.3	16.9	30.4	32.4
1985-86	21.8	7.0	22.4	15.6	33.2	27.4	21.0	23.6	28.0
1986-87	24.3	9.2	22.0	14.3	30.2	28.4	26.5	20.4	24.7

conti.

1	2	3	4	5	6	7	8	9	10
1987-88	27.6	7.7	17.1	14.0	33.6	32.6	31.1	33.4	2.9
1988-89	27.8	6.9	17.0	15.8	32.5	27.9	28.0	40.9	3.2
1989-90	24.6	6.3	19.7	15.9	33.5	24.9	25.9	45.6	3.6
1990-91	24.9	4.1	16.4	16.1	38.5	22.7	23.2	50.4	3.7
1991-92	24.5	3.9	17.4	18.1	36.1	19.7	20.0	54.2	6.1
1992-93	23.0	8.0	17.5	21.2	30.3	18.1	22.9	52.3	6.7
1993-94	26.8	7.0	20.3	18.7	27.2	22.8	29.2	40.3	7.7
1994-95	30.0	7.8	16.4	15.4	30.4	36.9	16.2	41.0	5.9
1995-96	30.9	7.6	19.7	14.0	27.8	40.4	11.2	45.7	2.7

Source: 'Indian Labour Statistics—Various Issues' Ministry of Labour, Government of India, Labour Beuro, Shimla.

Appendix Table A-27: Production and Wages Loss Due to Industrial Disputes in Registered Industries

Year	No. of Disputes	Mondays Lost ('000)	Wage loss (Rs. Crore)	Production loss (Rs. Crore)	Wages loss per manday	Production loss per manday
1	2	3	4	5	6	7
1973-74	3370	20626	31.91	153.86	15.47	74.60
1974-75	2938	40262	31.64	209.63	7.86	52.07
1975-76	1943	21901	33.81	177.6	15.44	81.09
1976-77	1459	12746	12.33	92.31	9.67	72.42
1977-78	3117	25320	21.81	284.48	8.61	112.35
1978-79	3187	28340	24.89	285.32	8.78	100.68
1979-80	3048	43854	46.14	443.02	10.52	101.02
1980-81	2856	21925	27.56	297.14	12.57	135.53
1981-82	2589	36584	46.83	628.76	12.80	171.87
1982-83	2483	74615	33.24	357.42	4.45	47.90
1983-84	2488	46858	50.05	430.07	10.68	91.78
1984-85	2094	56025	67.2	528.05	11.99	94.25
1985-86	1755	29239	36.42	374.5	12.46	128.08
1986-87	1892	32748	45.31	823.59	13.84	251.49
1987-88	1799	35358	53.88	639.69	15.24	180.92
1988-89	1745	33947	61.95	694.23	18.25	204.50

1	2	3	4	5	6	7
1989-90	1786	32663	49.97	495.31	15.30	151.64
1990-91	1825	24086	33.39	348.35	13.86	144.63
1991-92	1810	26428	39.36	579.87	14.89	219.42
1992-93	1714	31259	35.3	533.41	11.29	170.64
1993-94	1393	20301	37.68	660.66	18.56	325.43
1994-95	1201	20983	29.22	481.99	13.93	229.70
1995-96	1066	16290	54.31	454.59	33.34	279.06

Source: 1. 'Indian Labour Statistics—Various Issues' Ministry of Labour, Government of India, Labour Beuro, Shimla.
2. Last two column are calculated using other columns of table.

Appendix Table A-28: Weights Assigned to the Wholesale Price Index for the Input Groups for Calculation of Input Price

Input Group	Sugar	Paper & Paperboard	Fertiliser & Pesticide	Motor & Vehicles	Watches & Clocks
1	2	3	4	5	6
Textile and Textile Products	0.0033	0.0122	0.0003	0.0034	0.0015
Petroleum and Coaltar	0.0044	0.0093	0.0274	0.0191	0.0360
Rubber and Plastic	0.0003	0.0034	0.0162	0.0710	0.0076
Basic Industrial Chemicals	0.0100	0.0618	0.2408	0.0152	0.0182
Chemical Products	0.0020	0.0539	0.0875	0.0480	0.0016
Non-Electric Machinery	0.0052	0.0073	0.0107	0.0306	0.0028
Electricity	0.0115	0.1298	0.0691	0.0483	0.0447
Services and Others	0.0854	0.0936	0.0879	0.1076	0.4680
Misc. Manufacturing	0.0011	0.0138	0.0155	0.0138	0.0057
Paper and Paper Products	0.0019	0.4359	-	0.0109	0.0051
Wood and Wood Products	0.0004	0.0014	-	0.0017	0.0055
Coal and Lignite	0.0032	0.0453	0.0153	0.0005	-
Non-Metallic Mineral	0.0033	0.0016	0.0979	-	0.0123
Non-Metallic Mineral Products	0.0054	0.0029	0.0010	0.0041	-
Metal Products	-	0.0071	0.0079	0.0913	0.0022

conti.

1	2	3	4	5	6
Basic Metal Alloys	-	0.0028	0.0009	0.1508	0.0495
Non-Ferrous Metal	-	0.0019	0.0040	0.0312	0.0480
Electric Machinery	-	0.0018	0.0031	0.0233	0.0084
Forestry and Logging	0.0030	0.0924	-	0.0016	-
Crude Oil and Natural Gas	0.0013	0.0000	0.1400	-	-
Jute, Hempa and Mesta Textiles	0.0199	0.0108	0.0422	-	-
Prime Articles	-	0.0110	0.0018	-	-
Same Category	Sugar cane .8317	-	Fertiliser .1304	Motor vehicles .3073, Two Wheeler .0203	Watches & Clocks .2830

Source: Calculated from 'Input Output Transaction Table-1989-90' Central Statistical Organisation, New Delhi, 1997.

Note: Weights are calculated after excluding transport and trade charges.

Appendix Table A-29 : Gross Net Ratio (GNR) for Components of Fixed Capital, 1960

Industry	Gross Net Ratio			Current to
	Building & Construction	Plant & Machinery	Other Equipment	Purchase price ratio
Sugar and Gur	1.6555	2.2164	2.4659	1.3963
Paper and Paperboard	1.4501	1.6906	1.8135	1.3963
Fertilisers and Pesticide	1.2760	1.5382	1.6507	1.3963
Motor Vehicles	1.7376	1.6846	1.8238	1.1674
Watches and Clocks	1.5455	2.705	1.8143	1.1674

Source: Column 2, 3, 4 are extracted from Hasim and Dadi (1973) and column 5 is calculated from data given in Dadi (1971)

Notes:
1. Gross Net Ratio for chemicals and watches and clocks are taken same as for Chemicals and Miscellaneous respectively.
2. Current to purchase price ratios are of the two digit classification to which these three digit industries belongs.

Appendix Table A-30 : Frequency Distributions of Factories by Year of Initial Production and Industries

Industry	Before 1900	1900 -10	1911 -20	1921 -30	1931 -40	1941 -50	1951 -60	1961 -70	1971 -80	1981 -90	1991 -94
Sugar	2	3	6	5	73	13	41	48	97	75	23
Paper and Paper-board	0	0	0	1	5	8	33	99	200	515	135
Fertiliser and Pesticide	0	0	4	4	2	7	24	101	200	257	48
Watches and Clocks	0	1	0	0	0	3	5	21	58	91	13
Motor vehicles	1	0	0	4	4	31	110	238	457	687	122

Source: Extracted from Annual Survey of Industries 1994-95, Vol. 1, pp. 4-60.

Bibliography

Books

Aggarwal, S.C. (1998[a]) *Human Resources in Public Enterprises: A Wage-Productivity Approach.* New Delhi: Anmol Publishing Pvt. Ltd.

Ahluwalia, I.J. (1985) *Industrial Growth in India: Stagnation Since the Mid-Sixties.* Delhi: Oxford University Press.

Ahluwalia, I.J. (1991) *Productivity and Growth in Indian Manufacturing.* New Delhi: Oxford University Press.

Akerlof, G. and Yeller, J. (1986) *Efficiency Wage Models of Labour Market.* Cambridge: Cambridge University Press.

Allen, D. (1969) *Fringe Benefits: Wages or Social Obligation.* New York: Cornell University, Ithaca.

Banerji, A. (1975). *Capital Intensity and Productivity in Indian Industry.* New Delhi: Macmillan Co. of India Ltd.

Beckman, J. (1959) *Wage Determination—An Analysis of Wage Criteria.* New York: D. Van Nostrand Company Inc.

Beri, G.C. (1962) *Measurement of Production and Productivity in Indian Industry.* Bombay: Asia Publishing House.

Bodkin, R.G. (1966) *The Wage-Price-Productivity Nexus.* Philadelphia: University of Pennsylvania Press.

Bowen, W.G. (1966) *The Wage-Price Issue: A Theoretical Analysis.* Princeton: Princeton University Press.

Brahmananda, P.R. (1982) *Productivity in the Indian Economy:*

Rising Inputs for Falling Outputs. Delhi: Himalaya Publishing House.

Chakraborty, P. (1966) *Indian Central Wage Boards Analysis.* Calcutta: Gupta and Company Pvt. Ltd.

Chinchankar, P.Y. (1969) *Wage and Productivity in Indian Industries,* Bombay: Vora and Co.

Chitale, V.P. (1986) *Capital-Output Ratio in Indian Industries.* Delhi ESRF, Radiant Publishers.

Christensen, L.R., Cummings, D. and Jorgenson, D.W (1980) 'Economic Growth, 1947-73: An International Comparison,' in Kendrick, J.W. and Vaccara, B.N. (Eds.) *New Development in Productivity Measurement and Analysis:* New York: National Bureau of Economic Research.

Dadi, M.M. (1973) *Income Share of Factory Labour in India.* New Delhi: Shri Ram Centre of Industrial Relation and Human Resources.

Denison, E.F. (1967) *Why Growth Rates Differs: Post War Experience in Nine Western Countries.* Washington DC: The Brookings Institution.

Denison, E.F. (1974) *Accounting for United States Economic Growth, 1929 to 1969.* Washington DC: The Brookings Institution.

Desai, M. (1976) *Applied Econometrics.* New York: McGraw Hills.

Diatchenkp and Dunlop, J.T. (1964) *Labour Productivity.* New York: McGraw Hill Publication.

Dickens, W.T. and Katz, L.F. (1987) Inter-Industry Wage Differences and Industry Characteristics, in Lang, K. and Leonard, J.S. (Eds.) *Unemployment and the Structure of Labour Markets.* London: Basil Blackwell.

Dunlop, J.T. (1957) *The Theory of Wage Determination.* New York: Macmillan and Co.

Economic and Scientific Research Foundation (1969) *Productivity, Wages and Prices in Indian Industry: 1953-63.* New Delhi: Federation House.

Fabricant, S. (1959) *Basic Facts on Productivity Change.* New York: Columbia University Press, National Bureau of Economic Research.

Fabricant, S. (1981) 'The Productivity Issue: An Overview' in Rosow, J.M. *Productivity Prospect for Growth.* Van Nostrand Reynolds Co.

Fonesca, A.J. (1964) *Wage Determination and Organised Labour in India.* Bombay: Oxford University Press.

Fonesca, A.J. (1975) *Wage Issues in a Developing Economy.* Bombay: Oxford University Press.

George, R. (1959) *Industrial Changes in India.* Bombay: Asia Publishing House.

Goldar, B.N. (1986) *Productivity Growth in Indian Industry.* New Delhi: Allied Publishers Pvt. Ltd.

Griliches, Z. (1967) Production Function in Manufacturing: Some Preliminary Results, in Brown, M. (Ed.) *The Theory and Empirical Analysis of Production.* New York: National Bureau of Economic Research.

Griliches, Z. and Ringstad, V. (1971) *Economies of Scale and Form of the Production Function.* Amsterdam: North Holland Publishing House.

Gujrati, D.N. (1995) *Basic Econometrics (Third Edn.).* Singapore: McGraw-Hill Book Company.

Gupta (1987) *Productivity, Investment and Import Substitution in Indian Industries Case Study of Non-Ferrous Metals.* New Delhi: Anmol Publication.

Hajra, S. (1993) *Productivity Growth in Industry for Price Stability and Higher Export.* Delhi: Allied Publishers Limited.

Hart, R.A. (1984) *Economics of Non-Wage Labour Cost.* London: George Allen and Unwin.

Hasim, B.R. and Dadi, M.M. (1973) *Capital-Output Relationship in Indian Manufacturing (1946-64).* Baroda: M.S. University of Baroda.

Hebden, J. (1983) *Application of Econometrics.* Philips Allen Publishers Ltd.

Hicks, J.R. (1964) *The Theory of Wages.* Landon: Macmillan and Company Limited.

Jose, A.V. (1994) 'Earnings, Employment and Productivity Trends in the Organised Industries in India' in Despande, L.K. and Rodgers, Gerry. (Eds.) *The Indian Labour Market and Economic Structural Change.* Delhi: B.R. Publishing Corporation.

Kandall, M.G. (1969) *Hand Book of Central Wage Board Recommendations.* Bombay: The Employers Federation of India.

Kehar, S. (1964) *Productivity and Economic Growth.* Bombay: Asia Publishing House.

Kendrick, J.W. (1961) *Productivity Trends in United States.* Princeton: Princeton University Press, National Bureau of Economic Research.

Kendrick, J.W. (1973) *Post War Productivity Trends in U.S. 1948-69.* New York: National Bureau of Economic Research

King, J.E. (1990) *Labour Economics.* London: Macmillan.

Krishna, K.L. (1987) 'Industrial Growth and Productivity in India' in Brahmananda, P.R. and Panchmukhi, V.R. (Eds.) *The Development Process of the Indian Economy.* Delhi: Himalaya Publishing House.

Lucas, R.E.B. (1988) 'India's Industrial Policy', in Lucas, R.E.B. and Papanek, G.F. (Eds.) *The Indian Economy: Recent Development and Future Prospectus.* New Delhi: Oxford University Press.

Madan, B.K. (1977) *The Real Wages of Industrial Labour in India.* New Delhi: Management Development Institute.

Mahapatro, B.B. (1993) *Industrial Wage Regulation in India.* New Delhi: Mittal Publications.

Mehta. S.S. (1980) *Productivity, Production Function and Technical Change: A Survey of Some Indian Industries.* New Delhi: Concept Publishing Co.

Misra, S.S. (1981) *Money, Inflation and Economic Growth.* New Delhi: Oxford and IBH Publishing Co.

Mohanty, K. (1993) *Wages and Productivity in a Developing Economy.* New Delhi: Discovery Publishing House.

Mohnot, S.R. (1998) *CIER's Industrial Databook.* New Delhi: Sage Publications.

Palekar, S.A. (1962) *Problem of Wage Policy for Economic Development with Special Reference to India.* Bombay: Asia

Publishing House.

Papola, T.S. (1970) 'Productivity and Wage Structure in Indian Industries, in Sandesara, J.C. and Despande, L.K. (Eds.) *Wage Policy and Wage Determination in India.* Bombay: Bombay University Press.

Papola, T.S. (1970) *Principles of Wage Determination: An Empirical Study* Bombay: Somaiya Publications Pvt. Ltd.

Ramjas (1992) *Trade Union and Productivity in Indian Industries.* New Delhi: Radha Publication.

Rao, P. and Miller, R.L. (1971) *Applied Econometrics.* New Delhi: Prentice Hall of India Ltd.

Rosow, J.M. (1981) *Productivity Prospects for Growth.* Van Nostrand Reynolds Co.

Salter, W.E.G. (1969) *Productivity and Technical Change.* Cambridge: Combridge University Press.

Sandesara, J.C. and Despande, L.K. (Eds.) *Wage Policy and Wage Determination in India.* Bombay: Bombay University Press.

Sanga, K. (1964) *Productivity and Economic Growth.* Bombay: Asia Publishing House.

Sattinger, M. (1980) *Capital and the Distribution of Labour Earnings.* Amsterdam: North Holland Publishing Company.

Singh, M.K. (1989) *Labour Productivity in Indian Industry.* New Delhi: National Publications.

Singh, N. (1984) *Sharing of Productivity Gains in Indian Industry.* Delhi: B.R. Publishing Corporation.

Singh, R.R. (1955) *Movement of Industrial Wages in India.* Bombay: Asia Publishing House.

Sinha, J.N. and Sawhney, P.K. (1970) *Wages and Productivity in Selected Indian Industries.* New Delhi: Vikas Publishing House.

Sinha, P.R.N. (1971) *Wage Determination.* New Delhi: Asia Publishing House.

Sreenivasan, K. (1964) *Productivity and Social Environment.* Delhi: Asia Publishing House.

Srivastva, S.C. (1984) *Wages, Profits and Productivity in Selected*

Industries in India Since 1950: An Econometric Study. Delhi: Himalaya Publishing House.

Subramaniam, K.N. (1977) *Wages in India.* New Delhi: Tata McGraw Hill Publishing Co. Ltd.

Sundaram, S.I. (1987) *National Wage Policy.* Delhi: B.R. Publishing Corporation.

Suri, G.K. (1976) *Productivity, Wages and Industrial Relations.* New Delhi: Affiliated East-West Press Pvt. Ltd.

Thomas, R.L. (1985) *Introductory Econometrics: Theory and Application.* New York: Longman Inc.

Verma, P. (1980) *Wage Determination: Concept and Cases.* New Delhi: Wiley Eastern Ltd.

Articles

Agarwal, K.K. and Agarwal, R. (1986) Fringe Benefits and other Auxiliary Wage Issues. *Indian Journal of Industrial Relations,* Vol. 22, No. 1, pp. 14-35.

Aggarwal, S.C. (1988[b]) Wages and Productivity in Indian Public Enterprises. *The Indian Journal of Labour Economics,* Vol. 41, No. 4, pp. 911-16.

Akaike, H. (1969[a]) Statistical Predicator Identification. *Annals of the Institute of Statistical Mathematics,* Vol. 21, pp. 203-18.

Akaike, H. (1969[b]) Fitting Autoregressions for Prediction. *Annals of the Institute of Statistical Mathematics,* Vol. 21. pp. 243-47.

Alam, S.N. (1971) Marginal Productivity Theory of Distribution—A Survey. *Indian Economic Journal,* Vol. 18, No. 2, pp. 230-48.

Apte, P. (1988) Relationship Between Sub-Period and Total Period Regression. *Artha Vijnana,* Vol. 30. No. 3, 277-86.

Arrow, K.J. (1962) The Economic Implications of Learning by Doing. *Review of Economic Studies.* Vol. 29, June, pp. 155-73.

Arrow, K.J., Chenery, H.B., Minhas, B.S., and Solow, R.M. (1961) Capital-Labour Substitution and Economic Efficiency. *Review of Economics and Statistics,* Vol. 43, August, pp. 225-50.

Arya, I.C. (1983) Technology and Productivity of Cement Industries in India—A Case Study. *Artha Vijnana,* Vol. 25, No. 3, pp. 259-70.

Balakrishnan, P. and Pushpangadan K. (1995) Total Factor Productivity Growth in Manufacturing Industry. *Economic and Political Weekly,* March 4, pp. 462-64.

Balakrishnan, P. and Pushpangadan K. (1996) Total Factor Productivity Growth in Manufacturing Industry. *Economic and Political Weekly,* pp. 425-28.

Balakrishnan, P. and Pushpangadan, K. (1998) What Do We Know about Productivity growth in Indian Industries? *Economic and Political Weekly,* August 15-22, pp. 2241-46.

Balakrishnan, P. and Pushpangadan, K. (1994) Total Factor Productivity Growth in Manufacturing Industry: A Fresh Look. *Economic and Political Weekly,* July 30, pp. 2028-35.

Beckman, M.J. and Sato, R. (1969) Aggregate Production Function and Type of Technical Progress. *American Economic Review,* Vol. 59. pp. 88-96.

Bhardwaj, V.P. and Papola, T.S. (1967) Productivity Gains and Distributive Shares. *The Indian Journal of Labour Economics,* Vol. 9, No. 4, pp. 367-77.

Bhasin, V.K. and Seth, V.K. (1978) Estimation of Production Function for Indian Manufacturing Industries. *Artha Vijnana,* Vol. 20, pp. 395-408.

Bhat, S. (1993) Effects of Technology Transfer on Productivity of Indian Automobiles Industry. *Asian Economic Review,* Vol. 35, pp. 337-76.

Bhatnagar, V. (1988) Wage-Productivity Relationship in Indian Industries. *Productivity,* Vol. 28, No. 4, pp. 405-12.

Bhattacharya, B.B. and Mitra, A. (1994). Employment, Labour Productivity and Wage Rate in Public and Organised Private Sectors in the Context of Structural Reforms. *The Indian Journal of Labour Economics,* Vol. 37, No. 2, pp. 163-73.

Brown, D.G. (1962) Expected Ability to Pay and Inter-Industry Wage Structure in Manufacturing. *Industrial and Labour Relation Review,* Vol. XII, No. 1, October.

Bruno, M. (1978) Duality, Intermediate Inputs and Value Added, in Fuss, M. and McFadden, D. (Eds.) *Production Economics: A Dual Approach to Theory and Applications.* Amsterdam: North Holland Publishing Co.

Bruno, M. (1984) Raw Materials, Profits and the Productivity Slowdown. *Quarterly Journal of Economics,* Vol. 1, pp. 1-29.

Chakraborty, D. (1982) CES Production Function—A Review of Recent Literature. *Artha Vijnana,* Vol. 24, No. 3, pp. 220-47.

Chakraborty, D. (1983) Translog Production Function—A Review of Recent Literature. *Artha Vijnana,* Vol. 25, No. 2, pp. 116-46.

Chandy, K.T. (1973) Keynote Address in the Seminar on Sharing the Gains of Productivity and Productivity Agreements (Trivendrum) Published in National Productivity Council (1973), p. 8.

Chaudhuri, T.D. and Bhattacherjee, D. (1994) A Structural Model of Strikes and Wages in Indian Industries. *Indian Journal of Industrial Relations,* Vol. 30, No. 2, pp. 144-53.

Christensen, L.R., Jorgenson, D.W. and Lau, L.J. (1973) Transcendental Logarithmic Production Frontiers. *Review of Economics and Statistics,* February, pp. 28-45.

Dash, J. (1995) Productivity of Manufacturing Industries and its Linkages with Wages. *The Indian Journal of Labour Economics,* Vol. 38, No. 2, pp. 322-30.

Denison, E.F. (1961) 'Measurement of Labour Input: Some Question of Definition and Adequacy of Data' in Output, Input and Productivity Measurement. *Studies in Income and Wealth,* Vol. 25, pp. 347-87. New York: National Bureau of Economic Research.

Denison, E.F. (1962) The Sources of Economic Growth in the US and the Alternative before US. *Committee for Economic Development.* New York: Library of Congress.

Denison, E.F. (1964). The Unimportance of the Embodiment Question. *American Economic Review,* Vol. 54, March, pp. 80-94.

Denison, E.F. (1969) Some Major Issues in Productivity Analysis. *Survey of Current Business,* Vol. 49(5), May, pp. 1-28.

Diwan, R.K. and Gujarati, D. (1968) Employment and Productivity in Industries. *Artha Vijnana,* Vol. 10, No. 1, pp. 29-67.

Dixon, R.P. and Macdonald, D. (1992) A Decomposition of Changes in Labour Productivity in Australia: 1970-71 to 1989-90. *Economic Record.* March, pp. 105-17.

Fallen, P.R. and Lucas, R.E.B. (1991) The Impact of Changes in Job Security Regulations in India and Zimbabwe. *World Bank Economic Review,* Vol. 5, No. 3.

Gangopadhyay, S. and Wadhwa, W. (1998) Economic Reforms and Labour. *Economic and Political Weekly,* May 30, pp. L42-48.

Ghosh, A. (1984) Efficiency and Productivity of Indian Manufacturing Industry: A Few Case Studies. *Economic and Political Weekly,* Annual Number.

Ghosh, A. (1988) Industrial Productivity: Some Issues Relevant for Policy Making. *Productivity,* Vol. 29, No. 3, October-December, pp. 303-10.

Ghuman, R.S. and Singh, L. (1998) Employment, Wages and Productivity in Public Sector Enterprises in India. *The Indian Journal of Labour Economics,* Vol. 41, No. 4, pp. 923-33.

Goldar, B.N. (1987) Employment Growth in Indian Industry. *Indian Journal of Industrial Relation,* Vol. 22. No. 3, pp. 271-85.

Gordon, R.J. (1982) Why U.S. Wage and Employment Behaviour Differs from that in Britain and Japan. *The Economic Journal.* Vol. 92, pp. 13-44.

Gordon, R.J. (1987) Productivity, Wages and Prices Inside and Outside of Manufacturing in Britain and Japan. *European Economic Review,* Vol. 31, pp. 685-739.

Goyal, R.C. (1974) Productivity—A Neglected Word in Industrial Relation Policy. *Productivity,* Vol. 15, No. 3, pp. 345-52.

Granger, C.W.J. (1969) Investing Causal Relations by Econometric Models and Cross-Spectral Methods. *Econometrica,* Vol. 37, pp. 424-38.

Griliches, Z. and Jorgenson, D.W. (1966) Sources of Measured Productivity Change: Capital Input. *American Economic Association Papers.* May.

Griliches, Z. and Jorgenson, D.W. (1967) The Explanation of Productivity Change. *Review of Economic Studies,* Vol. 34, July, pp. 249-84.

Gupta, D. (1995) Productivity Growth in Indian Capital Goods Industry. *Artha Vijnana,* No. 2, pp. 172-83.

Heubes, J. (1969) Time Series CES Presentation: Functions for Primary Production and Manufacturing, Federal Republic of Germany—1950-65. *German Economic Review,* Vol. 7, pp. 346-60.

Hojler, H.J. (1990) The Determinants of Employees Productivity and Earnings. *Industrial Relations,* Vol. 29, No. 3, pp. 403-22.

Hsiao, C. (1987) Autoregressive Modeling and Money Income Causality Detection. *Journal of Monetary Economics,* Vol. 7, pp. 85-106.

Iyer, K.V. (1982) Linking Wages with Productivity. *Financial Express,* April 21.

Johri, C.K. and Agarwal, N.C. (1966) Inter-Industry Wage Structure in India, 1951-61: An Analysis. *Indian Journal of Industrial Relations,* Vol. 1, No. 4, pp. 379-413.

Jorgenson, D.W. and Griliches, Z. (1967) The Explanation of Productivity Change. *Review of Economic Studies.* Vol. 34, July, pp. 249-84.

Jorgenson, D.W. (1966) The Embodiment Hypothesis. *Journal of Political Economy,* Vol. 74(1), February, pp. 1-17.

Jose, A.V. (1992) Earnings, Employment and Productivity Trends in the Organised Industries in India, *The Indian Journal of Labour Economics,* Vol. 35, No. 3, pp. 205-26.

Kadak, A.M. (1985) Growth, Employment and Choice of Technique—A Survey. *Anveshak,* Vol. 15, No. 1. pp. 59-90.

Kadak, A.M. (1986) Growth and Employment in Some Selected Industries of Indian Manufacturing Sector. *Anveshak,* Vol. 16, No. 1, pp. 1-32.

Kannan, K.P. (1994) Leveling Up or Leveling Down?: Labour Institution and Economic Development in India. *Economic and Political Weekly,* July 23, pp. 1938-45.

Kazi, U.A. (1978) Production Function with a Variable Elasticity of

Substitution: Analysis and Some Empirical Results. *Artha Vijnana,* Vol. 20, No. 2, pp. 168-95.

Kazi, U.A. (1974) Estimation of Elasticity of Substitution with Stock of Capital from the Constant Elasticity of Substitution Production Function (CES). *Anveshak,* Vol. 20, No. 2, pp. 207-38.

Kazi, U.A. (1980) The Variable Elasticity of Production Function: A Study for Indian Manufacturing Industries. *Oxford Economic Papers* (New Series), Vol. 22, No. 1, pp. 163-75.

Kendrick, J.W. (1956) Productivity Trends: Capital and Labour. *Review of Economics and Statistics,* Vol. 38, August, pp. 248-57.

Kendrick, J.W. (1964) Measuring the Nation's Wealth. *Studies in Income and Wealth Series.* Vol. 29, New York: National Bureau of Economic Research.

Kennedy, C. and Thirlwall, A.P. (1972) Survey in Applied Economics: Technical Change. *The Economic Journal,* Vol. 82, No. 325, pp. 12-72.

Khader, S.A. (2000) Strategic Perspective for Building Productivity Culture. *Yojna,* Vol. 44, No. 5, pp. 10-17.

Kmenta, J. (1967) On Estimation of the CES Production Function. *International Economic Review,* Vol. 8, No. 2, June, pp. 180-89.

Mehrotra, S.N. (1967) Sharing Gains in Productivity. *The Indian Journal of Labour Economics,* Vol. 9, No. 4, pp. 389-93.

Mehta, F.H. (1966) Sharing the Gain of Productivity. *The Indian Journal of Labour Economics,* Vol. 9, No. 1, pp. 80-110.

Mehta. S.S. (1974) Growth and Productivity in Indian Industries. *Anveshak.* Vol. 4, No. 1, June, pp. 1-11.

Nadiri, M.I. (1972) Some Approaches to the Theory and Measurement of Total Factor Productivity: A Survey. *Journal of Economic Literature,* Vol. VIII, pp. 1137-77.

Nagraj, R. (1989) Growth in Manufacturing Output Since 1980. *Economic and Political Weekly,* Vol. XXIV, No. 26, July, pp. 1481-84.

Nagraj, R. (1994) Employment and Wages in Manufacturing Industries: Trends, Hypothesis and Evidence. *Economic and Political Weekly,* January 22, pp. 177-86.

National Productivity Council (1973) *Seminar on Sharing the Gains of Productivity and Productivity Agreement.* Vol. 14, No. 1

Nazmuddin, M. (1994) Factors Responsible for Inter-Regional Differentials in Industrial Wages. *The Indian Journal of Labour Economics,* Vol. 34, No. 2, pp. 122-35.

Nelson, R.R. (1965) Recent Exercises in Growth Accounting: New Understanding or Dead Ends? *American Economic Review,* Vol. 63, June, pp. 462-68.

Neogi, C. and Ghosh, B. (1998) Impact of Liberalisation on the Performance of Indian Industries: A Firm Level Study. *Economic and Political Weekly,* February 28, pp. M 16-24.

NPC Research Division (1997) Capital Productivity in Indian Manufacturing Industries (1973-94). *Productivity,* Vol. 37, No. 4, pp. 719-28.

Oliker, L.R. (1988) Productivity and Inflation. *Productivity,* Vol. 29, pp. 11-15.

Oomen, M.A. and Evenson, R. (1977) Scale Economies, Elasticity of Substitution and Productivity Change in Agro Based Industries in India. *Asian Economic Review,* Vol. 19, No. 1, pp. 10-34.

Oxley, L. and Greasly, D. (1998) Vector Autoregression, Cointegration and Causality: Testing for Causes of the British Industrial Revolution. *Applied Economics,* Vol. 30, pp. 1387-97.

Papola, T.S. (1972) Inter-Industry Wage Structure: Technology Hypothesis. *Anveshak, June*, pp. 50-74.

Patel, N.T. and Gandhi, M. (1998) Wage-Productivity Relations in Agro-Based Industries. *The Indian Journal of Labour Economics,* Vol. 41, No. 4, pp. 917-22.

Pathak, P.G. (1994) CES Production Function for Gujrat Industries—A Study of Factor Use Pattern. *Anveshak,* Vol. 24, No. 1, pp. 1-43.

Perumai, S.V. (1992) The Missing Links of Labour Productivity: A Review. *The Indian Journal of Labour Economics,* Vol. 35, No. 4, pp. 421-26.

Pradhan, B.K. and Saluja M.R. (1998) Industrial Statistics in India: Sources, Limitations and Data Gaps. *Economics and Political Weekly.* May 23, pp. 1263-70.

Pradhan, G. and Barik, K. (1998) Fluctuating Total Factor Productivity in India: Evidence from Selected Polluting Industries. *Economic and Political Weekly.* February 28, pp. M 25-30.

Raj Krishnan and Mehta, S.S. (1968) Productivity Trends in Large-Scale Indian Industries. *Economic and Political Weekly,* Oct. 26.

Rajalakshmi, K. (1985) Productivity Comparison of Manufacturing Sectors of All-India and Rajasthan. *Artha Vijnana.* Vol. 27, No. 1, pp. 55-66.

Rao, J.M. (1996a) Manufacturing Productivity Growth: Method and Measurement. *Economic and Political Weekly,* November 2, pp. 2927-36.

Rao, J.M. (1996b) Indices of Industrial Productivity Growth: Disaggregation and Interpretation. *Economic and Political Weekly,* December 7, pp. 3177-88.

Raychaudhuri, B. (1996) Measurement of Capital Stock in Indian Industries. *Economic and Political Weekly,* May 25, pp. M2-6.

Reddy, C.S.R. (1987) Measurement of Non-Neutral Technological Change in Cotton, Jute and Woollen Industries. *Prajnan,* Vol. 16, No. 2, pp. 127-43.

Reddy, M.G.K. and Rao, V. (1962) Functional Distribution in the Large Scale Manufacturing Sector in India, *Artha Vijnana,* Vol. 4, No. 3, pp. 187-89.

Ruggles, R. and Ruggles, N. (1961) Concepts of Real Capital Stocks and Services, in Output, Input and Productivity Measurement. *Studies in Income and Wealth,* Vol. 25, pp. 387-411. New York: National Bureau of Economic Research.

Saibaba, G. and Rao Mohan, L.K. (1992) Labour Productivity and Trade Unions in India. *The Indian Journal of Labour Economics,* Vol. 35, No. 4, pp. 406-11.

Sawhney, P.K. (1969) Inter-Industry Wage Differentials in India. *Indian Economic Journal,* July-September, pp. 28-47.

Sen, S.K. (1985) Inter-Industry Differentials in Growth of Real Earnings: Some Implication for Wage Policy. *Economic and Political Weekly,* Vol. 20, No. 13, March, pp. 556-64.

Seshaiah, S.V. and Reddy, V.K. (1993) Andhra Pardesh Manufacturing Sector: Productivity Trends. *Productivity.* Vol. 34, No. 1, pp. 112-15.

Sheshinsky, E. (1967) Test of Learning by Doing Hypothesis. *Review of Economics and Statistics.* November.

Shivamaggi, H.B., Rajgopalan, N. and Venketachalam, T.R. (1968) Wages, Labour Productivity and Cost of Production. *Economic and Political Weekly,* Vol. 3, No. 18, May, pp. 710-16.

Sidhu, H. (1995) Factor Productivity in Manufacturing Sector of Gujrat. *Productivity,* Vol. 36, No. 1, pp. 270-75.

Sidhu, H. (1997) Wage Differential in SSI Sector in Gujarat. *Indian Journal of Industrial Relations,* Vol. 33, No. 2, pp. 211-21.

Singh, N., Kochak, A.K. and Malhotra N.J. (1990) Paper and Paperboard Industry: Productivity, Structure and Related issues. *Productivity,* Vol. 31, No. 3, pp. 421-35.

Singh, R.R. (1966) Productivity Trends and Wages. *Eastern Economists,* April 29.

Singh, R.R. (1973) Labour's Share in National Income. *Productivity,* Vol. 14, No. 1, pp. 106-11.

Singh, T. and Ajit, D. (1995) Production Functions in the Manufacturing Industries in India. *RBI Occasional Papers,* Vol. 16, No. 2, pp. 125-55.

Singh, L. and Singh, K.C. (1987) Economies of Scale and Technical Change. *Productivity,* Vol. 28, No. 3, pp. 291-296.

Solow, R. (1957) Technical Change and Aggregate Production Function, *Review of Economics and Statistics,* Vol. 39, No. 3, August, pp. 312-20.

Somayajulu, V.V.N. and George, J. (1983) Production Function Studies of Indian Industries—A Survey. *Artha Vijnana,* Vol. 25, No. 4, pp. 402-18.

Soni, K.C. and Jani, B.B. (1987) VES Production Function with Neutral Technical Change—A Comparative Study of the Industrial Sectors of Gujarat vs. All India. *Anveshak,* Vol. 17, No. 2, pp. 59-75.

Subrahmanyam, G. (1984) Some Conceptual Issues in Productivity Measurement. *Prajnan,* Vol. 13, No. 2, pp. 173-85.

Suri, G.K. and Sastry, C.M. (1974) Determinants of Workers Money Earnings and Income Policy. *Productivity,* Vol. 15, No. 1, pp. 97-112.

Swamy, T.L.N. (1993) Vedroon's Law of Productivity Growth. *Productivity,* Vol. 34, No. 1, April-June, pp. 109-11.

Tulpule, B. and Datta, R.C. (1988) Real Wages in Indian Industries. *Economic and Political Weekly,* October 29, pp. 2275-78.

Upender, M. (1996) Elasticity of Labour Productivity in Indian Manufacturing. *Economic and Political Weekly,* May 25, pp. M7-10.

Verma, P. (1971) Inter-Industry Wage Structure in India: Further Evidence. *Indian Journal of Industrial Relations,* January, pp. 289-95.

Verma, P. (1977) Wages In India: Towards a National Policy. *Indian Journal of Industrial Relations,* Vol. 20, No. 3, pp. 109-22.

Verma, P. (1992) Trends and Structure of Wages in Indian Industries. *Productivity.* Vol. 33, No. 2, pp. 270-75.

Verma, P. and Subbayamma, G. (1985) The Inter-Industry Wage Structure in India: Recent Experience. *The Indian Journal of Labour Economics.* Vol. 32, No. 3.

Yellen, J.L. (1984) Efficiency of Wage Models of Employment. *American Economic Review,* Vol. 74, pp. 200-05.

Thesis/Mimeo/Working Paper

Dadi, M.M. (1971) *Income Share of Factory Labour in India.* Ph.D thesis submitted to the M.S. University of Baroda.

Goldar, B.N. (1981) *Some Aspects of Technological Progress in Indian Industries.* Ph.D. Dissertation submitted to the University of Delhi.

Gumaste, V.M. (1982) *Technology and Productivity in Indian Manufacturing Industries.* Ph.D. Thesis Submitted to University of Bombay.

Ho, K.J. (1986) *Wage, Employment and Income Distribution in South Korea: 1960-1983.* New Delhi: ILO-ARTEP.

Mitra, A. (1999) Total Factor Productivity growth and Technical

Efficiency in Indian Industries: A Study Based on Panel Data for Fifteen Major States. *Institute of Economic Growth*, Working Paper No. E/ 203.

Palekar, S.A. (1974) Wages under Planning—A Case Study of India. *Monograph, Sastry Indo-Canadian Institute*, Monetreal.

Ramjas (1988) *Trade Union and Productivity—A Study of Selected Industries in India*. Ph.D; Thesis submitted to University of Delhi.

Seraphim, Rina (1988) *The Problem of Productivity in Iron and Steel Industry in India: A Management Perspective*. Ph.D. Thesis submitted to Patna University.

Srivastava, S.K. (1978) *Wage-Productivity Relationship in Engineering Industries of Kanpur Region*. Ph.D. Thesis submitted to Kanpur University.

Tiwari, R.M (1971) *Labour Productivity in Indian Cotton Textile Industry with Special Reference to Kanpur*. Ph.D. Thesis submitted to Lucknow University.

Government Publications/Reports

Government of India (1949) *Report of the Committee on Fair Wages*. Ministry of Labour.

Government of India (1966) *Report on the Trends in Utilisation of Labour and Other Inputs in Selected Industry*. Ministry of Labour and Employment, Shimla: Labour Bureau.

Government of India (1969) *Report of the National Commission on Labour*. Ministry of Labour. Chandigarh: Shram Bureau. Chairman: Dr. P.B. Gajenderagadkar.

Government of India (1993) *Wage Fixation in Industry and Agriculture in India*. Chandigarh: Labour Bureau, Ministry of Labour.

Government of India (1997) *Input-Output Transaction Table 1989-90*. New Delhi: Central Statistical Organisation, Ministry of Planning and Programme Implementation.

Government of India. *Eighth Five Year Plan 1992-97- Vol. I & II*. New Delhi: Planning Commission.

Government of India. *Index Number of Wholesale Prices in India*. New Delhi: Ministry of Industry.

Government of India. *Index Number of Wholesale Prices in India: A Time Series Presentation (1971-1986)*. Office of Economic Adviser, New Delhi: Ministry of Industry.

Government of India. *Seventh Five-Year Plan 1985-90*. New Delhi: Planning Commission.

Government of India. *Sixth Five-Year Plan 1980-85*. New Delhi: Planning Commission.

Government of India: *Annual Survey of Industries (Various Issues)*. Central Statistical Organisation, New Delhi: Ministry of Planning.

International Labour Organisation (1951) *Methods of Labour Productivity Statistics*, Geneva.

International Labour Organisation (1954) *Higher Productivity in Manufacturing Industries*, Geneva.

International Labour Organisation (1956) *Problems of Wage Policy in Asian Countries*, Geneva.

International Labour Organisation (1961) *Wages: A Worker's Educational Manual*, Geneva.

Miscellaneous

Different issues of *Yojana*

Different issues of *Kurukshetra*

Different issues of *Economic and Political Weekly*

Different issues of *Financial Express*

Different issues of *Business India*

Index